SOCIAL WORK IN JUVENILE
AND CRIMINAL JUSTICE SETTINGS

SOCIAL WORK IN JUVENILE AND CRIMINAL JUSTICE SETTINGS

Edited By

ALBERT R. ROBERTS, D.S.W.

Associate Professor of Social Work
Seton Hall University
South Orange, New Jersey

With a Foreword by

Vernon Fox, Ph.D.

Professor and Founder
School of Criminology
Florida State University
Tallahassee, Florida

CHARLES C THOMAS • PUBLISHER

Springfield • Illinois • U.S.A.

Published and Distributed Throughout the World by
CHARLES C THOMAS • PUBLISHER
2600 South First Street
Springfield, Illinois 62717

© *1983 by CHARLES C THOMAS ○ PUBLISHER*

ISBN 0-398-04862-2

Library of Congress Catalog Card Number: 83-4246

With THOMAS BOOKS *careful attention is given to all details of manufacturing and
design. It is the Publisher's desire to present books that are satisfactory as to their physical
qualities and artistic possibilities and appropriate for their particular use.* THOMAS
BOOKS *will be true to those laws of quality that assure a good name and good will.*

Printed in the United States of America
SC-R-1

Library of Congress Cataloging in Publication Data
Main entry under title:

Social work in Juvenile and criminal justice settings.

Includes index.
1. Social work with delinquents and criminals—United
States.   I. Roberts, Albert R.
HV7428.S5745   1983   364.6   83-4246
ISBN 0-398-04862-2

CONTRIBUTORS

ALBERT S. ALISSI, D.S.W., M.S.L.
Professor
School of Social Work
University of Connecticut
West Hartford, Connecticut

GLORIA CUNNINGHAM, Ph.D.
Assistant Professor
Loyola University of Chicago
School of Social Work
Chicago, Illinois

DAN W. EDWARDS, Ph.D.
Chair, Fields of Social Work Practice
School of Social Welfare
Louisiana State University
Baton Rouge, Louisiana

SUSAN HOFFMAN FISHMAN, M.S.W.
Executive Director
Women in Crisis
Hartford, Connecticut

JOHN T. GANDY, Ph.D.
Associate Dean and Associate Professor
College of Social Work
University of South Carolina
Columbia, South Carolina

SHELDON R. GELMAN, Ph.D., M.S.L.
Professor and Director
Social Welfare Major
Department of Sociology
The Pennsylvania State University
University Park, Pennsylvania

KAY SEELEY HOFFMAN, Ph.D.
Director, Social Work Program
Marygrove College
Detroit, Michigan

MARIAN HUNSINGER, L.B.S.W.
Social Worker
Mental Health Unit
Kansas State Penitentiary
Lansing, Kansas

H. WAYNE JOHNSON, M.S.W.
Professor and Director
Undergraduate Social Work Program
University of Iowa
Iowa City, Iowa

JAMES D. JORGENSEN, M.S.W.
Professor
The Graduate School of Social Work
University of Denver
Denver, Colorado

JOHN A. LACOUR, M.S.W.
Assistant Professor
School of Social Welfare
Louisiana State University
Baton Rouge, Louisiana

C. AARON McNEECE, Ph.D.
Associate Professor and Assistant Dean
School of Social Work
The Florida State University
Tallahassee, Florida

CAROLYN NEEDLEMAN, Ph.D.
Associate Professor
The Graduate School of Social Work and
Social Research
Bryn Mawr College
Bryn Mawr, Pennsylvania

JOSEPH E. PALENSKI, Ph.D.
Assistant Professor
Department of Sociology
Seton Hall University
South Orange, New Jersey

JACK G. PARKER, Ed.D.
Professor
School of Social Welfare
Louisiana State University
Baton Rouge, Louisiana

JANET L. PRAY, M.S.W.
Associate Professor and Director
Social Work Program
Department of Sociology and Social Work
Gallaudet College
Washington, D.C.

FRANK B. RAYMOND, III, D.S.W.
Professor and Dean
College of Social Work
University of South Carolina
Columbia, South Carolina

ALBERT R. ROBERTS, D.S.W.
Associate Professor
Department of Social Work
Seton Hall University
South Orange, New Jersey

TOM ROY, M.S.W.
Associate Professor
Department of Social Work
University of Montana
Missoula, Montana

ROBERT P. SCHEURELL, M.S.W.
Coordinator
Undergraduate Social Work Program
School of Social Welfare
The University of Wisconsin-Milwaukee
Milwaukee, Wisconsin

DAVID SHOWALTER, L.M.S.W.
Former Associate Director
Mental Health Unit
Kansas State Penitentiary
Lansing, Kansas

HARVEY TREGER, M.S.W.
Professor
Jane Addams College of Social Work
University of Illinois at Chicago Circle
Chicago, Illinois

JUDITH F. WEINTRAUB, M.A.
Consultant in Criminal Justice and
Executive Secretary
Alliance of Non-governmental Organizations
United Nations
Section on Crime Prevention and Criminal Justice
New York, New York

FOREWORD

Social Work as a profession is a twentieth century development, but it has a long legacy in private philanthropy and religious movements. The "Good Samaritan" (Luke 10: 30–37) was only one example during ancient times of compassion for less fortunate people that can be traced from primitive man to the present day. The monasteries provided services to children and minor offenders through the Middle Ages. Welfare programs began in England on a small scale after Henry VIII closed the monasteries in 1636 to 1639. Concern for the welfare of children and minor offenders was included in the Elizabethan Poor Law of 1601, which made use of the "bridewells" begun in 1557 to house debtors, dependent children, and others who needed governmental care. In 1648, concern for children in trouble was shown by the establishment of a home for wandering children in Paris by St. Vincent de Paul and the establishment of a church-affiliated institution in Milan to house boys with behavior problems. Pope Clement XI established the Hospice di San Michele (House of St. Michael) in 1704, in Rome, to care for children now referred to as "delinquent." That institution still stands and is still used for its original purpose. While there had been places for detention, including rooms in the ancient temples, there were jails and private prisons from the twelfth through the eighteenth centuries, prior to the beginning of prisons as they are known today.

The first prison was introduced at Simsbury, Connecticut, in 1773, when an old copper mine was converted into an institution for detaining "criminals"; George Washington used it as a military prison. In 1787, the Quakers started the Philadelphia Society for Alleviating the Miseries of the Public Prisons. The goal of the Society was to improve the sad plight of convicts by advocating that imprisonment in solitary confinement be substituted for the death penalty and physical torture. As a result, the "penitentiary movement" began with the Walnut Street Jail in 1790. The name of the Philadelphia Society was changed to Pennsylvania Prison Society in 1887.

John Howard (1726–1790) and Elizabeth Gurney Fry (1780–1845) initiated lay visiting in England's jails and prisons that marked the beginning of private social work in prisons. Fry was known for lending material aid to individual prisoners, while John Howard was most concerned with improving the overall prison condition. The Correctional Association of New York was formed in 1844. The Prisoners' Aid Association of Maryland was formalized in 1869, but its beginnings went back to 1829, when the rector of St. Paul's Church in downtown Baltimore provided food and other assistance to men leaving the penitentiary. The Massachusetts Correctional Association was established in 1889 as the John Howard Society. The first John Howard Society had been established in England in 1866. Since that time, there have been prisoners' aid societies functioning around the world that handle all probation and parole functions in many countries.

A group of Quakers opened a halfway house for women in New York City in the 1880s, which continues today as the Isaac T. Hopper House and now houses the American Correctional Association for Women. Settlement houses began to appear in London in the 1880s. The first settlement house in the United States was the "Neighborhood Guild" in New York City in 1887, an outgrowth of the London Movement founded in Toynbee Hall. The most significant and influential settlement house was Hull House, founded in 1889 by Jane Addams and Ellen Gates Starr. Addams and Starr rented a house built by Charles G. Hull at 800 South Halsted Street in Chicago. Although it was geographically replaced in January, 1961, by the University of Illinois at Chicago Circle, the original Hull House still remains as a museum, and in 1967 it was designated a national landmark. The present Jane Addams School of Social Work is a part of the University of Illinois.

Social work had its beginnings as a profession around 1904. Charles Booth participated in the Charity Organization Movement, studied social conditions in London from 1886 to 1903, and his *Life and Labour of the People of London*, published in 1904, became a monumental contribution of the time, and others in England and America followed its tradition in social work. With Paul Kellogg, Charles Booth's most ambitious work was the Pittsburgh Survey in 1909 to 1914, financed by the Russell Sage Foundation. Summer training courses for charity workers were begun by the New York Charity Organization Society in 1898. By 1904, the first School of

Social Work was established at Columbia University as a one-year program, then called the New York School of Philanthropy. As of 1919, the fifteen Schools of Social Work had organized into the Association of Training Schools for Professional Social Work, including nine programs operating within university auspices and six independent schools. Adoption of a minimum curriculum had taken place by 1932. In 1935, the American Association of Schools of Social Work ruled that only those schools connected with universities could be accredited. By 1940, the Association required graduate-level education as part of all social workers' professional development. Social work had emerged as an accepted profession.

From the beginning, the field of corrections had been an anathema to professional social work. Problems of the poor, family services, child protective services, philanthropy, and general social welfare became the primary concern of social work. Some writers, such as Warner, Queen, and Harper, in 1935, date the beginning of professional social work back to 1893, when settlement workers were trying to gain recognition just to be on the program of the National Conference of Charities and Correction. This group subsequently gained recognition and "blundered" into the emerging professionalism of social work.

Correctional work had always been part of philanthropy and preprofessional social work. As social work became recognized as a profession, however, the field of corrections was excluded from its purview as being beyond its concern. While professional social workers did work with families, settlement houses, low-income families, and the new child guidance clinics begun in Philadelphia in 1897, and worked with predelinquents and delinquents in that context, they were moving away from the criminal offender. In 1917, Mary Richmond's *Social Diagnosis* (published by the Russell Sage Foundation) established the guidelines and the norms for professional social work. It was aimed at, "those processes which developed personality through adjustments consciously effected, individual by individual, between men and their social environment." Among the dicta were that caseworkers worked with individual "cases," not large groups and—most damaging to corrections—the doctrine of self-determination, which meant that social workers help people help themselves. Since corrections is coercive through enforcement and confinement, "self-determination" is automatically excluded from the field of professional social work, which cannot function in an authoritative setting. The "constructive use of authority" was seen as withdrawing services when the individual became ineligible for any reason.

Professional social work had moved out of corrections. Attention continued in family problems and social welfare concerns, but the emphasis began to focus toward mental health. In 1921, the American Association of Social Workers was founded to provide an organizational base for professional social workers. In 1922, the Commonwealth Fund created scholarships for professional "Social Workers" to become assistants to psychiatrists in the mental health field, and this funding continued through 1928. With the coming of the Great Depression, social work was inundated with income maintenance problems, but continued its other functions in private Family Welfare Associations, the Child Welfare League of America, the National Federation of Settlements, and other private organizations, while governmental concerns primarily focused on poverty and income maintenance as a result of the Depression. In the meantime, social work remained away from corrections because of (1) the large caseloads, (2) the doctrine of self-determination that prevented them from working in an authoritative setting, (3) the definition of "authority" as a withholding of services, rather than as an authoritative person or agency, and (4) the belief that social work techniques should remain the same, regardless of the clientele and the circumstances of the host agency, which is an oversimplification in the correctional setting.

In 1945, Dr. Kenneth Pray, Director (frequently called Dean) of the School of Social Work at the University of Pennsylvania, was a major speaker at the annual meeting of the American Association of Social Workers in Chicago, where he had been elected president. His speech was revolutionary. Dean Kenneth Pray contended that professional social workers *could* and *should* work in corrections. All that was needed was an extra step in the early confrontations to "sell" or "motivate" the client into wanting to help "reform" himself. The response was vitriolic. Traditional social workers engaged Dean Pray intensely and almost viciously. Some of the debate can be read in the issues of the *Social Service Review* after that 1945 meeting and several years afterward. His papers were subsequently published posthumously as *Kenneth Pray; Social Work in a Revolu-*

tionary Age and Other Papers by the University of Pennsylvania Press in 1949. The debate continued for years.

In 1959, the famous thirteen-volume Curriculum Study was made under Werner W. Boehm in order to consolidate the social work curriculum. Volume V on *Education for Social Workers in the Correctional Field* was done by Elliot Studt, who concluded that, "no separate specialty seems required in order to prepare social workers to take their place in correctional service." The last sentence was that, "professional education should elect and prepare students for early leadership responsibility." Even this writer entered the fray with an article on "The University Curriculum in Corrections" that appeared in the September, 1959, issue of *Federal Probation*. The article presented two possible curricula, one for corrections and another for social workers interested in corrections. The Council on Social Work Education had a five-year Corrections Project (1959–1964) financed by The Ford Foundation. Throughout its deliberations, the debate involved whether additional information should be added to the curriculum for corrections or whether it should not. Those in favor of adding new information referred to the problems resulting from Mary Richmond's *Social Diagnosis* in 1917. The project reached the same conclusions that Elliot Studt had made in the curriculum study, that no separate or additional information was needed.

An outgrowth of that project, however, was the Arden House Conference on Manpower and Training for Corrections, held June 24 to 26, 1964, at Harriman, New York, involving over sixty national organizations. Outgrowths from this conference included the Correctional Rehabilitation Study Act of 1965, the Prisoner's Rehabilitation Act of 1965, and the Joint Commission on Correctional Manpower and Training, which was funded by The Ford Foundation, 1966 to 1969. The social work profession continued to maintain that no new information was needed to serve social workers working in corrections. This history of social work practice in corrections has been one of bouncing back and forth between expressing inability to work in an authoritative setting, to having state legislative committees demanding that the M.S.W. (master's degree in social work) be the basic requirement for the correctional position, particularly in probation. The push for the M.S.W. requirement was successful in several states, such as New York, Michigan, Wisconsin, Minnesota, and others. Some long-term probation officers were surprised when the M.S.W. probation workers in New York discharged persons who had violated probation as "not eligible for probation," rather than recommending that the judge revoke probation and send them to the institution, as had been their custom. But the social work concept of "constructive use of authority" is based on ineligibility for service, rather than further punishment. Such conceptual misunderstandings have occurred between social workers in corrections and some correctional personnel and administrators with backgrounds in other areas.

This is the first book of major importance that covers professional social work in the field of corrections. It covers all the fields in which social work functions in just about the amount proportionate to their functioning in practice. The reentry of social work was first in the juvenile area, particularly in the court and the community, followed by adult probation. Parole took a little longer, as did medium and minimum security institutions for adults. The maximum security prison has been the last to experience this reentry. This book reflects this progression in its text and in its format. More than the first half of the book is devoted to social workers in the juvenile field, the point of reentry. Probation, parole, and court settings are discussed next. Finally, the maximum security prison is discussed well, although there are more restrictive settings in some stronger maximum security institutions in which some of the examples used could not have taken place—the setting of the writers of this chapter was the Mental Health Unit of the Kansas State Penitentiary, rather than the maximum security unit. This fits into the scheme and reflects the progression of social work back into the correctional field as it actually did happen. The other three chapters in the prison section involved volunteers and family relations. In summary, then, this book reflects almost exactly the way social work came back into corrections and discusses the problems of working with authority, the problem of client self-determination, the problem of caseloads, and the problem of specialization in social work, as it relates to the entire field of corrections. Ellen Handler's excellent article (published in *Criminology: An Interdisciplinary Journal*, August, 1975) focuses on corrections and social work being "an uneasy partnership." This is only one example of the thorough breadth of literature that characterizes the support for this book.

Dean Kenneth Pray would have been proud to see this book after his being embroiled in turmoil and debate following his revolutionary speech in Chicago in 1945 when he said that social work *could* and *should* work in the field of corrections. As a participant in and a follower of the field of corrections and welcoming the assistance of any legitimate profession for many years of turbulent and frenzied efforts to stay even with the challenge, this writer is also proud of this book. It has been, in fact, "an uneasy partnership," but it should not have been. There are still many professionals working in practices based in the behavioral sciences who have difficulty in working with authority and want to "help the client help himself" and have other troubles in working with offenders. Even so, the number of people who can work comfortably in corrections is increasing—even in maximum security prisons— which is a rewarding observation after these many years of frustration. It is a gross disservice to the client for a professional to *wait* for the client to become "motivated" so he can "help him help himself" when that client is so "beat down" and angry that he will never achieve that kind of motivation. There are some who consider this kind of aloofness as downright immoral in a "helping" profession. There are now professional social workers who can talk about "aggressive casework," "hard-to-reach groups," "reaching out," and motivating people "to help themselves." While this book is important to help social workers understand corrections, it is far more important that all correctional administrators and practitioners read it to gain an understanding about what the *new* professional social worker has to offer and how he or she functions. *This book is the most significant contribution in many years to the mutually rewarding understanding of the alliance between professional social work and corrections.*

Vernon Fox
Professor
School of Criminology
Florida State University
Tallahassee, Florida

PREFACE

There is a growing need for social services for juvenile and adult offenders, as well as for their unfortunate victims. My purpose in preparing this book was to provide a comprehensive description of what social workers in the juvenile and criminal justice system are currently doing and what they should be doing to become more effective in humanizing the justice field.

Social work students at the undergraduate and masters levels are being prepared for entry level positions in the delivery of treatment and rehabilitation services to clients of the justice system. This role must include more than the provision of services to offenders after crimes have already been committed. It must include early identification of problem youths, intervention with families at risk, coordination with community agencies, and participation in influencing policy aimed at increased funding for needed services.

This book focuses on the role of the social worker and counselor in juvenile and criminal justice settings. It responds to the rapidly rising interest in the reform of policies and programs in juvenile justice, law enforcement, adult corrections, probation and parole, and the courts. In view of budget cutbacks and problems in processing offenders and changing their behavior, justice professionals are searching for improved methods of delivering social services to juvenile and adult offenders and their victims. This volume was written to meet the needs of practitioners as well as social work and criminal justice educators.

The topics selected for inclusion in this book were chosen following an extensive needs assessment study, which I began in the late spring of 1981. I developed a two-page questionnaire that was mailed to the Directors of the 303 CSWE-accredited undergraduate programs and the Deans of the eighty-seven graduate schools of social work. The purpose of the survey was twofold: (1) to identify the number and content of courses related to social work practice in the justice arena and (2) to locate the experts who had

the practice experience, knowledge base, and motivation to prepare a chapter especially for this volume. The outcome was that
I was deluged with reprints of published articles, conference
presentations, and outlines of proposed chapters, which colleagues
from throughout the country so graciously shared with me.

The chapters selected for inclusion in the book represent those
that were the most readable, while also providing a balanced
presentation of the knowledge, skills, and guidelines essential for
efficacious practice in the justice system. My goal has been to
make this book as up-to-date and practical as possible.

I gratefully acknowledge the vital assistance of the authors who
prepared individual chapters. In almost all cases, these authors
met the deadlines for submission of initial drafts and chapter
revisions. The end result is a series of comprehensive analyses
developed by a number of extremely capable scholars who are
intimately familiar with the policies, issues, and practice skills
applicable to a specific segment of the justice system.

I wish to thank Payne Thomas and his fine staff for their care
and efficient handling throughout all phases of the book's pro-
duction. On a personal level, I am grateful to my wife, Beverly, for
her valuable help. As always, she provided countless hours of
editing and indexing assistance, in addition to emotional support.

I hope that this book will stimulate the reader to apply and
improve upon the justice social work perspectives presented here.
I also hope that this book will serve as a catalyst for the further
development and improvement of specific programs that will
ultimately lead to a more humane and safe society.

Albert R. Roberts

INTRODUCTION

These are difficult times for the social work profession, which is laboring under the onus of severe budget cuts in social programs. At the same time that programs are being slashed, the crime rate is increasing and the juvenile and adult correctional systems are handling more individuals than ever before. The issues of punishment, deterrence, and changing the law breaker, long the topics of public debate, have never been more relevant than they are today. The type of treatment that the accused receives during and after arrest, adjudication, and conviction will have a profound effect on the individual and society.

The juvenile and adult criminal justice systems are experiencing unprecedented strain due to the following:

1. the steady upward trend in the rate of most major offense categories;
2. the backlog, inconsistency, and often ineffectual processing and sentencing of convicted felons;
3. the lack of adequate professional personnel, overcrowding, and antiquated conditions at the institutional level;
4. the excessive caseloads of probation and parole agents; and
5. the lack of comprehensive diversion, restitution, and victim assistance programs.

In decades past, social workers helped perpetuate a regressive, antiquated, and punitive correctional system. The neglect of correctional social workers was most evident in their tendency

1. to search for individual pathology among offenders and develop treatment plans accordingly;
2. to ignore cultural norms and social structures that perpetuate social injustices;
3. to avoid working in direct service roles in police departments, training schools, correctional facilities, and parole offices;
4. to disregard the impact on the client of his environment; and

5. to overlook the daily pressures resulting from social conditions over which individuals have no control (Costin et al.,
1973).

Social workers have not been alone in their disregard for the
daily pressures, oppression, and degrading conditions characteristic of many correctional environments—particularly maximum-
security penitentiaries. Classification officers, correctional psychologists, prison teachers, and probation and parole officers have
also perpetuated the status quo.

According to Brodsky and Horn (1974):

> The counselor finds himself cast in the role of a social control agent
> seeking to make persons compliant and manageable. Primary allegiance
> and loyalty are expected and demanded to correctional policies which are
> often antiquated and oppressive. The correctional helper is thus placed in a
> position of ambivalent loyalty. If he accepts the rehabilitation rhetoric of
> the prison, he feels a sense of obligation to the prisoner client. If he is aware
> of the political process of "taking sides" within the institution, he is
> impelled toward being a representative of the warden. The ways in which
> the ambivalence is resolved vary, depending on the counselor himself, the
> particular prisoner, and the situation. There are some situations in which
> there clearly is no conflict; the interests of the institution and the prisoner
> coincide fully. This type of situation occurs only in the very few open institu-
> tions in which policy and objectives are fully shared by all concerned (p. 73).*
>
> The correctional treatment personnel in prisons are placed in a precari-
> ous position between responsibilities to prisoners and institutional loyalties.

With increasing frequency, social workers are providing services
to individuals handled by police departments, public defender
programs, probation and parole agencies, group homes, and correctional facilities. Because of the coercive and social control nature
of these agencies and programs, many social workers are reluctant
to enter this field of practice. In addition, the doubts and uneasy feelings of many social work students and professionals toward offenders
is a reflection of society's view of offenders as loathsome and sinister.

During the past decade, significant strides have been made in
broadening the role of social workers in the justice system. Social
workers can serve an important function in many different criminal justice settings including police departments, victim service

---

*For a thorough discussion of the counselor's role in different types of correctional
institutions. including a counselor typology, see Stanley L. Brodsky and Charles L.
Horn. The politics of correctional treatment. In Albert R. Roberts (Ed.) *Correctional
Treatment of the Offender.* Springfield, Illinois: Charles C Thomas, 1974, 72–80.

agencies, court settings, probation and parole offices, institutional facilities, community-based facilities, and family reintegration projects. Social work practice roles have expanded greatly from traditional caseworker to client advocate, crisis counselor, program developer, program evaluator, and broker of services.

Most social workers are heavily involved in their day-to-day practice responsibilities and activities. As a result, it is easy for them to lose sight of the policy issues. In order to better understand the implications of social work practice in justice settings, the editor has focused his attention on the community level as well as on society-at-large. In developing this book, the editor has adopted a multidimensional perspective that will help the reader better understand the total social system. The systems perspective of justice social work can enhance our understanding of the client, the client's family, the social worker, the agency, and society.

Social work has broadened its focus by placing greater emphasis on the institutional and societal factors that often impact on lawbreakers. Social workers have begun to look beyond the intrapsychic processes that operate within the individual client to those that operate within social systems and act as causative factors of crime and delinquency (Handler, 1975). Social workers should be aware that delinquency is often an outgrowth of factors in the social structure. These factors should be dealt with at the level of social policy and the delivery of social services (Kahn, 1965).

Social workers who enter this field of practice have many obstacles to overcome:

1. the authoritarian, custody-oriented environment of many correctional facilities;
2. the rigidity of many custody-oriented staff who view offenders as unreachable and incapable of positive change;
3. oversized caseloads and time-consuming, bureaucratic responsibilities (e.g. filling out numerous forms);
4. resistant clients whose social-emotional problems are often compounded by the uncertainties of an inconsistent and unpredictable system of justice;
5. limited resources and lack of cohesive relationships with other staff members; and
6. few opportunities for professional growth (through quality staff supervision and comprehensive in-service training).

The inadequacy of resources for changing the offender are noted by criminologist Vernon Fox:

> Correctional caseloads are so high that treatment remains crisis-oriented and superficial. The inadequacy of resources in terms of treatment personnel and facilities contributes to the high recidivism rates in American prisons and the high re-arrest rates in the communities. Classification and treatment programs are really delivery systems that do not deliver the intended results because there is so little to deliver; they are used to processing people and warehousing prisoners.

Excessive caseloads for probation and parole officers are a major problem, particularly in large cities:

> Caseloads in probation and parole are too large for *treatment*. Thus the work of probation and parole officers generally becomes mostly paperwork and writing pre-sentence investigation reports, progress reports, monthly reports, and crisis intervention, when a probationer or parolee in their caseloads gets into trouble (Fox, 1974, p. 311).

The juvenile and criminal justice arenas are posing new challenges to the social work profession. The changes of the 1980s thrust social workers into a demanding, yet potentially promising field of practice. These changes have implications for social work practice in justice settings. Correctional social work has been primarily based upon the rehabilitative ideal in an authoritarian setting; however, this rationale has been found to be basically ineffective, resulting in the need for social workers to reexamine the nature of their practice in criminal justice settings.

Social work's reorientation has already begun with the development of several new models, policies, and programs.

THE JUSTICE MODEL AND ITS IMPLICATIONS FOR SOCIAL WORKERS: One of the most significant is David Fogel's justice model in which social workers become advocates for "just deserts"— penal sanctions that are consistent and proportional to the seriousness of the offense. The recent passage of determinate sentencing legislation by several states is in accord with the "just deserts" model. The basic premise of this model is that the criminal justice system needs to provide humane and fair treatment to all offenders. Accordingly, social work advocates are calling for the development of alternative forms of punishment.

There is a trend in a number of states toward expanding the sentencing alternatives available to judges. The most common alternatives to traditional sentences are split sentences, shock probation, intermittent confinement, restitution through unpaid community service, diagnostic studies followed by probation, bench parole, and jail as a condition of probation. The purpose of some forms of alternative sentencing is to shock or jolt the offender by means of a brief period of confinement lasting from a few days to several months. The goal is to deter the offender from repeating his or her offense. By having the offender experience a brief period of incarceration, it is anticipated that he will not easily forget the consequences of committing a crime. Prolonged periods of incarceration only enrage offenders, isolating them from their families and community, in addition to the financial burden for taxpayers.

Fogel (1979) states that if sentencing is based on fairness and honesty, there is a greater likelihood that offenders will acquire similar values. Galaway (1982) acknowledges that social workers "may be initially uncomfortable with the notion of imposing punishments for reasons other than rehabilitation." However, he cautions that if social workers refuse to handle this responsibility, other staff will do so—staff who may be "less likely to impose punishments humanely and fairly."

RESTITUTIVE JUSTICE AND ITS IMPLICATIONS FOR SOCIAL WORK: Restitutive justice offers a promising alternative to traditional processing and punishment of the offender. Restitutive justice partially meets society's need to punish the offender by helping restore the victim's losses and contributing to community well-being. It provides a mechanism for reconciliation between the wrongdoers and their victims. These programs are unique because they involve both the victim and the offender. The two parties are often brought together to develop and mutually agree on a contract.

Restitution programs allow the offender an opportunity to rectify some of the hurt, injury, or damage he has caused the victim. There are three major types of restitution:

1. monetary payments made by the offender to the victim(s);
2. payments by either replacing damaged goods or providing service to the victim (which is often related to the offense); and
3. providing a service to the general community.

The special knowledge and skills that social workers possess is particularly well-suited for restitution work. As a result, a number of social workers have become administrators and direct service providers in these programs. The role of the worker in fostering a joint agreement between the victim and offender is crucial to the success of restitution efforts. The development of restitution programs is providing new roles for social workers as advocates, mediators, arbitrators, dispute settlers, and program managers. In recent years, we have also seen the increased development of victim service programs, which provide psychological and financial assistance to victims. These programs have also resulted in increased opportunities for justice social workers.

EMERGING ROLES IN PROBATION AND PAROLE: A new role for the probation and parole officer is that of a broker of services and manager of community resources. The emerging Community Resources Management Team (CRMT) has been referred to as "a coming mode of operation for probation and parole throughout the United States" (Wilson, 1978). It is unrealistic to expect the probation and parole officer to be able to resolve all of the offender's major problems. There already are many individuals and agencies in the community that have vast experience in solving particular problems. In fulfilling the role of community resource manager, the social worker first helps the offender identify his needs and problems and then helps him gain access to the most appropriate services. To be an effective coordinator of services, the officer needs to remain up-to-date on the nature, policies, and personnel changes of the specialized services.

Team supervision of probationers and parolees is also being utilized with increasing frequency, particularly in large cities. It is difficult for any one probation officer to be knowledgeable about the vast number of problem-solving strategies and specialized services available in large urban centers. As a result, probation and parole departments are utilizing team specialists with a shared decision-making approach. Thus, the individual probation or parole agent coordinates a single set of problem-solving services, such as employment services, training and education, alcohol or drug abuse treatment, and mental health services. One agent is responsible for determining the offender's needs and coordinating the negotiation of service plans with the other team specialists. Depending upon the size of the agency and the number of agents, one particular agent in a team, or a group of agents in an office, specialize in certain services.

PURCHASE OF SERVICES FROM THE PRIVATE SECTOR: Involving the private sector in corrections offers great promise of filling the gaps in state and locally operated services. By contracting with private community organizations and industrial corporations for the purchase of services, public agencies will be better able to deliver a wide range of cost-effective services to their clients (Fox, 1977; Lindquist, 1980; Salvation Army Correctional Services Department, 1978; Skoler, 1976).

Social work in justice settings has been a neglected area in the professional literature. Specifically, the literature is lacking information on the knowledge and skill base necessary for effective social work practice in the justice arena. Although there is a dearth of professional literature on this topic, a surge of interest has begun. A number of social work education programs (with faculty who have practice experience in criminal justice) are beginning to develop this area of the social work curriculum. This is in response to strong student interest for a sequence of courses and field placement opportunities that would lead to a career as a social worker in settings such as probation and parole, a restitution program, a diversion program, a group home, jail, prison, or community correctional center.

Justice social workers need to learn the theories, skills, and competencies that are specifically applicable to this field of practice. This knowledge will enable them to

— design and implement more effective programs;
— become more adept at handling various direct and indirect service roles; and
— become more effective in facilitating change for their clients, agency, and society.

Traditionally, social work practice has focused mainly on the direct service roles; yet, in juvenile justice and correctional settings, the indirect, social support tasks consume most of the social worker's time. Therefore, this volume presents the detailed knowledge base and skills necessary to the justice social worker in his/her direct and indirect service roles. There is a need for including the following curriculum content in justice social work courses:

1. Theory and practice of crisis intervention and other forms of short-term counseling.

2. Developing skills in advocacy, dispute settlement, conflict resolution, and mobilization of resources.
3. Understanding the special needs of minority clients in the justice system.
4. Learning the methods of interprofessional cooperation.
5. Doing legal research and giving expert testimony in court.
6. Learning program planning, management, and evaluation.
7. Understanding community analysis and organizational change techniques.

This text provides a comprehensive overview of social work policies and practices in juvenile and criminal justice settings. It examines the role of social workers in the delivery of social services to victims and perpetrators of crime and delinquency. It further provides the most current information about policies, programs, and services for clients of the justice system.

This handbook is the first authoritative reference in the important but neglected social work specialization of justice social work. This book will equip students and practitioners with the most up-to-date knowledge and methods used in the delivery of social services to status offenders, delinquents, convicted felons, ex-offenders, their victims, and their families. This volume offers no panacea, but it does provide detailed information and practical approaches for working with victims and offenders.

The essays in this book reflect the varied dimensions of social work's contributions to the well-being of juvenile and adult offenders, particularly the humanizing of juvenile justice and criminal justice processing. A new breed of dedicated social work professionals have become involved in the development of nontraditional programs for offenders and their families. Challenging opportunities for social workers are emerging in all components of the juvenile and criminal justice system. The progressive reforms and innovative program developments documented in this book reinforce the need for recruiting increased numbers of social workers to work in justice settings.

REFERENCES

Costin, Lela B. *et. al.* Barriers to social justice. in Bernard Ross and Charles Shireman (Eds.) *Social Work Practice and Social Justice*, Washington, D.C.: National Association of Social Workers, Inc., 1973.

Fogel, David. *We are the Living Proof: The Justice Model for Corrections.* Cincinnati: Anderson Publishing Co., 1979.

Fox, Vernon. The future of correctional treatment. in Albert R. Roberts (Ed.), *Correctional Treatment of the Offender*, Springfield, Illinois: Charles C Thomas, 1974.

Fox, Vernon. *Introduction to Corrections* (second edition). Englewood Cliffs, New Jersey: Prentice-Hall, Inc., 1977.

Galaway, Burt. Restitutive Justice: Policies, Programs and Services, 1982, mimeographed.

Galaway, Burt and Hudson, Joe (Eds.) *Perspectives on Crime Victims*. St. Louis: The C.V. Mosby Co., 1981.

Handler, Ellen. Social work and corrections. *Criminology*. August, 1975, *13*.

Hussey, Frederick A. and Duffee, David E. *Probation, Parole, and Community Field Services*. New York: Harper and Row Publishers, 1980.

Kahn, Alfred J. Social work and the control of delinquency: Theory and strategy. *Social Work*. April, 1965, *10*, 8–12.

Lindquist, Charles A. The private sector in corrections: Contracting probation services from community organizations. *Federal Probation*, March, 1980, *44*, 58–64.

Salvation Army Correctional Services Department. *The Salvation Army Misdemeanant Probation Program*. Jacksonville, Florida: The Salvation Army, 1978.

Skoler, D. Private sector delivery of criminal justice services — the hidden impact. *Criminal Justice Digest*, 1976, *4*, 1–3.

Wilson, Rob. Probation/parole officers as resource brokers. *Corrections Magazine*, June, 1978, *4*, 48–49.

CONTENTS

Page

Section I
POLICY ISSUES

Section II
THE ROLE OF POLICE SOCIAL WORKERS

Section III
VICTIM ASSISTANCE WORK

SOCIAL WORK IN JUVENILE AND CRIMINAL JUSTICE SETTINGS

Section I

POLICY ISSUES

INTRODUCTION

The development of national and local social policies in juvenile and criminal justice is a crucial step in meeting the social needs of juvenile and adult offenders, their families, and their victims. The purpose of social policies is to improve the quality of life in a society, the circumstances of living of individuals and groups, and the nature of human relationships (Gil, 1973). Social policy can lead to alleviating social problems, creating an environment in which individuals, groups, and communities can flourish and protecting the public from the pain and suffering inherent in violent communities.

This section analyzes social policy perspectives in the justice arena. It examines the social and political systems that shape the complex interactions between the social worker, the client, and the environment.

In Chapter 1, Harvey Treger emphasizes the need to understand and use two major concepts—interprofessional cooperation and social change. These types of systematic efforts can result in improving direct practice, planning, management, and evaluation. When interprofessional relationships such as the ones examined in Chapter 1 are developed, the results are a sharing of resources, increased referrals, and the ripple effect of other agencies seeking involvement in the new service.

Social work's leadership in the initiation of collaborative programs has the potential of significantly affecting public policy and program development in the justice system. Treger explores the potential of his model for advancing social work education, particularly justice social work. A strong relationship between educational institutions and the community may well provide a cost-effective model for stimulating the kind of interchange that will provide multiple benefits to a number of systems, i.e. the justice system, the social service system, the educational system, and the community.

Although there is constant change in the kinds of issues that constitute the public agenda in juvenile justice, a number of major policy issues have been at the top of the juvenile justice agenda for several years. In Chapter 2, C. Aaron McNeece focuses on the following contemporary issues: diversion, detention, status offenders, violent juveniles, new treatment alternatives, delinquency prevention programs, and due process. Permeating all of these issues is the broad question of whether the juvenile court should retain jurisdiction with certain types of cases, or refer them to mental health or other social service systems for appropriate treatment. McNeece's chapter also examines recent improvements in the juvenile justice system and problems and abuses that still remain.

In Chapter 3, Sheldon Gelman examines a somewhat disconnected set of issues in a systematic way so as to identify the context in which correctional policies develop and operate. He draws on a range of correctional, social work, and legal literature as well as judicial decisions and media reports to illustrate factors that determine policies in the correctional field. Conflicting value premises underlying correctional policies, societal perceptions regarding the threat of criminal behavior, and economic and political considerations play key roles in the development of correctional policies. The intent of correctional policies is mixed, reflecting both "rehabilitative" and "just deserts" elements. While a given perspective may become dominant at a given time in history, elements of the other perspective are always present. As the factors identified above shift over time, demands for reform are heard, different policies are developed, and resources available for correctional activities are modified. An examination of this process is crucial to understanding correctional policies.

Chapter 4, written by H. Wayne Johnson, explores the community context of crime and delinquency and the community responses to this social problem that are collectively termed criminal justice. The responses of society are formalized through the court, probation and parole, detention centers, institutions, and community-based alternatives. The responses of the different segments of the criminal justice system are examined in both rural and urban contexts. The basic trend has been for urban and rural communities to become more alike. Rural crime, which is growing at a disproportionate rate, seems to be catching up to the urban rates. Similarly, there is a convergence of both traditional and nontraditional methods of handling crime and delinquency in rural and urban areas.

REFERENCE

Gil, David G. *Unraveling Social Policy.* Cambridge, MA: Schenkman Publishing Co., 1973.

Chapter 1

SOCIAL WORK IN THE
JUSTICE SYSTEM: AN OVERVIEW

HARVEY TREGER

The practice of social work and social work education have had a long and somewhat tenuous association with the criminal justice system, particularly in the field of corrections. One has but to review the history of social work to recall the early National Conference on Charities and Corrections. Since the beginning of professional social work training, corrections, particularly probation, has recruited professionally trained social workers.[1] Oftentimes this was a difficult task, as professional social workers tended to view those who chose to work with offenders as "auslanders," i.e. outsiders to the profession. By working in an authoritarian setting with nonvoluntary unmotivated clients, the social worker in corrections was often looked upon as a violator of professional values and a coercer of people. This perception of the correctional social worker as a kind of borderline professional continues among many academicians, practitioners, and students who may feel uncomfortable about the nature of the work and the setting in which it is practiced. Nevertheless, a small core of professional social workers has continued to work in the field and has recently extended the boundaries of social work practice.

Traditionally, social work practice has related only to the corrections component of the justice system, after a person had been adjudicated and was already halfway through the system. Within the past two decades, social work has extended its services and usefulness from courts and institutions to the entire spectrum of criminal justice process to include law enforcement, the prosecution,

---

[1]Ben S. Meeker, Former Chief Probation Officer, Northern District of Illinois and Director of the Federal Probation Training Center, was a prominent leader in this effort.

and the defense. Social work is now the only profession in all parts of the justice system. Innovative programs in which social workers team up with the police, public defenders, legal aid lawyers, prosecutors, and magistrates have resulted in new relationships and opportunities for public service (Treger et al., 1975; Senna, 1975; Treger et al., 1972; *Speedy Trial Act*, 1979), new knowledge, and a workable model for system change. As a result of these new programs, social work's involvement in the justice system has been broadened and social justice has been extended, especially to minority and low income groups, many of whom are now diverted from the justice system into the social service system. In the years to come the introduction of social work in additional parts of the justice system may be looked upon as a significant social reform. At present, some of the observable positive outcomes have been new opportunities for social work employment and service and cooperation with professions, disciplines, and systems that have had little contact in the past. As a result of these developments, social work is now faced with a new challenge — to reconceptualize the evolving field of practice from corrections to "social work in the justice system" — to build upon the landmark conceptualizations and analysis begun by Elliot Studt (Studt, 1965; Studt, 1959). As cooperation with other professions continues, they too will need to examine the effects of interprofessional cooperation with social work on their practice and education.

Social workers in the justice system are now working with adjudicated and nonadjudicated people, juveniles, families, and adults who come to the attention of the system for a variety of reasons. They present a range of problems and predicaments, e.g. minor violations, personal, social, bureaucratic problems, and the reluctance of agencies to provide services because of restrictive and inflexible policies. The justice system has become a comprehensive juvenile, adult, and family service bureau for people with predicaments for which no single social agency, e.g. Child Welfare, Mental Health or Family Service, would offer services.

The Jane Addams College of Social Work has had a heavy investment in the development of innovative justice system programs, starting in 1970. "The Police-Social Work Team," a model program, developed in three Chicago area communities for diversion of juveniles and adults with misdemeanant and socially oriented noncriminal problems is now operational in forty-five Illinois communities, various parts of the United States, West Germany, England, and Israel. In 1975 to 1978, the "Prisoners Legal-Social Services Project" has also broken new ground in the area of law-social work interprofessional relationship, as well as offered multiprofessional services to incarcerated adults and their families in Illinois. Lawyer-social worker teams offered intervention to prisoners and their families in the areas of divorce, parole preparation and representation, child custody conflicts, and obtaining physical and mental health care in the prisons. This included individual casework as well as system intervention, thus utilizing the community organization skills of the social workers. More recently in the "Public Defender-Social Work Project" at the Juvenile Court of Cook County, social workers and public defenders teamed up to provide services to indigent parents in cases of child abuse and child neglect. Social workers were involved in client evaluation, obtaining services for families accused of abuse or neglect, developing and implementing alternative disposition plans for public defender attorneys to present to the court, direct service to defendant-parents, and expert testimony in court.

Another project, funded by the Law Enforcement Assistance Administration, was called the "Criminal Defense Project." This project utilized social workers to provide services to indicted persons prior to trial, including pretrial diversion plans, probation alternatives, and jury selection assistance.

The learning from these experiences now needs to be brought back into the classroom. Curriculum development that will support and extend social work practice in the justice system is urgently needed so that social work education will not be so fragmented and the gap between education and practice can be narrowed. When social workers can demonstrate their effectiveness in innovative and traditional settings, the social work profession will be perceived more positively and will achieve an increasingly significant role in influencing the direction of public policy in the justice system. Two major concepts, cooperation and social change, underpin the learning that has resulted from community-university innovation at the Jane Addams College of Social Work in the past decade.

COOPERATION

Experience indicates that achieving successful interdisciplinary cooperation is a dynamic process that requires a very sensitive, knowledgeable, and experienced approach. These are some basic guidelines to be followed toward achieving this goal:

1. Recognition and definition of a realistic achievable mutual goal with specific emphasis on the benefits for each profession.
2. Role definition of each profession; special emphasis should be given to clarify and point out the uniqueness as well as the similarities of each discipline to enable a careful, logical, and operative recognition of the boundaries between them.
3. Working toward a mutual commitment to achieve positive attitudes, removing myths, and establishing a contract of good will.
4. Identification and a beginning toward resolution of critical areas, e.g. communication, coordination, decision-making, etc.
5. Understanding and coping with the process of social change, i.e. the "chain reaction" and the disequilibrium of established community services that result from introducing new programs of interprofessional cooperation (Treger, 1981).

One of the discoveries of the social service project in working with law enforcement was that there was a lack of experience in working together. As a consequence, negative biases and preconceptions developed about each other. Social workers and police lacked knowledge and understanding of each other's professional subculture and system of organized services. They also lacked clarity about the problems of central concern for each of the professions, their values, ethics, and methods as well as attitudes of diverse client groups regarding their contact with each of these professions in different communities (Bartlett, 1961). As a result, both professions did not know how they could work together and be useful to each other and the community. By working together, the police and social workers learned from each other about their systems, perceptions of each other and the community, and areas where cooperation could be beneficial to all concerned. Similar relationships and service arrangements could be developed between other professionals both within and outside the justice system. As a result, energies can be freed up for investment in the provision of comprehensive, integrated services instead of being consumed in interrelationship problems and fragmentation.

Experience indicates that community situations and predicaments are frequently complex and interlocking. They require input from many professionals and systems working cooperatively as a team to maximize their impact on the problem. In this way, each profession may add to its knowledge as well as provide increased services to its clients. The expansion of social work services in the justice system thus requires cooperation with other professions and systems.

Interprofessional and intersystem efforts are not without risks, as differing orientations, values, and professional needs for status and control in decision-making areas can be conflictual. The issue of cooperation is a real one. The potential for one party to be swallowed up or taken over by the other exists. We are basically dealing with differences and the discomfort over differences. Sensitive areas such as these require personal and professional security, flexibility, and the capacity for mediation and change. The resolution of these issues will either inhibit or develop cooperative efforts. The idea of extending one's own professional practice by working with other disciplines has been neatly stated in another context by the great Russian cellist and recently turned conductor, Mstislav Rostropovich, "Once he has achieved a certain level, a physicist or a mathematician often must move outside his own discipline in order to make a leap in imagination—in other words to grow" (Feifer, 1978). Working with other professions may provide social work with a vehicle for growth. Social work has a tradition of interprofessional teamwork and the coordination of services with medicine, nursing, psychiatry, psychology, education, law, architecture, and the military. Much can be drawn from this body of knowledge and experience and utilized in current practice and education for social work in the justice system. Our new relationships with law enforcement, others in the justice system, community, and various departments in the university can further build upon and enhance social work's established competencies, develop new models for interprofessional and intersystem cooperation, and lead the way to further knowledge building and theory for professional practice and education in the justice system. The bottom line is, "Can we establish a true interdependent relationship that will result in improved services to people?" However, before cooperation between professions, disciplines, or system can begin, there must be a need, a desire and capacity for change, and systems that will permit openness and the interchange of ideas. As a result of cooperation social change can occur.

SOCIAL CHANGE

Social change is a key concept that is increasingly appearing in social science and other professional and scholarly literature. As Norval Morris points out, " . . . it is a result of the congruence of a wide diversity of personal and political pressures" (Morris, 1974). The process of change itself requires careful study and attention to the different reactions people have in moving from the known to the unknown. "While in the process of searching for suitable sites for the Police-Social Work Project and before funding was received a progression of obstacles were presented:

> 1st—It was a good idea but might not get funded, as there were too many pieces to put together.
> 2nd—No police department would ever accept this proposal.
> 3rd—It won't work out. There are too many new relationships and the Project challenged traditional police roles; social workers would lose their identities by working in a police department; clients would see social workers as part of the police organization and, therefore, would be unable to accept services.
> 4th—Once in the police department, we would become involved in a power struggle" (Treger, 1975).

The anxieties of colleagues revealed themselves through such comments as, "Are you in jail yet? Will you be in plain clothes or uniform? I heard you are helping the police to repress people." The students, who were in the process of developing a professional social work identity, revealed their anxieties about cooperation in working with the police by giving the project director a badge inscribed "Special Police" and a pair of handcuffs with an attached note saying, "To the Chief, Chief of the Social Service Project, from your line officers." The senior social worker received a toy club and a whistle. A police lieutenant revealed his anxieties over the project director's educational background when he said he had known college men before but, "they didn't know too much." The Chief also revealed some anxieties about teachers by his tone of voice and expression when he introduced his eight-year-old son to the project director and said, "This is a professor." We need to recognize our own feelings in moving into new situations and be sensitive to how others are reacting to change so that we can develop positive relationships. This is an area where direct practice skills can be applied to program development.

Inkles has stated, "Changes in one part of society have important implications for other parts of the system (thereby) enabling us better to understand why so often innovations are so slowly adopted" (Inkles, 1954). If system reactions to contemplated policy decisions are not planned for, unexpected and undesired reactions and impediments to a program can arise in a seemingly unrelated context.

The Police-Social Work Program has developed interest in other countries, e.g. West Germany, England, and Israel, where the problems in cooperation and social change also have relevance for them. When the Police-Social Work Program became operational in Hanover, West Germany (August, 1979), the Lord Mayor expressed concern about the political consequences of such cooperation. The professional social work association reacted strongly to the idea of police and social work cooperation. They distrusted the police (which was historically related to the police role in Nazi Germany) and feared the police would coopt the social workers. The police feared the social workers were communists and would radicalize them. Some social agencies even decided to boycott the program. Information revealed that the social agencies in the community had not been involved in the planning and did not fully understand the nature of the program, what the social workers would be doing, and the kinds of informational safeguards that were built into the program. Although there were interorganizational conflicts in the social work association, the leaders found an external issue, police-social work cooperation, that could unite their group. One dynamic was clear—some of the social agencies were feeling left out and were expressing their fears and anger. It was apparent that a step in the process of social program development was left out and now needed to be made up. Rather than respond to the social work association's threat of boycott directly, and thereby risk the chance of uniting them against the program, the police-social workers utilized a more effective strategy. They contacted the individual agencies, obtaining the support and influence of the Lord Mayor to further interagency cooperation. The resistance to the program was being resolved. An unexpected consequence to this event was that the attack on the project by the social work association brought project social workers closer to the police, facilitating the development of a positive relationship. The police, an often beleaguered group, could easily identify with the social workers in this situation. Experience indicates that obstacles in program development are frequently first viewed as problems, but in retrospect they may be recognized as opportunities to demonstrate competence to the community and further the development of interagency relationships, thus facilitating social change. The process of social change takes place because of the interaction and struggle people have with each other and the need for common goals.

When new programs are introduced into a community, they can affect change in other agencies; for example, the Police-Social Work Team seemed to produce a "ripple effect." Shortly after the program began in Maywood, Illinois, social and mental health agency executives contacted the police chief to determine if their agencies could offer services to the police department. The Chief remarked, "I have never seen these people before—they know that you're here and now they want to get into the act." Shortly thereafter a number of crisis services, e.g. hot-lines and twenty-four-hour mental health emergency services, began to emerge in the Maywood community. It seemed that the Police-Social Work Team program had stimulated the changing of service delivery patterns and encouraged the development of new services. This illustration demonstrates the effect innovation in the justice system can have in producing change in the larger community (Treger, 1981). Carter described the impact of social change in a system when he stated,

... If substantial numbers of offenders are diverted by local law enforcement to community based agencies there will be, in all likelihood, reduced inputs to prosecution, adjudication and correctional agencies. Lessened inputs will alleviate some of the backlog in the judicial system and reduce caseload pressure in probation and parole and size of institutional population. While these occurrences are desirable, at some point in time the bureaucratic instinct for survival may be threatened, reactions protective of the establishment may set in. (Carter, 1972)

Although the desire for new ideas and new programs to solve system problems are verbalized by educational, criminal justice, and community leaders, they are also resisted because invariably they challenge established norms and relationships creating conflict and disequilibrium in a system and threatening spheres of influence and power. It is this effect that change has on a system that must be understood and planned for by involving people who will be affected by the change at every step of the way. Students need to learn that when people are included, kept informed, and derive some benefits from the program, innovation will have a firm foundation for being sanctioned, supported, and developed. The literature indicates that the process of codifying and synthesizing some of the factors influencing organizational and community change has already begun.

CURRICULUM FOR SOCIAL WORK IN THE JUSTICE SYSTEM

Social workers entering the field of criminal justice should have knowledge of legal aspects and organizational systems unique to social work practice in the justice system as well as knowledge, skills, and values generic to all social work. The field requires a social worker capable of developing new services where patterns have not yet been defined and where the contribution of social work is not yet readily accepted. Social workers need to be skilled in designing and implementing as well as in delivering and critically evaluating services. The curriculum requires a holistic approach to social work, including knowledge of other human service professions, cooperation, and the process of achieving social change. The practice wisdom gained from experiences in innovative justice system programs should be captured and utilized as inputs for ongoing research and development in social work education and social work practice in the justice system.

OBJECTIVES

The general objectives for education in social work in the justice system should be to offer students the opportunity for classroom and field learning experiences to prepare for professional social work practice in the justice system. Specific objectives should include the following:

1. A knowledge base for direct practice with clients and for the planning, administration, and management of social services in the justice system.

2. The opportunity to develop skills in the justice system through use of internships to gain direct practice experiences or experiences in planning, administration, or management.
3. Experience in interdisciplinary study and opportunities for working with a range of professionals in the justice system.
4. Orientation to public policy, program development, and evaluation needs of the justice system.

The university as a community and system has an established structure that has been very resistant and slow to change. The implications for creating cooperative relationships between professions and disciplines to begin the development of a new educational model for social work in the justice system would affect the major academic areas: teaching, research, and community service.

While the university is not a public policymaking agency, it does provide an environment in which alternative solutions can be proposed and evaluated. The urban university can fulfill its public service role by providing leadership in the development of innovative ideas and effective programs as well as prepare its graduates for the realities of professional practice. Further, the community, by indicating its particular needs and resources, will challenge and stimulate the university to apply and develop its knowledge in new and creative ways. When education involves itself with contemporary problems, issues, and concerns, it may become more effective in improving the conditions of life in our society.

During this time of resource scarcity, it is necessary to try out innovative ideas that may induce multiple social and educational benefits. Indeed, cooperation between the university and community can result in more efficient use of available resources and greater impact on urban problems than each could achieve by working alone. It is likely that with closer relationships between universities and communities a cycle for innovation and service will be put into motion—a shuttle from theory to practice will be initiated. Social work can play a key role in these new arrangements by bringing new groups of people together and coordinating their special contributions to resolve community issues.

If social work is to become relevant to the justice system, it must reconceptualize the field of practice and narrow the gap between education and the needs in the field. A mutually useful relationship between educational institutions and the community may provide a cost effective model for stimulating the kind of interchange and development that provides multiple benefits to a number of systems.

REFERENCES

Bartlett, Harriet. *Analyzing Social Work Practice by Field*, National Association of Social Workers: New York, 1961.

Carter, Robert. The Diversion of Offenders. *Federal Probation*, 1972, *36*, 35.

Feifer, George. Slave To His Friends. *London Telegraph*, Sunday Magazine Section, April 16, 1978, p. 30.

Inkles, Alex. *What is Sociology?* Models of Society in Sociological Analysis: Prentice Hall.

Morris, Norval. *The Future of Imprisonment*, University of Chicago Press: Chicago, 1914.

Senna, Joseph J. Social Workers in Public Defender Programs. *Social Work*, 1975, *20*, 271–276.

Speedy Trial Act of 1974, Administrative Office of the U.S. Courts: Washington, D.C., 1979.

Studt, Elliot. *A Conceptual Approach to Teaching Materials: Illustrations from the Field of Corrections*, Council on Social Work Education: New York, 1965.

Studt, Elliot (ed). *Education for Social Workers in the Correctional Field*, Volume V of the Social Work Curriculum Study, Council on Social Work Education, New York, 1959.

Treger, Harvey and Associates. *The Police-Social Work Team*. Charles C Thomas, Publisher: Springfield, Illinois, 1975.

Treger, Harvey, Collier, James,.Henninger, Carl F. J. Deferred Prosecution: A Community Treatment Alternative for the Non-Violent Adult Misdemeanant. *Illinois Bar Journal*, 1972, *60*, 922–931.

Treger, Harvey. Police-Social Work Cooperation. *Social Casework: The Journal of Contemporary Social Work*, 1981, *62*.

Chapter 2

JUVENILE JUSTICE POLICY

C. AARON MCNEECE

E very American youth is a potential candidate for processing, labelling, and treatment by our juvenile justice system.
Certain kinds of delinquent behavior are so common among our
children that we consider them to be simply a part of "growing up"
(Gold, 1970). Those few children who never violate a criminal law
may still come into contact with the system by skipping school,
refusing to obey their parents, or running away from home. In
fact, these "status offenders" who violate no criminal laws are often
dealt with more harshly than juvenile lawbreakers (National Institute for Juvenile Justice, 1980).

Whether a particular child comes into contact with the juvenile justice system often depends more on chance than any
other factor. Only a fraction of juvenile crime is detected and
reported, and an even smaller fraction of those crimes reported
result in official handling by law enforcement agencies and the
courts (Gold, 1966). Even when detected or observed by police, juvenile crime is often ignored, especially if it is perceived to be of a trivial or nonserious nature (Williams & Gold,
1972).

Nevertheless, delinquent behavior occurs so commonly that
over three million youths per year are taken into custody by
police, and half of them are referred to juvenile courts (Cavan &
Ferdinand, 1975). At the present rate of referral, approximately
one child in ten will be officially processed by a juvenile court
before his or her eighteenth birthday (Bureau of Justice Statistics,
1981). These figures do not include the millions of juveniles who
are dealt with informally by either law enforcement agencies or
the courts. The potential of the system for influencing the lives of
the nation's youth, for good or bad, is obviously very great.

19

MAJOR SYSTEM COMPONENTS

The first justice system official that a juvenile is likely to encounter is the local policeman. The police are the major gate-keepers of the juvenile courts in over three-fourths of all cases (Rubin, 1976; Cohen, 1975). The police, generally acting on citizen complaints, apprehend juveniles and decide whether to take any further action. Many cases end with the police simply warning and releasing the offender. Depending on the jurisdiction and the structure of the local system, the police may transport the juvenile to a detention facility and file a petition or a complaint or they may release the juvenile to a parent or guardian and then file a petition with the court.

Each judicial district has at least one court designated to handle "juvenile cases," usually delinquency and juvenile status offenses —and possibly dependency and neglect cases. In some districts this court will be an independent juvenile court; in others a family court (which may also handle divorce and child support procedures), and in still others it may be a district court *sitting as* a juvenile court. Even in those cases where district judges process delinquency cases, however, the laws under which decisions are made concerning adjudication and disposition are different than the laws under which adult criminal offenders are tried (Rubin, 1976).

The juvenile court has several options available in processing an alleged delinquent or status offender. The court's options may range from dismissal of the charges to placement under probation supervision to confinement in a secure institution. The major choices made by the court are either to take no further formal action or to place a youth on probation. Relatively few juvenile offenders are institutionalized (Cohen, 1975; Hasenfeld, 1976).

Treatment/rehabilitation/correctional agencies are the other major component of the juvenile justice system. These programs are sometimes operated directly by the court itself, but more frequently the court may contract with another agency to provide services and transfer the legal custody of the juvenile to that agency. Some children under probation supervision may be allowed to remain at home or placed in foster care and also be referred for treatment to another agency. (This is especially true of juveniles who are adjudicated on drug abuse charges.) Thus, more than one agency or program may be used as a disposition for a youth (Empey, 1978).

The "end of the line" for an adjudicated delinquent is a juvenile correctional institution. The quality of care and treatment available in the facilities is generally not good (Bartollas et al., 1976; Polsky, 1962). Institutions are usually public rather than private, provide only moderate security, and are quite ineffective in "rehabilitating" their clients (Jessness, 1970; Seckel, 1975).

MAJOR COMPONENTS OF THE SYSTEM'S ENVIRONMENT

A number of agencies and organizations that we do not ordinarily define as being part of the juvenile justice system nevertheless have important consequences for that system. Foremost among those agencies are the schools, who refer to the courts a large number of status offenders known as "truants." Schools also provide both law enforcement agencies and the courts with much useful information about juvenile offenders. Probation officers commonly use schools as a meeting place for interviews with their clients. Since the juvenile frequently *must* attend school as a condition of probation, the probation officer can depend on the school as a place to locate him (McNeece, 1976).

On another level, schools are an important agency in the justice system's environment because a large proportion of juveniles who are "failures" at school eventually become clients of the system. Schools routinely and, rather illogically, ask law enforcement and judicial agencies to correct shortcomings of the educational system (Polk & Schafer, 1972).

Social service agencies may sometimes refer clients to the juvenile justice system, especially to the courts, but they are more important on the "output" side of the system. As mentioned above, courts frequently contract with and refer (or commit) to social service agencies those clients who are believed to be in need of services. State or local public welfare agencies, youth service bureaus, or community mental health agencies are commonly used. Private agencies can also be used, but many of them are reluctant to accept juvenile offenders as clients. They may fear that acceptance of these juveniles will reduce opportunities to serve more "desirable" clients (McNeece, 1976).

There are many reform groups and client advocacy groups that also have a strong influence on the juvenile justice system. On the national level, the League of Women Voters has been quite active in studying juvenile justice systems and issuing recommendations for reform. The Junior League and The National Council of Jewish Women have also been active in the same policy arenas at the state and local levels. Many local reforms have been accomplished because of the attention these groups focused on the problems of unnecessary or prolonged detention, illegal jailing of juveniles, violation of legal rights, etc. Other important organizations in the juvenile justice system are indicated in Figure 2-1. Because of its important role in receiving, processing, and distributing clients, the court is perceived as the focal point of the system.

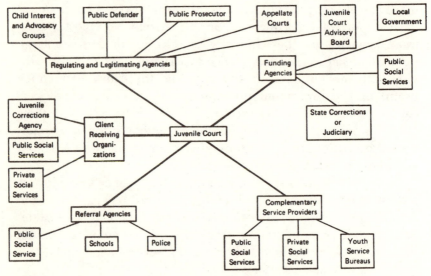

Figure 2-1. The Juvenile Court and the Juvenile Justice System.
Adapted from Yeheskel Hasenfeld, "The Juvenile Court and the Task Environment," in Rosemary Sarri and Yeheskel Hasenfeld (Eds.), *Brought to Justice?: Juveniles, the Courts, and the Law* (National Assessment of Juvenile Corrections, University of Michigan, 1976).

MAJOR POLICY ISSUES IN JUVENILE JUSTICE

A social problem is defined as a social issue when there is disagreement over the choice of a proposed solution for the problem (Eyestone, 1981). Although there is constant change in the kinds of issues that constitute the public agenda, a number of major policy issues have been at the top of the juvenile justice agenda for several years. These issues include diversion, detention, the handling of status offenders, the development of new treatment alternatives, and due process. Permeating all of these issues is the broad question of whether the court should retain jurisdiction in many cases or simply refer certain juveniles to mental health or other social service systems for appropriate treatment.

Critics of formal court processing of juvenile offenders generally cite three arguments against it: (1) the court consistently fails to protect the legal rights of its clients, (2) official court processing has a stigmatizing effect on juveniles, and (3) legal sanction is ineffective in compelling treatment, i.e. that the client must be willing to accept help freely in order for treatment to be effective (Schur, 1973).

Formal Versus Informal Processing

Opponents of formal processing believe that " ... it would probably be better for all concerned if young delinquents were not detected, apprehended or institutionalized" (Samuels, 1971), since too many of them get worse while under the care of the court and the juvenile justice system.

On the other hand, proponents of formal court handling of juvenile offenders view the diversion of a client from the court as a denial of the client's right to *help* from the court. Without the coercive effect of the court's legal sanction, children who are in need of help might not get it. Some feel that the court would be abdicating its responsibility if it did not support " ... parents with its authority ... " (Martin & Snyder, 1976). "Otherwise we are putting the burden of change on those who have shown that they can bear it least well." Another argument against the elimination of formal processing is that the legal rights of the client may be even *less* protected under informal arrangements such as diversion (Nejelski, 1976).

The most radical critics of the juvenile court argue that the juvenile justice system is unable to reform itself either to adhere to the rule of law or to ensure that children under its jurisdiction receive the type of care that should be provided. Their solution is to allow children accused of "criminal" offenses to be tried in adult court, while status offenders would be completely removed from the legal system and sent elsewhere for services (Guggenheim, 1978). More moderate proposals would reform the juvenile court rather than abolish it. Rubin (1979) suggests changes such as removing the court's jurisdiction over status offenders and prohibiting the waiver of counsel for a juvenile at any stage of the legal process.

There is no simple way of determining whether formal or informal processing is more effective in dealing with juvenile clients. The kind of social experimentation necessary to allow a more-or-less definitive answer is not possible. In comparing systems that use formal court processing with systems that use other methods to handle juvenile offenders (South Australia, Norway), there is some reason to believe that while the use of non-court alternatives may reduce stigma for the client (Sarri & Bradley, 1980), there are as many problems inherent in administrative solutions as in judicial solutions (Dahl, 1976).

Diversion

Despite the debate over formal versus informal methods of processing, there is a widespread feeling among most scholars and practitioners of juvenile justice that the more serious juvenile offenses must continue to be referred to law enforcement agencies and to the courts for handling and that diversion is more appropriate for first offenders and juveniles accused of "trivial" offenses. Beyond that, however, there seems to be little agreement on the matter of diversion, including an acceptable definition of diversion (Cressey & McDermott, 1973). To some, diversion simply means that the police and the courts should adopt a "hands-off" policy—leaving children alone wherever possible (Schur, 1973). To others it means that juveniles must not only be diverted *from* the police or the court but that they must also be diverted *to* other agencies which provide appropriate services. This kind of diversion would, "involve the mobilization of greater, not fewer, programs for children ... " although official court processing would be reduced (Empey, 1978).

Theoretically, diversion programs could reduce much of the secondary deviance that is created by the effect of labelling a juvenile as a "delinquent" through formal court processing (Lemert, 1951). The success of a diversion policy depends on whether the referral of a client to a non-court alternative (mental health, family service agency, youth service bureau, etc.) is less stigmatizing than formal court handling and whether recidivism rates for diversionary programs are lower than for official court-operated programs such as probation.

The evidence on these two points is mixed. While some research indicates that non-court programs are less stigmatizing (Sarri & Bradley, 1980) and that clients of diversion programs have fewer rearrests than those handled formally (Quay & Love, 1977; Nejelski, 1976), other studies show that there are no significant differences in the recidivism rates of diversionary clients and officially processed clients (Sarri & Bradley, 1980; Spergel & Reamer, 1981). Still other research indicates that despite widespread diversionary efforts, the volume of officially processed cases recorded by the courts has not decreased. Several jurisdictions that began diversion programs have watched their official court caseloads grow *along with diversion caseloads* (Sarri & Bradley, 1980; Spergel & Snapp, 1977).

While the goal of diversion is laudatory, it appears that its overall effect may have been to extend control where none existed before (Lemert, 1981). It may have "widened the net" of social control and brought more children into the juvenile justice system who would not otherwise be there (Blomberg, 1975; Graecen, 1975; Klein et al., 1976; Kutchins & Kutchins, 1973; Mattingly & Katlin, 1975; McNeece, 1976; Vorenberg & Vorenberg, 1973). The increase in the number of clients in the system despite the growth of diversion programs raises the possibility that diversion programs may be attracting new clients who previously would not have been selected for formal court processing. Now that less stigmatizing options are available, however, the courts may be willing to accept additional cases for referral to diversion programs. This would not be undesirable if additional clients are getting help, if they are not being drawn further into the juvenile justice system through diversion programs, and if their legal rights aren't being violated.

On the other hand, if *coerced* treatment is taking place in situations where it is inappropriate, it could present another major problem for a diversion policy. There is a strong feeling among some critics that the protection of clients' legal rights is even less adequate in diversion programs than in official court handling. The essence of the problem, as Nejelski sees it (1976), is that, " . . . voluntary diversion is a contradiction in terms." Clients often attend diversion programs under a direct or an implied threat of formal court sanctions, but clients who are not formally processed are rarely provided adequate legal counsel.

Status Offenders

Since the creation of the juvenile court system in the United States, certain kinds of juvenile behaviors of a noncriminal nature were defined as appropriate matters of concern for the juvenile justice system (Platt, 1969). In 1967, the President's Commission on Law Enforcement and the Administration of Justice (1967) expressed the opinion of many reform groups when it suggested that, "Serious consideration . . . should be given to the complete elimination of the court's power over children for noncriminal conduct." Juveniles who were accused of such offenses as truancy, incorrigibility, or sexual promiscuity were processed in juvenile courts along with their peers who had committed criminal offenses. They were detained in the same detention facilities, provided the same services, and given the same label—"juvenile delinquents." Many recent studies have shown that the noncriminal offenders ("status offenders") actually received harsher dispositions than those juveniles adjudicated delinquent for criminal behavior (Gibbons & Griswold, 1957; Lerman, 1968; National Institute for Juvenile Justice, 1980).

For at least twenty years, there has been concern that the indiscriminate labelling and mixing of status offenders with other juvenile offenders might result in unwarranted stigmatization of children who were not accused of criminal activity. A new legal code in California in 1961 provided for a separate legal status for status offenders, and during the next decade many other states followed suit. Children who previously had been classified as juvenile delinquents for certain noncriminal behaviors were now reclassified as CHINS, PINS, JINS, or MINS—meaning children, persons, juveniles, or minors in need of supervision. In a few instances archaic terms such as "wayward" children or ungovernable were used (Levin & Sarri, 1974). Unfortunately, most of these states did not require the separate handling of juvenile status offenders but simply a different legal designation. A number of organizations and reform-minded individuals continued to press for change, however, and federal legislation was finally passed that placed much pressure on the states to separate status offenders and delinquents. The Juvenile Justice and Delinquency Prevention

Act of 1974 required that states receiving federal funds to fund juvenile offender programs must agree to remove all status offenders from places of detention or incarceration within two years. Unfortunately, even those state systems that readily agreed to comply with this Act have had considerable difficulty in doing so (National Institute of Juvenile Justice, 1980). There is some evidence that certain jurisdictions have even resorted to "name games" such as simply changing the labels under which offenders are processed in order to route them into legally acceptable disposition alternatives (McNeece, 1980).

Concern over the treatment of status offenders in the juvenile justice system prompted the National Council on Crime and Delinquency to issue a policy statement in 1975 calling for the removal of such cases from the jurisdiction of the juvenile court (NCCD, 1975). Instead, the Council asserted that status offenders and their families, " . . . should have community resources available for their voluntary use . . . "

Detention

The purpose of detaining a youth awaiting a court hearing is *control*: either to prevent the youth from harming himself or others or to insure a court appearance. Recent studies vary widely in their estimates of the use of detention. Pawlak (1977) and Cohen (1975) estimate that about one quarter of all youths are held in detention while awaiting a court hearing, while the President's Commission (1967) and Sarri (1974) estimate that perhaps two-thirds or more of such youths are sent to a detention facility. Even more disturbing is the fact that as late as 1967, 93 percent of the nation's counties, serving 50 percent of the youth population, had *no* detention facilities (National Council on Crime and Delinquency, 1967). The major alternatives for detaining children in these jurisdictions are adult jails and police lockups (Empey, 1978). Despite the fact that state laws generally require the separate maintenance of juvenile and adult prisoners, the incidence of juvenile-adult mingling in adult jails is a national embarassment (Sarri, 1974).

Although it perhaps makes sense to detain juveniles accused of serious crimes, the severity of the offense is only one factor considered in detention decisions. Actually juvenile status offenders are far more likely to be detained in certain jurisdictions than are juveniles accused of crimes, especially if they are females, and especially if they are females accused of promiscuity (Chesney-Lind, 1977; Sarri, 1974). Detention decisions seem to be strongly influenced by parents, schools, and welfare agencies who frequently request the detention of status offenders as a way of reinforcing their control over these children (Cohen, 1975). A frequent problem with status offenders is that the lack of family willingness or availability to take custody results in their being sent to detention by default. Altogether, status offenders tend to have a higher rate of detention than other juvenile offenders (National Institute for Juvenile Justice, 1980).

There are other problems of sex discrimination in detention, too. Not only are girls detained for moral reasons, especially morals related to sexual behavior, far more often than boys but their treatment in detention is often discriminatory. It is a common practice to check girls in detention for pregnancy or veneral disease, but boys are rarely subjected to any type of sexual examination (Chesney-Lind, 1977; Wakin, 1975).

In many jurisdictions detention is used for purposes other than pretrial control of a juvenile. In most states, punishment is not defined as a legitimate function of juvenile detention, although local authorities often use it as such. Wisconsin began allowing limited use of detention as a postadjudication dispositional alternative several years ago, however, and a recent Senate bill in Florida (which already has the nation's highest rate of juvenile detention) would have allowed judges to "sentence" juveniles to detention as punishment. These events seem to underscore the frustration of local authorities in attempting to cope with the delinquency problem. It should be kept in mind, however, that juvenile detention facilities usually have even fewer resources available for the treatment or rehabilitation of juvenile offenders than do the juvenile correctional programs. Even if they did, it would still be unwise to mix youths awaiting a court hearing with those "sentenced" for punishment.

Social workers who are concerned with juvenile detention, especially those who work as intake officers for the court, should attempt to use the least restrictive detention alternative necessary to guarantee a juvenile's appearance in court or to protect the community. Whenever possible, a juvenile should be remanded to the custody of his family or placed in a foster home or other nonsecure detention alternative.

Treatment Alternatives

Juvenile justice philosophy is based on the assumption that juvenile offenders are susceptible to rehabilitative efforts and that society has an obligation to provide appropriate treatment whenever possible (Empey, 1978). The juvenile codes of the states reflect clearly the belief that the primary purpose of bringing an accused juvenile under the protection of the court is to provide special diagnosis and treatment, not to mete out punishment (Levin and Sarri, 1974). The courts have sought to provide treatment to their clients through institutional programs, probation, and other community-based alternatives. Despite decades of experiences in attempted rehabilitation programs, there is little evidence that anything works (Bartollas et al., 1976; Jessness, 1970; McCord & McCord, 1959; McCachern & Taylor, 1967).

The evidence is most clear in institutional programs, where research has consistently shown that outcomes of incarceration are likely to be increased resistance to authority (Bartollas et al., 1976; Cressey, 1960; Sykes, 1965), exploitation and abuse (Polsky, 1962), and high readmission rates (Jessness, 1970; Rossebaum et al., 1971; Seckel, 1965). Studies of probation programs have shown that clients on experimental intensive caseloads fare no better than those on regular caseloads (Adams, 1970) or those who received *no* probation supervision (McEachern & Taylor, 1970). In fact, there is some evidence that more intensive supervision is associated with greater risks of recidivism (Lipton et al., 1975). Probation officers who are able to pay closer attention to the behavior of their probationers are apparently more likely to notice their failure to follow the conditions of their probation.

Studies of community-based treatment alternatives have also failed to yield firm evidence of their effectiveness. One study of the Community Treatment Program in California claimed a high success rate (in terms of lower parole revocation) for experimental clients who were diagnosed, classified, and assigned to a caseworker who was trained to meet their needs. The control group, who were incarcerated and then released on regular parole, actually committed fewer new offenses than the experimental group, however (Lerman, 1968; Palmer & Warren, 1967). It may be that the lower recidivism rates as well as the higher offense rates of the experimental group may simply reflect the greater tolerance of the caseworkers who were assigned to that group, while the regular parole officers were not as tolerant of new offenses.

Despite the rather dismal state of knowledge that currently exists concerning the rehabilitation of juvenile offenders, the research has yielded several facts that have important policy implications for their treatment. First, we know that institutional programs do not work. If they must be used at all, we should recognize that the purpose is control or punishment, not rehabilitation. To continue committing children to institutions for *treatment* simply guarantees additional failure and increased disenchantment with the concept of rehabilitation.

Second, we know that while the evidence on probation effectiveness is not convincing, the great majority of probationers do not commit new offenses (England, 1957; Grunhut, 1948; Scarpitti & Stephenson, 1968). At the same time, we also know that probation programs are more humane and less expensive than institutional programs. It would seem reasonable to suggest that a presumption be made in every juvenile case that probation (or another community-based alternative) is the preferred disposition except when the nature of the offense indicates a need for protecting the community or controlling the juvenile.

Due Process

Our concern with the provision of rehabilitative services to juvenile offenders has actually interfered with the protection of legal rights. The benevolent ideology surrounding the juvenile court has been so pervasive that we have often forgotten that courts are primarily *legal processing institutions*, not treatment institutions. Juvenile court philosophy has justified the trying of juvenile cases in formal hearings, without defense counsel, with no sworn testimony, and with great reliance on hearsay evidence, because the goal of the court was to *treat* children and not to *punish* them (Empey, 1978). It was not until 1966 that the Supreme Court recognized in the *Kent* case (383 U.S. 541, 1966) that a child "receives the worst of two possible worlds: that he gets neither the protections accorded to adults nor the solicitous care and regenerative treatment postulated for children."

The following year, the Supreme Court accepted the position that at least some of the procedural safeguards granted to adults should also be provided to juveniles (*In re Gault, 387* U.S. 1). A fifteen-year-old boy, Gerald Gault, was charged with making an obscene phone call and committed to an institution where he could have been held until the age of twenty-one. (The maximum punishment for an adult would have been a $50 fine and two months in jail.) Gerald was held in detention without notification of his parents, and no official petition outlining the charges was presented to his parents prior to the trial. The petition, in fact, made no reference to any factual basis for the court action other than stating that "said minor is a delinquent minor."

The complaint originally filed with the police was only verbal, and the complainant never appeared in court to provide sworn testimony. No one was sworn in at the hearing, nor were any transcripts of the proceedings maintained. Gerald was alleged to have confessed his guilt to the police, but his "confession" was never put in writing, was obtained without the presence or advice of either his parents or legal counsel, and without forewarning him of his legal rights. Gerald was not represented by an attorney at any point in the adjudication or disposition process. There was, in fact, a total disregard of due process.

The court once more reaffirmed juvenile's rights to due process in the *Winship* case (397 U.S. 358) and added a further requirement that proof of guilt beyond a reasonable doubt be used as a standard in juvenile courts. The Supreme Court has stopped short of saying that juvenile courts must provide exactly the same due process guarantees as adult courts, however. "The observance of due process standards, intelligently and not ruthlessly administered, will not compel the States to abandon or displace any of the substantive benefits of the juvenile process" (*In re Gault*, 1967:21).

We have corrected a serious deficiency in the juvenile justice system by requiring closer attention to matters of procedural rights, but it will take much more than a mere declaration of those rights by appellate courts before much real change should be expected; for example, insuring that accused juveniles are provided legal counsel will not per se make any significant difference in case outcomes. Several recent studies have shown that there is no substantial difference in adjudication or disposition decisions when attorneys are assigned to represent juveniles (National Institute of Juvenile Justice, 1980). In fact, some studies show that juveniles who are represented by legal counsel are more likely to receive a harsh disposition (McNeece, 1976; Stapleton & Teitlebaum,

1972). The problem is the prevailing attitude concerning procedural rights that still exists in the juvenile justice system. Many attorneys who represent juvenile clients remain convinced that because the juvenile court is really an institution for providing treatment to their clients, they should not aggressively pursue the protection of their legal rights. After all, the court is still presumed to act "in the best interests of the child."

The roots of the juvenile court are still deeply embedded in the principles of equity jurisprudence, a branch of law that provides remedies where the common law does not apply, and juvenile judges are accustomed to exercising tremendous discretion. There are few watchdogs surrounding the juvenile court, and extraordinary remedies via the appeals process are rarely sought. U.S. Supreme Court decisions are often inconsequential if the juvenile court chooses not to incorporate those decisions into its own decision-making. Unfettered by statutory, institutional, or systemic constraints, the juvenile court can be expected to continue ignoring procedural rights (McNeece, 1976).

ANALYZING JUVENILE JUSTICE POLICY

Our understanding of the juvenile justice policy development process will benefit from the use of a paradigm or model, which will help us relate current policies and programs to structural, environmental, and situational factors that impinge on the policy-making process. Such a model is systems theory. Before explaining that model, however, definitions are in order:

> *Policy*—guiding principles or courses of action adopted and pursued by societies and their governments (Gil, 1976).
>
> *Social Problem*—a condition identified by significant groups as a deviation from social standard or a breakdown of some important facet of social organization, a widely felt deficiency or disappointed expectation (Eyestone, 1978).
>
> *Social Issue*—a conflict between two or more identifiable groups over procedural or substantive matters relating to the allocation of values (resources, positions, authority, wealth, etc.) (Cobb & Elder, 1972).

An issue arises when a significant public with a problem seeks or demands governmental action, and there is public disagreement over the best solution for the problem. If action is taken by legislators, judges, or agency officials that serves to guide future decision-making on that or similar issues, a *policy* has been formulated.

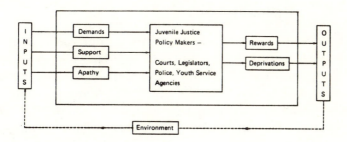

Figure 2-2. The Juvenile Justice Policy Process.

Systems Theory

Systems theory stresses the interrelationship of all the elements in the policy process. Policy is not made in a vacuum. Policymakers respond to and are influenced by inputs from organizations in the task environment (Figure 2-1) and from the larger social, cultural, and physical environment (Figure 2-2). Policy responses of the official decision-makers have a corresponding influence on the environment, which consequently influences inputs.

The policy formulation process may be triggered by a sudden event, such as the abuse of a child in a detention facility, which focuses attention on the existence of the problem. If a significant group defines the problem as such, it becomes a *social* problem. If the group is able to expand the problem to a larger audience and *demand* that government take action to change the policy regarding juvenile detention (and there is no general agreement on what should be done), the problem then becomes a social *issue* and is placed on the public agenda for consideration (Cobb & Elder, 1972).

At the same time, there also may be *support* for continuing the current policy. Unless the issue becomes highly politicized, however, the most frequent citizen response will be *apathy*. (The degree of apathy determines how much freedom official decision-makers have in formulating policy.) Constraints on the range of policy alternatives possible are partly determined by the environment. Some alternatives, such as building a new juvenile shelter, may be precluded because of the lack of financial resources. Other alternatives, such as increasing the use of foster care for serious offenders, may not be possible because of prevailing social values regarding social control and punishment.

A change in policy, such as a decision to divert juvenile offenders from detention, has repercussions throughout the system; for example, the police may respond by refusing to arrest offenders if they expect that they will not be detained. A reduction in the use of detention might also allow the transfer of resources to be used in another program, such as probation supervision. The actual policy decision may be compared to a stone tossed into a pond, with the policy repercussions represented by the concentric ripples flowing out from the point of impact.

Trends in Juvenile Justice Policy

Changes in juvenile justice policy may be identified in at least two different ways. First of all, one might analyze changes that have occurred in official written policies or examine proposals for reform in those policies. If one were to follow that method, it would appear that major trends in juvenile justice policy have occurred in the areas of diversion, decriminalization, and deinstitutionalization. A second method is to determine by observation what actually happens to children. We would conclude that policy changes had occurred only if patterns of policy outcomes had changed. That method might lead us to quite different conclusions about policy trends.

The enthusiastic application of "diversion" programs actually has resulted in the creation of a new semilegal, semiwelfare bureaucracy, which has broadened the effective social control mechanisms of the juvenile justice system without paying much attention to the legal rights of children (Empey, 1978). While many juvenile offenses have been decriminalized and separate dispositional alternatives for status offenders have been created, it is difficult to say that children are being treated much differently than they were before, apart from the changes in the labels they now wear. Approximately half of all of the juveniles in institutions prior to the passage of the Juvenile Justice and Delinquency Prevention Act of 1974 were status offenders. The implementation of this act

resulted in a relatively small reduction in institutional populations (McNeece, 1980).

Most of the states have at least one loophole that allows the
continued incarceration of status offenders; the most common is
the provision that allows status offenders to be placed under probation supervision. Violations of probation supervision may result
in the offender being reclassified as a juvenile *delinquent*. Official
statistics show that the number of juveniles held in public institutions did decrease between 1971 and 1977 (Bureau of Justice Statistics,
1981), but there was a corresponding increase in *private* institutional
programs. There has been increased use of private correctional
facilities, residential treatment programs, and psychiatric units of
hospitals to serve juvenile offenders. In 1976, 40 percent of all
AFDC foster care maintenance funds were spent for institutional
care for juveniles with mental or delinquency problems (Lerman,
1980).

It is interesting that certain policy reforms have spilled over
into the juvenile justice system from the adult criminal justice
system. The state of Washington recently adopted a determinate
sentencing policy for juvenile offenders. Under that policy, juvenile offenders are sentenced to a specific term of incarceration that
is related to the severity of the offense. The attempt is to "make the
punishment fit the crime" (Sevill, 1980). This concept obviously is
not congruent with the rehabilitative ideal so prevalent in our
juvenile justice system, but many reformers believe that it will be
more equitable and just.

Changes such as this may also reflect a general sense of frustration and powerlessness in dealing with juvenile offenders. Even
worse, it may also indicate a change in the public mood, which is
becoming more favorable to punishment rather than rehabilitation.
Recent evidence of this changing mood is reflected in legislation
introduced in Florida in 1981 that would facilitate the transfer of
juveniles to adult courts and allow judges to sentence juvenile
offenders to local detention centers as punishment (S.B. 243,
1981). Similar legislation has also been introduced in several
other states.

Another useful way to analyze policy changes in juvenile justice
is to examine the changes in funding patterns, because financial
support for programs is one of the keys to successful implementation. If decision-makers are serious about making changes in

policy, those changes will be reflected in budgets. The major change in funding programs in the area of juvenile justice occurred with the passage of the Law Enforcement Assistance Act in 1965 (P.L. 89-197) and the Omnibus Crime Control and Safe Streets Act of 1968 (P.L. 90-351). Together, these two laws provided the money and the administrative apparatus for providing new grants to state and local agencies for law enforcement and related programs. In 1974 the Office of Juvenile Justice and Delinquency Prevention was created within LEAA to coordinate efforts to control delinquency (P.L. 93–415). For the fiscal years 1975 through 1977, 89,125 JJDP formula grants to state and local agencies were approved (Office of Juvenile Justice and Delinquency Prevention, 1979). In 1977, 47,625,000 dollars was available through OJJDP for delinquency control and prevention programs.

Budget authority for the Office of Juvenile Justice and Delinquency prevention was scheduled to increase to 100 million dollars in FY 1981 and 135 million dollars in FY 1982 under the proposed Carter budget (Office of Management and Budget, 1981). The actual expenditure for juvenile justice formula grants in 1980 was 68,000,000 dollars (OMB, 1981).

Meanwhile, the disenchantment of Congress with LEAA resulted in a mandate to dismantle the agency well before the end of the Carter administration. While the actual expenditure for all Law Enforcement Administration Programs in FY 1980 was 444,781,000 dollars, the executive budget request for FY 1982 was only 159,691,000 dollars. The few remaining LEAA grants are expected to end in 1982 (OMB, 1981a), but President Reagan has proposed that the funds that would have been allocated as grants through the Office of Juvenile Justice and Delinquency Prevention be converted to block grants to the states (OMB, 1981c). Whether the Congress approves this transfer and whether the states will use that money for the same purposes remains to be seen.

Meaningful statistics on the state and local funding of juvenile justice programs are not readily available, but we do know that state and local expenditures for all corrections programs (adult and juvenile), police protection, and judicial operations increased between 75 to 90 percent during the period from 1971 to 1976 (National Criminal Justice Information and Statistics Service, 1979). Much of the funding increases during the past decade have been for community-based programs. A much greater amount of the increased funding probably has been needed just to continue old programs at higher inflated costs. After discounting the above-mentioned figures for inflation, "real" increases in funding would be much smaller.

Many of the original advocates of the federal cost-sharing approach to crime and delinquency programs now believe that a serious mistake was made in allowing billions of dollars to be spent on criminal and juvenile justice programs. Some even believe that not only was this money wasted, but also that it might have made matters worse. Wilson (1975) believes that these billions of dollars did not even add much to our knowledge about which approaches and programs were more effective and that rather than testing our theories about rehabilitation and prevention we were merely "funding our fears."

For better or worse, it appears that the federal largess in juvenile corrections has ended. States and localities will continue to bear the bulk of the financial burden for institutional programs and other postadjudication dispositions, while cities and counties will finance most law enforcement programs, and courts and probation staff will be supported by both state and local revenues (Bureau of Justice Statistics, 1980). Because federal money was largely responsible for the development of delinquency prevention programs and many noninstitutional alternatives to incarceration, there is some fear that states and communities may return to their previous patterns of funding only the more "traditional" juvenile programs, i.e. institutions and probation.

There was also a disturbing intrusion of congressional politics in the funding of programs for runaways in 1981. Prior to this year, federal funds were provided under The Runaway Youth Act of 1974 (P.L. 93–415) to the states on the basis of the number of runaways that were served in each state. States such as California and Florida, which had unusually large numbers of runaway youth, received proportionately larger shares of these funds. However, in 1981 the funding formula was changed by Congress so that each state now receives a share proportional to its *youth* population, not its *runaway* population. Now states from which children run away receive as much as the states to which they go. These changes were championed by representatives from states having relatively few runaways. Their intentions seem obvious.

CONCLUSIONS AND RECOMMENDATIONS

Despite the improvements that have been made in the juvenile justice system in recent years, there are still many problems and abuses to correct. Despite federal legislation in 1974, status offenders are still detained and institutionalized in secure facilities. Despite court decisions guaranteeing procedural rights, juveniles who are represented by legal counsel are just as likely to be institutionalized. Training and experience of personnel who work in the juvenile system seems to make little difference in case outcomes, and there is virtually no literature on how to *classify* juveniles for treatment. Little is known about how juvenile policy is made, and written policy is rarely available to guide persons at any level of the juvenile justice system when classifying juveniles or making dispositional decisions. Officials in almost every system component (law enforcement, courts, institutions, etc.) have almost unlimited discretionary authority in labelling and case dispositions, which increases the probability of inconsistent labelling (National Institute for Juvenile Justice and Delinquency Prevention, 1979).

The most important factors that influence decision-making on juvenile cases are the referral incident, the juvenile's statement, the juvenile's attitude and demeanor, and the number of prior police contacts. Decisions to detain juveniles prior to adjudication are strongly influenced by the availability of alternatives to secure detention. Detention rates tend to be lower and more referrals are made to community programs where twenty-four-hour centralized intake service is available (National Institute for Juvenile Justice, 1979). Given these conditions, a number of recommendations are in order:

1. *The juvenile court should make decisions only regarding the culpability of its clients (adjudication) and the appropriate degree to which its clients' freedom should be curtailed.* Treatment decisions should not be made by the juvenile court but by agencies who are better prepared to make those kinds of decisions. Even so, we must realize that we know very little about the effective treatment of delinquency.
2. *We should endeavor to keep as many juveniles as possible out of the juvenile justice system.* We know that most first offenders, if not formally processed and labelled, will not be recidivists. Formal handling increases the likelihood of recidivism.

Toward this end, juvenile courts should handle trivial cases unofficially whenever possible, and should not retain jurisdiction over juvenile status offenses. Truancy, running away, and failing to obey one's parents are noncriminal problems that should not be dealt with by courts utilizing criminal sanctions. School problems are best handled by schools, and family relationship problems are best handled by family service or community mental health agencies.

3. *Juveniles should never be allowed to waive their legal rights, and attorneys should be assigned to every juvenile referred to court.* Legal counseling may be most helpful *prior* to any formal processing, since one of the most important decisions made by the court is whether to process a juvenile through formal proceedings. Whatever the outcome of those proceedings, the juvenile may suffer from the consequences of the labelling that grows out of formal processing.

4. *Until we do know how to provide effective treatment for juvenile offenders, we should concentrate on making the juvenile justice system as equitable, just, and humane as possible.* Achieving these objectives will not lead to their rehabilitation, but it will insure that they are treated better than they are in our present system. Surely that is a goal worth pursuing.

REFERENCES

Adams, Stuart. "Correctional Caseload Research." Pp. 721–732 in Norman Johnston et al. (Eds), *The Sociology of Punishment and Correction* (2nd ed.). New York: John Wiley, 1970.

Bartollas, Clemens, Miller, Stuart J., and Dinitz, Simon. *Juvenile Victimization: The Institutional Paradox.* New York: John Wiley, 1976.

Blomberg, T. G. "Diversion: A Strategy of Family Control in the Juvenile Court Process." Tallahassee: School of Criminology, Florida State University (mimeo), 1975.

Cavan, Ruth Shonle and Ferdinand, Theodore N. *Juvenile Delinquency, Third Edition.* Philadelphia: J. B. Lippincott Co., 1975.

Chesney-Lind, Meda. "Judicial paternalism and the female status offender." *Crime and Delinquency*, April, 1977, 23: 121–130.

Cobb, Roger W. and Elder, Charles D. *Participation in American Politics.* Boston: Allyn and Bacon, 1972.

Cohen, Lawrence E. *Delinquency Dispositions: An Empirical Analysis of Processing Decisions in Three Juvenile Courts.* Utilization of Criminal Justice Statistics Project, Analytic Report 9, National Criminal Justice Information and Statistics Service, Law Enforcement Assistance Administration. Washington, D.C.: U.S. Government Printing Office, 1975.

Cressey, Donald R. *The Prison*. New York: Holt, Rinehart and Winston, 1960.

Cressey, Donald R. and McDermott, Robert A. *Diversion From the Juvenile Justice System*. National Assessment of Juvenile Corrections. Ann Arbor: University of Michigan, 1973.

Dahl, Tove Stang. "The Scandinavian system of juvenile justice: a comparative approach." pp. 327–347 in Margaret K. Rosenheim (Ed.), *Pursuing Justice for the Child*. Chicago: University of Chicago Press, 1976.

Empey, LaMar T. *American Delinquency: Its Meaning and Construction*. Homewood, Illinois: The Dorsey Press, 1978.

England, Ralph. "What is responsible for satisfactory probation and post-probation outcome?" *Journal of Criminal Law, Criminology, and Police Science*, March-April, 1957, 47: 667–677.

Executive Office of the President, Office of Management and Budget, *Budget of the United States Government, Fiscal Year 1982, Appendix*. Washington, D.C.: U.S. Government Printing Office, 1981b.

Executive Office of the President, Office of Management and Budget. *Budget of the United States Government, Fiscal Year, 1982*. Washington, D.C.: U.S. Government Printing Office, 1981a.

Executive Office of the President, Office of Management and Budget. *Fiscal Year 1982 Budget Revisions: Additional Details on Budget Savings*. Washington, D.C.: U.S. Government Printing Office 1981c.

Eyestone, Robert. *From Social Issues to Public Policy*. New York: John Wiley and Son, 1978.

Gibbons, Don C. and Griswald, Manzer J. "Sex differences among juvenile court referrals" *Sociology and Social Research*, November/December, 1957, XL11: 106–110.

Gil, David G. Unraveling Social Policy, *Revised Edition*. Cambridge, Mass.: Schenkman Publishing Co., 1976.

Gold, Martin. "Undetected Delinquent Behavior." *Journal of Research in Crime and Delinquency*, January, 1966, 3: 27–46.

Gold, Martin. *Delinquent Behavior in an American City*. Belmont, CA: Brooks/Cole Publishing, 1970.

Graecen, John M. "Pitfalls and possibilities in juvenile justice reform." Paper presented at the National Conference on Juvenile Justice, Los Angeles, 1975.

Grunhut, Max. *Penal Reform*. New York: Clarendon Press, 1948.

Guggenheim, Martin. *A Call to Abolish the Juvenile Justice System*. New York: American Civil Liberties' Union, June, 1978.

Hasenfeld, Yeheskel. "Youth in the juvenile court: input and output patterns." pp. 60–72 in Rosemary Sarri and Yeheskel Hasenfeld (Eds.), *Brought to Justice? Juveniles, the Courts, and the Law*. National Assessment of Juvenile Corrections. Ann Arbor: University of Michigan, 1976.

Jesness, Karl F. "The Preston typology study." *Youth Authority Quarterly*, Winter, 1970, 23: 26–38.

Kassebaum, Gene, Ward, David and Wilner, Dan. *Prison Treatment and Its Outcome*. New York: John Wiley, 1971.

Klein, Malcom W., et al. "The explosion in police diversion programs." pp. 101–120 in Malcom W. Klein (Ed.), *The Juvenile Justice System*. Beverly Hills, Ca.: Sage Publications, 1976.

Kutchins, H. and Kutchins, S. "Pretrial diversionary programs: new expansion of law enforcement activity camouflaged as rehabilitation." Paper presented at the Annual Meetings of the Pacific Sociological Association, Honolulu, Hawaii, 1973.

Lemert, Edwin M. "Diversion in Juvenile Justice: What hath been wrought?" *Journal of Research in Crime and Delinquency*, January, 1981, 18: 34–46.

Lemert, Edwin M. *Social Pathology*. New York: McGraw-Hill, 1951.

Lemert, Edwin M. "The juvenile court—quest and realities." pp. 91–106 in the President's Commission on Law Enforcement and Administration of Justice, *Task Force Report: Juvenile Delinquency and Youth Crime*. Washington, D.C.: U.S. Government Printing Office, 1967.

Lerman, Paul. "Trends and issues in the deinstitutionalization of youths in trouble." *Crime and Delinquency*, July, 1980, 26: 281–298.

Lerman, Paul. "Evaluating institutions for delinquents." *Social Work*, 1968, 13: 55–64.

Levin, Mark M. and Sarri, Rosemary C. *Juvenile Delinquency: A Comparative Analysis of Legal Codes in the United States*. University of Michigan: National Assessment of Juvenile Corrections, 1974.

Lipton, Douglas, Martinson, Robert, and Wilks, Judith. *The Effectiveness of Correctional Treatment*. New York: Praeger Publishers, 1975.

Martin, Lawrence H. and Snyder, Phyllis R. "Jurisdiction over status offenders should not be removed from the juvenile court." *Crime and Delinquency*, January, 1976, 22: 44–47.

Mattingly, J. and Katkin, D. "The Youth service bureau: a reinvented wheel?" Paper presented at the Society for the Study of Social Problems, San Francisco, 1975.

McCord, Joan, and McCord, William. "A follow-up report on the Cambridge-Somerville youth study." *Annals of the American Academy of Political and Social Science*. March, 1959, 322: 89–98.

McEachern, Alexander W. and Taylor, Edward M. *The Effects of Prison*. Probation Project Report No. 2, Youth Studies Center. Los Angeles, University of Southern California, 1967.

McNeece, C. Aaron. *Juvenile courts in the Community Environment*. Ph.D. Dissertation, University of Michigan, May, 1976.

McNeece, C. Aaron. "'Justice' in the juvenile court: some suggestions for reform." *Journal of Humanics*, May, 1980b, 8: 77–97.

McNeece, C. Aaron. "The deinstitutionalization of juvenile status offenders: New Myths and old realities." *Journal of Sociology and Social Welfare*, March, 1980a, 7: 236–245.

National Council on Crime and Delinquency, Board of Directors. "Jurisdiction over status offenders should be removed from the juvenile court: a policy statement." *Crime and Delinquency*, April, 1975, 21: 97–99.

National Council on Crime and Delinquency. "Corrections in the United States." pp. 115–212 in President's Commission on Law Enforcement and Administration of Justice. *Task Force Report: Corrections*. Washington, D.C.: U.S. Government Printing Office, 1967.

Nejelski, Paul. "Diversion: unleashing the hound of heaven?" pp. 94–118 in Margaret K. Rosenheim (Ed.), *Pursuing Justice for the Child*. Chicago: The University of Chicago Press, 1976.

Palmer, Theodore and Warren, Marquerite Q. Community Treatment Project. CTP Research Report, No. 8, Part 1. Sacramento: California Youth Authority, 1967.

Pawlak, Edward J. "Differential selection of juveniles for detention." *Journal of Research in Crime and Delinquency*, July, 1977, 14: 1–12.

Platt, Anthony M. *The Child Savers: The Invention of Delinquency*. Chicago: University of Chicago Press, 1969.

Polk, Kenneth, and Schafer, Walter E. (Eds.) *School and Delinquency*: Englewood Cliffs, N.J.: Prentice Hall, 1972.

Polsky, Howard W. *Cottage Six*. New York: Russell Sage, 1962.

President's Commission on Law Enforcement and Administration of Justice. *Task Force Report: Juvenile Delinquency and Youth Crime*. Washington, D.C.: U.S. Government Printing Office, 1967.

Quay, Herbert C. and Love, Craig T. "The effect of a juvenile diversion program on rearrests." *Criminal Justice and Behavior*, December, 1977, 4: 377–396.

Rubin, Ted. "The Juvenile Courts," Chapter 4 in *The Courts: Fulcrum of the Justice System*. Pacific Palisades, CA: Goodyear Publishing Co., 1976.

Samuels, Gertrude. "When children collide with the law." *New York Times Magazine*, Sec. 6, pp. 44 ff., December 5, 1971.

Sarri, Rosemary and Bradley, Patrick W. "Juvenile aid panels: an alternative to juvenile court processing in South Australia." *Crime and Delinquency*, January, 1980, 26: 42–62.

Sarri, Rosemary C. *Under Lock and Key*. Ann Arbor: University of Michigan, National Assessment of Juvenile Corrections, 1974.

Scarpitti, Frank R. and Stephenson, Richard M. "A study of probation effectiveness." *Journal of Criminal Law, Criminology, and Police Science*. September, 1968, 59: 361–369.

Schur, Edwin M. *Radical Nonintervention: Rethinking the Delinquent Problem*. Englewood Cliffs, N.J.: Prentice-Hall, 1973.

Seckel, Joachim M. Experiments in Group Counseling at Two Youth Authority Institutions. Research report N. 46. Sacramento: California Youth Authority, 1965.

Serrill, Michael S. "Washington's new juvenile code." *Corrections Magazine*, February, 1980, 7: 36–41.

Spergel, Irving A. and Reamer, Frederic G. "Deinstitutionalization of status offenders: individual outcome and system effects." *Journal of Research in Crime and Delinquency*, January, 1981, 18: 4–33.

Spergel, Irving A. and Snapp, Thomas. *The Illinois Status Offender Service Evaluation Quarterly Progress Report*. Chicago: The University of Chicago School of Social Service Administration, April, 1977.

Stapleton, Vaughn and Teitlebaum, Lee. *In Defense of Youth*. New York: Russell Sage, 1972.

Sykes, Gresham M. *The Society of Captives*. New York: Antheneum Press, 1965.

Teittlebaum, Lee E. and Gough, Adrian R. (Eds.) *Beyond Control: Status Offenders in the Juvenile Court*. Cambridge, Mass.: Ballinger Publishing Co., 1977.

Thompson, James D. *Organizations in Action: Social Science Bases of Administrative Theory*. New York: McGraw-Hill Book Co., 1967.

U.S. Department of Justice, Law Enforcement Assistance Administration, Office of Juvenile Justice and Delinquency Prevention, National Institute for Juvenile Justice and Delinquency Prevention. *A National Assessment of Case Disposition and Classification in the Juvenile Justice System: Inconsistent Labeling, Vol. 1, Process Description and Summary*. Washington, D.C.: U.S. Government Printing Office, 1979.

U.S. Department of Justice, Law Enforcement Assistance Administration, Office of Juvenile Justice and Delinquency Prevention, National Institute for Juvenile Justice and Delinquency Prevention. *A National Assessment of Case Disposition and Classification in the Juvenile Justice System: Inconsistent Labeling, Vol. 11, Results of a Literature Search*. Washington, D.C.: U.S. Government Printing Office, 1980.

U.S. Department of Justice, Law Enforcement Assistance Administration, Office of Juvenile Justice and Delinquency Prevention. *Second Analysis and Evaluation, Federal Juvenile Delinquency Programs, Vol. 1*. Washington, D.C.: U.S. Government Printing Office, 1979.

U.S. Department of Justice, Bureau of Justice Statistics. *Sourcebook of Criminal Justice Statistics*, 1980. Washington, D.C.: U.S. Government Printing Office, 1981.

U.S. Department of Justice, Law Enforcement Assistance Administration, National Criminal Justice Information and Statistics Service. *Trends in Expenditure and Employment Data for the Criminal Justice System, 6971-76*. Washington, D.C.: U.S. Government Printing Office, 1979.

Vorenberg, Elizabeth W. and Vorenberg, James. "Early diversion from the criminal justice system: practice in search of a theory." pp. 151-183 in Lloyd E. Ohlin (Ed.), *Prisoners in America*. Englewood Cliffs, N.J. Prentice-Hall, 1973.

Wakin, Edward. *Children Without Justice*. New York: National Council of Jewish Women, 1975.

Williams, Jay R. and Gold, Martin. "From Delinquent behavior to official delinquency." *Social Problems*, Fall, 1972, 20: 209-229.

Wilson, James Q. *Thinking About Crime*. New York: Basic Books, 1975.

Chapter 3

CORRECTIONAL POLICIES: EVOLVING TRENDS[1]

SHELDON R. GELMAN

W hen attempting to deal with the topic of correctional policy, one is immediately confronted by a dilemma. The dilemma arises from two distinct yet interrelated sets of issues. The first issue involves the question, "What is policy?" while the second centers on whether there is something that can be identified as correctional policy. The first issue can be readily addressed through a definitional exercise in which various authors' perspectives on policy are set out (e.g. Gilbert & Specht, 1974; Morris, 1979; Gil, 1973; Kahn, 1973; Rein, 1970). One or several formulations can then be selected that encompass the range of activities that are identified as policy.

Basically, every industrialized society, as part of its organizational structure, attempts to meet the needs of its constituents through a system of formal principles. These principles, laws, or policies attempt to create some degree of order so that the society and its members can reach or achieve their full potential. A society's policies are designed to assist with meeting social needs, alleviate social problems, create an environment in which individuals and the society can grow, and provide a measure of safety to its members. According to Gil, social policies deal with the quality of life in a society, the circumstances of living of individuals and groups, and the nature of intrasocietal human relationships (Gil, 1973). Kahn describes policy as, "the explicit or implicit core of principles, or the continuing line of decisions and constraints, behind specific programs, legislation, administrative practices, or priorities" (Kahn, 1973). Some writers see policy as a process in

---

[1]This chapter is dedicated to the memory of Frederick A. Hussey, a friend and colleague whose many contributions to the field of criminal justice will remain as only a glimmer of what could have been.

45

which problems or needs are identified, choices made, and strategies developed, while others view policy as the outcome or product of this process. Generally, the evolution of policy involves a goal or series of goals that are developed in response to an identified or anticipated problem. Policy is both process and outcome and can be viewed not only as potential solutions to perceived social problems but also as a cause or perpetuating factor in social problems.

The second issue identified above is somewhat more problematic since there appears to be no single policy but a variety of policies developed and implemented at various levels in the field of corrections. According to Allen F. Breed, Director of the National Institute of Corrections, "the fact that corrections is beset with significant problems despite all our prior efforts is perhaps best explained by the absence of any foundation of policy upon which our standards efforts could be built" (Breed, 1981). Correctional policy has been and is developed by many groups and agencies that function in a semiautonomous fashion in various governmental and political jurisdictions. The policies formulated are usually arrived at through political compromise and are more often than not contradictory in terms of direction and focus. The direction of policies is determined by formal and informal negotiations among various interest groups. The position taken by any interest group is determined by its particular value orientation. Policy is, in the end, a reflection of the values of the public as voiced through its political representatives and implemented through various professional functionaries. Therefore, while it is possible to discuss correctional policies in some detail, any effort to identify a single correctional policy or to assess the effectiveness of policies or policy outcomes in the field of corrections is more problematic.

Additionally, since the development of policy is conceptually and administratively distinct from the implementation process, understanding the impact and effect of correctional policies is far from easy (Levine, Musheno, & Palumbo, 1980). Implementation of correctional policy, like policies in other areas, is subject to a range of discretionary actions that color the outcome or impact of policies. The process is further complicated, according to Duffee, by the fact that the notion of a unitary or coherent "criminal justice system" is an ideal that does not really exist (Duffee, 1980).

Therefore, although reference throughout this chapter will be made to the criminal justice "system," I do not want to give the impression that a unitary, easily identifiable system actually exists. I use the word "system" in its broadest sense, referring to a range of activities occurring in the criminal justice field.

Given this background, we now can attempt to rationally discuss a somewhat disconnected set of issues in a way that attempts to explain the context in which correctional policies develop and operate. In order to gain a comprehensive understanding of correctional policy, a systematic approach that identifies issues and outcomes is indicated. The approach must define the nature of the problem that requires the development of a correctional response, underlying value premises and theoretical approaches to the problem, goals and objectives, historical responses to the problem, cost, related policies impacting on the correctional field, and intended and unintended effects. Special attention to resources and the issue of "rights" within the correctional field must also be examined.

THE NATURE OF THE PROBLEM

Every society has been confronted with the problem of individuals who violate or are perceived as violating the norms of that society. As a result, all societies have developed policies to deal with norm violating behavior. Death, physical maiming, ostracism, and incarceration have been utilized as policy choices aimed at curbing norm violating behavior. Similarly, penitence and rehabilitation (treatment) have also been selected as appropriate policy responses to be applied to law violators. History illustrates that societal responses in terms of policy development tend to be cyclical with preference being given to different forms of intervention at different times. Harsh, if not cruel and inhumane, sanctions and punishments have been balanced or replaced with more humanitarian and rehabilitative measures and vice versa.

Theorists have long debated the cause of criminal activities, i.e. norm violating behavior, and the type of response that is needed in order to protect and maintain a functioning society. The cause of law violating behavior has been viewed as either a defect within the individual and/or caused by an oppressive or unjust society. Neither perspective in terms of cause or response has won out over the other perspective on a permanent basis. No consensus has ever been reached as to which form of intervention is most effective in eliminating, deterring, or limiting rule violation or in creating a just and harmonious society. Dissatisfaction with one or the other perspective is based on perceptions regarding the effectiveness of the intervention in reducing or eliminating criminal activities.

A key element in the development of correctional policies is societal perceptions relating to the threat of crime but not whether interventions are effective; for example, society perceives that there has been a drastic increase in criminal activity on the basis of media reports and the FBI Uniform Crime Reports, which indicates a 33 percent increase in reported offenses between 1973 and 1979. However, the National Crime Survey, a poll of 60,000 households and 50,000 businesses conducted by the Law Enforcement Assistance Administration and the U.S. Census Bureau, reports a far more moderate increase in violent crimes (approximately 6%) (Lieber, 1981). The perception of crime, the perceived threat of crime, and the belief that current efforts to curb crime are ineffective rather than an actual increase in crime is sufficient to create a demand for correctional reform. Shifts in correctional policy occur in response to the fear of the public at large and general dissatisfaction with existing practices.

UNDERLYING VALUE PREMISES

Policies in the correctional field deal with the perceived rights and responsibilities of society towards and in behalf of its members. Implicit in all correctional policy is the protection of society and its members from potential law breakers. Social order and the preservation of the public peace, health, and safety are of prime concern. Law breakers, with the possible exception of some who claim political motivation and justification, are viewed as deviating from accepted societal norms and values. Such deviation is perceived as a threat to the established order and therefore requires the development of a variety of institutions that act as a means of social control. Societal institutions, whether they be legislative decrees or physical structures, serve as a stabilizing factor in societies undergoing change (Ponsioen, 1969). They provide an ordered and continuous framework for realizing group values and are the most important vehicle through which the sanctions of society are brought to bear upon the individual (Merrill, 1961).

It has long been recognized that the criminal justice system is faced with the often conflicting objectives of protecting society and rehabilitating the offender. One way of looking at these conflicting objectives is to contrast what has become known as the "just desert" (Von Hirsch, 1976; Dershowitz, 1976) or "justice model" (Fogel, 1975) approach to that of the "rehabilitative ideal" (Allan, 1959). The "just deserts" or "moralist" perspective holds that criminal justice activities should not be concerned with rehabilitation, the remaking or remolding of the individual to better fit the norms of society, but should focus on exacting from each offender "deserved" punishment that is proportional to the offense that has been committed against society or its members (Duffee, 1980).

The moralist approach to criminal justice is one in which the system is seen as upholding the morals and value of society. The system is viewed as having a deterrent force towards law breaking. Individuals are encouraged to adhere to societal mandates to avoid retributive sanctions. Punishment is viewed as a major element of the criminal justice system. The threat and application of punishment is viewed as necessary to preserve order. According to Packer, "When the threat of punishment is removed or reduced, either through legislative repeal . . . or through the inaction of enforcement authorities, conduct that has previously been repressed . . . tends to increase" (Packer, 1964). Individuals who violate the law are viewed as deserving punishment, and society is best served by delivering punishment and deterring potential law breakers. Sentencing offenders is based on their past behavior and actions and the nature of the offense.

The above approach can be contrasted to the "rehabilitative ideal" or "social welfare" perspective. The social welfare perspective favors the notion of rehabilitation and views retribution and punishment as having little impact on criminal behavior. According to Duffee, the overriding characteristics of those who assume the social welfare perspective is the "insistence that the criminal justice system must be evaluated in terms of its ability to improve the conditions as well as the behavior of people against whom it directly intervenes" (Duffee, 1980). The emphasis within the welfare perspective is on the offender and the treatment or handling of the offender. It is intimately related to society as a whole and to its welfare. The primary cause of criminal behavior is viewed as rooted in the political and economic system rather than within the individuals themselves. Rehabilitation must take place on two fronts. Rehabilitation of the individual who has committed crimes against society and, second, rehabilitation of society to eliminate the necessity of an individual engaging in criminal activity. It has been frequently asserted that the welfare of society is and can only be protected through humane treatment and appropriate rehabilitative activities. According to Hussey (1979),

> ... When an offender has been convicted of a criminal act, the welfare of society and of the offender are of concern and that both could be served best if the sanction received by the offender could be informed by a study of that particular offenders needs. Indeed, it was believed that the criminal justice response should be tailored to the unique offender. In a phrase, the system adopted the positivists position and treated the offender, not the offense.

Integral to the "rehabilitative ideal" are the presentence investigation and the discretionary use of probation and parole, which can be used to individualize interventions and help rehabilitate the offender with the overall goal of improving functioning within society.

GOALS AND OBJECTIVES

There are two fundamental premises that underly all correctional policy. The first relates to a concern for the safety and protection of the community, the second with a concern for the individual offender. These concerns or policy premises can be combined to yield four general policy objectives with respect to corrections:

1. *Restraint*, in which corrections provides a holding action for the offender. Incarceration and punishment are used as a means of retribution, thus protecting society.
2. *Reform*, in which there is a low emphasis on the offender and a high emphasis on the community; this perspective has a deterrent focus and aims for conformity with dominant societal beliefs and values.
3. *Rehabilitation*, wherein correctional efforts are directed toward changing the pathology of the offender and bringing about conformity to societal norms.
4. *Reintegration*, in which there is a high level of concern for both the offender and the community with attempts being made to enhance opportunities for community interaction and involvement (Duffee, 1975).

Similarly, four traditional objectives can be identified that have been associated with correctional activities:

1. *Incapacitation,* the prevention of those crimes that would have been committed during the period of incarceration;
2. *Deterrence* of future criminal actions by the convicted offender or by others in the community by way of example;
3. *Retribution,* or punishment proportional to the seriousness of the committed offense, and;
4. *Rehabilitation,* in which the offender, not the offense, is the primary focus of intervention.

Since neither the Duffee policy orientations nor the traditional objectives of corrections exist in pure form, the actual operation of correctional activities generally reflect a mixture of these often competing orientations. The objective of the criminal justice system is therefore not singular in nature. "The plethora of objectives served by the system makes it difficult to talk about any one of them as if it were the overriding objective" (Hussey, 1979). In spite of these mixed objectives, the rehabilitative emphasis reached its modern day peak during the late 1960s and early 1970s. It was during this period that an emphasis on individual rights, civil liberties, due process, deinstitutionalization, educational opportunities, community alternatives, and various treatment and counseling modalities developed. The uses of punishment and incarceration were viewed by many with disdain (Menninger 1969; Clark, 1970; Mitford, 1973).

THE SCOPE OF THE PROBLEM

The validity of statistics relating to criminal activity has long been the subject of debate. As indicated previously, counting and perceptions are subjective enterprises and vary according to the "counter" (e.g. FBI, National Crime Survey) and the purposes for which statistics are being collected. Nevertheless, each and every one of us is a potential perpetrator or victim of criminal activity, a reality that brings us all into contact with the criminal justice system. The problem of law breaking affects us all. We pay either directly, as a victim of crime, or indirectly, as a taxpayer. While perceptions rather than actual number of crimes or criminals determine the nature of correctional responses, it should be clear that there has been a real increase in the number of criminal offenses reported in recent years. Whether this increase is the result of better reporting or an actual increase in criminal activity, the result has translated into public outrage and a drastic increase in the numbers of individuals incarcerated in local, state, and federal penal facilities.

According to the most recent statistics, there are currently 23,735 adult federal prisoners (Federal Bureau of Prisons, 1980), 299,134 state adult prisoners (Krajick, 1981), and 151,551 adults in local jails (LEAA, 1978). The number of individuals incarcerated in state and federal prison facilities has grown from 196,000 in 1973 to a total of 314,000 in 1981 (Lieber, 1981). Over the same time period, there has been an increase in the number of female prisoners from 6,329 to 12,927 (Lieber, 1981; GAO, 1980). These figures represent only those adults (not juveniles) who have been convicted and actually incarcerated. They do not represent either the number of individuals involved in adult criminal activity or those who have been apprehended, diverted or sentenced, and then diverted via probation in the criminal justice system, nor do they represent individuals who have been paroled and are presently under the supervision of correctional authorities.

Although statistics related to the sentencing of felons to community alternatives are difficult to locate, they can be extrapolated from existing data sources. About 40 percent of the criminal defendants convicted and sentenced in Federal District Courts in 1978 and 1979 received probation and/or were diverted to community based programs (Hindelang, Gottfredson, & Flanagan, 1981). A comparison of individuals incarcerated in federal correctional facilities with those under the supervision of federal parole authorities indicates that there are three times as many convicted felons under community supervision as there are in prisons (Federal Bureau of Prisons, 1980; Hindelang, Gottfredson, & Flanagan, 1981). There were a total of 1,461,459 individuals under state and local probation or parole supervision in 1976, again approximately three times the number of individuals incarcerated (Hindelang, Gottfredson, & Flanagan, 1981). Therefore, despite the heavy emphasis on incarceration, there remains a majority of offenders and former offenders who must be programmed for in the community rather than institutional context.

With the apparent rise in criminal activity and growing prison populations has come an increased demand by the public at large and by politicians in particular for correctional reform. Support for rehabilitative efforts has given way to an increasing emphasis on confinement and punishment. The belief in "just deserts" has again come into prominence pushing rehabilitative and social welfare efforts aside.

Dissatisfaction with the "rehabilitative ideal" can in part be traced to the increase in crime, a growing fear among citizens, difficulties with predicting future behavior-dangerousness (Underwood, 1979), and to the utilization of social science research in correctional policymaking. This last item is illustrated in an article by Robert Martinson that appeared in the Spring 1974 issue of *The Public Interest*. Martinson reported on a review of more than 200 studies on correctional treatment and concluded that, " . . . with few and isolated exceptions, the rehabilitative efforts that have been reported so far have had no appreciable effect on recidivism." Although Martinson's conclusions were challenged by Palmer and others on the basis of methodology, facts, and interpretation (Palmer, 1975), the seeds of doubt regarding the efficacy of rehabilitative efforts quickly bore fruit. Politicians and the public at large faced with growing unemployment, inflation, and crime wanted results— a reduction in criminal activity and safety for the public. If rehabilitative efforts had little or no impact and if prediction is so difficult, then more effective or at least more satisfying forms of intervention would have to be found. Short range solutions, regardless of cost, that appear as different than those that have gone on before were needed to soothe the public ire.

The move away from rehabilitative activities has been accompanied by a shift in sentencing procedures in more than a dozen states. The shift, to determinate sentencing, is designed to bring about uniformity in the sentences that are imposed on offenders and limit the discretionary power of judges, which had permitted the imposition of individualized, custom sentences (Hussey, 1981). Objections to indeterminate sentences centered in part on the widely disparate periods of imprisonment meted out within and among various jurisdictions and claims of racial and socioeconomic bias. Uniformity, equality, fairness, and certainty in the sentences imposed is the desired outcome. However, it is most difficult for individualized justice and equal justice to exist simultaneously (Levine, Musheno, & Palumbo, 1980). In other words, "rehabilitation" and "just deserts" may be mutually exclusive premises on which to operate a criminal justice system.

SHIFTING POLICY PERSPECTIVES

Although the emphasis in correctional policy in the 1980s
appears to have shifted once again toward the "just deserts" premise,
the existence of mixed policy objectives continues. References to
rehabilitation, with its concern for civil rights, due process, and
individualized treatment, continues to dominate much of the professional social work and correctional literature, while the media
and legislative task forces increasingly are calling for a "hard line"
approach to deal with criminal activity; for example, the 1977
issue of the *Encyclopedia of Social Work* contains four articles dealing with crime and delinquency. The second article, prepared
by Elliot Studt, identifies six directions for correctional reform:
(1) deinstitutionalization, (2) decriminalization and diversion,
(3) reduction of time spent in institutions, (4) alternatives to
institutionalization, (5) making the period of institutionalization
fully productive, and (6) restoring civil and personal rights. In a
similar vein, the 1977 Delegate Assembly of the National Association of Social Workers passed an extensive policy statement dealing with juvenile delinquency and adult crime. The policy statement
identifies seventeen areas of reform ranging from prevention to a
moratorium on the construction of prisons (NASW, 1980). Reform
of the correctional enterprise is perceived as proceeding in two
directions: helping the offender adjust to the community and
helping the community accept the returning offender. Successful
efforts to combat crime are believed to be dependent on society's
ability and willingness to eliminate poverty and discrimination,
overcome the alienation of young people, develop and administer
just laws, and create rational and coherent law enforcement, courts,
and correctional systems. Community-based treatment is the treatment of choice for the overwhelming majority of offenders, with
institutions being used only for those who present a clear and
present danger to society.

Another professional perspective is provided by Allen F. Breed,
Director of the National Institute of Corrections, who in his opening address to the 1981 American Correctional Association's Mid-
Winter Conference identified two major problems confronting the
field of corrections. The first involved overcrowding of correctional
facilities and the second dealt with the classification of institutionalized offenders. He urged the members of the American Correc-

tional Association to undertake as a goal a project that would propose a National Corrections Policy. To give direction to that challenge, he proposed two policies:

1. The right of the states to confine offenders does not include the right to house more offenders in a particular institution than the facility is certified to hold.
2. The right of the states to incarcerate prisoners implies the obligation to utilize a modern, empirically tested classification system that ensures that no offender is placed in a level of security that is greater than is required for personal safety and public protection (Breed, 1981).

While these policy recommendations are systems oriented and have received support from professional correctional personnel, they, like the social work proposals, do not coincide with current public concerns or present pressures in the correctional field. The difficulty of shifting correctional perspectives is explained in part by Parker when he notes that, " . . . the theory of rehabilitation has merely been imposed upon the theories of punishment" (1975). This phenomenon is dramatically illustrated through the issue of prison overcrowding and whether overcrowding constitutes "cruel and unusual punishment" under the Eighth and Fourteenth Amendments of the United States Constitution.

Under an order issued by Federal District Judge Frank M. Johnson in 1972, *Newman v Alabama*, 349 F. Supp. 278 (M.D. ALA, 1972), Alabama's prisons were placed under Federal court jurisdiction. Alabama prison authorities were ordered to meet minimal standards set forth by the court, which included a reduction in inmate population. On July 15, 1981, some nine years after the litigation began, Federal District Judge Robert E. Varner ordered Alabama prison authorities to release 400 inmates in order to relieve overcrowding of "grossly inadequate facilities." An effort to block Judge Varner's order by State Attorney General Charles Graddick proved unsuccessful when Associate Justice Lewis F. Powell of the United States Supreme Court lifted a temporary stay of the early release order and 222 inmates were freed. The early release of state prisoners who were not considered dangerous or were nearing parole or release eased the pressure on more than 1500 Alabama state prisoners housed in overcrowed county jails (Rawl, 1981).

It should be noted that Mr. Graddick had campaigned on a law-and-order platform stressing tough policies, long prison sentences, and a reduction in the number of prisoners granted parole. This position, although currently a popular one, is quite interesting given Levin's findings that, "offenders who receive probation have significantly lower rates of recidivism than those who have been incarcerated, and incarcerated offenders receiving shorter sentences generally have a somewhat lower recidivism rate than those receiving longer sentences" (1972). Levin's conclusion is based on his evaluation of more than fifteen separate studies of recidivism, which involved tens of thousands of offenders in more than twenty jurisdictions (Levin, 1971). Each of these studies demonstrated the same pattern: the milder the sentence, the lower the rate of recidivism. He notes that, "with few exceptions, these differences persist when one controls for the type of offense, type of community, and offender's age, race, or number of previous convictions" (1972). Longer sentences and fewer releases tend to increase overcrowding, lessen the already minimal opportunities available for treatment or rehabilitation, and heighten prison tensions, which have in the past led to inmate uprisings and violence.

The push for longer prison sentences and construction of additional prison beds is not unique to Alabama, whose legislature recently voted to provide 45 million dollars for the construction of two new prisons. The New York State Legislature, like legislatures in forty-six of the fifty states, have passed legislation to enable the construction of additional cells or prisons. In the instance of New York, a 500 million dollar prison bond issue was authorized for construction and renovation of prison facilities (*N. Y. Times,* July 12, 1981).

Comparative cost data related to institutional versus community supervision, while inconclusive, generally views community supervision as being less costly. Cost data from New York State for 1978 indicates that while the annual cost for parole supervision in the community was 1,090 dollars and 273.00 dollars for probation supervision, the cost for incarceration was a minimum of 14,065 to a maximum of 24,855 dollars per inmate (*Jericho,* Summer 1980). The state of Georgia is able to operate its ten community residential centers, which combine restitution with community service, at a cost of 1,560 dollars per inmate per year while the cost of imprisonment is 26,000 dollars (*Jericho*, Winter 1979/80). Some authorities feel that the cost of an "ideal" community-based correctional service network would cost as much if not more than the current cost of operating primarily custodial institutions. However, if an "ideal" institutional setting was developed, one with a range of educational, training, and treatment components, the cost would exceed that of the "ideal community" program.

According to the National Moratorium on Prison Construction, 533 new facilities with an estimated capacity of 162,466 beds have been proposed or are currently under construction. Eight new federal facilities, 169 state, and 376 local locked facilities are included among the total (*Jericho*, Spring 1981). The April 1981 issue of *Corrections Magazine* reported a 4 percent increase in state prison populations from January 1980 to January 1981. State prison populations have grown by more than 42 percent over the past five years (Krajick, 1981). The rise in state prison populations is attributable to three major factors: (1) the implementation in twenty-seven states of some type of mandatory sentencing policy, (2) determinate sentencing legislation, which has been adopted in fourteen states, and (3) reduction in the number of paroles granted to inmates. All are indicative of dissatisfaction with past correctional activities.

Another example of this hard-line approach is evident in the recent report of the Attorney General's Task Force on Violent Crime (*N. Y. Times*, 7/26/81). According to Jeffrey Harris, executive director of the Task Force, the panel agreed that, "the single most important thing necessary for the criminal justice system is more prison space in state prisons." In addition to the expansion of housing units, the Task Force endorsed the easing of restraints on the use of illegally obtained evidence in criminal trials, the abolition of parole for federal prisoners, and high or no bail for defendants who are considered dangerous. These recommendations are consistent with projected expansion of state and county correctional facilities and the elimination of parole in a number of states that have moved to a determinate sentencing structure. The Task Force proposal includes a recommendation that an additional 2 to 4 billion dollars be provided to the states for the construction of additional jail space. It is felt that these reforms will, "shift the balance in the criminal justice system in a way that will make enforcement more effective and provide greater protection for the public" (*New York Times*, 7/26/81).

Probably the clearest example of this hard-line approach to offenders is illustrated in Senate Bill 114 (1981), the federal death penalty bill, which has again been introduced and is a top priority of the Senate Judiciary Chairman Strom Thurman. The imposition of the death penalty would be permitted with certain non-homicidal offenses and allows the death penalty to be imposed if a death occurs during the commission of or in flight from the offense even though death was not intentional or committed by the defendent (ACLU, 1981).

Henry Miller (1981) in his recent analysis of changing perspectives summarizes what has occurred in the correctional field:

> They did a really slick number with the prisons, and most of us didn't even notice it. Remember when we used to think that the crooks and the hoodlums could be reformed? No more. Forget about rehabilitation—it didn't work all that well ... Punishment's the thing now. Pay the price. Debt to society and all of that equity stuff. It happens to be cheaper, of course, but that's just a coincidence isn't it.

The shift is real, but not really real and not really cheaper. Not in the short run and not in the long run. The correctional field has always, or at least in modern times, delivered mixed messages, with punishment and custody playing a crucial role. Despite the avowed goal of rehabilitation, approximately 95 percent of all correctional expenditures are for custody, with only 5 percent of funds utilized for health services, education, vocational training, and other rehabilitation services (Clark, 1970). When outcomes didn't correspond to desired goals, more often than not because we were never really clear as to what those goals were, one needs only to shift slightly and go back to basics. An eye for an eye. Cost, which has always been of primary concern in terms of rehabilitative efforts, no longer need be of concern because protection is the key no matter what the cost. Besides, it makes us feel better to vent frustrations and get even, no matter what the cost. A point graphically depicted in the film, " ... And Justice for All," by Judge Flemming, in his swimming pool soliloquy. "Blaming the victim" has long been a popular pastime. Blame the Democrats, blame social service personnel, blame liberals, extract retribution from those who dare to violate the law.

RELATED LEGISLATURE POLICIES

Additional policies supportive of this hard-line approach are evident in a number of federal legislative proposals. Since the Criminal Justice Construction Reform Act of 1980 (S186) was introduced by Senator Robert Dole (R-Ks), eight additional bills related to correctional activities have been introduced in the House and Senate. While differing slightly in focus, the intent of the legislation is clear, the construction of additional institutional beds by the states. These bills include Justice Assistance Act (HR 3359), Criminal Justice Assistance Amendments (HR 2972), Correctional Services Improvement Act (HR 791), The Corrections Construction and Program Development Act (HR 658), State Justice Institute Act (HR 2407 and S 537), National War on Violent Crime Act (S 953), The Federal Death Penalty (S114), and the Omnibus Criminal Code Recodification (S1722).

The direction of current legislature reform proposals are supportive of the "just deserts" perspective and are in opposition to those "rehabilitative" reforms advanced by social work and correctional professionals. However, in spite of these correctional reforms, those who support rehabilitation have not gone away; their turn will come again.

RESOURCE DEVELOPMENT AND UTILIZATION

As indicated previously, just as the numbers of individuals incarcerated has grown over the past five years, so have the number of facilities and beds to hold these individuals. As indicated earlier, an estimated 162,466 additional jail and prison beds are now under construction or proposed: 1,843 Federal, 160,623 state and local (*Jericho*, Spring 1981). These figures do not reflect the additional 2 billion dollars recommended by Attorney General William French Smith's Task Force on Violent Crime for prison expansion. It is estimated that the total cost of prisoner care and custody amounted to 5.52 billion dollars in 1978 (*Jericho*, Spring 1981). The cost of construction of the additional 162,466 beds is estimated to cost 8.73 billion dollars. The average cost of each newly constructed prison bed ranges from 30,000 to 50,000 dollars, depending on auspices and level of security (*Jericho*, Spring 1981).

While there is no evidence to indicate that the availability of additional correctional beds will affect criminal behavior or the crime rate one way or another, a recently released study by Abt Associates entitled *American Prisons and Jails* suggests that the numbers of individuals incarcerated corresponds to the number of beds available and that the availability of space may diminish reliance on and utilization of noncustodial alternatives (Abt, 1980).

Correctional resources, i.e. funds made available for correctional activities, are closely linked to the goals and objectives to be achieved at any given period in our history. As noted previously, the development of correctional goals and objectives are part of a political process and are quite divergent in expected impact and outcome. Political considerations also have an economic dimension, with total resources available being limited. When resources are directed or invested in certain types of programs to achieve a specific set of goals, those resources are not available for other purposes. When incarceration or custody become paramount in the minds of politicians and the public, resources for treatment services and community-based options are unavailable or limited. Resources devoted to custodial purposes divert already limited resources away from rehabilitative and/or less restrictive alternatives.

From a historical perspective, it is interesting to note that the rate of incarceration is directly related to social, political, and economic circumstances of the country. Incarcerated populations increase during periods of economic hardship and diminish in times of economic growth, often associated with a war-time economy (Farber, 1968; Abt, 1980). When unemployment is high, demands on the correctional enterprise increase. It is estimated that a 1 percent rise in unemployment results in a 4 percent jump in the rate of imprisonment (Lieber, 1981).

PROTECTING RIGHTS

During the last two decades, a great deal of interest in the issue of "rights" has evolved. A series of activist judicial decisions was handed down affirming the rights of various groups (i.e. racial minorities, the mentally retarded, juveniles, and the physically handicapped) who believed that as citizens they were entitled to standing and to protection from discriminatory actions. Included among the groups requiring protection were prisoners, parolees, and probationers. The courts were called upon to assure that governmental agencies (i.e. the police and correctional authorities)

acted according to law and did not exceed their delegated authority
by broaching what has come to be known as the individual's "fundamental rights." These rights, in addition to the right to due process
and equal protection have been expanded to include the right

1. To have equal educational opportunity;
2. To be free from inappropriate educational classification,
   labeling, and placement;
3. To receive community services and treatment in the least
   restrictive environment;
4. To be free from peonage and involuntary servitude;
5. To be free from restrictive zoning practices;
6. To have free access to buildings and transportation systems;
7. To be free from unconstitutional commitment practices;
8. To procreate; and
9. To have equal access to adequate medical services (Gelman,
   1981).

The Supreme Court in *Miranda v. Arizona*, 384US 436 (1966), set
requirements to be followed in arrest procedures, in *Morrissey v.
Brewer*, 408US 471 (1972), specified due process requirements for
parole revocation hearings, and in *Gagnon v. Scarpelli*, 411US 778
(1973), establish guidelines for the provision of legal counsel during parole and probation revocation proceedings. The federal
district court in *Newman* (1972), which was discussed earlier, set
forth minimal standards for Alabama prisons and in *James V.
Wallace*, 406 F Supp. 318 (M.D. Ala. 1976), addressed the adequacies
and availability of prison medical care.

Support for these judicial decrees was most often heard from
inmates, citizen groups, and correctional personnel who wanted to
limit the discretionary power of administration and who supported
the notion of rehabilitation. Opposition to these "liberal" reforms
came from those who believed in "justice" or "just deserts" and
viewed these changes as leaving the public at large in a vulnerable
position. Prisoners were perceived as having more rights and
protections than the potential victims of their criminal behavior.

In more recent years, as previously discussed, there has emerged
a countertrend that seeks to assure the safety of the public and the
security of correctional institutions. This is to be achieved in part
by reestablishing "order" and again applying the notion of "just
deserts." This hard-line approach is apparent in the limitations on

how much process is due inmates eligible for parole (i.e. *Greenholtz v Inmates of Nebraska Penal and Correctional Complex*, 995. CT. 2100, 1979), the move to determinate sentencing, the abolition of parole, and limitations on the immunity of parole board members. The U.S. Court of Appeals for the 5th Circuit in *Payton v. United States*, 49 LW 2521 (1981), held that parole board members are not necessarily insulated from liability suits that claim that the board negligently released a dangerous person who harmed another.

Further support for this protective posture can be found in Justice Rehnquist's opinion in *Bell v. Wolfish*, 441 U.S. 520 (1979), where in a case involving pretrial detainees still presumed innocent, he stated that, "even when an institutional restriction infringes a specific constitutional guarantee, such as the First Amendment, the practice must be evaluated in light of the central objectives of prison administration, safeguarding institutional security."

The Supreme Court held in both *Wolfish* and *Rhodes v. Chapman* (Docket No. 80-332, decided June 15, 1981) that the practice of "double celling," in these specific cases, did not constitute cruel and unusual punishment. According to the opinion delivered by Justice Powell, "To the extent such conditions are restrictive and even harsh, they are part of the penalty that criminals pay for their offenses against society."

The expansion of prison and jail facilities, rather than being an effort to (1) overcome prison overcrowding, (2) assure prisoner rights, or (3) improve upon rehabilitative programs, can be viewed as supporting the removal from society for a period of time those individuals whom the public fears, i.e. incapacitation. The emphasis on "rights" shifts as does the value premise and goals underlying correctional activities. Rights granted or guaranteed to one group are accompanied by real or perceived limitations or restrictions on the rights of others. Whether or not rights and protective safeguards can be equally distributed in the future among all people remains to be seen. Current practice in the correctional field is dependent upon the dominate or currently acceptable value premise on which correctional policy is built.

CONCLUSION

I have attempted in the foregoing presentation to identify factors that determine policy in the correctional field. Conflicting if not mutually exclusive value premises regarding the role and function of correctional activities, coupled with economic and political considerations, play crucial roles. The intent of correctional policies is mixed, reflecting both "rehabilitative" and "just deserts" elements. At different times in history, one or the other perspective becomes dominate. While one perspective may be dominate for a period of time, the other perspective maintains its presence through the support of various constituencies. Over time, fears subside, positions moderate, and concerns shift. Society becomes more liberal or conservative with its resources. Abuses are corrected and new problems are identified requiring new protections associated with the rights of individuals and society. Efforts are made to maintain a dynamic balance.

The real dilemma in terms of understanding correctional policy is explained by Duffee when he notes, " . . . Actual demonstration of consensus about policy and outcome is not sought nor is achievement of it really expected" (1980). Until we know what we want, there will be no satisfaction with correctional policies.

CASES

Bell v. Wolfish, 441 U.S. 520 (1979).

Gagnon v. Scarpelli, 411 U.S. 778 (1973).

Greenholtz v. Inmates of Nebraska Penal and Correctional Complex, 99 S. Ct. 2100 (1979).

James v. Wallace, 407 F. Supp. 318 (M.D. Ala. 1976).

Miranda v. Arizona, 384 U.S. 436 (1966).

Morrissey v. Brewer, 408 U.S. 471 (1972).

Newman v. Alabama, 349 F. Supp. 278 (M.D. Ala. 1972).

Payton v. United States, 49LW 2521 (1981).

Rhodes v. Chapman (Supreme Ct. Docket No. 80-332, **decided June 15, 1981.**

REFERENCES

Abt Associates. *American Prisons and Jails.* Washington, D.C.: U.S. Government Printing Office, 1980.

Allen, F. A. "Criminal Justice, Legal Values and the Rehabilitative Ideal," *Journal of the Criminal Law, Criminology, and Police Science, 50* (1959) 226–232.

American Civil Liberties Union. "Senate Moving Quickly on Death Penalty Bill." *Civil Liberties Alert, 4,* 8 (May 1981).

Breed, Allen F. "A National Corrections Policy: Formulation and Implementation," *Corrections Today*, (March/April 1981) 56–67.

Clark, Ramsey. *Crime in America*. New York: Simon & Schuster, 1970.

Dershowitz, Alan M. *Fair and Certain Punishment*. New York: McGraw-Hill, 1976.

Duffee, David. *Correctional Policy and Prison Organization*. New York: Sage, 1975.

Duffee, David E. *Explaining Criminal Justice: Community Theory and Criminal Justice Reform*. Cambridge, Mass.: Oelgeschlager, Gunn & Hain, 1980.

Farber, Bernard. *Mental Retardation: Its Social Context and Social Consequences*. Boston: Houghton Mifflin, 1968.

Federal Bureau of Prisons. "Monday Morning Highlights," 12-29-80.

Fogel, David. *We Are the Living Proof . . . The Justice Model for Corrections*. Cincinnati, Ohio: W. H. Anderson, 1975.

Gelman, Sheldon R. "Who Should Administer Social Services," *Social Work, 26*, 4 (July 1981) 327–332.

General Accounting Office. *Women in Prison: Inequitable Treatment Requires Action*, Report #GGOD-81-6, December 10, 1980.

Gil, David G. *Unravelling Social Policy*. Cambridge, Mass.: Schenkman, 1973.

Gilbert, Neil and Specht, Harry. *Dimensions of Social Welfare Policy*. Englewood Cliffs, N. J.: Prentice-Hall, 1974.

Hindelang, Michael J., Gottfredson, Michael R., and Flanagan, Timothy J. *Sourcebook of Criminal Justice Statistics—1980*. Washington, D.C.: U.S. Dept. of Justice, Bureau of Justice Statistics, U.S. Government Printing Office, 1981, 422–429, 472–473.

Hussey, Frederick. "Just Deserts and Determinate Sentencing: Impact on Rehabilitation," *The Prison Journal, 29*, 2 (Autumn-Winter, 1979) 36–47.

Hussey, Frederick A. and Lagoy, Stephen P. "The Impact of Determinate Sentencing Structures," *Criminal Law Bulletin, 17*, 3 (May-June, 1981) 197–225.

Kahn, Alfred J. *Social Policy and Social Services*. New York: Random House, 1973.

Krajick, Kevin. "Annual Prison Population Survey: The Boom Resumes," *Corrections Magazine, 7*, 2 (April 1981) 16–20.

Law Enforcement Assistance Agency. *Census of Jails*, Preliminary Report—February 1978.

Levin, Martin A. "Crime and Punishment and Social Science," *The Public Interest, 27* (Spring 1972) 96–103.

Levin, Martin A. "Policy Evaluation and Recidivism," *Law and Society Review, 6* (August 1971) 17–45.

Levine, James P., Musheno, Michael C., and Palumbo, Dennis J. *Criminal Justice: A Public Policy Approach*. New York: Harcourt Brace Jovanovich, 1980.

Lieber, James. "The American Prison: A Tinderbox," *New York Times Magazine*, (March 8, 1981) 26–61.

Martinson, Robert. "What Works? Questions and Answers About Prison Reform," *The Public Interest, 35* (Spring 1974) 22–54.

Menninger, Karl. *The Crime of Punishment*. New York: Viking, 1969.

Merrill, Frances E. *An Introduction to Sociology, Society and Culture*. Englewood Cliffs, N. J.: Prentice Hall, 1961.

Miller, Henry. "Dirty Sheets: A Multivariate Analysis," *Social Work, 26*, 4 (July 1981) 268–271.

Mitford, Jessica. *Kind and Unusual Punishment: The Prison Business*. New York: Knopf, 1973.

Morris, Robert. *Social Policy and the American Welfare State: An Introduction to Policy Analysis*. New York: Harper & Row, 1979.

National Association of Social Workers. "Juvenile Delinquency and Adult Crime," *Compilation of Public Social Policy Statements*. Washington, D.C.: NASW, 1980.

National Moratorium on Prison Construction. "United States Incarceration and Prison Growth," *Jericho, 24* (Spring 1981) 6–7.

National Moratorium on Prison Construction. "Research and Reports: Dollars and Sense," *Jericho, 21* (Summer 1980) 8.

National Moratium on Prison Construction. "Community Service: Promise and Peril," *Jericho, 19* (Winter 1979–80) 5.

New York Times, July 2, 1981.

New York Times, July 26, 1981.

Packer, Herbert. *The Limits of the Criminal Sanction*. Stanford, Calif.: Stanford University Press, 1968.

Palmer, Ted. "Martinson Revisited," *Journal Research in Crime and Delinquency, 12* (1975) 133–152.

Parker, William. *Parole*. College Park, Md.: American Correctional Association, 1975.

Ponsioen, J. A. *The Analysis of Social Change Reconsidered*. Paris: Mouton, 1969.

Rawls, Wendell J. "Powell Lifts Alabama Stay and 222 Prisoners Go Free," *New York Times*, July 26, 1981.

Rein, Martin. *Social Policy*. New York: Random House, 1970.

Studt, Eliot. "Crime and Delinquency: Institutions," *Encyclopedia of Social Work*. Washington, D.C.: National Association of Social Workers, 1977, 208–213.

Underwood, Barbara D. "Law and the Crystal Ball: Predicting Behavior with Statistical Inference and Individualized Judgment," *Yale Law Journal, 88*, 7 (June 1979) 1408–1448.

Von Hirsch, Andrew. *Doing Justice*. New York: Hill and Wang, 1976.

Chapter 4

RURAL AND URBAN CRIMINAL JUSTICE

H. Wayne Johnson

INTRODUCTION

In exploring a subject as vast and complex as criminal justice settings and social work, it is not surprising to discover that there are many dimensions to consider. One of these is the community context of both the behavior that is defined (by the community/society) as deviant and the organized societal responses to this social problem that are collectively termed criminal justice. While it is possible to study social welfare settings in criminal justice without dealing with this variable, it is unwise to do so because the community plays such a profound part in social problems and in social policies and programs directed to these conditions.

URBAN AND RURAL AS CONCEPTS

To understand this dimension, it is useful to divide communities into rural and urban areas, and this necessitates definition of terms. Rural communities are defined by the U.S. Bureau of the Census as those under 2,500 population. Other important lines, however, are drawn by the same federal organization at 50,000 inhabitants. "Standard Metropolitan Statistical Areas" (SMSA) are units generally following county lines surrounding cities of 50,000 and larger sharing certain metropolitan characteristics (Johnson, 1980). "Urbanized areas" consist of "a central city or twin cities with a total population of 50,000 inhabitants or more, together with contiguous closely settled territory or urban fringe" (Johnson, 1980).

There are compelling reasons to utilize, for our purposes, the 50,000 population figure as the dividing line between urban and rural, in spite of the lower figure generally used. In significant respects, communities of several thousand people are generally more rural than urban and should be thought of as such.

Several things should be kept in mind in this distinction. Communities, like people, are unique and have their own individual characteristics and, therefore, while generalizing upon them is essential, it is also hazardous. There is always the possibility of overgeneralization. Some communities with 30,000 population may be more urban in important ways than many others double or triple that size. Similarly, there are cities that technically are urban that in actuality are quite rural sociologically and in other respects.

Furthermore, "rural" encompasses both farm and nonfarm communities, with the latter being a large majority currently. To equate rural with farm is inaccurate; most rural dwellers live in towns and small hamlets. By the same token, there is a world of difference between cities of 50,000, 500,000, and 5 million, all technically urban. Suburbanization is just one of many further considerations in this picture.

CRIME AND DELINQUENCY: RURAL AND URBAN

Before examining criminal justice services found in the two groups of communities, it should be worthwhile to review the major types of crime and delinquency found in each. There is an image of the rural community as crime-free. Social problems in general are seen as aspects of urban life and nonmetropolitan areas are thought of as pure, clean, unpolluted, and untainted. This idyllic picture is less fact than fancy, however, because rural communities experience essentially the same social problems found in the cities, including behavior proscribed by law.

Crime rates are generally higher in cities than in the country and, according to Gibbs (1979), the differences between urban and rural rates are greater for violent victimization than for theft victimization. A new statistical indicator developed by the U.S. Department of Justice in 1981 termed Households Touched by Crime found that one of three metropolitan households is likely to be touched by crime in a year compared to one of four small town or rural households (Bureau of Justice Statistics, 1981).

The FBI's Uniform Crime Reports for 1979 includes the following crime rate table (Table 1) showing quite clearly that the rate is higher in urban contexts than rural, but also that there is a substantial amount of crime in nonmetropolitan areas as well. A breakdown is included for each of the eight so-called index offenses for which detailed information is compiled by the FBI.

Table 1[+]

Crime Rate by Area, 1979

(Rate per 100,000 inhabitants)

Offense	Total United States	Metropolitan area	Rural area	Other cities
Crime Index total Modified Crime Index total	5,521.5	6,313.1	2,167.5	4,948.6
Violent	535.5	640.6	187.4	329.9
Property	4,986.0	5,672.5	1,980.1	4,618.7
Murder	9.7	10.9	7.4	5.7
Forcible rape	34.5	41.1	15.1	18.3
Robbery	212.1	276.2	22.1	57.9
Aggravated assault	279.1	312.5	142.8	248.0
Burglary	1,499.1	1,708.8	770.8	1,134.4
Larceny-theft	2,988.4	3,353.1	1,072.2	3,218.0
Motor vehicle theft	498.5	610.6	137.1	266.3
Arson				

[+] Adapted from Webster, W.H. Uniform Crime Reports 1979. Washington: Federal Bureau of Investigation, p.38.

Arson has just recently been added to these offenses and complete data was not yet available for this crime category.

Rural and urban *arrests* are reported by the FBI for 1978 to 1979 as follows (Table 2). This table also shows that between 1978 and 1979 there was a greater *increase* in arrests for index offenses within rural areas (1.6%) than in cities (0.5%).

Table 3 provides a more detailed breakdown of arrests in 1979 as related to communities grouped by size from largest to smallest.

From Table 2 it can further be determined that in 1979 almost a quarter (24.5%) of rural arrests were for violent crimes whereas in urban communities less than one-fifth (19.4%) were for such acts. This single year data is consistent with some other findings (e.g. the 1978 Uniform Crime Reports) but inconsistent with others (e.g. Smith & Donnermeyer; Warner, 1978) that suggest that there is proportionately more violent crime in cities.

The Table 4, comparing rural and urban arrests by sex, shows that arrests are of males even more overwhelmingly in rural than in urban areas.

Table 2[+]

Arrest Trends by Area, 1978-1979

Offense charged	CITY[*]			RURAL[**]		
	1978	1979	Percent change	1978	1979	Percent change
TOTAL	7,027,634	7,064,147	+.5	867,052	880,797	+1.6
Murder and nonnegligent manslaughter	12,108	12,478	+3.1	2,189	2,096	-4.2
Forcible rape	19,103	20,854	+9.2	2,545	2,694	+5.9
Robbery	105,447	107,243	+1.7	4,275	4,434	+3.7
Aggravated assault	175,259	183,925	+4.9	25,003	26,512	+6.0
Burglary	335,954	334,062	-.6	43,088	43,387	+.7
Larceny-theft	863,246	890,152	+3.1	47,813	53,005	+10.9
Motor vehicle theft	108,252	107,706	-.5	11,648	11,569	-.7
Arson	11,912	12,692	+6.5	1,907	1,908	+.1

* (8,221 agencies; 1979 estimated population 139,316,000)

** (2,241 agencies; 1979 estimated population 26,957,000)

[+] Adapted from Webster, W.H. Uniform Crime Reports 1979. Washington: Federal Bureau of Investigation, pp.203, 221.

Table 3[+]

Number and Rate of Arrests by Population Group, 1979

Offense charged	Total[1]	Total city arrests[2]	CITIES						COUNTIES	
			Group I[3]	Group II[4]	Group III[5]	Group IV[6]	Group V[7]	Group VI[8]	Suburban counties[9]	Rural counties[10]
TOTAL	9,488,212	7,223,415	2,497,122	848,518	853,111	979,108	1,030,732	1,014,824	1,290,917	973,880
Rate per 100,000 inhabitants	4,636.9	5,046.0	6,098.9	5,135.6	4,709.4	4,431.1	4,305.0	4,713.3	3,898.4	3,434.3

[1] 11,758 agencies; total population 204,622,000
[2] 8,555 cities; population 143,151,000
[3] 55 cities 250,000 and over; population 40,944,000
[4] 116 cities 100,000 to 249,999; population 16,522,000
[5] 263 cities 50,000 to 99,999; population 18,115,000
[6] 640 cities 25,000 to 49,999; population 22,096,000
[7] 1,547 cities 10,000 to 24,999; population 23,943,000
[8] 5,934 cities under 10,000; population 21,531,000
[9] 833 agencies; population 33,114,000
[10] 2,370 agencies; population 28,357,000

[+] Adapted from Webster, W.H. Uniform Crime Reports 1979. Washington: Federal Bureau of Investigation, p.188.

Table 4[+]

Arrests by Sex and Area, 1979

Offense charged	Percent male	Percent female	Percent male	Percent female
TOTAL	83.8	16.2	87.5	12.5
Murder and nonnegligent manslaughter	86.5	13.5	86.1	13.9
Forcible rape	99.2	.8	99.3	.7
Robbery	92.6	7.4	92.5	7.5
Aggravated assault	87.1	12.9	89.6	10.4
Burglary	93.6	6.4	94.0	6.0
Larceny-theft	68.5	31.5	83.8	16.2
Motor vehicle theft	91.1	8.9	90.9	9.1
Arson	88.3	11.7	90.5	9.5

* (8,555 agencies; 1979 estimated population 143,151,000)

** (2,370 agencies; 1979 estimated population 28,357,000)

[+] Adapted from Webster, W.H. <u>Uniform Crime Reports 1979</u>. Washington: Federal Bureau of Investigation, pp.207, 225.

The fact that illegal behavior may be increasing more in rural than in urban communities, in spite of traditionally higher rates and amounts in the latter, is also seen in juvenile court records. *Juvenile Court Statistics* divides areas into urban (70% of the total population must live in an urban area), semi-urban (30 to 70% of the total population must live in an urban area), and rural (less than 30% of the total population must live in an urban area). Using these definitions, it was found that, over the three year period 1976–78, urban and semi-urban delinquency cases declined whereas there was a marked rural increase both in number of cases and rates. "This sharp rise in delinquence rates demonstrates a growing similarity between the delinquency characteristics of rural and non-rural areas" (Dahma, Snyder, & Sullivan, 1981). In contrast to cities where the decrease in female cases accounted for a large part of the delinquency decrease from 1976–77, female cases grew in rural areas during the same time period. Male cases in rural communities increased similarly (Dahma et al., 1981).

Property offenses, as compared to crimes against the person or violent acts, predominate in both rural and urban areas. Theft in various forms is among the most common illegal acts in both kinds of communities. The nature of the acts differs, however, as does what is stolen. In farming areas at the present time, it is fairly common to find theft of livestock, grain and farm equipment occurring. Cities, rural nonfarm, and farm areas all experience burglary/breaking and entering of homes, out-buildings, business places, and other facilities.

There is some evidence that rural areas have proportionately as much crime as urban centers, although they do not have as much *reported* crime. Two of the reasons that have been advanced for the nonreporting of rural deviance are that rural communities are strongly independent and intolerant of proactive law enforcement strategies except in unusual circumstances. Second, in rural areas there is reliance on social control agencies other than the police to handle minor transgressions (Karr, 1978). On the other hand, Newman (1978) found no differences in attitudes toward the police or the courts between rural and urban persons and that these attitudes did not appear to affect the likelihood of reporting.

CRIMINAL JUSTICE SETTINGS

In responding to the problems of crime and delinquency, society has developed a criminal justice system (actually more a nonsystem) encompassing three subsystems of measures aimed at controlling or changing behavior: law enforcement, judicial, and correctional. While the social control features of these provisions are rather conspicuous, they differ only in degree from the social control aspects of many other social welfare instruments generally.

Law Enforcement Subsystem

As far as law enforcement is concerned, municipal police are the major consideration in urban centers. Rural areas are served by county sheriffs' units and towns by marshalls, with these two working together and supplementing each other. Beyond these, there are various state and federal officials. State police are important in both urban and rural environments, dealing with traffic control, public safety, emergencies, and other activities.

A principal difference between urban and rural law enforcement has to do with distance and time. Typically, an urban officer is only a very few minutes from a cover car to help in the event of a problem as compared to the nearest deputy sheriff's car, which may be forty-five minutes away. This makes the job of the rural law enforcement person a lonely one and may place the officer in a position of feeling especially isolated and vulnerable with few supportive resources (Haafke, 1981).

Traditionally, urban law enforcement was more sophisticated than rural, technically and in training. Significant changes have occurred, however, and present-day rural law enforcement organizations run a wide range of sophistication. Law Enforcement Assistance Administration (LEAA) funds have helped departments modernize in communities of all sizes, especially with regard to hardware. In fact, this was one of the criticisms of LEAA earlier, that it granted too large a portion of federal crime funds to police hardware.

Judicial Subsystem

There are parallels between the rural-urban similarities/ dissimilarities in law enforcement and those in the judicial realm. Here, too, rural adjudication has often been rather unsophisticated in the past and may continue to be in some communities today. Some of the factors in this are the fact that the rural prosecuting attorney is more likely to be only part-time in this role and also maintaining a private law practice concurrently. Being unable to devote oneself totally and exclusively to being a district or county attorney may detract from performance of the role. By the same token, fewer rural attorneys develop practice expertise as criminal or trial lawyers serving defendants.

In some cases, a person charged with committing an offense retains an attorney with a reputation in criminal law from an urban center at considerable distance. Similarly, a state Attorney General may send someone from that office to a local county in any part of the state to lead or assist with a case and its prosecution. Judges in a city may serve for years in one building whereas in a nonmetropolitan environment the judge may "ride a circuit" covering a number of county court houses or other facilities.

Corrections Subsystem

The most important of the three subsystems generally for social work is corrections. One significant exception to this statement is the juvenile court, which, because it is a court, belongs under the judicial group. But, because of the extensive involvement of counseling and probation attached to many juvenile courts, it actually is a hybrid entity bridging the judicial and correctional subsystems.

Juvenile Court

The juvenile court was urban in its Chicago and Denver origins at the turn of the century and most separate courts exclusively hearing juvenile cases are still today located in urban settings. Regardless of community size, however, the cases of young offenders are usually handled by a court acting on its juvenile jurisdiction and authority.

Often this is a person sitting as a juvenile judge on only a part-time basis, hearing non-juvenile cases a greater share of the time. This arrangement particularly characterizes rural communities. Another practice allows one or more judges or referees in mostly rural counties to specialize in juvenile cases by traveling to multiple counties in the course of a week or several weeks. It has been contended (Levin & Sarri, 1974) that juvenile court judges should hear enough such cases to develop expertise in this practice. Depending upon how a system is organized, this is possible even in rural areas.

Detention

One important aspect of corrections is temporary detention of persons (1) being held by the police during investigations, (2) awaiting hearings or trials, (3) following a commitment or sentence by a court to a longer term institution, awaiting transportation and admission to that facility, and (4) in the case of mainly adults, incarceration locally for shorter penalties often up to one year. In the instance of youth, this is a juvenile detention facility and for adults it is jail, either municipal or county.

Most counties have jails and these are among the oldest and frequently most neglected correctional institutions. Paradoxically, the closest-to-home facilities (except for municipal lock-ups) are often overlooked in the interest in and concern about the more publicized state prisons and institutions. There are immense liabilities in county jails generally given their age, decrepit crumbling conditions, poor sanitation, inadequate staffing, and virtual dearth of any meaningful programming for inmates. This picture is characteristic of both rural and urban jails, the major difference being simply one of size. Here and there around the country there are newer, generally better facilities, some of which are freestanding jails and others part of law enforcement centers, justice buildings, or other more modern structures. The solution for most rural counties and many small cities may lie in regionalization.

A serious problem in this nation is the lack of specialized detention facilities for juveniles, the result being that often youngsters are held in jails. All too frequently there are destructive results for young people. Most separate juvenile detention facilities are in cities, just as is true of independent juvenile courts. The majority of rural counties do not have positive routine arrangements for detaining juveniles. A solution for nonmetropolitan areas is regional detention facilities serving multiple counties. Regional jails are a parallel version for adults. These should be centrally located in a geographical area small enough so that all sections are accessible within reasonable driving time, yet sufficiently large to contain a population base warranting a jail or detention facility constituting an efficient operation.

There is a question as to whether a single detention facility can be utilized for both juveniles and adults. This happens often in the case of traditional jails and should be prohibited because of what happens all too often to younger persons—homosexual rape, assault, suicide, and generalized contagion in an environment with often older, more sophisticated, and hardened offenders. But regional facilities in rural areas could be designed and operated to handle both age groups while maintaining their total separation, visually, auditorily, and in absolutely all respects. At the same time, economies can result, e.g. a single kitchen preparing food for both groups and centralized medical and social services and so forth. There is some beginning move in the United States toward regional facilities for adults, juveniles, or both.

A caveat is necessary relative to erecting new correctional facilities, jails, juvenile detention centers, and especially prisons. Experience demonstrates that, if available, they will be used and filled. All too often these are overused, and many people are institutionalized for short or long periods of time who do not actually require such structure and security. This is true in both urban and rural environments.

Probation

Another traditional correctional program, this one community-based, is probation, both adult and juvenile. Probation agencies and services are found in both rural and urban areas but, again, they differ because of the population density. Often officers in rural environments serve two or more counties, whereas a probation worker in a large city may be assigned to only one portion of the single community. This means that the rural probation officer may spend an inordinate amount of time traveling to see only a few clients. It also means that he or she may not work out of an "office" in the usual sense much of the time, doing more home visits and meeting clients in municipal or county facilities, schools, and other arrangements. Structurally, many juvenile probation officers are county employees, while often those working with adults are state agents, although there are numerous variations in such patterns around the country. Both urban and rural probation officers typically carry excessive caseloads (President's Commission, 1967). Whereas the President's Commission recommended caseloads of thirty-five and other organizations have suggested fifty, figures as recently as 1976 show adult probation loads nationally double to triple these standards (National Criminal Justice Information and Statistics Service).

Institutions

Long-term correctional institutions include training schools and variations thereof for juveniles and camps, reformatories, prisons, and prerelease centers for adults. In all of these, a common pattern is incarcerating mainly urban offenders in institutions frequently located, if not usually, in rural settings. Many problems result.

Years ago when legislatures established public state institutions for offenders, the mentally ill, the retarded, and other special groups, these facilities were typically placed in out-of-sight, out-of-mind rural areas. From the point of view of contemporary modern America, they were often not well situated in central locations close to population centers. But in a horse-and-buggy era, the location often made sense; for example, in Iowa, a rural state, there are four state mental hospitals, each centrally located in the four quarters of the state. But none of these and none of the correctional facilities are in or adjacent to today's largest cities. Often state institutions were originally designed in conjunction with a farm. More recently the farms have sometimes been sold or have ceased operation and clientele are less likely to work on the farm.

Problems of urbanites being incarcerated in rural institutions are numerous and are exemplified by the notorious Attica, New York prison eruption of 1971. Distance for visitors is an obstacle, yet visits from interested supportive family members is important, as is maintenance of family ties. Remembering that many offenders are poor and/or from financially poor families, the great distances become a serious financial burden whether the costs are bus fare, driving, or some other mode of transportation. Time is a consideration also including loss of income resulting from time away from work for visitors, when necessary.

Because such institutions are in rural environments, people employed to staff them in most nonprofessional levels such as guards, correctional officers, or youth workers tend to be from the immediate farm and small town vicinity. Typically, these are white, middle-class people employed to work with a population heavy in racial and ethnic minorities and the poor, and they have the greatest amount of direct contact with the incarcerees. For institutions to attempt to employ more blacks and other minorities is extremely difficult generally because so few such persons reside in the area from which most employees are customarily drawn.

It has been observed that there is little communication between rural staff and urban residents in a juvenile training school setting and that the communication that does exist tends to be directive toward the residents. This directiveness is an easy way for staff to deal with situations, but it creates hostility and prevents change on the part of the residents (Towley, 1981).

Another problem is attracting and retaining experienced professionals for positions in rural institutions (Towley, 1981). While this may be slightly easier currently with the back-to-the-country movement and rural growth, generally it is difficult to recruit physicians, psychologists, psychiatrists, social workers, and other professionals to institutions in rural environments. Part of this is probably resistence to the idea of working in a correctional institutional context, but some of it is due to the rural setting, which may be perceived by prospective employees as lacking cultural opportunities and professional stimulation.

The growing number of institutions or units termed security medical facilities or some such designation present special issues (Clemens, 1981). These vary in purpose but usually are for the diagnosis and treatment of mentally ill offenders and/or evaluation of persons for courts, institutions, and parole authorities. Sometimes mental and physical health activities are combined in a single facility. Because of these particular functions, they require more specialized personnel, e.g. psychiatric and medical, than the usual prison. This is the kind of program that may be located within the vicinity of a university at least partially because of the professional personnel needs as well as for other reasons. Universities, too, run the gamut with regard to urban and rural settings.

College and university environments not only bring together professionals, they also afford an opportunity to utilize students in a variety of ways—residents, interns, and practicum and field experience students from a variety of fields including social work. Furthermore, it is not uncommon for criminal justice programs to employ persons, part-time or full-time, who may simultaneously be students.

Parole

The last traditional correctional service is parole for adults, often termed after care for youth who have been institutionalized. Much of what has been noted previously relative to probation also characterizes parole. Parole officers are more likely to be state employees than county or local, and parole tends to be more uniform within a state relative to its administration. With both probation and parole, urban agencies often have such large caseloads that most of the time is spent just attempting to fit clients as a group into the agency mainstream. Rural officers/workers, on the other hand, may handle their smaller loads in a more individualized personable way with more procurement of services and more mediation. The other side of this is that the rural worker may be assigned such an expansive territory that a great deal of time is consumed in travel.

Thus far, we have examined traditional correctional services, both community-based field services and institutions, with regard to their rural/urban similarity and dissimilarity attributes. There is a danger of overstating the dissimilarities, especially in terms of stressing the image of rural areas as totally lacking services. Elsewhere, the author has suggested (Johnson, 1980) that, rather than a simple dearth of resources in rural environments, more accurately what exists is a difference in the nature of services, in how they are delivered. Of course, many of the differences are ones of degree. Everything considered, urban and rural criminal justice are much more alike than unalike.

COMMUNITY-BASED ALTERNATIVES

We turn our attention now away from the traditional criminal justice programs to those newer alternatives that are community-based. Only a few will be considered in interest of space limitations. At the outset, it should be noted that innovation has occurred and is taking place currently in both metropolitan and rural communities in spite of the fact that criminal justice generally is a conservative, slow-to-change field.

In recent years, considerable attention has been given to *diversion* of accused or convicted juveniles and adults from the usual channel of procedures and practices that all too often in the past have led to negative labeling, destructive consequences, and high recidivism. The major unofficial diverters traditionally, without using the term, have been the police. But now as diversion has begun to be structured and institutionalized, special projects have appeared. In many programs, diversion comes much later in the process than with the police. In one county of 80,000 population, including a city with 50,000, a project provides diversion for juveniles early, at the time of a "preliminary inquiry," which is similar to an arraignment for adults. At this hearing, the judge refers the youth to the diversion unit (Souter, 1981). In other communities, both rural and urban, diversion comes later.

Pretrial and related services are another group of community-based programs. In fact, the first project in the nation to be awarded the "Exemplary Program" designation by LEAA was a community based correctional endeavor in Des Moines, Iowa, a city of 190,000 in a county of 300,000, the largest community in a rural state. "The Exemplary Projects Program (National Institute of Justice, 1981) is a systematic method of identifying outstanding criminal justice programs throughout the country, verifying their achievements, and publicizing them widely" toward the goal of replication. To be eligible for consideration, projects must demonstrate goal achievement, replicability, measurability, efficiency, and accessibility. The four components of the Des Moines program, "pre-trial release screening; a pre-trial community supervision effort; a county administered probation unit; and a community-centered corrections facility" (National Institute of Law Enforcement, 1973) operate from a single administrative unit. It is fairly simple in design, relatively low cost, and effective.

The first two of these measures made it possible to reduce the number of persons being held prior to trial in an ancient and overcrowded county jail. At the same time, the number of persons who were released without bond and appeared later for their trials was impressively high. This was true both for the group based on the Vera-Manhattan Bail Project and another group presenting greater risks released under supervision in the community (National Institute of Law Enforcement, 1973).

The *community centered correctional facility* in Des Moines is also noteworthy, though not a pretrial program. It consists of an abandoned army barracks on a military reservation within the city and is used as an alternative to incarceration in a state prison. Education and work release are its major programs for a population that was 90 percent felon and 20 percent heroin addicts in 1972. The facility works closely with community resources and is well staffed. Without spending large amounts of public funds on brick and steel erecting a bastille, the facility maintains a relatively low escape rate. During its first year of operation (1972) there were ten escapes when a total of 148 residents were admitted (National Institute of Law Enforcement, 1973). All four aspects of this "Court Services" program could be duplicated in communities both larger and smaller, almost regardless of size. Sparsely populated counties may need to combine to have a sufficiently large base and this is done in multicounty judicial districts now. The local small institution idea can be implemented generally. Most counties or judicial districts could locate an inexpensive building, abandoned or otherwise, that could be leased or purchased and converted into a local institutional facility.

Very much related to the community centered correctional facility are *partial confinement* (von Hirsch, 1976) and *work release*. These programs are most likely in municipal or county jails or other local residential facilities. Such provisions are found in large and small communities. The idea is to incarcerate offenders at certain times, e.g. nights and/or weekends, and permit them to obtain or continue employment concurrently. A number of advantages are inherent in this kind of arrangement, several of which are economic. There is reduced need for public assistance or welfare for the family of an offender who is employed. Similarly, the work releasee or partial incarceree may be charged for his/her public "board and room," thus relieving the taxpayer. There are other potential gains as well and all can benefit the rural and urban communities offering such services.

Another community-based program that is regaining popularity is the sanction of *restitution*, related both to the growing concern with crime victims as well as the recognition that repayment by offenders to persons who have suffered loss at the hands of the perpetrator can have significant restorative value for both the offender and the victim. By its very nature, restitution lends itself almost equally well to both rural and urban contexts. In fact, it is found in both, whether administered by courts, probation/parole, or some other arrangement.

Community service is another sanction being used in some places in several variations. Offenders are required, in this plan, to do stipulated amounts of work in nonprofit organizations such as charitable or governmental. As with any program, this one is no panacea and there are problems to be resolved, but its potential is considerable in both urban and nonmetropolitan areas. Its benefits for the public may be doubly significant in rural communities when townspeople perhaps more directly observe and experience offenders constructively occupied repairing or maintaining public buildings, facilities, and grounds or working with "charity" organizations. To the extent that this produces more positive public attitudes toward offenders (improved offender attitudes are reciprocal in these dynamics) the potential payoff for everyone concerned is substantial (Harris, 1979).

The author has been involved with senior college students in social work who staffed a community service project in a university community. Among the latters' duties were screening, training, and supervising the activities of sophomore level student volunteers in the same program, recruiting new community agencies to participate in the program, providing liaison to participating agencies, and overall monitoring. Activities included interviewing, data collection, record keeping, case management, and working with resources. In another corrections setting, a security medical facility, a graduate practicum social work student interested in supervision, administration, and teaching provided supervision and instruction for an undergraduate field experience student functioning as a generalist. All of this involving the author's participation has occurred in small cities. This is significant when one realizes how many of the colleges and universities with Council on Social Work Education (CSWE) accredited undergraduate programs (276 in 1980) are in smaller communities (Council, 1980). The same thing is true of eighty-four graduate schools. The point is that the potential for innovative impacting on criminal justice is considerable if fully exploited.

Group homes for juveniles and *halfway houses* for adult offenders exist in various patterns in urban and rural areas. Some are in lieu of institutionalization in more secure facilities. Others serve to smooth the transition from institutions back into the community and others serve still additional purposes. There is a common phenomenon when the establishment of group homes and halfway houses is proposed—neighborhood opposition. This is seen in communities of all sizes and kinds. Some of the expressed fears are reduction of property values, danger due to the presence or bad example of offenders, and similar notions. Interestingly, however, when there is a proposal to close or reduce in scope a state institution in a rural community, there is as much or more opposition. In some towns, an institution is literally the largest employer in the community and the major "industry." To lose it can be quite damaging economically to the local community.

In recent years, there have been a number of developments having to do with *runaway* youth often taking the form of *shelters* for short-term care. This population is relevant for juvenile justice to the extent that running away is defined as delinquency, albeit a status offense. Such acts are being substantially redefined nationally to decriminalize. This does not completely solve the problem, however, of the needs of youth on the run. A directory of shelters (Office of Juvenile Justice, 1979) suggests that they are present in all sections of the U.S., more so in urban centers but even in quite small communities.

The same thing is true of *shelters* for persons experiencing *spouse abuse* and family violence. These even newer facilities are distributed unevenly in various parts of the nation but are found in communities ranging widely in size. Rural towns would have trouble maintaining such a facility because it is usually important that the location remain unidentified and unknown and this is difficult to do in a nonmetropolitan community. Directories of spouse shelters reflect largely urban locations. While the general approach in child abuse is to help parents rather than punish, the act of abuse is itself illegal and hence can and sometimes does become a matter for criminal justice.

Rape crisis programs are another recent innovation. This offense occurs in all regions but it may be more difficult to establish relevant social services in rural areas because of the community's propensity to ignore or deny some of its problems such as this one. Part of the rural social worker's challenge is often to sensitize the community to its own needs and enable it to take constructive action in programming (Davenport).

THE SOCIAL WORK ROLE IN URBAN
AND RURAL CRIMINAL JUSTICE

The function of the social worker in criminal justice is essentially the same as that in other major fields of service: applying the helping or problem-solving process with offenders. The involuntary nature of the clientele makes some significant differences, but the principal activities are basically the same. These generally are conceptualized as study (often called investigation in criminal justice), assessment, formulating a plan of action, implementation or intervention, and evaluation.

Common social work roles in criminal justice are probation/parole officer, institutional counselor or social worker, pretrial worker, police social worker (as discussed by Treger in another chapter), or one of the other newer, more specialized roles such as those having to do partially or entirely with restitution or community service. Most social workers in criminal justice are in direct service with individuals, families, and/or small groups (casework and groupwork in traditional terminology), but there are those in administration at various levels including state director of corrections, and in research, teaching and other aspects.

The literature on rural social work stresses the need for a generalist worker in nonmetropolitan areas. This is true in rural corrections also. Such a professional is one skilled in the major methods who is able to provide direct service, engage in some program development, and operate with self-help activities. He or she is very much attuned to the nature of the community, its customs, and its traditional service network, often involving law enforcement persons, clergy, school officials, clubs and lodges, and others and to the existent "natural helpers." This is a worker who can function autonomously without much supervision or professional stimulation.

In contrast to the rural generalist, there is more specialization (and formalization) in urban settings. This does not necessarily mean that such programs are therefore better or more effective, however. Actually, upon examination, criminal justice is seen to be largely a hodge-podge nonsystem rather than a well organized and smoothly integrated social mechanism. This is true when considering the urban or rural situations separately or both together.

Many social workers from noncriminal justice settings encounter offenders in the course of their practice just as many offenders experience social workers, in and out of criminal justice. Therefore, it is important that social service professionals be able to deal comfortably and competently with this client group.

TRENDS AND THE FUTURE

As far as crime and delinquency are concerned, the basic trend is for urban and rural communities to come together and be more alike. Rural crime and delinquency are growing at a disproportionate rate and appear to be catching up with urban. Although there are offenses characteristic of each kind of community, most types of offenses are now found in central cities, suburbs, and rural areas.

Traditional criminal justice provisions are present in both rural and urban areas and innovative programs exist in communities of various size. Not surprisingly, more community-based measures are established in cities, but the latter certainly have no monopoly on these. Some promising programs are present in sparsely populated areas. There is every indication that these developments will continue in at least the near future although shrinking funds, both federal and state, may negatively impact on the picture, rural, and urban.

SUMMARY AND CONCLUSION

In this chapter we have considered the concepts urban and rural as related to crime and delinquency. The three subsystems of criminal justice and a variety of settings, both traditional and nontraditional, have been examined as these are found in rural and urban areas. Community-based alternatives to institutions have been included. The social work role in both metropolitan and rural criminal justice was explored.

While some distinctiveness has been noted in urban and rural crime problems and criminal justice programs, it has been seen that these differences are easily exaggerated. There appears to be convergence taking place between large and small communities with regard to deviancy and criminal justice. Stereotyped and inaccurate notions of communities in general and of their problems such as crime and their social welfare services like corrections require balancing and reason. Programs, whether in the law enforcement, judicial, or correctional realm, are more likely to be of maximum benefit if properly understood in their rural and urban environmental contexts. Most program ideas can be adapted to communities of various sizes and characteristics.

REFERENCES

Bureau of Justice Statistics. *The Prevalence of Crime*. Washington: U.S. Department of Justice, 1981.

Clemens, C. Personal Communication, Oakdale, Iowa, September 3, 1981.

Council on Social Work Education. *Colleges and Universities with Accredited Undergraduate Social Work Programs*. New York, 1980.

Dahma, L., Snyder, H. N., & Sullivan, D. *Juvenile Court Statistics 1976–78*. Pittsburgh: National Center for Juvenile Justice, 1981.

Davenport III, J. "Rape Crisis Service in Rural Areas" (a video-tape). University of Kentucky, Appalachian Education Satellite Program, 1978.

Gibbs, J. J. *Crime Against Persons in Urban, Suburban and Rural Areas: A Comprehensive Analysis of Victimization Rates*. Albany: Criminal Justice Research Center, 1979.

Haafke, R. L. Personal Communication, Sioux City, Iowa, August 13, 1981.

Harris, M. K. *Community Service by Offenders*. Washington: U.S. Department of Justice, National Institute of Corrections, 1979.

Johnson, H. W. (ed). *Rural Human Services*. Itasca, Illinois: F. E. Peacock Publishers, 1980.

Karr, J. T. *Rise of Proactive Police Strategies — An Alternative Approach to Bureaucratic Rationalization and Rural-Urban Crime Differentials*. Unpublished doctoral dissertation, University of Kansas, 1978.

Levin, M. M. & Sarri, R. C. *Juvenile Delinquency: A Study of Juvenile Codes in the U.S.* Ann Arbor, Michigan: University of Michigan, National Assessment of Juvenile Corrections, 1974.

National Criminal Justice Information and Statistics Service. *State and Local Probation and Parole Systems.* Washington: U.S. Department of Justice, Law Enforcement Assistance Administration, 1978.

National Institute of Justice. *Exemplary Projects.* Washington: U.S. Government Printing Office, 1981.

National Institute of Law Enforcement and Criminal Justice. *Community Based Corrections in Des Moines.* Washington: U.S. Department of Justice, Law Enforcement Assistance Administration, 1973.

Newman, J. H. *Differential Reporting Rates of Criminal Victimization.* Unpublished doctoral dissertation, Washington State University, 1978.

Office of Juvenile Justice and Delinquency Prevention. *Runaway Youth Program Directory.* Washington: U.S. Department of Justice, Law Enforcement Assistance Administration, 1979.

President's Commission on Law Enforcement and Administration of Justice. *The Challenge of Crime in a Free Society.* Washington: U.S. Government Printing Office, 1967.

Smith, B. L. & Donnermeyer, J. F. *Victimization in Rural and Urban Areas — A Comparative Analysis,* 1979.

Souter, J. Personal Communication, Iowa City, Iowa, September 2, 1981.

Towley, J. F. Personal Communication, Iowa City, Iowa, August 27, 1981.

von Hirsch, A. *Doing Justice.* New York: Hill and Wang, 1976.

Warner, Jr., J. R. *Rural Crime — A Bibliography.* Monticello, Illinois: Vance Bibliographies, 1978.

Webster, W. H. *Crime in the United States 1979: Uniform Crime Reports.* Washington: Federal Bureau of Investigation, 1980.

Section II

THE ROLE OF
POLICE SOCIAL WORKERS

INTRODUCTION

Section II focuses on a promising area in the delivery of justice social services: police social work. Social workers employed by law enforcement agencies interface with a most difficult and complex environment. In the past, police social work was synonymous with police women's bureaus. Female social workers who were employed by police departments were frequently subjected to the prejudices of sexist and antagonistic male police officers.

In Chapter 5, the Editor documents the history of the police social work movement. It is important to explore the humble beginnings of police social work in the early 1900s, the marked growth period from 1920 to 1950, and the political obstacles that led to the downfall of most police women's divisions. Much remains to be done before the law enforcement community can be said to be responding fully to the acute need for social work intervention within their area of responsibility.

Chapter 6 describes the significant accomplishments of Harvey Treger and his associates in developing the "Police-Social Work Team" model. Based on Treger's experiences throughout the state of Illinois, the chapter provides step-by-step guidelines for those social workers interested in developing a police-social work program in their community.

Chapter 5

THE HISTORY AND ROLE OF
SOCIAL WORK IN LAW ENFORCEMENT[1]

ALBERT R. ROBERTS

The history of police social work is almost exclusively one of policewomen providing social work services and, consequently, is closely intertwined with the emergence of policewomen, many of them having social work backgrounds. In the early 1900s, at a time when policemen were mostly assigned to patrolling the streets and to the other duties traditionally associated with law enforcement, the first police social workers were policewomen who were responsible for providing certain social services, usually to women and juveniles. There is no evidence that policemen were ever assigned to perform social work functions during the first quarter of the twentieth century. At that time, social work was a predominantly female profession, and it is understandable that the first police social workers were women.

Although the police social worker movement had a spirited beginning, accounts of police social work faded from the literature after approximately forty years. By the end of World War II, it seemed to have been almost completely forgotten. Although a new surge of interest is now emerging and several police departments have demonstrated their concern for helping people in need of social and medical services, much remains to be done before even the most enlightened and humanistic police departments can be said to be responding fully to the acute need for social work intervention within their areas of responsibility.

The author's interest in expanding the points of entry into social service delivery systems led to extensive research into the history of police and social work collaboration. The review of the

[1] Adapted from *Social Work*, 1976, 21(4), 294–299 with the permission of the National Association of Social Workers, Inc.

literature presented here was undertaken to discover and synthe-
size the widely scattered information on the police social work
movement and determine what has impeded its development in
this country. Briefly, the development of this movement has been
hampered by various forms of misconception, resistance, and
ignorance, and because the documentation is at best sketchy, an
integrated assessment of its history must consist of piecing together
many obscure threads in the literature.

The research did not uncover specific evidence that during the
first half of this century police departments specifically allocated
positions for social workers. However, many of the early policewomen had social work training prior to being hired by the police
departments, and they performed police social work roles in their
protective work with children and youth. Although there is no
clear-cut means of distinguishing between the early policewomen
and the first police social workers, the author has determined that
the history of police social work is often synonymous with that
of women's bureaus in police departments and of policewomen
generally. Indeed, the origin of the police social worker movement can be traced to the establishment of women's bureaus in
police departments during the first quarter of this century. The
establishment of these women's bureaus was, in turn, a direct
result of a desire for better protective and preventive social services
for women and children.

It is the author's belief that by studying the problems that
impeded the police social worker movement from flourishing
similar mistakes can be avoided as the social work profession
attempts to reestablish these services. This chapter includes a discussion of the origin and growth of the women's bureaus that
became the prototypes of police social work, an analysis of the
problems leading to the decline of police social work, and finally,
several recommendations for planning and developing much needed
collaborative efforts between police and social workers.

WOMEN'S BUREAUS AND POLICE SOCIAL WORK

Police departments have traditionally been concerned with,
among other things, protective services for women and children,
and as a result, they have provided some social services, particularly for juveniles. A crucial step in the gradual evolvement of the
police social worker movement was the establishment of Women's

Bureaus within police departments during the 1910s and 1920s.

Although the first protective service for young girls was developed as early as 1905 in Portland, Oregon (Pigeon, 1939), the year 1910 is frequently cited as the origin of the policewomen profession in the United States. In September of that year, Mrs. Alice Stebbins Wells was appointed a police officer in Los Angeles. Prior to her employment in police work, Mrs. Wells had made a study of crime and concluded that there was a strong need for women in police service (Graper, 1920). However, she did not acquire her position without the concerted effort and support of many local citizens, a hundred of whom she had persuaded to sign a petition to the mayor requesting that she be put on the police force. Fortunately, Mrs. Wells had been able to keep the knowledge of the petition from both the local press and politicians until its actual presentation, which allowed the mayor and the aldermen to grant her request in an unpressured climate (Darwin, 1914). Only one year after Mrs. Wells had obtained her position on the Los Angeles police force, the position of policewoman became classified under civil service, thus enabling other women to be recruited to work with juveniles.

While these events were taking place in Los Angeles, similar developments occurred in Chicago. Minnie F. Low (1911) reported that a social worker was on duty at the Chicago police station. Many people had been coming to the police station to air their grievances, both real and imagined, and the social worker was assigned to doing away "with petty, degrading litigation and adjust [ing] the less serious complaints." Because of the social worker's efforts, such litigation was considerably reduced, and this arrangement won favorable comments from the courts. As a result, within two years (in August, 1913) the Chicago Police Department had appointed ten policewomen with social work experience under civil service regulations. By 1919, the number had increased to twenty-nine (Minor, 1919).

Initially, there was strong opposition among policemen in most departments to the hiring of female officers. However, this overt opposition gradually faded, at least on the surface, and the hiring of policewomen spread. By 1915, it was reported by the United States Census Bureau that twenty-five cities employed policewomen who were paid from police appropriations. The largest number of policewomen in any city, a total of twenty-one, was reported in Chicago, while the cities of Baltimore, Pittsburgh, Los Angeles,

San Francisco, Minneapolis, Seattle, Portland, St. Paul, Dayton, and Topeka had each hired from two to five policewomen.

At the Conference of Charities and Correction in 1916, Alice Stebbins Wells, who had become the President of the International Association of Policewomen, spoke on the topic of the policewomen movement. She stated that the impetus for women to become policewomen had derived from a desire to care for young people who needed help. Mrs. Wells also remarked that many troubled women who had been able to confide in policewomen may have had difficulty relating to a policeman. "The power of the policewomen to counsel and protect fills a real need," she said, and urged the expansion of recruitment and training of women for this field.

By 1920, the prospect of policewomen serving in social work advocacy roles (particularly dealing with juveniles) seems to have taken hold. In a speech before the National Conference of Social Work, Mina Van Winkle (1920), Director of the Women's Bureau at the Metropolitan Police Department in Washington, D.C., clarified the role of policewomen serving in her Bureau, saying, "Policewomen are aiming to bring about a close relationship between social workers, the public and the police." Van Winkle further described the Women's Bureau as, "a separate unit in the police department with a women as director responsible to the head of the department and giving entire time to all cases in which women and children are involved as well as to preventive and protective work." Her stated goal was to have a Women's Bureau, directed by a woman, in every large city throughout the country. Van Winkle distinguished four types of responsibilities— protective, preventive, corrective, and general police work—and specified the activities in which the policewomen were involved as, "follow-up work for women and girls, securing employment, improving and changing environment that causes delinquency, voluntary probation, ... physical and psychopathic examinations, careful investigation of questionable circumstances ... locating missing girls, assistants in case work for the police, juvenile and criminal courts." She also mentioned other responsibilities for policewomen such as searching for runaway girls, helping policemen secure evidence against prostitutes, and providing temporary boarding where necessary (Van Winkle, 1920).

Between 1915 and 1920, the number of policewomen had increased sufficiently to support an International Association of Policewomen. The original constitution of this Association set forth standards including the following:

> ... to act as a clearinghouse for compilation and dissemination of information on the work of women police, to aim for high standards of work and to promote preventive and protective service by police departments.

> ... the use of policewomen chiefly for protective and preventive work, the employment of professionally trained women, the establishment of courses of instruction in universities or schools of social work, and the keeping of proper records. (Pigeon, 1934)

However, the growth of the International Association of Policewomen was limited because the police social worker movement was prevalent only in a few large urban areas such as Washington, D.C., Berkeley, Chicago, Detroit, Cleveland, Indianapolis, New York City, Los Angeles, Seattle, and St. Louis.

In the decades following the inception of a corps of policewomen, there was a steady increase in their numbers. By 1930, for example, there were 509 policewomen in 200 police departments throughout the United States (U.S. Department of Labor, 1931). By 1949, employment statistics of the Women's Bureau of the U.S. Department of Labor indicated that there were over one thousand policewomen in the United States. Yet, this group comprised less than 1 percent of the total number of police officers in the country. Although the numbers of those early policewomen were small, their work was important and the level of their education remarkably high. This can be illustrated by the Detroit Police Department, which in 1944 had fifty-eight policewomen in its Women's Division. They had all attained a college degree or the equivalent and had two years of practical experience in youth work prior to employment with the Women's Division. Broadly defined, a large part of the work carried out by these educated women could have been classified as social work intervention. Although the policewomen were required to perform patrol work and investigative duties, they were also able to provide early case finding and referral to appropriate social agencies.

Two case examples from the records of the Women's Division of the Detroit Police Department from the early 1940s will serve as an illustration of the intervention strategy utilized by these policewomen (Connolly, 1944).

The first is a vivid account of a policewoman, Miss Kidder, picking up in her patrol car a young runaway girl, just as she is about to be taken to a hotel by a stranger. Despite some initial lying and subterfuge on the girl's part, Miss Kidder's "kind, expert questioning" back at police headquarters brings out the whole, sad story of a seventeen-year-old girl who, having run away from a drunken father and stepmother in Akron, Ohio, comes to Detroit hoping to live with her aunt, only to find out that the latter has left town. Unable to keep her job in a cheap vaudeville theater, the girl is now penniless, homeless, hungry and cold, and vulnerable to transients and pimps who want to pick her up. At this point, let us turn to the actual dialogue between the police-woman and the girl as it was recorded:

> "Where was he taking you when we picked you up?"
> "He was going to rent a room for me."
> "You mean—for both of you?"
> "No. He said not. He promised. . . . "
> Miss Kidder turned directly to the girl. "Jean, have you had anything to do with men or boys, sexually? If you have, you should be examined for venereal disease."
> "No," was the vehement protest. "I never have. Never! But go ahead, examine me. I don't mind."
> "Good. Now, Jean, we'll have to detain you here at headquarters while your case is investigated. You'll be in a clean, private room. Not with anyone else. And you are *not* being arrested or given a police record. You are just being protected.
> "Don't send me home!" the girl begged.
> "Your home will be investigated. If it's what you claim it is, you won't have to go back. If you do stay in Detroit, we'll help you get adjusted. Social agencies will find you a clean place to live, a job, some young friends and some fun. You'd like that?"
> Tears of relief sprang to the girl's eyes. "Yes," she said huskily.

This case is representative of police social work during the early 1940s, in which timely assistance was provided to juveniles in danger of becoming involved in delinquent acts.

A second case, also from the records of the Detroit Police Department, shows perhaps even more forcefully the critical need for timely intervention on behalf of young and troubled girls.

> In Detroit, a girl of eleven, missing from her home for a week, was found by policewomen as a result of dogged day and night searching. This child, Helen, left alone evenings, had wandered downtown to a movie, been picked up by a young procuress of fourteen, lured to her apartment and

dressed up to look eighteen. She had been offered to sailors as a V-girl. But
though she looked eighteen, the men had decided, from her childish voice,
that she must be very young and had let her alone. Her hostess then turned
her out. Helen escaped rape almost by a miracle (Connolly, 1944).

Mrs. Coolidge, lieutenant of the Detroit women's division, was
appalled by the fact that the number of rapes was on the increase
and that policemen were being assigned the difficult and delicate
task of questioning the victims. The lieutenant strongly believed
that because of the strain on the young victim of recounting
the horrid events, all rape investigations should be handled by
policewomen.

Van Winkle (1924) was in the vanguard of those urging collaboration between social work and police work; as early as 1924, she
was recommending that social workers enter the police force. She
called for employing social work techniques when working with
juveniles with the goal of preventing delinquent acts and proposed that educated police social workers be hired to work toward
that end. Van Winkle hoped that this would lead to a reduction in
the continuing controversy between police, courts, and probation
personnel as to which agency was responsible for reducing the
delinquency problem.

Van Winkle further recognized and deplored the tendency of
some agencies to be concerned only with their own specific function,
without being concerned with the overall service delivery system.
She concluded that all agencies were at fault in this regard, stating
emphatically that:

> Each group is only too prone to see the question of delinquency from its
> own angle without reference to the problem as a whole, and certainly
> without reference to society. Let us, therefore, join hands. Police work is
> social work, and until you include it in social service we shall continue to
> pass delinquents from one agency to another, and then from reformatory to
> jail, workhouse, and prison. Socialized policework is but a further exten-
> sion of the government's responsibility for public welfare (Van Winkle, 1924).

As has been seen then, beginning in 1910, women had become
an important part of police departments in several urban areas
across the United States by providing social service oriented
police work, dealing particularly with juveniles and women. The
emergency of a corps of well-educated police social workers was,
however, fraught with unresolved problems.

The next section of this article will deal with these problems and misconceptions before discussing recommendations for the future.

MISCONCEPTIONS AND PROBLEMS

Throughout the early 1900s, policewomen had to contend with publicized misconceptions of their role. Published accounts of their responsibilities frequently overlooked the social work functions that policewomen carried out. Caricatures of policewomen appeared in the newspapers, which depicted them as tight-lipped, masculine-looking creatures, with "billy" clubs swinging at their sides and a revolver in hand. The adverse treatment in the press reached such proportions that in 1919 the Executive Secretary of the New York Probation and Protective Association, Maude E. Minor, responded by declaring emphatically that policewomen did not police a beat and make arrests as the men did. Policewomen's major responsibilities, as Maude Minor explained them, were in the realm of protective work with juveniles.

In addition, and even more damaging to the police social worker movement than the resistance of the press toward policewomen, was the resistance from male police officers and police administrators. Policemen had difficulty accepting the presence of females within their department. Their antagonism toward the police social workers seems to have stemmed not only from the chauvinistic view that women belonged in the home but also from prejudices against social workers. The powerful, authoritarian role in which policemen perceived themselves was diametrically opposed to the human service casework orientation of most police social workers.

In studying and analyzing the police social worker movement during the first quarter of the twentieth century, it is important to remember that in those years a certain amount of contempt was directed at all women who were pursuing a professional career; therefore there was even greater disdain for women who chose to enter a traditionally male profession such as policework. Policewomen were continually faced with criticism, i.e. that they were attempting to do a "man's job" by arresting hardened criminals, when in fact, the early policewomen were far more interested in providing social work intervention services than they were in doing patrol work. It comes as no surprise, then, that policewomen's energies were often diverted from working full-time in areas such as protective services to repeatedly defend and explain their true purpose and function.

In addition to the harassment the early policewomen endured from the press and their male co-workers, there were other obstacles that impeded the expansion of the police social worker movement. These were the most significant stumbling blocks: political considerations; lack of interest and support from citizens groups; lack of funds from private organizations and foundations with which to publicize the accomplishments of police social work and expand staff; insufficient support from elected officials for larger appropriations; lack of coordination with and participation in local, state, and national social welfare and police organizations; and limited opportunities for students in schools of social work to take course and field work in the structure and function of police departments.

Political obstacles, especially at the local level, frequently prevented the growth of the police social worker movement; for example, the election of a new mayor or city manager often occasioned the appointment of a new police commissioner, and it was not unusual for such turnovers to result in new policies that restricted the hiring of police social workers and threatened the work of women's bureaus.

The chain of events resulting from new city leadership frequently went like this: direct or indirect pressure caused the director of the women's bureau to resign; internal changes occurred whereby policemen stopped referring appropriate cases to the women's bureau and attempted to handle those cases by themselves; and, as an end product resulting from policemen's lack of knowledge of community resources, the number of referrals to child guidance clinics, traveler's aid, and other social agencies would fall off.

These developments were often, of course, reflections of a lack of police interest in social work objectives. In some cases, policemen had merely been paying lip service to the police social worker movement, and when the support of the police chief began to wane, they were quick to verbalize their opposition to the work of the women's bureau. Also, the stereotyped exaggerations of policewomen that appeared periodically in local newspapers reinforced many policemen's prejudices against the social work responsibilities carried out by female police officers.

In recent years, only limited use has been made of collaboration between social work and law enforcement professionals in the

United States. Few areas of the country have utilized the relatively untapped potential of police social workers in providing immediate intervention services to troubled juveniles, adults, the elderly, and families. At the present time such programs are operating in Haywood, California, Honolulu, Hawaii, Lyndhurst and Trenton, New Jersey, Yonkers, New York, Pawtucket, Rhode Island, and several areas throughout the state of Illinois (Carr, 1979, 1982; Michaels & Treger, 1973; Treger, 1972, 1974, 1983). Programs in other locations should also be developed.

In a number of locations across the nation, a more humanistic perspective among police chiefs is becoming apparent. Among the police programs that seem to be realistic indicators of police departments' concern about social service objectives are the training of police officers in family crisis and social work intervention and the development of crime-specific rape crisis centers.

RECOMMENDATIONS

The history of police social work lends support to the view that social workers can make a significant contribution to broadening the role of police departments as human service agencies, especially in crisis intervention work with juveniles and their families. Consequently, the question becomes this: What should be the relationship between social workers and law enforcement personnel in the 1980s?

Both types of professionals have expanded their respective functions from what they were in the early 1900s. Social work services are, and should continue to be, provided mostly by social work agencies, and law enforcement functions are properly the province of police departments. However, if police officers are to do their jobs most effectively, it is essential that they gain a basic knowledge of crisis intervention strategies, an awareness of appropriate referral sources in their community, and a sensitivity toward the social problems faced by community residents.

The recommendations put forth here are actually geared to two types of programs. One is aimed at providing training for all police officers to enable them to be more effective in helping the troubled persons they encounter while on patrol. Such skills are particularly important during the evening, weekend, and holiday periods when most social agencies are closed. The problems on which crisis intervention training should focus include child abuse, suicide, alcoholism, violent family quarrels, and juvenile offenses.

Police officers' knowledge and skill need to be broadened beyond just transporting an abused child to the local hospital emergency room. They need training in human relations and mental hygiene, sensitivity training, and to know how to recognize personality disorders. They need training not so that they can take the place of experienced social workers, psychiatrists, and psychologists, but to be able to provide immediate crisis intervention when emergencies arise and the other professionals are not available. Many of the larger police departments already provide some of this training to new recruits. However, there is a need for a more thorough handling of these topics during training sessions and for more standardization to reduce the wide variation that presently exists from one department's training program to the next.

The other area of recommendation encompasses the development of social work teams within police departments. Such teams would be staffed by experienced social workers who are knowledgeable about police procedures, and they would be assigned the following responsibilities: (1) to establish solid working relationships with agencies providing emergency medical, psychiatric, and social work services in the community; (2) to provide the initial diagnostic assessment of clients referred to them by police officers, make appropriate referrals to local agencies, and follow-up to ensure that service was rendered; (3) to provide police officers with in-service training in crisis intervention techniques; and (4) to be on the job twenty-four-hours-a-day to serve as a back-up resource for the policemen and policewomen on patrol.

National and state-wide training models and research grants should be given high priority and receive the necessary financial support, through federal and private foundation funding. Schools of criminal justice and schools of social work could provide invaluable support by expanding or reallocating their resources—faculty, curriculum, videotape equipment, and computer time—into demonstration, training, and research projects geared toward assembling practice models for social worker-police collaboration.

Without the development of national standards and goals, the mistakes of history may be repeated. The social work profession can learn from past mistakes. A concerted effort must be initiated now so that national leaders in social work practice and police science can provide the unified leadership necessary for building working models of cooperation between police and social workers. Together these recommendations can, in part, provide the initial blueprints for national models of practice.

REFERENCES

Bard, Morton and Berkowitz, Bernard. "Training Police as Specialists in Family Crisis Intervention: A Community Psychology Action Program." *Community Mental Health Journal, 3* (1967) 315–317.

Bard, Morton. *Training Police as Specialists in Family Crisis Intervention.* Washington, D.C.: U.S. Government Printing Office, Law Enforcement Assistance Administration, 1970.

Bard, Morton. "Family Intervention Police Teams as a Community Mental Health Resource." *Journal of Criminal Law, Criminology and Police Science, 60* (June, 1969) 247–250.

Carr, John J. "Treating Family Abuse Using a Police Crisis Team Approach," in Maria Roy (Ed), *The Abusive Partner.* New York: Van Nostrand Reinhold Co., 1982, 216–229.

Carr, John J. "An Administrative Retrospective on Police Crisis Teams." *Social Casework, 60*:7 (July, 1979) 416–422.

Connolly, V. "Job for a Lady: Detroit's Women Police Tackle the Girl Delinquency Problem." *Colliers, 113* (June 10, 1944) 19–20, 48.

Darwin, M. "Police Women and Their Work in America." *Nineteenth Century,* (June, 1914) 1370–71.

Graper, E. D. *Police Organization and Methods of Administration in American Cities.* Doctoral dissertation, Columbia University, Faculty of Political Science, New York, 1920.

Low, M. F. "Report on Joint Section Meetings." *Proceedings of the Thirty-eighth Annual Session of the National Conference of Charities and Correction.* Boston, Mass., 1911.

Michaels, Rhoda A. and Treger, Harvey. "Social Work in Police Departments." *Social Work, 18* (September, 1973) 67–75.

Minor, M. E. "The Policewoman and the Girl Problem." *Proceedings of the Forty-sixth Annual Meeting of the National Conference of Social Work.* Atlantic City, N.J., 1919.

Pigeon, H. D. "Policewomen." *Social Work Yearbook, 1933.* N.Y.: Russell Sage Foundation, 1934.

Pigeon, H. D. "The Role of the Police in Crime Prevention." *National Probation Association Yearbook,* 1939.

Shimota, Kenneth L. *Police Social Worker, Eau Claire Police Department: A Summary Report.* Madison, Wisc.: Wisconsin Division for Family and Youth, mimeographed.

Treger, Harvey, Thomson, Doug, and Jaeck, Gordon S. "A Police-Social Work Team Model." *Crime and Delinquency* (July, 1974), 281–290.

Treger, Harvey. "Breakthrough in Preventive Corrections: A Police-Social Work Team Model." *Federal Probation 36,* (December, 1972) 53–58.

Treger, Harvey. "Guideposts for Community Work in Police Social Work Diversion." *Federal Probation*, 44 (September, 1980) 3–8.

United States Census Bureau. *General Statistics of Cities*. Washington, D.C.: U.S. Government Printing Office, 1915.

U.S. Department of Labor. *Juvenile Court Statistics*. Publication No. 200. Washington, D.C.: U.S. Government Printing Office, 1931.

U.S. Department of Labor, Women's Bureau. *The Outlook for Women in Police Work*. Bulletin No. 231. Washington, D.C.: U.S. Government Printing Office, 1949.

Van Winkle, Mina. *Standardization of the Aims and Methods of the Work of Policewomen*. Proceedings of the National Conference of Social Work at the Forty-seventh Annual Session, New Orleans, La., 1920. Chicago, Ill.: University of Chicago Press, 1920.

Van Winkle, Mina. *The Policewomen*. Proceedings of the Fifty-first Annual Session of the National Conference of Social Work, Toronto, Ont., 1924, Chicago, Ill.: University of Chicago Press, 1924.

Wells, Alice Stebbins. *The Policewoman Movement, Present Status and Future Needs*. Proceedings of the Forty-third Annual Session of the National Conference of Charities and Correction, Indianapolis, Ind., 1916, Chicago, Ill.: Hildman Printing Co., 1916.

Chapter 6

GUIDEPOSTS FOR COMMUNITY WORK IN POLICE SOCIAL WORK DIVERSION[1]

HARVEY TREGER

When the Jane Addams College of Social Work, University of Illinois at Chicago Circle, placed social workers and graduate students in community police departments, it was as if a pebble were thrown into the water. A widening ripple effect was created. The consequences of this innovation provided new relationships and opportunities for public service; new knowledge was developed and a workable model for systems change was discovered.

"The Police-Social Work Team" Model is an example of fitting university resources and innovation with community needs and problems in a mutually acceptable arrangement for public service. For the profession of social work, "The Police-Social Work Team" extended the tradition of cooperation and facilitation to new professions and disciplines and offered services to previously unserved populations.

The experience in innovating and directing this pioneer effort in police-social work beginning in March 1970 through 1977 provided the basis for developing some generalizations and guideposts in community work that may be useful to others contemplating similar efforts in community-based corrections.

The process of entry into a community, developing working relationships, and becoming a partner in social welfare program development is something of a mystery to many professionals in the field of human services. The literature is lacking in such reports so that a description of the process can begin to fill a knowledge gap in this area. Beyond this, it may provide some

[1]From *Federal Probation*, 44 (September, 1980) 3–8. Reprinted with the permission of the publisher.

practice skills capable of routinization, evaluation, and further elaboration.

Structures such as the police, the criminal justice system, and the political arrangements in a community are essentially based on levels of authority. An understanding of the nature of authority and its interrelationships in a specific community system is necessary if ideas are to be translated into programs. The first step is always very important, as it can influence and affect subsequent actions. An association of mental health agency directors recognized this when they asked, "How did you get into the police department?" Entry into the police department, as with any system, is not simple. To the uninitiated, it may appear that way, particularly if one enters the system from another discipline.

The first task of a program developer is to talk with the agency head—in this instance it was the chief of police. In one community, an attempt was made to develop a police-social work diversion program by beginning with the juvenile officer. The program got started but failed to receive ongoing support. The juvenile officer did not have the authority to establish an ongoing program in a police agency without the approval of his chief and the sanction and support of senior officers in the department.

GUIDEPOST NO. 1. If you want to start a program in a community agency, you must first talk with the head of the agency in which your program will be lodged and "sell" him on your idea.

If someone the chief knows and trusts introduces you to the chief, it may be helpful at least in "getting the ear" of the chief. Once the chief is interested in your ideas and believes they are congruent with his philosophy of police work or human services and would be useful to the department and community, he may plan for you to meet with supervisory staff to explain the program and how it would work. In this way, senior ranking officers are involved to elicit their reactions and how they think the staff would receive such a program.

If after meeting with the chief and supervisory staff it is still "go," the chief will start you through the political system to gain the necessary support, sanction, and appropriation. It is important for the social program developer to be alert and monitor this experience with the system as it progresses. You will want to observe relationships, identify the center(s) of power and control, and note the official concerns and personal characteristics and interests of people you may be working with. You will also want to see how decisions are made and observe the customary ways of doing business in this community. You may wish to use this information about "how this system works" at a later date to achieve your program objectives. Once you learn how to "operate" in more than one system, it is easier to learn a third and a fourth, etc. As a result, you will likely develop deeper insights into your own organizational interrelationships, as well as have greater facility and confidence in working cooperatively with a variety of systems.

GUIDEPOST NO. 2. Follow the guidance of the agency head. They usually know their community and political system, as well as the process of introducing new people and programs into existing structures.

The chief of police can identify key community influentials—and groups—whose support will be useful in the planning and development or later operational phase. Preliminary meetings may occur with the city manager and the mayor and sometimes later with several key members of the city council before a meeting with the board. It is important to prepare yourself for each meeting just as a direct practice person would with an individual or family. Ask yourself, "Why are you getting together? What are your goals? What do you hope to accomplish? What is your strategy? What information will be required to 'sell' the idea? What kind of format will be most effective to influence your audience? Is there any preparation in the way of information, etc., that would be useful for the group to know prior to the meeting?" In one instance, a village president had not prepared the council for the program developer's presentation. The outcome was literally a disaster. It was later learned that the village president was himself ambivalent toward the suggested program. He had some commitment and loyalty to an already existing program that a few board members felt wasn't working as well as expected. Some prior preparation with the village board could have insured a better reception to the new idea or else they might have decided not to entertain a proposal for a new program thereby making the meeting with the program developer unnecessary.

Village officials usually have at least several concerns:

(1) What is the program? How will it work?
(2) Has it been tried anywhere else and with what results?
(3) Why did you come to this community?
(4) What will the program cost?

(5) Does our community need this program?
(6) Does the program developer have ample time and competence to direct the program, e.g. is he or she a person who has the personal attributes to work cooperatively with the political system and diverse groups in the community?
(7) What are the projected political consequences of introducing this new program, i.e. how will it affect interprofessional relationships and other city departments as well as impact on the target population?

It may be useful to offer an illustration that will demonstrate how the program might work with a specific problem. Take your audience through the system so they can get a feeling for the program. Allow lots of time for questions. You will be more likely to obtain interest and even commitment when people are involved and you contribute ideas and suggestions and clarify areas of uncertainty.

Questions No. 6 and No. 7 will be answered by the city officials and department heads as they assess the program and the program developer. They will be keenly interested in knowing what kind of a person you are, i.e. are you thoughtful or impulsive? Are you evenhanded or arbitrary? Do you have fixed, rigid ideas or are you flexible and openminded? They will want to know how you make decisions. Are you authoritarian or do you involve others in matters of mutual concern? How do you work with your peers and those in authority? How do you handle your own authority? Are you a team player? Will you consult on policy issues with governmental officials?

The process here is akin to being interviewed for a job. Of course, this is a two-way street and you will be making your own assessments too:

(1) Can the key political leaders obtain the needed sanction and support to launch and maintain the program?
(2) How much involvement and commitment can be mobilized? What assistance is needed in obtaining supplementary outside funding? How much will the political leaders help?
(3) How stable are the political arrangements in terms of the life of the project?

GUIDEPOST NO. 3. Involvement and commitment is an essential ingredient for effecting beginning and continuing support by community officials. An illustration of this principle can be seen in the recent development of a police-social work program in Hanover, West Germany. The program was initially sponsored by the Minister of Justice for Lower Saxony, Professor Hans-Dieter Schwind, with partial funding from the German Marshall Fund. Since the program was in the City of Hanover, sanction and support by the Lord Mayor, Herbert Schmalstieg, was necessary. The achievement of this objective was an important step. The situation was particularly sensitive as the Minister of Justice and the Lord Mayor were of opposing political parties. A two-phase plan was designed:

(1) A meeting with the Lord Mayor, the Minister of Justice, program director, and consultant to discuss the Lord Mayor's concerns regarding the program and to encourage his involvement.
(2) To plan a visit for the Lord Mayor to the United States for a "firsthand" view of a police-social work program.

At the meeting, the Lord Mayor expressed three concerns about a police-social work program in Hanover:

(1) The political concern, i.e. the potential for role conflict and cooperation between police and social workers.
(2) The impact of social work on community problems, e.g. are social workers theoretical or are they pragmatic, too?
(3) The problems of minorities (Afghanistans, Greeks, Yugoslavians, Italians, etc.) and the ability of the program to relate to the problems of these people, e.g. housing, medical care, parent-child culture conflict problems, problems of alienation, etc.

The Lord Mayor's concerns were similar in many respects to the experience with governmental officials in the United States when the program first began in their community. The background of the American social worker who would work in the Hanover program for the first year included experience as a police-social worker and work with minorities and displaced persons.

The Lord Mayor subsequently visited the United States and was exposed to a number of programs. He talked with governmental officials and practitioners to learn about problems and issues as well as to get a feeling of confidence in the capability of police-social work diversion.

Later, the Lord Mayor reported he was well pleased with his visit and that he had learned a great deal. Correspondence from Hanover indicates the Lord Mayor is now feeling involved and is committed to the program. He has offered to assist the project in obtaining cooperation from some referral agencies that are reluctant to work with the police-social work program.

After most of the initial planning phase is completed, the program developer must himself begin to get more involved in the community.

GUIDEPOST NO. 4. The goals and objectives of the program and their priorities should serve as a guide to the nature and degree of community involvement at various points in time.

The kinds of information and relationships needed in beginning program development require careful thought and planning. The collection of information and the development of supportive and service relationships often go hand in hand. A useful reference point for getting to know a community is your own experience in relocating from one community to another. Most everyone can relate to this, as they have moved at some time in their life. Ask yourself what kinds of information did you want to know before and after the move and what additional would have been useful to know? Transportation, schools, churches, banks, shopping, safety, reputation of police, fire departments, city services, and the quality of life are a few of the things most people are interested in. What resources are available for obtaining this information? A few information resources are the Chamber of Commerce, City Hall, the library, the International City Managers Association publication, "The Municipal Year Book," community influentials, and directors of agencies and institutions, especially those with whom you will work.

The police are a natural resource, a storehouse of community data that has been little appreciated and used in social planning. The police chief can identify community influentials whose support may be needed for program development. He knows how people relate to each other and how they behave organizationally and therefore can be a key leader in community development.

In the areas of delinquency prevention and crime control, the police are especially knowledgeable about the financial and political aspects of the community, history of community problems, available resources, gaps in services, and general information about the ambiance of life in the community.

GUIDEPOST NO. 5. In order to successfully develop a program, the social program developer must have workable relationships and become a partner in community development. They must become invested in the life and concerns of the community, i.e. attend community meetings, social affairs, serve on agency boards, and be available for advice to city officials in their area of expertise. This kind of progressive and ongoing investment is the substance of successful program development. When you invest in the life of a community, your relationship with the community will deepen. Experience indicates that a new person or program in a community is like a "new kid on the block." Agency executives will want to know, Who is he, why is he there, what does he hope to accomplish, and how long does he plan to stay? Furthermore, they want to know what their relationship will be, i.e. what can he do for them and what effect will his actions have on their program? Will they work cooperatively and in what area? Will they compete for funds and/or clients? Will this new program be threatening to the existence of established agencies? Will agency functioning change?

Experience in developing police-social work programs demonstrated that two things emerged from community contacts early on:

(1) That some people had ambivalent feelings about the presence of the project in their community. These feelings were typical of the feelings of some police officers, social workers, university colleagues, and people from the funding agency. From the communities' point of view, they were reacting to a stranger in their midst, an outsider from the big state university, of whom one community influential said, "you don't even know the names of the streets." Others expressed a fear the program would permit criminals to roam the streets.

(2) That early contacts later proved worthwhile, when requests were made for client services.

"The ability of the program developer to deal with community reactions to a new situation is observed and evaluated and helps the social program developer to establish an identity as well as his competence" (Treger, 1976). This dynamic interaction is part of a continuum of change. Community and agency relationships will develop as the program becomes operational and service requests are initiated. The consequences of being interdependent with many agencies and systems is that you tend to broaden the base of understanding and support for your program while building linkages for service delivery; you also learn about additional resources and gaps in services. Furthermore, the broader the resource base, the more impact and choices a system has. Community problems and situations are frequently complex and interlocking. They require inputs from many professionals and systems working cooperatively as a team to maximize its impact on the problem. In this way, each profession may add to its knowledge and expand its services to new populations. As a result, better coordinated and more comprehensive services could be offered. Interprofessional-intersystem efforts, however, are not without risks, as differing orientations and values can be conflictual and there may be sensitive borderline areas where flexibility and mediation are required.

GUIDEPOST NO. 6. Programs of social provision should be designed to fit the needs of the people being served.

The experience of developing programs in a variety of communities with different populations including working class, middle class, upper middle, and minority groups has created a sensitivity to the uniqueness of the life-styles of each community. It's not like setting up a franchise hamburger or fried chicken establishment. If it is, chances are you will not be in business long. It takes time to get on board with a community, just as it does with a client. The collection of significant information about the community being served is cumulative and requires assessment for it to become a useful input in planning and program development. An example is Maywood, Illinois. Maywood has very large working class and minority group populations. Approximately 30 percent of the police-social work program clients were either receiving some form of public aid or had income that was just above the public assistance level. To establish an effective program in this community, the staff and students needed to demonstrate their interest and availability to the population referred for services. Minority group populations tend to be distrustful of government and authorities and are reluctant to become involved in government-sponsored programs in traditional settings. To stimulate motivation for social services, most people referred to the Maywood Project were seen as soon as possible in their own homes rather than in the police department, unless social assessment indicated otherwise. Unavailability of child care arrangements and lack of transportation and funds were additional reasons for the frequent use of home visits as the setting of choice for offering services in this community. It is believed that if services were not tailored to the life style and needs for this community, the utilization of services would have been markedly diminished. Furthermore, interpretation to referral agencies of acceptable service patterns and follow-up with the agencies and clients was necessary to insure a high level of referral acceptance.

An open house in the beginning phase of the program was helpful in broadening our acquaintance with the community and for bringing diverse groups, e.g. agency directors, funders, university officials, police, and social workers, together in an informal evening where new relationships and follow-up opportunities could develop. Representatives of a Black Muslim group attended the Maywood open house and wrote a letter supporting the program, which was used as evidence of community support when second year funding was sought.

GUIDEPOST NO. 7. The development of a new program in a community can be understood from a systems perspective.

The police-social service program is actually a system within systems (Treger, 1951). When working with a range of professionals in different systems, it becomes necessary to be sensitive to the impact of decision-making upon the interrelationship of their respective systems, e.g. the police-social service program was in the law enforcement system part of the justice system working within the university system, and within the systems of professional social work and social welfare. A decision in one program could affect the interrelationships of the program with other parts of the system(s).

Inkles has stated, "Changes in one part of society have important implications for other parts of the system (thereby) enabling us better to understand why so often innovations are so slowly adopted" (1964). If system reactions to contemplated policy decisions are not thought through and planned for, unexpected and undesired reactions and impediments to a program could occur. When the police-social work program became operational in Hanover, West Germany (August 1979), the professional social

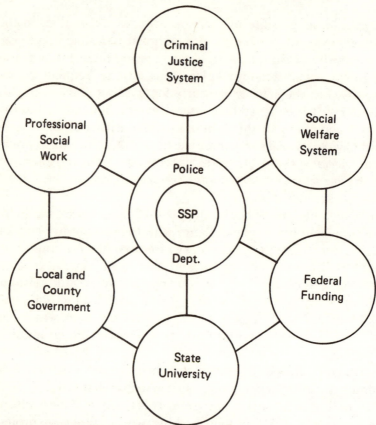

Figure 6-1. The Social Service Project — A System.

work association reacted strongly to the idea of social work and police cooperation. They feared the police would coopt the social workers and decided to boycott the program. Information revealed that the agencies in the community had not been involved in the planning and did not fully understand the nature of the program and what the social workers would be doing. They were feeling left out, and like an orphan, they were expressing their fears and anger. It was apparent that a step in the process of community involvement was left out and now needed to be made up. An unexpected consequence was that it brought the social workers closer to the police who could identify with them as a beleaguered group under external threat.

Another example of system interaction occurred when an irate judge stormed down to a community police department to lecture juvenile officers that he didn't want youths who should properly be before him referred by police officers to the project. Some prosecutors are also concerned that police officers and social workers may invade their area of discretion. It has been stated that, "if substantial numbers of offenders are diverted by local law enforcement to community based agencies (or to units such as a police-social work program) there will be in all likelihood reduced inputs to prosecution, adjudication, and correctional agencies. Lessened inputs will alleviate some of the backlog in the judicial system and reduce caseload pressure in probation and parole and size of institutional population. While these occurrences are desirable, at some point in time the bureaucratic instinct for survival may be threatened. Reactions protective of the establishment may set in" (Carter, 1975). Although new programs to resolve community problems are desired by community leaders, they are also resisted because invariably they challenge established norms and relationships creating conflict and disequilibrium in a system. It is this effect that innovation has on a system that must be anticipated and coped with if a new program is to be sanctioned and supported. Any new group or program must either become integrated into the fabric of the system, assimilated, or expelled. The development of interprofessional and intersystems cooperation requires mutual involvement in planning and program development that relates to the concerns and sensitivities of the various professions and systems involved as well as client groups in a dynamic and ongoing manner.

Getting into a community and knowing what to do when you get there is something akin to learning to drive a stick shift car. You begin with shifting the *first gear*—getting into the agency and political community; *second gear*—becoming acquainted with the community, its influentials, agencies, institutions, and systems; and then shifting into *third gear* with ongoing communication, information dissemination, and input into the wider area of social welfare program development. You put it all together in a continuous manner with fine tuning as new information develops and situations change over time. This dynamic process can help achieve the goal of a true partnership, with reciprocal benefits to the program, the cooperating professions, the political structure, the funding and sponsoring agencies, and the client.

REFERENCES

Carter, Robert M. "The Diversion of Offenders." *Federal Probation, 36*:4 (1972) 35.

Inkles, Alex. *What is Sociology?* Englewood Cliffs, N.J.: Prentice-Hall, 1964.

Treger, Harvey. "Process in Development of the Project." *The Police-Social Work Team.* Springfield, Ill.: Charles C Thomas, 1975.

Treger, Harvey. "Wheaton-Niles and Maywood Police-Social Service Projects." *Federal Probation*, (September, 1976) p. 34.

Section III

VICTIM ASSISTANCE WORK

INTRODUCTION

One of the most overlooked areas of justice social work has been services for victims. Historically, victims of crime have been ignored by the courts, social welfare policymakers, and those in social work practice. In the recent past, some attention has been given to victims. This victim concern trend is quite significant and consists of programs that provide client services to victims of crime as well as programs that actively involve victims in the actual administration of justice.

The recent proliferation of programs to aid crime victims came into being as a result of federal and state grants. The Law Enforcement Assistance Administration (LEAA) was the major sponsor for victim-witness assistance programs and safe neighborhoods and crime prevention programs. Rape crisis centers were developed as a result of funds from the now defunct LEAA and from the National Center for the Prevention and Control of Rape (of the National Institute of Mental Health). Programs for victims of wife abuse received substantial staffing support as a result of CETA funding. Other funding sources for victim services were Community Development and ACTION grants, as well as state human service grants. Most of these funding sources have been disbanded or substantially cut back as a result of Reagan's economic and social policies. Only time will tell whether these victim assistance programs will be able to locate alternative sources of funding. Fiscal cuts at the state and local level also will affect the stability of safe neighborhoods and crime prevention programs. The primary sponsor of these prevention programs is usually a city or county police department or a community agency.

In Chapter 7, John Gandy discusses a number of innovative victim service programs. Such programs include victim-witness assistance, safe neighborhoods and crime prevention, restitution, pretrial settlement, and victim-offender reconciliation. After exploring the general area of services to victims, Gandy discusses programs that necessitate direct services to victims. Considerable attention is devoted to programs that involve victims in the criminal justice process. The remainder of the chapter is devoted to the role of the social worker in the delivery of services. A brief historical perspective is provided concerning the involvement of social work in criminal justice. Advocacy, mediation, and arbitration are discussed as roles assumed by social workers, as is involvement in dispute settlement and conflict resolution.

Throughout history, deaf persons have encountered major communication barriers within the justice system. These barriers can be eliminated by using *qualified* interpreters and telecommunication devices for deaf persons (TDD's). Although Section 504 of the Rehabilitation Act of 1973 and Department of Justice Regulations require agencies receiving federal financial assistance to provide qualified interpreters, there are many places in the justice system where interpreters are not provided.

In Chapter 8, Janet Pray examines the special problems encountered by deaf persons when they come into contact with criminal justice agencies. She informs the reader that the social work profession, which already has a place in the justice system, has a responsibility to educate both deaf clients and the justice system with respect to the legal requirements and the benefits derived from use of interpreters and TDD's. Social workers can also develop skills and become knowledgeable about resources that make it possible for deaf persons to experience the justice system in a way that is more comparable to that of hearing persons than has been true in the past.

Chapter 7

SOCIAL WORK
AND VICTIM ASSISTANCE PROGRAMS

JOHN T. GANDY

INTRODUCTION

The notion that criminal offenders are a disenfranchised group should not surprise anyone, it's fact. What might be of some surprise, however, is the idea that victims are also a disenfranchised group. It is ironic that social work has attempted to respond to the needs of offenders, yet it has traditionally ignored victims. The concern for victims is a fairly recent occurrence. Historically, victims have received minimal, if any, concern by the courts, the public, social welfare policymakers, and those in social work practice. A very recent trend in criminal justice is the increasing attention being devoted to victims, which in itself is quite significant. Included in this trend are efforts to provide services to crime victims as well as efforts to more actively involve victims in the actual administration of justice.

The author will discuss social work practice in several innovative programs that focus on the victim: victim-witness assistance, safe neighborhoods and crime prevention, restitution, pretrial settlement, and victim-offender reconciliation. It should be noted that several of the programs that will be discussed involve the offender as well as the victim such as restitution, pretrial settlement, and victim-offender reconciliation. As we continue to move away from traditional social welfare programming in the justice arena, these innovative developments will become even more significant for victims as well as offenders.

SERVICES TO VICTIMS

In a general sense, victim service programs have been in operation for some time. These services have been targeted historically at specific populations and generally ones that elicit considerable emotion and feeling. Such programs include services to victim groups related to child abuse, rape, family violence, etc. While such programs and related social services are obviously crucial, the concern for victims in the general sense has been a rather recent phenomenon.

In examining services and programs designed for crime victims, it is helpful to conceptualize them in relation to the larger perspective, i.e. the functions they serve. A discussion of such functions contributes to our examination of the role of the social worker in victim assistance programs and the delivery of social services through such programs.

In relation to functions, Dussich has discussed victim services programs in terms of primary, secondary, and tertiary functions (1981):

Some primary functions include:
—Taking immediate responsibility for the victim
—Ensuring that the victim is provided with emergency medical or social services
— . . .
—Addressing the client's family needs
— . . .
—Following up on the delivery of public assistance to clients

Some secondary functions include:
—Helping victims in their role as witnesses
—Providing advice to reduce the victim's risk of revictimization
—Establishing volunteer efforts to augment victim service units
—Rendering aid to victims and their families with aftermath arrangement, such as funerals, insurance, and victim compensation
— . . .
—Arranging with victims convenient times for court appearances
—Maintaining a victim-witness courtesy center where victims can wait for their court appearance
— . . .

Some tertiary functions include:
—Studying individual victimizations for use in preventive planning
—Developing public awareness programs for target hardening
—Conducting periodic victimization surveys for use in planning
—Developing victim awareness throughout the community
— . . .
—Setting up periodic victim-awareness seminars for middle and upper management criminal justice personnel

— . . .
— Publishing a community services directory tailored to victim needs
— . . .
— Assisting in developing restitution and compensation programs

In the victim assistance programs that are discussed, the role of the social worker and the delivery of services relates directly to the functions that the program is serving. Victim service programs incorporate at least one function and at times two or three functions, i.e. primary, secondary, and tertiary. Since social work practice can embrace all three functions, the role of the social worker as well as the delivery of social services vary depending on the specific victim assistance program.

An intriguing orientation to discussing victim services concerns whether or not the victim is involved in the criminal justice process. The author conceptualizes services to victims as actually two issues. One type of service involves only the provision of direct services to the victim with the focus being meeting the needs of that individual. The second type of service is concerned with actual involvement of the victim in the criminal justice process. In effect, the victim becomes a significant party in the process.

DIRECT SERVICES TO VICTIMS

The first concern for victims of crime was manifested in rudimentary programs of a crisis nature. These programs usually were targeted at specific population groups, i.e. victims of child abuse, rape, etc. We are now witnessing an awareness and recognition of the needs of other groups, such as victims of family violence and the aged victims of crimes.

It is interesting to note that the concern for such victim groups developed in large part from the community or lay groups. These programs are concerned with meeting the needs of the victims and not with the purpose of involving the victim in the criminal justice system. They serve primary functions for the most part, although some secondary functions are also involved. In such programs, direct services are utilized to a great extent. Crisis intervention as well as more traditional one-to-one and group services are incorporated into such programs. Emergency shelters for various victim groups, such as child abuse, rape, and family violence, are widely used in programs concerned with primary and some secondary functions. The aged victims of crime are just beginning to emerge as an issue, and specific programs are being initiated to respond to this need.

In victim assistance programs providing direct services to victims, the social worker functions in a rather traditional role. The social worker is primarily concerned with the immediate needs of the victim. Such crisis intervention usually includes the provision of emergency medical care for cuts, lacerations, bruises, etc. It may also consist of emergency psychiatric services, which is a new and developing arena. Another primary concern of the social worker at this phase of intervention is the provision of emergency social services. This is an important role for the social worker, since the delivery of social services through such programs is crucial. Such services include meeting the needs of the client's family. If children are involved it might necessitate the use of temporary care. The social worker may need to respond to the emotional and physical issues involved in the victimization of a family member. In such emergency situations, many times the social worker is required to make very quick decisions regarding removal of the victim to ensure that repeated victimization does not occur.

Direct services provided by the social worker are not limited to emergency situations. The social worker has a significant role in delivering ongoing social services to the victim and the victim's family. Such services include, but are not limited to, ongoing individual and family counseling. Issues that are addressed include the meaning of being victimized, the feeling of being vulnerable to victimization, the lasting inpact on one's self and family, and the victim's role in the event, etc. The aftermath of a victimization is very difficult and a crucial time to obtain some resolution to these issues.

The role of the social worker in the provision of direct services is primarily crisis intervention. This is a difficult and demanding role with considerable pressure and stress.

Programs involving direct services to victims can be under the auspices of a variety of agencies. Services may be provided by the prosecutor's office, the mayor's office, city or county police departments, social service agencies, and nonprofit community agencies. Nationwide programs providing direct services can be found under all of the auspices mentioned. Generally, direct services are provided by police departments, social service agencies, and non-profit community agencies. Although these agencies serve primary, secondary, and tertiary functions, there is a similarity in the direct nature of the services they provide. We are apt to see the focus on the provisions of services to the victim and the family from a social service context as opposed to a strictly legal or administrative perspective.

Although direct services to victims are a significant part of the social worker's role in victim assistance programs and in the delivery of social services, another important role is developing. This role concerns the actual involvement of the victim in the criminal justice process.

INVOLVEMENT OF VICTIMS
IN THE CRIMINAL JUSTICE PROCESS

In the past few years, the role of the victim has evolved from being only the recipient of services to being an active participant in the legal process. Most such programs remain in the developmental or formative stages, although a number of programs are in existence at the present time.

Victim-witness assistance programs were initiated to aid the treatment of victims and witnesses by the system and enhance the effectiveness of the criminal justice system by the establishment of more helpful relationships between the system and victims and witnesses. Historically, victims as well as witnesses were left standing alone without any support whatsoever from the criminal justice system. They were to navigate the murky waters of the justice proceedings without any assistance, and needless to say, this has proven to be disastrous for both parties. Neither victims nor witnesses had experience with criminal justice matters, and they were overwhelmed, terrified, and confused.

Victim-witness assistance programs were developed in response to this reality. Such programs offer support to the victims and witnesses, and staff are liaisons with the system as well as guides through the complicated justice quagmire. Victim-witness programs also assist the individual in coping with the inconveniences of the justice process, such as conflicts between work schedules and court demands, loss of income, etc. Program staff also help dispel a number of fallacies and myths about the system as well as respond to the anxieties and apprehensions of the victims and witnesses.

Safe neighborhood and crime prevention programs are also a part of the victim movement. Various neighborhood watch programs, which depend on neighbors having responsibility for others' property, have experienced tremendous growth. These are well organized and many are scientifically designed and tailored to neighborhood and community needs.

Crime prevention programs in neighborhoods as well as in relation to specific properties are also developing rapidly. Police and even ex-offenders involved in community service restitution work with neighborhoods and individual property owners in, for example, burglary-proofing houses, installing break-in proof locks and windows. The fear of being victimized or being repeatedly victimized has led to the development and improvement of these programs.

Several developing programs are unique in that they involve the victim and the offender. In fact, in many instances the two parties are brought together in developing a contractual relationship. The general term utilized in relation to such programs is restitution, although it is more accurate now to refer to them as monetary restitution, community service restitution, and personal service restitution (John T. Gandy, James H. Bridges, & James D. Jorgensen, 1979).

Monetary restitution involves payments made by the offender to the victim of the crime, community service involves the offender providing a service to the community for the general community good; and personal service restitution involves the victim performing a service, preferably related to the offense for the victim. Monetary restitution and community service have experienced considerable success, and programs involving these concepts are expanding, while personal service has been utilized on a very limited basis.

All three types of restitution involve a contractual relationship. Monetary and personal service restitution dictate a contractual relationship between the offender and the victim. This contract is an important and critical element, as it is through this contract that the amount, as well as the form, of the restitutional act will be decided. This contractual relationship, in bringing together the offender and the victim, serves as the vehicle for behavior change for both parties. In many cases, such as victimless crimes, lack of victim participation in a restitution contract, or in the case of groups of institutionalized offenders, it is possible for the offender to provide a service to the larger community that might ideally be related to the offense. Thus far, offenses included in restitution programs have been limited to property offenses and have included both adults and juveniles. Social workers have assumed administrative as well as direct service positions in a number of restitution programs, since the skills needed in such programs appear particularly well suited to social work. Not only are there rather obvious rehabilitative benefits present for the offender, the victim is also benefiting greatly by the "new" role assumed in this process.

Pretrial settlement programming is an innovative mechanism in involving the victim in the criminal justice proceedings. Such programs bring together victim, defendant, judge, and possibly others. It is perceived by some as a reform in plea bargaining (Anne M. Heing & Wayne A. Kerstetter, 1981). Pretrial settlement programs offer a number of benefits to all parties involved and dramatically alter traditional criminal justice processes. The following describes one such program (Heing & Kerstetter):

> The pretrial settlement conference in Dade County, Florida created a more open, formal arena for plea negotiations. The procedure increased the number of participants, including nonprofessionals, and thereby lowered information costs. Information needs were quite low. The sessions were brief, lasting an average of ten minutes. At the conclusion of the conference three-quarters of the cases had reached either a settlement or the outlines of a settlement.
>
> The conference assumed the characteristics of an administrative proceeding whose goal was to fit the case into a category and then apply existing legal rules. Such a procedure appears appropriate for most criminal cases, where the issues in dispute are minimal. It also helped to identify the "difficult" cases (those that were most serious or where guilt was disputed) so that alternative procedures could be followed, such as further discovery and trial. This is facilitated by the presence of the disputing parties. For example, one defendant brought in a surprise witness which resulted in a continuance for further discovery.

A number of benefits are evident in such pretrial settlement programs: reduced time in closing cases and impact of proceedings on parties involved, i.e. victim, defendant, police, etc., reduced court costs, and the furthering of justice (Anne M. Heing & Wayne A. Kerstetter). Particular benefits appear evident to the parties involved due to the face-to-face format of the proceedings. With the tremendous criticisms of the criminal justice system, pretrial settlement appears to be a viable option with numerous payoffs.

Victim-offender reconciliation projects are also relatively new and innovative. Not only are the services that are involved unique, but the project purposes deserve attention (Dorothy Edmonds McKnight, 1981):

1. To provide an alternative method for dealing with crime in the community.
2. To bring the victim and offender together in an attempt to reach reconciliation and come to a mutual agreement regarding restitution.
3. To use a third party who could foster reconciliation between victim and offender.
4. To deal with crime as a conflict to be resolved.

Again, the strategy of bringing together the victim and the offender is crucial in this program. Also, a third party, possibly a social worker, is an important element in reconciliation work. Prior to the meeting with all parties involved, the worker meets separately with the offender and the victim. As with all such meetings between offenders and victims, considerable groundwork needs to be laid by the worker. Direct work with the two parties requires and demands special skills on the part of the social worker.

THE ROLE OF THE SOCIAL WORKER
IN THE DELIVERY OF SERVICES

Victim assistance programs that involve the victim in the criminal justice process necessitates a re-examination of the role of the social worker. Historically, social work's involvement in criminal justice has been based on the rehabilitative justification for punishment (Burt Galaway & John T. Gandy, 1980). This rationale has been criticized, and criminal justice is being challenged to examine its purpose and function. In response to this critical evaluation, a number of innovative alternatives such as victim assistance programs have been developed.

In order to discuss the role of the social worker in victim assistance programs that involve the victim as well as the delivery of social services through such programs, we need to briefly discuss the historical orientation. The provision of services in criminal justice has in the past been based on the following (Galaway & Gandy):

1. A coercive orientation to treatment systems.
2. An illness or medical orientation to behavior change.
3. An adversarial orientation in the entire system.
4. An orientation to offenders, with a total neglect of victims.

We as a society are witnessing the initial changes in our entire criminal justice system. Programs and services are being conceptualized and developed that are based on the following: a voluntary treatment versus a coerced treatment orientation, a fairness versus an illness or medical orientation, a dispute versus an adversarial orientation, and a developing concern for victims of crime.

The role of the social worker in victim assistance programs that involve the victim in the criminal justice process represents a dramatic departure for service delivery. The traditional rehabilitation oriented role assumed by social workers has been under intense and broad based criticism. As Empey so succinctly states, "the rehabilitative philosophy of the past century has been a failure. There is almost no evidence that we can successfully rehabilitate offenders" (1978). Such criticism has been increasing and is beginning to reach a crescendo and, in fact, has become apparent that a movement away from the rehabilitation rationale for the imposition of criminal sanctions has emerged. Numerous recognized scholars and experts (Morris, Wilks; Martinson, Wilson, Van den Haag) have advocated the elimination of the rehabilitative orientation (La Mar T. Empey, 1978).

The criticisms of rehabilitation in criminal justice are emerging from a variety of sources, not just scholars and experts in the field. Of particular significance is the general public's perception and attitude in relation to criminal justice. Research regarding the general public and their attitudes toward criminal justice has produced findings indicating a high level of dissatisfaction with the present system (Burt Galaway & John T. Gandy, 1979). This dissatisfaction appears to be related to a number of issues including rehabilitation, punishment, and the purposes of various sanctions in criminal justice. Not only are public attitudes reflective of this movement away from the rehabilitation rationale for the imposition of criminal sanctions, but the trend can be observed in newspaper editorials, legislative bills, and statements by public officials.

The roles being assumed in the developing programs that

involve the victim in the criminal justice process are as advocate, mediator, and arbitrator. Victim assistance programs such as victim-witness assistance, safe neighborhood and crime prevention, restitution, pretrial settlement, and victim-offender reconciliation necessitate by their very nature advocacy, mediation, and arbitration. These programs serve mainly secondary functions, although some tertiary functions are also involved. In addition to advocacy, mediation, and arbitration, the developing roles for social work include involvement in dispute settlement and conflict resolution.

Victim-witness assistance programs are unique from a historical perspective, since usually such programs are based in the prosecutor's office and have the purpose of easing the hardships and difficulties victims and witnesses experience. Obviously, a related purpose of such programs and one that is unique for social work relates to assisting the prosecutor's office in the prosecution of offenders. As was discussed earlier, our society's history of concern for crime victims as well as witnesses has been very poor. Victim-witness assistance programs represent the first effort in meeting the needs of both parties.

The primary role of the social worker in the delivery of services in such programs is that of an advocate and mediator. Such advocacy and mediation functions are organized to provide emotional support for the victim both immediately after the victimization and throughout the criminal justice process. The social worker's victim advocate role is to pursue the rights entitled to the victim and ease the hardships experienced by the victim as well as the witness. The supportive role, which supplements advocacy and mediation, is crucial, since the majority of victims have had little or no experience in criminal justice and are bewildered and anxious. Many victims not only have little or no knowledge of the system and what to expect but subscribe to fallacies and myths about the system and the procedures. The mere presence of a social worker mediating between the victim and the system contributes to a more therapeutic and responsive milieu. One aspect of the social workers role is purely educational, which in many cases is what is desired and needed by the victim.

Safe neighborhood and crime prevention programs are elements in the range of victim assistance programs, although they are somewhat unique. Such programs serve mainly tertiary functions, and community organization skills are vital for a social worker in programs of this nature.

This is an excellent example of a primary prevention program with a number of secondary benefits. In the process of developing safe neighborhood programs, communities are involved in the actual process of building a feeling of community spirit. Individuals as well as neighborhoods may, for the first time, be forced to work closely together. The building of relationships is a significant product of many such safe neighborhood and crime prevention programs. The social worker performs enabling and organizing functions in programs of this nature. Such programs do not have the traditional social work rehabilitative focus, and in fact, there is minimal delivery of supplemental social services. The purpose of safe neighborhood and crime prevention programs is rather narrow, although this is not to discount the very significant secondary benefits to the community produced by such programs. Programs of this nature usually operate under the auspices of city or county police departments and nonprofit community agencies. Police departments have sponsored a number of safe neighborhood and crime prevention programs, which contribute to the unique nature of these programs as they are operated in nonsocial work agencies. The social worker brings to the program knowledge and skills in working with people and communities while police have the technical expertise in crime prevention. It creates a unique working relationship and is different from other programs providing victim assistance services.

Restitution programs are unique in that they benefit victims and offenders. As was previously discussed, restitution is really a broad concept for three discrete programs involving monetary, community service, and personal service. Programs involving restitution serve the full range of functions, i.e. primary, secondary, and tertiary, although secondary and tertiary functions are prominent.

A number of roles are assumed by the social worker in restitution programs, including advocacy, mediation, arbitration, dispute settlement, and conflict resolution. Prior to a discussion of social work roles in specific restitution programs, the issue of contracts needs to be addressed.

Although the issue of contracts was previously discussed it needs to be discussed in relation to restitution services. Contracting is crucial in restitution programming in that, "negotiation of a contract means that what will happen between another system and the social worker will be determined by joint agreement" (Allen Pincus & Anne Minahan, 1973). The contract is developed by the social worker and is a formal agreement between the two parties. One party being the offender and the other, depending on whether restitution is monetary, personal service, or community service, may be the victim or the community. Skills in negotiating and developing contracts are very significant and can be related to specific elements in contracting (Pincus & Minahan):

1. Establishing an initial relationship with another system.
2. Identifying the purpose of the contract.
3. Clarifying contract terms.
4. Identifying disagreements with the other system.

Both parties must be involved in the development of the contract. The role of the social worker is absolutely crucial, for example, in bringing together the offender and the victim face to face. Without the proper preparation of both parties the result might be disastrous.

In monetary restitution programs, although a number of roles may be utilized, the social worker is primarily involved in advocacy and mediation. Rather traditional social work skills such as relationship building are also involved. The social worker works directly with the offender and maintains an ongoing relationship. Programs such as monetary restitution are unique in victim services because there is some inherent therapeutic value for the offender.

Community service restitution necessitates the use of mediation skills on the part of the social worker. Community organization skills also tend to serve the social worker well in developing community service projects. The social worker may need to "sell" the idea to the community as well as develop specific projects such as restoration of older houses owned by the elderly.

Although personal service restitution is quite limited, it represents an exciting development. The role of the social worker in such programs involves mediation and arbitration. The social worker should be more directly involved in personal service restitution, since this requires an ongoing, more direct relationship between the victim and the offender.

As in other victim assistance programs, many times the social worker has an administrative role. Restitution programs in particular involve a wider range of ancillary social services involving a variety of systems, such as the victim, offender, community, family, etc., than other victim assistance programs. Intervention in more traditional forms is involved in such programs, as is the more rehabilitative and therapeutic orientation. Restitution programs by their very nature are under the auspices of a variety of entities such as the prosecutor's office, the mayor's office, county or city police department, social service agencies, courts, or nonprofit community agencies.

Pretrial settlement represents another unique development in victim assistance programming. Such programs serve mainly secondary functions. One very significant secondary product of pretrial settlement programs concerns prevention. These programs direct people out of the prison system. Criminal justice disputes and conflicts are handled before trial, and thus the offender has minimal involvement in the criminal justice proceedings.

The social worker in programs of this nature is involved primarily in mediation, arbitration, dispute settlement, and conflict resolution. The worker plays a major role in these programs in mediating and arbitrating with all parties involved such as the victim, defendant, judge, and lawyers. It is of utmost importance to understand that the focus is not rehabilitation and therapy but rather fairness and equity in the settlement. The traditional social work rehabilitative orientation is absent; if such change takes place, it is secondary. Such a focus could signal dramatic changes in the criminal justice system.

The remaining program type to be discussed is quite similiar to pretrial settlement and the two need to be discussed together. Victim-offender reconciliation programs represent another unique departure for the criminal justice system. Such programs serve mainly secondary functions. The role of the social worker is quite similar to the role in pretrial settlement programs, since skills in mediation, arbitration, dispute settlement, and conflict resolution are utilized.

In victim-offender reconciliation, the focus is again on the settlement of disputes as opposed to the traditional notion of rehabilitation. The purpose is not to provide the full range of ancillary social services. As in other programs, the parties involved are not concerned with determining guilt and prescribing punishments. The following speaks to the role of dispute settlement in both pretrial settlement and victim-offender reconciliation programs (Galaway & Gandy, 1980):

> The process of determining guilt and carrying out punishment does very little to resolve these underlying disputes; recently a variety of dispute settlement projects have developed to provide offenders the option to engage in mediation or arbitration process designed to bring about a resolution of the dispute rather than to pursue criminal processes. Dispute settlement, as an alternative to criminal justice processing, may hold considerable potential in criminal situations arising from domestic disputes, neighborhood disputes, assaults (especially between people who know each other), and possibly, several categories of property crime including bad checks, larceny, vandalism, and so forth. In each of these situations there is clearly a dispute between an offender and a victim; procedures designed to resolve this dispute equitably may be much more useful to victims, offenders, and society as a whole than criminal justice processing.

The intriguing fact is that many offenses in criminal justice are basically disputes. The role of the social worker in pretrial settlement and victim-offender reconciliation programs concerns the arbitration and mediation of such disputes. The irony of it is that initially social workers question whether they have the expertise for such a role. Yet, social work historically has utilized conflict resolution strategies as well as arbitration and mediation skills in working with marital and family conflicts, interpersonal conflicts, and group and community conflicts (Galaway & Gandy, 1980). The dispute settlement experience that the profession has in more traditional settings is very appropriate to victim-assistance programming.

Both pretrial settlement and victim-offender reconciliation programs are usually under the auspices of a governmental body, in many cases the prosecutor's office. As in earlier discussed programs, social work's involvement is rather unique in that it is in the legal arena. Neither ancillary social services nor the traditional rehabilitation focus are primary concerns in such programs.

CONCLUSIONS

Although a societal victim orientation is relatively new, it provides very fertile ground for future development and exploration. The field of victim services will without question be growing and expanding. Several reasons for this exist; however, the primary one is the wide range of support that victim service programs receive. A number of studies demonstrate the strong support for services and programs for victims of crime (John T. Gandy, 1978). Conservatives as well as liberals support the concept, and in fact, articles concerning restitution have appeared in *Psychology Today* and *Newsweek*, as well as editorial statements by diverse commentators as the conservative James Kilpatrick and the liberal Nicholas Von Hoffman. The idea of victim services receives such support because people conceptualize and view it differentially. In other words, they see what they want to see in the notion of victims receiving services.

Social work has been involved in victim assistance programs to some extent, although it has been relatively minimal. There is absolutely no question in this writer's mind that, in this era of pessimism for the social work profession, victim services offers exciting potential. Interestingly enough, it offers an arena for social work to operationalize many concepts that we have only supported historically by lip-service. Victim service programming forces the worker to utilize skills in arbitration, mediation, negotiation, and conflict resolution. The victim advocate role is ideally suited to one with social work education and skills.

Traditionally, victims have been a disenfranchised minority. This historic fact is changing, and victims of crime are beginning to receive attention. Innovative programs and services are developing and emerging that not only are concerned with meeting the needs of victims but involving them directly in the criminal justice process.

REFERENCES

Dussich, J. P. J. "Evolving services for crime victims." In B. Galaway and J. Hudson (Eds.), *Perspectives on Crime Victims*. St. Louis: The C. V. Mosby Company, 1981.

Empey, L. T. *American delinquency its meaning and construction*. Homewood: The Dorsey Press, 1978.

Galaway, B., & Gandy, J. T. *Policy and practice in the justice arena: new directions for the curriculum in the 1980's*. New York: Council on Social Work Education, 1980.

Galaway, B. & Gandy, J. T. Restitution as a sanction for offenders. In J. Hudson & B. Galaway (Eds.), *Victims, Offenders and Alternative Sanctions*. Lexington: D. C. Heath and Company, 1980.

Gandy, J. T. Attitudes toward the use of restitution. In B. Galaway & J. Hudson (Eds.), *Offender Restitution In Theory and Action*. Lexington: D. C. Heath and Company, 1977.

Heing, A. M., & Kerstetter, W. A. Pretrial settlement conference: evaluation of a reform in plea bargaining. In B. Galaway & J. Hudson (Eds.), *Perspectives on Crime Victims*. St. Louis: The C. V. Mosby Company, 1981.

McKnight, D. E. The victim-offender reconciliation project. In B. Galaway & J. Hudson (Eds.), *Perspectives on Crime Victims*. St. Louis: The C. V. Mosby Company, 1981.

Pincus, A., & Minahan, A. *Social work practice: model and method*. Itasca: F. E. Peacock Publishers, Inc., 1973.

Chapter 8

SPECIAL PROBLEMS OF DEAF PERSONS AND CRIMINAL JUSTICE

JANET L. PRAY

A person who sees a prowler outside the house or who is the victim of a burglary is likely to telephone the police immediately. If arrested as a suspect in a crime, a person can expect to be advised of his or her rights. A witness to a crime is likely to be called to testify in court. It is probable that in one's lifetime a letter will be received with instructions to report for jury duty. Although the average citizen may consider few, if any, of these circumstances as desirable, and all may cause some amount of stress, none presents insurmountable problems. Would the same be true if the persons concerned were deaf? Could the deaf person telephone the police? Hear the Miranda Warning? Testify in court? Serve on a jury?

The questions posed here touch upon some of the barriers that deaf persons encounter when voluntarily or involuntarily entering any sector of the justice system. Fortunately, there are ways to overcome the barriers and, since implementation of Section 504 of the Rehabilitation Act of 1973, there are legal mandates to assure that effective communication is possible between deaf persons and hearing persons with whom they must interact in the justice system.

HISTORY OF THE LAW AND DEAF PERSONS

Understanding current problems may be facilitated by considering the response of the law to deaf persons within a historical context. In early Roman law, persons who were deaf from birth were assumed to be deficient in intelligence and unable to transact legal business and manage their own affairs. Sometimes a distinction was made between the person who was congenitally deaf and the one who was adventitiously deaf, the law looking more

137

favorably upon the competence of a person who had been "normal" at birth. Gaw (1907) suggests that in ancient Greece and Rome, deaf infants may have been spared death by exposure since deafness was (and is) rarely identifiable in infancy, the period during which "defective" children were left to die.

In early English law, a person born deaf who had not acquired speech was considered to be an "idiot," and in the early history of both English and American law the presumption was that such a person was unable to contract. Interestingly, in France, in the middle of the seventeenth century, the Code d'Instruction Criminelle made provision for the appointment of interpreters when a deaf person who was unable to write appeared in court as accused or as a witness (Gaw, 1907). This is of particular significance considering that in 1884, in the United States, a case was appealed when a "deaf-mute"[1] youngster who had witnessed a murder was permitted to testify in a New Mexico court using his mother as an interpreter. The decision to allow his testimony was reversed by the New Mexico Supreme Court and a new trial ordered (May an uneducated deaf child be a competent witness? 1886).

In 1829, a deaf man in Cologne, Prussia, was charged with murdering his employer. A physician of the court testified that because of his "defects of nature" the deaf person was unable to distinguish right from wrong and could not be held responsible for the murder. The defense added that the defendant must be regarded as a child. The jury found the man not guilty (Guilty or not guilty? 1871).

In 1883, a Missouri court found that a "deaf-mute" was assumed to be incapable of making a contract unless evidence could be presented to prove otherwise (Best, 1943).

In 1947, in Kentucky, a father placed his three young children in an institution after separating from his wife who was deaf. In 1952, the mother sought to obtain custody, but the court ruled that after five years in "normal" surroundings the children were in a better environment than they would be with the mother who lived with "deaf-mutes" (Mood, Frost, & Turner, 1962). By contrast, in Boston, in 1907, the court ruled in favor of the father when a

---

[1]Whenever "deaf-mute" appears in this chapter, quotation marks are used to indicate use of the term in the reference cited. Readers should be aware that "deaf-mute" and "deaf and dumb" are inaccurate designations and are considered offensive by most deaf persons.

grandmother attempted to obtain custody of her grandchildren because their father was deaf (Gaw, 1907).

In 1966, a Los Angeles judge refused to allow a deaf couple to adopt a newborn infant placed in their home because it was not a "normal" home. His decision was reversed on appeal nineteen months later (Lawrence, 1972).

Although some of the court decisions cited above indicate lack of understanding of the capabilities of deaf persons, it has been established during the twentieth century that deaf persons have the same legal privileges and responsibilities as hearing persons (Gaw, 1907; Palumbo, 1966). The major difficulty facing the justice system has been how to assure that deaf persons are able to exercise these privileges and responsibilities.

COMMUNICATION PROBLEMS

Because of the major communication problem imposed by deafness, the provision of interpreters is one of the greatest needs. One attorney expressed his conviction about the importance of interpreters by writing that if a deaf person is arrested, "first obtain a skilled interpreter and secondly, obtain a competent attorney . . . " (Lawrence, 1972). Rarely, if ever, will lipreading or written communication serve as an effective substitute. Approximately four percent of deaf people can be classified as proficient speechreaders (lipreaders) or speakers (Furth, 1966). Estimates are that the best speechreaders are able to understand no more than twenty-five to thirty percent of spoken English. The percentage of comprehension will decrease to as little as ten percent if the speaker has a moustache or beard, uses idiomatic expressions, speaks with an accent, does not face the deaf person directly, moves a hand across the mouth while speaking, fails to articulate clearly, etc. Further difficulties arise if the lighting is poor or there is a glare or the lipreader does not have good vision. Furthermore, it is known that forty to sixty percent of the sounds of English look the same as some other sounds on the lips (Jeffers & Bailey, 1971), creating a situation in which the deaf person must guess at many words based upon the context within which they are spoken. There is no doubt that such imprecise communication can lead to misunderstandings. The magnitude of the communication problem between deaf and hearing persons can have particularly disastrous consequences in a legal situation.

One might think that writing assures more accurate communication. At best, this method is tedious and impractical. More importantly, studies have shown that the average deaf adult cannot read and write well enough to communicate effectively. One study found that the average reading achievement of sixteen year olds was grade level 3.4 (Wrightstone, Aronow, & Muskowitz, 1963), hardly a reading level permitting effective communication, particularly if complex legal terminology or issues are involved. The Miranda Warning, for example, requires comprehension at a sixth to eighth grade reading level (Dubow & Geer, May 1981). The aforementioned data should not be interpreted to mean that deaf persons have limited intelligence nor that there are no deaf adults who read and write well. Many hard of hearing persons, persons deafened postlingually, and even some congenitally, profoundly deaf persons have good English skills. The fact is, however, that a congenitally deaf person will have great difficulty mastering a language he has never heard, a language most people learn from infancy by hearing it spoken regularly.

SELECTING AN INTERPRETER

When selecting an interpreter, care must be taken to be certain that the interpreter is skilled in the language of the deaf person. Many deaf people communicate most comfortably in American Sign Language (ASL), a language with a syntactical structure different from spoken English. An interpreter who knows only a signed English system will not be able to interpret competently for someone who uses ASL. Likewise, a deaf person may be "oral" and prefer an oral interpreter rather than a sign language interpreter. In that case, the interpreter will not sign but mouth the words and will be knowledgeable about synonyms for words not easily read on the lips.

Qualified professional interpreters can be identified through the Registry of Interpreters for the Deaf (RID). RID is a national organization that has established standards for interpreters, has a certification process for interpreters, has a professional code of ethics that includes a commitment to confidentiality, and maintains a register of certified interpreters that includes their level of certification. There is, for example, a special certificate for legal interpreting. RID has its national office in Silver Spring, Maryland, as well as state and local chapters throughout the country. Usually it is best to avoid using a friend or relative of the deaf person as an interpreter because of the danger that the interpreter may inject personal views, speak for the deaf person, or protect the deaf person by omitting or rewording some part of the communication. The foregoing concern notwithstanding, it is best to respect the deaf person's preference for an interpreter because the deaf person will know whether he or she understands the interpreter and is understood by the interpreter.

TELECOMMUNICATION DEVICES

Another area of concern with respect to communication is use of the telephone. How can deaf persons call the police or their attorney, for example? Telephone communication has been made possible through use of a telecommunication device for deaf persons (TDD), which permits transmittal of typewritten messages by telephone between two persons who have comparable devices. Police departments in many communities have installed TDD's, making it possible for deaf people with such devices to call the police just as normally hearing people. Some attorneys have purchased TDD's to facilitate communication with deaf clients. Unfortunately, not all deaf persons have a TDD because the cost is usually several hundred dollars. In a few areas, telephone companies will provide a TDD to a hearing impaired person at no cost or on a rental basis, but only a modest number are currently available in this way. It should be noted that a TDD is also beneficial to hearing persons with speech or communication disorders.

PROBLEMS ENCOUNTERED BY DEAF PERSONS IN THE JUSTICE SYSTEM

What happens when the various components of the justice system do not make accommodations for the deaf person? Frequently deaf persons remain in jail longer than hearing persons because no interpreter is provided, or they are denied access to prison rehabilitation programs because of failure to meet their communication needs (Goldberg, Gardner, & Dubow, February 1981).

A case example will illustrate some problems that can arise for deaf persons when there is lack of awareness and/or sensitivity to their communication needs and concerns. In the following case, the parents and adolescent are profoundly deaf and use sign language. The social worker is hearing and communicates with the clients using sign language.

> ... Mr. and Mrs. A. informed me that two months ago they were so fed up with Steve, age 15, because of his refusal to go to school and repeated episodes of running away from home that they decided to file a complaint in juvenile court. It had been difficult for them to understand the person who gave them the papers to sign, but they were so desperate to do something about Steve that they filled out the papers without comprehending what they were about. They were given a note to inform them that a probation officer would talk with them before the juvenile court hearing.
>
> The probation office (Mr. L.) visited the A. home during which time an awkward interview was conducted by exchanging written notes. Mr. and Mrs. A. did not always understand what the probation officer meant but they gave him no indication of that. Mrs. A. said she "hated it" because she knew her English was "bad" and she was ashamed having to write to a hearing person. 'I'll bet he thought we were real stupid!' I asked if they had thought about asking Mr. L. to bring an interpreter. Mr. A. said they had a friend who signs "pretty good," but they really didn't want him to know their personal business. I explained that I meant a professional interpreter who would be bound by confidentiality. Mr. A. laughed and said, 'I don't want *anybody* knowing our business.' He went on to explain how everyone knows everyone and everyone else's business in the deaf community and he just wasn't comfortable with the idea of an interpreter, regardless of who it was.
>
> They explained that Mrs. A. and Steve went to the juvenile court hearing alone because Mr. A. was unable to get time off from work. They hadn't understood much of what went on but the judge seemed to be asking the probation officer a lot of questions. The hearing was short, they had not been asked to participate in any way, and at the conclusion the probation officer handed them a note saying that Steve was on probation for six months, the family was to be referred for counseling, Steve must go to school every day, observe a curfew, and the probation officer would visit every two weeks to make sure that Steve was 'doing what he was supposed to.' When I asked Mr. & Mrs. A. what would happen if Steve violated his probation, they said they didn't know. They also did not know where Mr. L. would see Steve, if he would see the parents, and what they could or should do if Steve gave them further difficulties.
>
> Steve ran away again and shortly thereafter, the police found him with a girl friend and some other friends. All were caught smoking 'pot.' Steve was put in the house of detention pending another juvenile court hearing. I spoke with the parents again about the importance of their understanding what was happening during the court hearing. They said they would accept an interpreter if it were me. I said I understood they might feel comfortable with me because they knew me and I knew their situation, but that I was not a certified interpreter and furthermore it would be a conflict of roles to be the family's social worker and also their interpreter. After much

discussion they finally agreed to my calling Mr. L. about providing an interpreter.

When I telephoned Mr. L. he said it was o.k. with him if the family brought an interpreter. I clarified that I meant for the juvenile court to provide a professional interpreter. He didn't know what I was talking about so I explained about certification, etc. He wanted to know who would pay for it. I explained that it was my understanding that under Section 504 of the Rehabilitation Act, it was the court's responsibility, but more importantly, didn't he agree that it would serve both the court and the family best if there were clear communication? He said he thought they had done just fine without an interpreter before. I persisted and he said he'd have to talk with his supervisor and call me back. As the time approached for the court hearing he had not called me back and after several unreturned calls I finally reached him. He said his supervisor told him the family could have an interpreter if they insisted and how could he get one? I provided him with the name of the President of the local RID chapter and he agreed to make the arrangements. . . .

This case illustrates issues that arise frequently when deaf persons are involved with the justice system.

1. *Self-consciousness of deaf persons about their competence in English.* Deaf people who have difficulty with English are usually painfully conscious of the problem and often are reluctant to write extensively to a hearing person because of concern that they will be considered inferior.

2. *Deaf persons' passivity in relation to systems that are perceived as authoritarian (police departments, courts, etc.).* Typically, the passive behavior masks frustration and anger in relation to the barriers to communication and lack of consideration for the rights and needs of deaf persons.

3. *Limited understanding about professional interpreters.* Until recent years, a profession of interpreting did not exist and the only experience most deaf persons had with interpreters was the informal interpreting provided by friends and family. The National Registry of Interpreters for the Deaf was not established until 1964 (Quigley, 1965). Many deaf people are not aware of the existence of a certification process nor of the RID Code of Ethics, especially with respect to confidentiality. Furthermore, because of the rapid communication that occurs within the deaf community, there is sometimes a tendency to feel that an interpreter's knowledge of a personal situation will spread throughout

the community. Complicating matters is the reality that skepticism about confidentiality might be based upon prior experiences that were negative.

4. *Reluctance of the system to provide interpreters.* There is often both a lack of understanding of the extent of the deaf person's frustration with the barriers to communication and unfamiliarity with the requirements under Section 504 for the provision of interpreters. Cost is cited frequently as the reason for refusal to provide an interpreter.

5. *Role of the social worker.* The social worker often will need to educate both the system and the deaf person concerning interpreters, and advocate for the deaf person's rights as well. Education and willingness to help locate an interpreter can be more effective than confrontation about federal regulations. Sometimes the person in the justice system sees immediately the benefit to all concerned if a skilled interpreter were to be utilized.

Educating deaf people concerning their rights and helping them develop skills in advocating in their own behalf needs to be stressed. Organizations such as the National Association of the Deaf and National Center for Law and the Deaf have been instrumental in developing materials and workshops for deaf persons and for interested professionals. Although deaf social workers have been involved in these efforts, there has been infinitesimal participation on the part of hearing social workers. At a minimum, social workers can assume responsibility for informing individual clients of their right to have interpreters without cost to them and negotiating with the system to assure that the interpreting service is provided. To do this effectively, social workers should be knowledgeable about Section 504 of the Rehabilitation Act as well as the Department of Justice Regulations and Analysis of those Regulations.

SECTION 504 AND DEPARTMENT OF JUSTICE REGULATIONS

Section 504 provides that

no otherwise qualified handicapped individual in the United States . . . shall, solely by reason of his handicap, be excluded from participation in, be denied the benefits of, or be subjected to discrimination under any program or activity receiving Federal financial assistance. (*Federal Register*, May 4, 1977)

Social workers unfamiliar with the literature and terminology of the legal profession will find publications of the National Center for Law and the Deaf useful in highlighting and clarifying pertinent Department of Justice Regulations, court decisions, and state legislation with respect to requirements of Section 504 (see especially National Center for Law and the Deaf *Newsletter*, September 1980). There are some key components of Department of Justice Regulations and their Analysis that should be noted by social workers and other professionals whose deaf clients are involved with the justice system:

- —recipients of federal financial assistance with fifteen or more employees are required to provide sign language interpreters.
- —law enforcement agencies should inform the hearing impaired person of the agency's responsibility to provide a free qualified interpreter (certified when possible) and that a determination should be made as to whether the person communicates in ASL or Signed English
- —law enforcement agencies should have TDD's
- —qualified interpreters should be provided in civil and criminal proceedings in a court system that receives federal financial assistance
- —interpreters should be provided in detention and correctional facilities so that participation in rehabilitation programs is possible
- —when an indigent defendant is provided with a court appointed attorney, an interpreter should also be made available for all phases of preparation and presentation of the case
- —victims and complainants should also be provided with interpreters
- —interpreters should be provided upon request for educational programs sponsored by a law enforcement agency

DEAF PERSONS AND JURY DUTY

Lowell Myers, a deaf attorney, may be known to some as the attorney who defended Donald Lang, a deaf man accused of murdering a woman in Chicago. Myers' efforts in defending this man who could neither read nor write, lipread nor use sign language, exemplify his work in behalf of deaf persons in the criminal justice system. With respect to jury service, even he wrote in 1964,

> If a prospective juror is so deaf that he will not be able to hear all of the testimony, this is good grounds for either party to the case to object to having him serve as a juror ... It is obvious that such a person should not be permitted on a jury.

That a deaf person cannot serve on a jury is no longer "obvious," since in at least three states (Massachusetts, Washington, California), deaf persons have served successfully as jurors with the assistance of qualified interpreters.

GUIDELINES FOR THE SOCIAL WORK PRACTITIONER IN THE JUSTICE SYSTEM

Because the communication problems between the deaf person and the justice system are great, the major focus of this chapter has been upon identification and resolution of those problems through provision of interpreters and utilization of telecommunication devices. The question yet to be addressed is whether there are problems beyond the reach of these solutions that warrant the attention of social workers.

Social workers in correctional facilities are aware of the isolation and disruption in the life of the individual who is in a detention or prison facility. The problem is compounded for persons who cannot hear. Even when interpreters are provided, they are not available for the day-to-day informal communication that takes place with staff and among prisoners or detainees themselves. Complicating the situation is the discomfort experienced by hearing people when unaccustomed to interacting with deaf people, a phenomenon that frequently leads to avoidance. Deaf people as a minority group within a "hearing world" have had to struggle to communicate with hearing people throughout their lives. Most hearing people have not had to communicate with deaf people and often find the first experience anxiety producing. Social workers are not immune to this response and can find it particularly troublesome since communication is a hallmark of their profession. Since self-awareness is similarly important, social workers are advised to come to terms with any discomfort that may be experienced and face the challenge of the new experience.

If a social worker fluent in sign language is not available, the social worker on the case should secure a professional interpreter for anything more than superficial contacts if the deaf person's preferred communication system is sign language. Using an interpreter will facilitate communication, but the social worker must recognize that the presence of a third person in the interview will alter the nature of the relationship that can be established (Vernon, 1965). It is more difficult to establish rapport with a client when most of the visual contact is, of necessity, between deaf client and interpreter. This difficulty need not present insurmountable obstacles to the social worker determined to intervene effectively with and in behalf of the deaf client, particularly since there are possibilities for aiding the client outside of the interview itself. Staff can be educated with respect to seemingly obvious but often forgotten basics such as the importance of facing the deaf person directly when speaking to afford maximum opportunity for lipreading, encouraging use of natural gestures and body language, or learning the manual alphabet for short, simple communications. The manual alphabet would be tedious and impractical for lengthy communications but can be very useful for short exchanges. Its advantage is that it can be easily and quickly learned without making heavy time demands on an already burdened staff. Manual alphabet cards are available at no cost from organizations such as local and state associations of the deaf. Steve A., cited earlier, would have welcomed such an effort. His major complaint about his two stays at the juvenile detention facility was boredom related to his inability to communicate with anyone.

Interestingly, there have been situations in which a small group of inmates in an adult correctional facility have taken the initiative to learn sign language specifically to develop communication with a fellow inmate who was deaf and seen to be isolated from both prisoners and staff. In these situations, both the hearing and deaf prisoners benefited, the former from a sense of pride and achievement and the latter from the opening of meaningful communication. Such projects have the potential for alleviating the sense of boredom and worthlessness that typify so many who are incarcerated in correctional facilities.

Another resource upon which to draw are the numerous religious denominations that have clergy who are trained in ministering to deaf persons and know sign language. Some have congregations or special services for deaf parishoners—Assembly of God,

Church of Christ, Baptist, Episcopal, Jewish, Lutheran, Methodist. Roman Catholic, and others. If the deaf client has a religious interest or orientation, it may be appropriate to determine whether the community has such a congregation and enlist the assistance of the clergyman in visiting the deaf person. Such an effort considers the spiritual life of the person and also offers the possibility of a positive social contact. As with any other social work intervention, it is important not to impose this dimension but explore it as one would any other area of potential need and/or support.

What of the adult or juvenile offender who needs treatment by a social worker, psychiatrist, psychologist, or other mental health or human service professional? With increasing frequency, it is possible to find programs with qualified professionals, both hearing and deaf, who have knowledge and experience in the field of deafness. These programs may be found in a variety of settings including community mental health programs, family service agencies, psychiatric hospitals, and vocational rehabilitation agencies.

The A. case illustrates the potential for a working relationship between one component of the justice system and a community mental health program, even though that relationship was strained at times. It was the juvenile court worker who located a mental health program with a social worker who had knowledge about deafness and knew sign language. Despite the problems encountered securing an interpreter for the juvenile court hearing, the probation officer and the mental health program social worker worked collaboratively. The probation officer and the social worker had several joint meetings with the A's and Steve for the purpose of reviewing goals and progress in relation to the terms of Steve's probation. After six months, Steve was attending school regularly, his grades were somewhat improved, and he followed the curfew imposed by the juvenile court with only occasional infractions. Although the parents were uneasy about the loss of the external controls imposed by the juvenile court, Steve's probation was terminated and the A's and Steve continued to see the social worker in the mental health program to work towards consolidation of gains that had been made.

CONCLUSION

Hearing impairment is the single most prevalent disability in the United States, occurring more frequently than visual impairment or heart disease. A census of the deaf population indicated that there were 13.4 million persons in the United States with hearing impairment, of whom 1,767,000 were deaf (Schein & Delk, 1974). Despite the size of the deaf population, deaf people and their needs have been understood poorly and responded to inadequately by major systems in our society—the educational system, the social welfare system, the health care delivery system, and certainly the justice system. Throughout its history, the social work profession has addressed innumerable issues in all of these systems on both a policy and practice level. The profession now must become better educated about deafness, learn to communicate with deaf people (of which there are growing numbers within the profession), and work together with them to make the justice system and all systems as accessible and responsive to deaf persons as they are to hearing persons.

REFERENCES

Best, Harry. *Deafness and the deaf in the United States.* New York: Macmillan, 1943.

Dubow, Sy and Geer, Sarah. Eliminating communications barriers for hearing-impaired clients. *Clearinghouse Review,* May 1981, *15*(1), 36–44.

Federal Register. Wednesday, May 4, 1977, *42*(86), 22676.

Furth, Hans G. *Thinking without language: psychological implications of deafness.* Toronto: Collier-Macmillan, 1966.

Gaw, Albert C. *The legal status of the deaf.* Washington, D.C.: Press of Gibson Brothers, 1907.

Goldberg, Larry J., Gardner, E. Elaine and Dubow, Sy. Rights of the deaf. *Trial.* February 1981, *17*(2), 39–41.

Guilty or not guilty? *American Annals of the Deaf,* January 1871, *16*(1), 33–42.

Jeffers, Janet and Bailey, Margaret. *Speechreading (lipreading).* Springfield, Ill.: Charles C Thomas, 1971.

Lawrence, Ivan E. *Is justice deaf?* Florida Registry of Interpreters for the Deaf, 1972.

May an uneducated deaf child be a competent witness? *American Annals of the Deaf,* October 1886, *31*(4), 272–281.

Mood, Francis P., Jr., Frost, Mandeville A., and Turner, Lawrence, Jr. *The law relating to deaf mutes.* Virginia University Department of Law, 1962.

Myers, Lowell J. *The law and the deaf.* Washington, D.C.: U.S. Department of Health, Education, and Welfare, 1964.

National Center for Law and the Deaf. *Newsletter.* Washington, D.C.: Gallaudet College, September 1980.

Palumbo, Dolores V. *An investigation into the educational, social and legal status of the deaf in the 19th and 20th centuries.* Unpublished masters thesis, Southern Connecticut State College, 1966.

Section IV

JUVENILE JUSTICE PROGRAMS AND SERVICES

INTRODUCTION

This section examines the role of social workers in the context of the juvenile justice system. Juvenile justice programs concentrate on delinquent youth, as well as those youths who are labelled incorrigible, truant, and/or runaway. Social workers provide services for youths who are arrested, awaiting a juvenile court hearing, diverted to a special program, detained, processed through the juvenile court, placed on probation, and/or after adjudication to a juvenile facility or group home.

In this section, emphasis is placed on the settings in which social workers are most likely to intervene on behalf of troubled children and youth: the juvenile court, probation, and community-based group homes.

In Chapter 9, Carolyn Needleman points out that interpreting the practice problems faced by social workers in juvenile justice requires an understanding of the conflicting philosophies built into the system itself. This chapter reviews the rehabilitative ideals with which the juvenile court was founded and outlines three major sources of ideologically-based dissatisfaction with the court as an institution: Constitutionalist concerns about the lack of due process for the accused, retributive justice concerns about lack of deserved punishment for the offender, and humanitarian concerns about the gap that lack of resources has opened between the juvenile court's intentions and its reality. Each of these three critical perspectives has had an impact on the court's development in recent years. Each, however, implies a different kind of reform. As a result, current patterns of change in juvenile justice have been inconsistent and even contradictory.

Chapter 10 describes the activities and problems of social workers who deal with juvenile court, drawing on Carolyn Needleman's participant observation study of a New York Family Court. The pattern of social work involvement in juvenile court varies greatly by jurisdiction. Sometimes, social workers are directly employed by the court, usually as probation officers; sometimes, they work more independently, through social service agencies that have a close connection with the court. They serve the court in a variety of ways, including intake screening and preadjudication services, psychological assessment of accused juveniles, investigation of the accused juveniles' social circumstances, giving courtroom testimony, providing probation supervision, and providing court-assigned social services in agencies separate from the court. Three common sources of strain are discussed—role inconsistency, training incongruity, and interprofessional status tentions. Some practical suggestions are offered for making social workers' contributions to juvenile justice easier and more effective.

Chapter 11, by Tom Roy, examines social work practice in group care facilities within the juvenile justice system. Two forms of practice are identified: (1) the direct service, provider of care role, and (2) the indirect service, provider of social supports role. Within the direct service roles, Roy discusses specific care services that the social worker provides not only to the youth in group care but to the other staff and the youths' parents as well. In discussing the indirect service roles of the worker, he focuses upon the social worker as coordinator, program developer, interpreter, and trainer. Traditionally, social work education has centered upon the direct service-providing care roles, and yet, in group home settings, the indirect, social support tasks consume most of the social worker's time. This chapter presents a set of activities designed to provide on-the-job orientation to the social worker in his or her indirect service roles.

Chapter 9

CONFLICTING PHILOSOPHIES OF JUVENILE JUSTICE[1]

Carolyn Needleman

Many of the practice problems that social workers presently face in connection with juvenile justice have their roots in the ideological inconsistencies of the juvenile court itself. From its beginnings, juvenile court has differed from other parts of the United States legal system by explicitly combining criminal justice goals with social welfare concerns. As we shall see, the combination has been an uneasy one.

The court's emphasis on social welfare and rehabilitation was largely the contribution of a group of late nineteenth century social reformers, many of them feminists, who have been termed the "child savers" (Platt, 1969). Their ranks included individuals such as Jane Addams, prominent in the development of social work as a profession.

The tradition of juvenile justice the child savers set out to change was harsh indeed ("An Historical Overview," 1975). One of the by-products of that era's rapid immigration and extreme urban poverty was a large number of children who lacked the support of family and community; sometimes orphaned and often homeless, they lived by their wits, begging and stealing. When arrested, these children were confined with adult criminals. For serious offenses, they could receive the same penalties as adults, even capital punishment.[2] They often ended up in "Houses of Refuge," where they provided cheap labor for nearby manufacturers. Some

[1]The author would like to thank William W. Vosburgh, Miriam Vosburgh, Milton Speizman, and Martin Needleman for helpful comments on an earlier draft. Correspondence concerning this chapter should be addressed to Carolyn Needleman, Graduate School of Social Work and Social Research, Bryn Mawr College, 300 Airdale Road, Bryn Mawr, Pa. 19010.

[2]However, actual executions of children were apparently rare (Platt, 1969).

were forcibly apprenticed to whaling captains and farmers or sent west to work on ranches. Their natural parents, usually foreign and impoverished, had a difficult time regaining custody from the state. The child-saving movement sought to improve this pitiable situation by creating a separate juvenile court as a more humane means of dealing with delinquent and dependent children.

Besides compassion, the child savers also reflected a new philosophy of intervention in criminal behavior (Platt, 1969). Challenging the then-prevailing fatalistic view that criminals were born irreversibly depraved, they advanced a more developmental theory of crime: criminal behavior resulted not from biological heritage alone, but also from negative influences in the offender's family life and social environment. Thus for offenders young enough to be still malleable, it made sense to establish a separate court system that would seek not to punish, but to reform the offender.

The child savers successfully translated their ideals into a political movement, supported by allies such as the Educational Commission of Chicago, which saw an opportunity to further the cause of compulsory education and proclaimed,

> We should rightfully have the power to arrest all the little beggars, loafers and vagabonds that infest our city, take them from the streets, and place them in schools where they are compelled to receive education and learn moral principles (Harpur, 1899).

The fruit of their efforts was the creation of the nation's first official juvenile court in Illinois in 1899, based on a Juvenile Court Act that rapidly became a model statute for other states. Within the next twenty years, most states set up their own separate courts for children, and by 1932, the United States had over 600 independent juvenile courts (Platt, 1969).

In keeping with their nonpunitive aims, the new juvenile courts followed much more informal procedures than their adult counterparts. Hearings were nonadversarial and organized around the best interests of the child. As Jane Addams remarked enthusiastically, "The child was brought before the judge with no one to prosecute him and no one to defend him—the judge and all concerned were merely trying to find out what could be done on his behalf" ("An Historical Overview, 1975). The rationale of the new court was *parens patriae*: the state as a stern but benevolent parent, who would consider the child's entire situation sympathetically and arrive at an individually tailored treatment plan for rehabilitation.

Unfortunately, the new social welfare philosophy meshed poorly with other aspects of the juvenile court retained from the criminal justice system from which it derived. The resulting inconsistencies have given rise to three quite different kinds of criticism.

CONSTITUTIONALIST CRITICISMS

However benignly presented, the court's new philosophy posed some alarming threats to due process for young offenders (Platt, 1969; Fox, 1970; Schur, 1973; Ryerson, 1978; Sosin & Sarri, 1976; Lemert, 1967, 1970). Juvenile court was envisioned as a quite different institution from an adult criminal court, but the consequences of court action could still be just as serious. In fact, because of the practice of indeterminate sentencing for juveniles, a delinquent child could actually be incarcerated for a longer period than an adult convicted of the same crime (Lerman, 1970). In the juvenile court, children faced these consequences without the legal protections that they would have been entitled to as adults.

For half a century, evidence was allowed in juvenile court that in other courts would have been considered inadmissible hearsay; transcripts of court hearings were not regularly kept for appeal purposes; the juvenile offender was not represented by legal counsel. The court was not at all limited to the charged offense. Basic civil liberties such as the presumption of innocence, privilege against self-incrimination, and the right to remain silent were obscured by the court's informality.

Unease about this situation grew, and by the 1960s, it was clear to many that the concept of *parens patriae* has a dark side: by defining juvenile offenders as children in relation to the state as parent, it deprives them of their rights as citizens and grants to the state the arbitrariness allowed to actual parents in dealing with their own children. To constitutionalist critics, the due process disadvantages outweigh any social welfare benefits that might flow from the juvenile court's looseness of procedure and broad discretionary powers. As U.S. Supreme Court Justice Abe Fortas remarked, "Under our Constitution, the condition of being a boy does not justify a kangaroo court" (*In re Gault*, 1967).

RETRIBUTIVE JUSTICE CRITICISMS

A very different theme has been raised by other critics, who fear that the social welfare orientation of the juvenile court may prove damaging to the moral foundations of society (see Hirsch, 1976; van den Haag, 1975; Morris, 1974; Wilson, 1975). According to this argument, a legal system exists primarily to express and implement the social norms of a community. When norms are violated, the court has a duty to respond in a way that satisfies the community's sense of justice and provides moral education to the public. Therefore, when the juvenile court concentrates on the offenders' best interests and fails to punish their transgressions, the legitimacy of criminal law itself suffers. Potential offenders will not be deterred and the community will begin to lose confidence in its legal institutions because proper retribution is absent.

HUMANITARIAN CRITICISMS

A third line of criticism has come from humanitarians, among them a number of social work professionals, who are disturbed by the disparities they see between the juvenile court's social welfare ideology and its daily practice. For instance, consider the ideal of shielding child suspects from association with adult criminals. The stated intent of the court is to release juvenile offenders into their parents' custody pending trial if at all feasible or at least to keep the detained children out of adult jails. But over half of the children referred to court do get detained prior to their court hearings, rather than being immediately released to their parents or other guardians (Empey, 1978). Often there is no place to put them but in adult facilities (National Council on Crime and Delinquency, 1967; Children's Defense Fund, 1976). One investigator estimates that as many as 500,000 children spend time in adult jails each year (Sarri, 1974).

The results can be brutal. For one thing, the conditions in these facilities are typically quite poor. One report estimates that over 80 percent of the jails in which children are held are unfit even for their adult inmates (National Council on Crime and Delinquency, 1967). In addition, there are well documented cases of atrocities committed against the jailed juveniles by both guards and inmates — for instance, a fifteen-year-old in a maximum security cellblock in Virginia was teargassed for requesting medical help for a fellow prisoner who was a deaf mute and gravely ill; a seventeen-year-old kicked to death by his jail cellmates in Missouri; a seventeen-year-old murdered in a Miami jail; a runaway in Iowa, sixteen years old, who when left in isolation hanged herself in her cell (Goldfarb, 1976). This grim reality is a far cry from what the founders of juvenile court had in mind.

Humanitarian critics also find disturbing the mechanics of juvenile court hearings. The court is supposed to provide an opportunity for careful deliberation about a child's best interests by a dedicated, well-trained judge who is knowledgeable about helping children in trouble and can use the hearing to guide the offender. But the actual situation is often quite different. A Presidential Commission in 1967 reviewed a doleful list of shortcomings. Most juvenile court judges were not selected for their expertise and training, but rather were elected to office with no special background for the job; only about half of them had college degrees; the average juvenile court hearing lasted less than fifteen minutes; a third of all juvenile court judges lack staff assistance from probation officers who could assemble information about the child's social circumstances; 83 percent of the judges said there was no psychiatric or psychological assistance for the court; where probation officers were available to support the court's efforts at social investigation, their caseloads were unmanageably high (President's Commission, 1967). Others have reported that judges consider juvenile court a low prestige assignment to be avoided where possible (Rubin, 1976a). Most judges mix their juvenile work with service in other courts if the structure of the justice system in their jurisdiction allows it; a 1973 survey found that among 1,314 juvenile court judges, almost nine out of ten said they spent only half their time or less on juvenile matters (Smith, 1974).

Observing these deficiencies, humanitarian critics feel that juvenile justice has failed to deliver on its promise. While the original social welfare philosophy of the court is the correct one, the system as presently constituted cannot hope to implement it.

CONTRADICTORY REFORM EFFORTS

Because the critics of juvenile court are working from such vastly different perspectives, it is not surprising that their recommendations for reform point in different directions (see Empey, 1979).

Some of the most sweeping changes have been generated by the constitutionalists through a series of landmark Supreme Court decisions. In *Kent v. United States*, the Supreme Court expressed concern about the lack of constitutional guarantees for juveniles and declared that the tradeoff of criminal court's due process in exchange for juvenile court's benevolent treatment had been a poor bargain, exposing juvenile offenders to the "worst of both worlds" (383 U.S. 541, 1966:555–56). The *Gault* decision of the following year (387 U.S. 1, 1967) went further. This case involved a fifteen-year-old Arizona boy who had received an indeterminate sentence of up to five years in a state institution, for making an obscene phone call to a neighbor; had he been eighteen when he made the phone call, the maximum sentence he could have received would have been a 50 dollar fine or a two-month jail sentence. Quite apart from the harshness of the sentence itself, Gerald Gault's experience with juvenile justice was a classic example of arbitrary court practice. In ruling that his Fourteenth Amendment rights had been violated, the Supreme Court affirmed the right of juvenile offenders to be represented by legal counsel, know the specific charges, confront and cross-examine witnesses, and claim privilege against self-incrimination. Adding to these protections, the *Winship* case (397 U.S. 358) in 1970 addressed the process of fact-finding in a juvenile court, ruling that proof of guilt beyond a reasonable doubt is required for juveniles just as it is for adults (*In re Winship*, 1970:365).

These were notable victories, at least on paper. But the Supreme Court left plenty of ambiguity about just how hard it intended to push the juvenile justice system, declaring that due process standards should not be "ruthlessly administered" or allowed to replace "the conception of the kindly judge" (*In re Gault*, 1967:21). Constitutional rights have apparently been slow in coming to the juvenile court in many jurisdictions (Sosin & Sarri, 1976; Sosin, 1978).

Meanwhile, with quite a different goal in mind, retributive justice proponents have moved to make it easier for children charged with serious crimes to be stripped of the shelter of the juvenile court. Juvenile courts have all along had the authority to waive their jurisdiction and transfer particularly serious cases to criminal court, where the juvenile offender is prosecuted as an adult; in general, the application of this option has been restricted to offenders who are at least sixteen years old (National Advisory Commission, 1973a). But recent increases in serious youth crime, particularly in urban areas, have led some jurisdictions to lower the age limit for waiver to adult court—in some cases to as low as thirteen years old. The idea behind the change is to expose the offender to harsher and more certain penalties. Criminal court, organized around values of justice and retribution, is presumably less likely to "coddle" murderers, rapists, and professional thieves just because they happen to be children. Although there is evidence that waiver of juvenile jurisdiction still tends to be used only rarely (Sarri & Hasenfeld, 1976), the lowering of the minimum age standard represents an effort to reform juvenile justice by recriminalizing delinquency.

And what of the social work humanitarians? Their influence has inspired two other reforms that have little to do with either due process or retribution. The first is a move toward reorganizing the juvenile court into a new kind of institution—"family court." This organizational change, recommended by the National Advisory Commission on Court Standards (1973a), allows a single consolidated court to consider not only juvenile delinquency and status offenses[3] but also a range of family matters including child abuse and neglect, child custody, child support, paternity actions, adoptions, domestic violence, and family conciliation. The aim is to *de*emphasize the criminal dimension of juvenile justice by treating the juvenile offender's behavior as a type of family problem. Only a few states have taken this step (Levin & Sarri, 1974; Ketcham, 1978).

The second kind of humanitarian reform is an increased effort toward diversion in the early stages of court processing (see Lemert, 1971; Cressey & McDermott, 1973; Nejelski, 1976). There is a general feeling that status offenders, charged only with victimless noncriminal acts, are particularly appropriate subjects for diversion. Over half the states have already moved to make diversion of status offenders easier by creating special designations for them— PINS (persons in need of supervision) in New York; "601" children in California; UC (unruly child) in Georgia; and CHINS (child in need of supervision) in most of the rest (Empey, 1978;

---

[3]"Status offenses" are law violations by juveniles that would not be considered crimes if committed by adults, such as truancy, incorrigibility, and running away from home.

Levin & Sarri, 1974). The complete removal of all status offenders from court jurisdiction into social service agencies or nonjudicial "Youth Service Bureaus" regularly appears as a recommendation in reports by juvenile justice authorities (see President's Commission, 1967; National Task Force, 1977; Institute of Judicial Administration & the American Bar Association, 1977).

Here, then, is the institutional context in which social workers dealing with juvenile offenders must operate—a juvenile justice system that is inconsistent and confusing in its policies, deeply divided in its ideology and goals, characterized by great organizational variation from one jurisdiction to another, and subject to diametrically opposing kinds of reform effort. Let us now turn to the roles that social workers typically play in relation to the juvenile court.

REFERENCES

An historical overview of the establishment of the juvenile court system in the United States. *Landmarks in Criminal Justice, No. 6.* Haddam, Conn.: Connecticut Criminal Justice Training Academy, 1975.

Children's Defense Fund. *Children in Adult Jails.* New York: Washington Research Project, Inc., 1976.

Cressey, D. R., & McDermott, R. A. *Diversion from the Juvenile Justice System.* National Assessment of Juvenile Corrections. Ann Arbor: University of Michigan, 1973.

Empey, L. T. *American Delinquency: Its Meaning and Construction.* Homewood, Ill.: Dorsey Press, 1978.

Empey, L. T. (Ed.) *The Future of Childhood and Juvenile Justice.* Charlottesville: University Press of Virginia, 1979.

Fox, S. Juvenile justice reform: An historical perspective. *Stanford Law Review,* 1970, *22,* 1187–1239.

Goldfarb, R. *Jails: The Ultimate Ghetto.* New York: Anchor Books, 1976.

Harpur, W. R. *The Report of the Educational Commission of the City of Chicago.* Chicago: Lakeside Press, 1899.

Hirsch, A. von. *Doing Justice: The Choice of Punishments.* Report of the Commission for the Study of Incarceration. New York: Hill and Wang, 1976.

Horowitz, D. L. *The Courts and Social Policy.* Washington, D.C.: The Brookings Institution, 1977.

In re Gault. 387 U.S. 1, 18L. Ed. 2d 527, 87 S. Ct. 1428. 1967.

In re Winship. 397 U.S. 358, 25L. Ed. 2d 368, 90 S. Ct. 1068. 1968.

Institute of Judicial Administration and the American Bar Association (IJA/ABA). *Standards for Juvenile Justice: A Summary and Analysis.* Chicago: American Bar Association, 1977.

Kent v. United States. 383 U.S. 541, 16L. Ed. 2d i4, 86 S. Ct. 1045. 1966.

Ketcham, O. W. The development of juvenile justice in the United States. Pp. 9–42 in Stewart, V. L. (Ed.), *The Changing Faces of Juvenile Justice*, New York: New York University Press, 1978.

Klein, M. W. (Ed.). *The Juvenile Justice System*. Beverly Hills: Sage Publications, 1976.

Lemert, E. M. The juvenile court—quest and realities. Pp. 91–106 in President's Commission on Law Enforcement and Administration of Justice, *Juvenile Delinquency and Youth Crime*. Washington, D.C.: Government Printing Office, 1967.

Lemert, E. M. *Social Action and Legal Change: Revolution within the Juvenile Court*. Chicago: Aldine, 1970.

Lemert, E. M. *Instead of Court: Diversion in Juvenile Justice*. Chevy Chase, Md.: National Institute of Mental Health, Center for Studies of Crime and Delinquency, 1971.

Lerman, P. Beyond *Gault*: Injustice and the child. Pp. 236–250 in Lerman, P. (Ed.), *Delinquency and Social Policy*. New York: Praeger, 1970.

Levin, M. M., & Sarri, R. C. *Juvenile Delinquency: A Comparative Analysis of Legal Codes in the United States* National Assessment of Juvenile Corrections. Ann Arbor: University of Michigan, 1974.

Morris, N. The future of imprisonment: Toward a punitive philosophy. *Michigan Law Review*, 1974, *72*, 1161–1180.

National Advisory Commission on Criminal Justice Standards and Goals. *Courts*. Washington, D.C.: Government Printing Office, 1973. (a)

National Council on Crime and Delinquency. Correction in the United States. Pp. 115–212 in President's Commission on Law Enforcement and Administration of Justice, *Task Force Report: Corrections*, Washington, D.C.: Government Printing Office, 1967.

National Task Force to Develop Standards and Goals for Juvenile Justice and Delinquency Prevention. *Jurisdiction—Status Offenses*. Washington, D.C.: National Institute for Juvenile Justice and Delinquency Prevention, 1977.

Nejelski, P. Diversion in the juvenile justice system: The promise and the danger. *Crime and Delinquency*, 1976, *22*(4), 393–480.

Platt, A. *The Child Savers: The Invention of Delinquency*. Chicago: University of Chicago Press, 1969.

President's Commission on Law Enforcement and Administration of Justice. *Task Force Report: Juvenile Delinquency and Youth Crime*. Washington, D.C.: Government Printing Office. 1967.

Rubin, H. T. The eye of the juvenile court judge: A one-step-up view of the juvenile justice system. Pp. 133–159 in Klein, M. W. (ed.), *The Juvenile Justice System*, Beverly Hills: Sage Publications, 1976.

Ryerson, E. *The Best-Laid Plans: America's Juvenile Court Experiment*. New York: Hill and Wang, 1978.

Sarri, R. C. *Under Lock and Key: Juveniles in Jails and Detention*. National Assessment of Juvenile Corrections. Ann Arbor: University of Michigan, 1974.

Sarri, R. C., & Hasenfeld, Y. (Eds.), *Brought to Justice? Juveniles, the Courts and the Law*. National Assessment of Juvenile Corrections. Ann Arbor: University of Michigan, 1976.

Schultz, J. L. The cycle of juvenile court history. Pp. 239–258 in Messinger, S., et al. (Eds.), *The Aldine Crime and Justice Annual, 1973.* Chicago: Aldine, 1974.

Schur, E. M. *Radical Non-Intervention: Rethinking the Delinquency Problem.* Englewood Cliffs, N.J.: Prentice-Hall, 1973.

Smith, D. C. A profile of juvenile court judges in the United States. *Juvenile Justice,* 1974, *25,* 27–38.

Sosin, M. Due process mandates and the operation of juvenile courts. *Journal of Social Service Research,* 1978, *1,* 321–343.

Sosin, M., & Sarri, R. C. Due process—reality or myth? Pp. 176–206 in Sarri, R. C., & Hasenfeld, Y. (Eds.), *Brought to Justice? Juveniles, the Courts, and the Law.* National Assessment of Juvenile Corrections, Ann Arbor: University of Michigan, 1976.

van den Haag, E. *Punishing Criminals.* New York: Basic Books, 1975.

Wilson, J. Q. *Thinking about Crime.* New York: Basic Books, 1975.

Chapter 10

SOCIAL WORK AND PROBATION IN THE JUVENILE COURT*

CAROLYN NEEDLEMAN

This chapter examines the complicated and stressful role of social workers in juvenile court as they struggle to reconcile their child advocacy inclinations with the legalistic forms and traditions they deal with in the juvenile justice system. The purpose is to give the reader an overview of the wide variety of court-related services that social workers can provide. Drawing on my own two-year participant observation study of a suburban New York Family Court (Needleman, 1978) as well as the accounts of other researchers, I will review some typical court functions of social workers. I will then describe three widespread and predictable sources of role strain experienced by social workers in the juvenile court and suggest some immediate practical steps that could make their work more effective.

TYPICAL FUNCTIONS

An examination of how social workers participate in juvenile court must begin by acknowledging two related facts. First, since there is no consistency in the way juvenile courts are organized, the activities carried out by social workers in one jurisdiction may be nonexistent elsewhere or arranged quite differently. Second, social work functions in juvenile justice are not limited to professional social workers. Practically everyone gets involved in casework, child advocacy, and social service programming to some degree — police, probation officers, court psychologists, judges. Therefore

*The author would like to thank William W. Vosburgh, Miriam Vosburgh, Milton Speizman, and Martin Needleman for helpful comments on an earlier draft. Correspondence concerning this chapter should be addressed to Carolyn Needleman, Graduate School of Social Work and Social Research, Bryn Mawr College, 300 Airdale Road, Bryn Mawr, Pa. 19010.

165

it is somewhat arbitrary to separate those who are "officially" social workers by virtue of training and credentials from those who are practicing social work without clear identification with the profession.

The social work functions considered here will include intake screening and preadjudication services, psychological assessment, court investigations, courtroom testimony, probation supervision, and court-assigned social services. All of these are fairly common work assignments and are carried out at least some of the time by people who think of themselves as social workers and have professional training in social work or a related field such as counseling.

Intake Screening and Preadjudication Services

One of the major staffing innovations related to juvenile court has been the creation of special intake units to receive and screen the complaints referred to court by police, schools, parents, and social agencies. Occasionally, small courts may get along without such a unit, relying on "primary screening" by the referral sources. In jurisdictions that routinely handle status offenders[1] outside of court, the screening function largely devolves on social agencies (see Cressey & McDermott, 1973). But most larger jurisdictions have a well-established intake section, usually staffed by probation officers, or "POs" (National Advisory Commission, 1973b). The intake staff may number from one to over a dozen workers.

Social workers are intimately connected with the work of these intake units. For one thing, the intake POs may themselves be trained social workers. In my own research, I found that about forty percent of the intake workers had MSW degrees or a significant amount (over 30 credits) of graduate social work training; another twenty percent had graduate training in counseling or psychology and thought of themselves as "social work sympathizers" (Needleman, 1978). This proportion — over half the staff — is higher than is typical nationally (Eskridge, 1979), but many jurisdictions have at least a few social workers employed as POs in the court's intake unit.

---

[1]"Status offenders" are those juveniles arrested for offenses that would not be considered crimes if committed by adults — for example, truancy, incorrigibility, and running away from home. Many states now use a special designation such as "PINS" (Persons In Need of Supervision) to distinguish status offenders from delinquents. As explained in the previous chapter, some jurisdictions deal with all or most status offenders nonjudicially through social service agencies, with the court as a back-up if treatment efforts fail.

The intake POs deliver two services. The first is *screening*, to decide whether the case should go on to a formal hearing or be settled out of court; this option is permissible only with the consent of the injured party. The second intake service is "*informal adjustment*" of the cases diverted from court, consisting of a limited period (in New York, two months) of informal counseling and mediation with the juvenile offender and other parties in the case. The intake workers' monthly caseloads in the court I studied range from twenty to eighty-four cases, in various stages of screening/adjustment. Usually about half are minor delinquency charges, primarily shoplifting and burglary, a few are delinquency cases involving major damage and injury, and about a third are status offense cases—runaways, truants, and family discipline problems. For most, the POs simply give a stern lecture, provide information and referral services, and close the case. Where more intervention is felt necessary, they hold several office interviews with the child, the parents, and other relevant parties. In about 10 percent of the cases, they get heavily involved, holding weekly counseling sessions, and sometimes making home visits.

Intake preadjudication services represent the major element of diversion in the entire juvenile justice system. Nationally, about half the cases referred to court are screened out of the system by intake personnel and never reach a judge (National Center for Juvenile Justice, 1977). Those that do end up in court tend to be children with extensive prior records (Cohen, 1975), those who impress the intake officer as poor prospects for rehabilitation (Emerson, 1969; Cicourel, 1968), and those whose adjustment "fails" for a variety of reasons sometimes unconnected with the child's own behavior (Needleman, 1978). They are not necessarily the criminal offenders; children are just as likely to be sent to court for status offenses as for delinquency (Creekmore, 1976). Nor are they necessarily the cases involving the most serious offenses. In fact, the intake workers may choose to divert from court some juveniles charged with quite serious crimes, distrusting the court's capacity to deal appropriately with the juvenile's social welfare needs (Needleman, 1981).

An additional social work role associated with court intake is consultation. In the process of screening/adjustment, the intake POs frequently rely on information from social workers outside the court. They may call the child's school social worker or counselor, any youth programs or psychiatric services the child has been connected with, and any social services—such as mental health clinics, alcoholism programs, or welfare—that are working with the child's parents or other family members.

Relations between the intake officers and other social workers are usually cordial and collegial. Advice and information coming from social service agencies outside the court tends to be taken quite seriously (Lindner, 1977). However, some researchers have found the court's intake staff reluctant to refer adjustment cases to outside social service agencies for actual treatment, either because the POs lack information about the community's social service resources or they don't feel that outside agencies can handle the cases as effectively as the intake unit can (Cressey & McDermott, 1973).

Psychological Assessment

The resources of juvenile court are supposed to include a capacity for psychological evaluation of offenders who seem emotionally disturbed, to determine whether they need immediate hospitalization as a danger to themselves and others, and to aid the court in its deliberations. In many jurisdictions, such services are entirely absent, and the court either does without them or contracts with an outside agency (President's Commission, 1967a). But some large jurisdictions have a full-fledged mental health clinic attached to the court, staffed by psychiatrists, psychologists, and social workers (Lindner, 1977). Their function is to provide quick diagnosis only. If long-term therapy or observation seems indicated, the case is referred elsewhere, usually through court action.

Court Investigations

Once juveniles are declared delinquent or PINS in an adjudication (fact-finding) hearing, the judge may request a field investigation of their social circumstances. The purpose is to aid the court in making a disposition suited to the child's needs.

The agency that carries out these investigations for the court is typically another special unit of the Probation Department. POs assigned to investigations are—at least as found in my New York study—less likely than intake POs to be trained as social workers themselves. However, their work brings them into close contact with social workers outside the court as sources of information.

and they provide the court with a social report analyzing the child's family situation, peer relationships, neighborhood environment, school performance, and apparent moral character.

In theory, the content of the social investigation is available to the judge only for the child's second, or dispositional, court hearing, since it obviously has potential to prejudice the fact-finding activities of the initial adjudication hearing. This timing consideration is one of the rationales for separating investigations from intake services.

Courtroom Testimony

Social workers not officially attached to the court are sometimes called upon to testify as witnesses in juvenile court hearings. They may know the juvenile offender or his parents as clients and thus have special insights that the judge wishes to hear. They may be asked by a lawyer—the child's or the petitioner's—to testify on mitigating or aggravating circumstances. Or they may be asked to provide an expert opinion on the availability and advisability of some particular social service for the offender.

As courtroom witnesses, social workers often feel out of their element (Lindner, 1977; Bernstein, 1975). We shall see in a moment that this particular activity involves tremendous strain in terms of the social worker's status, allegiances, and self-image.

Probation Supervision

Nationally, about a fourth of the juveniles referred to court end up placed on probation (Empey, 1978).[2] Usually the judge sets up specific "conditions of probation"; some common ones are regular school attendance, part-time work, community service, participation in an alcoholism program, consultation with a family therapist or mental health clinic, and joining a recreation program. A key provision in the conditions of probation is, of course, staying out of further trouble with the law. The task of monitoring the child's behavior during the probationary period falls to the Probation Department's supervision unit. The child is assigned to a probation officer and is given a schedule of regular office appointments, which the PO may choose

---

[2] As we have seen, half are diverted from the court at intake. Most of the rest are dismissed with a warning from the judge (Hasenfeld, 1976). Only 4% to 7% are sentenced to a correctional institution, and very few (1%) are waived to adult court (Empey, 1978).

to supplement with home visits and other field site meetings.

While the purpose of probation supervision is fundamentally social control, it often develops into a casework or child advocacy role for the probation officer. Some of the POs in probation supervision will have social work training; most will not (Dietrich, 1979). However, their job clearly involves social work skills.

Court-Assigned Social Services

Social workers are also drawn into the probation aspects of the court as outside providers of court-assigned social services. Social service agencies must deal with the children, often hostile and defiant, who are sent to them as clients under threat of further court action. Sometimes the court's assignment will seem unrealistic or inappropriate, and the agencies' social workers will find themselves playing a broker role, referring the children and their families on to other social services better suited to their needs (Lindner, 1977). As we shall see, providing court-assigned services poses some special problems and dilemmas for social workers. It is unclear whether they are being expected to act as agents of the court, advocates for the client, or experts helping to refine the court's ideas about juvenile rehabilitation (Treger, 1965).

ROLE STRAINS

Most social workers seem to find working with the juvenile justice system personally difficult. As one social worker employed as an intake PO told me:

> I really think [juvenile justice] is such a rotten system, I can't relate my approach to it. I reject the whole crummy way that kids in trouble are handled here. . . . I don't go easy on kids who commit serious offenses, but I try to understand why and help with the real problems — not just punish [taped interview, New York Family Court].

Out of this general sense of unease can be isolated several typical, predictable sources of role strain that tend to make the work uncomfortable. I will focus here on three: role inconsistency, training incongruity, and interprofessional status tensions.

Role Inconsistency

Social workers in the juvenile justice system often find themselves torn between directly contradictory role requirements. For instance, social workers employed as POs are supposed to act as advocates for the child, but also as law enforcement agents. In intake processing, a particular child may in the PO's judgment need counseling and support, rather than a formal court hearing. But the petitioner (i.e. the victim) is legally entitled to recourse to the court if he or she insists. Exactly what client interests is the social worker responsible to here — those of the offender or those of the injured party, who may be as much in need of support and sympathy as the child? Should the social worker try to talk the petitioner out of pressing charges? Or evade the conflicting demands — and subvert the law — by avoiding contact with the petitioner altogether?

Probation officers working in supervision face the same kind of contradiction between the demands of rapport building and the demands of social control. Suppose that in a PO's casework interviews with a juvenile probationer it comes to light that the conditions of probation are being violated. Perhaps the child confesses to committing further offenses while on probation. What should happen? The PO has a legal obligation to report violations of probation. Should that obligation be ignored? Should the PO throw away months of rapport-building effort by betraying the child's trust? Should the PO tell the child from the first that all violations must be reported, thus making it impossible for the child to drop his guard in the counseling sessions? These can be agonizing dilemmas for the practitioner (see Dietrich, 1979).

Even social workers in agencies outside the juvenile justice system can be touched by these conflicts between treatment and control roles. They must make the same hard choices concerning client confidentiality when called upon to testify in juvenile court or to report back on the progress of a child receiving court-assigned services.

Training Incongruities

Much of the work that social workers do in juvenile court matches poorly with their training. For instance, most social workers feel they can exercise their skills to best advantage when there is *continuity* in their casework or problem-solving. They have been trained to move a problem through developmental stages and bring it finally to resolution. But the structure of the court makes this difficult by forcing an elaborate division of labor with episodic client contact and mandated cutoff dates for intervention at each level. The intake workers tend to feel time limitations most keenly, as their client contact is restricted to a couple of months.[3] In my research, I heard time after time the complaint that the PO was "just beginning to get through to the kid" when the time period expired or the case was forced to court by the petitioner's insistence. One worker summed it up sadly:

> Once it goes to court, it's out of your hands. As an intake worker, you can't have any more contact with them, or work with them—so it's just gone [taped interview, New York Family Court].

In their own ways, POs in the court's investigation and supervision units suffer the same frustration. Investigating POs, assigned to give diagnostic social reports only, are not supposed to provide service, even if they encounter urgent problems. Supervisory POs have assignments more similar to traditional casework or groupwork, but they also face cutoff dates that may not match the pace of the counseling relationship.

A second incongruity is that social workers are trained for working with clients who seek service *voluntarily*, or who at least view the practitioner as a helping agent. Quite the reverse is often true in juvenile justice work. Social workers employed as POs may try to persuade offenders and their families that their intervention is a benefit, but the clients don't always agree. This problem is especially troublesome for social workers outside the court who are providing court-assigned services (Abadinsky, 1979). They are seldom comfortable with coercing a client into unwanted treatment, particularly when the court-assigned treatment plan may not be the one they would have devised themselves.

One of the most frustrating mismatches of training and role assignment arises from the court's emphasis on the individual offender. Many court social workers define individual problems as part of a *system* of interpersonal relations and would prefer to work with the child's entire social network—at the very least, with the child's family. This is possible but not easy within the structure of juvenile justice, which is organized to judge and rehabilitate the

---

[3] In New York, the time limit on informal adjustment cases can be extended an additional two months, for a legal maximum of four months. However, the intake workers' heavy caseloads preclude frequent use of the time extension option.

child as an individual. Given large caseloads, POs have little time to track down and interview the offender's significant others. In trying to engage the family, they have few levers on parents who prove indifferent or uncooperative.

The social workers I interviewed in the Probation Department of the New York Family Court solved this problem by differentiating their case handling. They gave first priority to those cases most consistent with their training. Neighborhood disputes (which "everybody hates") got minimal crisis intervention only, as did the juveniles whose parents were uninterested in participating in the counseling. With the "boring" cases cleared out of the way, the POs were left with more time to spend on the professionally intriguing ones—usually PINS. As one intake worker explained:

> When somebody comes in and says "Yeah, I'm really having a problem with my child, I don't know what to do," then it's a different story. You really have something you can work with [taped interview].

She agreed that two different levels of service were being dispensed, and added, "It's a schizophrenic job." The unfortunate result of this kind of case sorting, of course, is that those offenders whose situation doesn't fit the family therapy model will get less support from the social worker.

A final training problem that plagues social workers in juvenile court is their *lack of preparation for the witness role*. Their whole approach to child advocacy is oriented toward conflict resolution and identification of the client's best interests as defined by professionals, consistent with the court's original *parens patriae* focus (see Davidson & Rapp, 1976; Gilbert & Specht, 1976). As the court has moved toward a greater emphasis on due process, a different kind of advocacy has appeared in court—legal advocacy, designed to further the child's best *legal* interests (Schultz, 1968). This latter approach is adversarial in tone, stressing principles that the social worker may see as unnecessary, such as limiting the testimony to the charged offense, and relying on strategies that may strike the social worker as wrongheaded, such as getting the case dismissed on a technicality (see Scherrer, 1976; Brennan & Khinduka, 1971). Untrained in how to present court evidence, social workers being questioned by a lawyer or a judge tend to be insufficiently prepared on the legally relevant details of the case, too wordy or indirect in reply to questions, too ready to volunteer information, unskilled in courtroom process, and too easily flustered by legal theatrics and hostile cross examination (Lindner, 1977). They may find themselves working at cross purposes with the offender's own legal counsel, even though both are there as advocates for the same child.

Interprofessional Status Tensions

Social workers in juvenile justice are operating in what often seems like alien professional territory. On the Probation Department staff, they are a minority. Moreover, they are concentrated in the juvenile court intake unit of probation, which tends to be seen by Department administrators as the soft, feminine part of an otherwise macho, law enforcement oriented system whose real work is service to the adult criminal courts. Despite the social welfare rhetoric of the juvenile court, social workers on the staff may find administrative support lacking for activities and programs that are explicitly social work in nature. In my research, for instance, I found a very bitter intake worker who had spent over a year trying to set up group counseling sessions in the evenings for juvenile offenders and their families. She was finally granted authorization to use the probation office facilities at night and compensation for her own extra worktime, but the Department showed little enthusiasm for the program and still expected her to carry a full caseload of individual juvenile offenders during the day. She was unable to get time off for attending social work institutes and workshops, even at her own expense, while other POs were being offered encouragement and compensation for attending in-service training seminars on the use of firearms and martial arts. "They hate social workers here," she claimed.

In part, the friction between probation personnel with social work training and those without it reflects a larger struggle between two professions competing for ascendancy in juvenile justice. The field of probation work, like social work, has developed its own professional associations and journals and is striving to build up its public visibility and upgrade standards among its practitioners. Since social work is older and better established, the overlap in content between the two fields poses a threat to the distinctiveness and legitimacy of probation as an emerging profession—a threat accentuated by social workers' tendency to describe probation patronizingly as a subfield of social work.[4] So even though probation work clearly borrows some of the skills of social work and employs POs with social work backgrounds, some—although certainly not all—probation authorities reject the idea that probation officers need graduate training in social work (Eskridge, 1979). It even has been suggested that probation officers might be better off without social work training, since they then wouldn't suffer the trauma of trying to reconcile their day-to-day tasks with the principles of casework as presented in schools of social work (Miles, 1965).

Social workers also experience status tensions with the lawyers they encounter in juvenile justice work. The higher pay and prestige of the legal profession hover in the background, and while the social worker usually respects the lawyer's expertise, that respect may not be reciprocated (Scherrer, 1976). The social workers' insecurity is only reinforced by the fact that their professional encounters with lawyers tend to occur on the lawyer's turf— the court—rather than in agency settings. The lawyer and the judge have in common a set of terms and procedural assumptions that the social worker does not usually share, making the social worker feel at a disadvantage in the courtroom.

Social workers may also feel conflicts with psychiatrists within the court's psychological assessment facilities. In the court I studied, the clinic—or "Court Consultation Unit," as it was called—was famous for returning innocuous reports on juvenile offenders. Even when the evaluations identified serious psychological symptoms, the stated diagnosis was almost always "adjustment reaction to adolescence." When I discussed this with a social worker assigned to the clinic, she laughed good naturedly and explained that the vagueness was intentional. In writing up the reports, the clinic's social workers used the psychiatrist's assessment but saw no need to "label these kids as schizophrenics and paranoids when we're going to be referring them to someone else anyway."

---

[4]For example: "Actually, a very encouraging aspect of the general probation field is its rapid movement toward professional status within the general field of social work" (Keve, in Rosenheim, 1972).

SOME PRACTICAL SUGGESTIONS

What can be done to make social workers' contributions to juvenile justice easier and more effective? One approach, of course, is through major policy changes such as abolishing court jurisdiction over status offenders, diverting more children away from court into social service agencies, and providing service programs open to the general youth population on a voluntary basis, thus reaching those children whose problems and crimes have gone undetected. As discussed in the previous chapter, this kind of change is on its way in juvenile justice, but at a slow pace and in a crazy-quilt pattern of variation among jurisdictions. It still remains to be seen whether and how well the European pattern of noncompulsory, nonjudicial treatment for most juvenile offenders can work in the United States (see Parsloe, 1978; Abadinsky, 1976; Schur, 1973; Martin & Snyder, 1976; Pabon, 1978; Bruce, 1975; Rosenheim, 1976; Howlett, 1973).

Let us end on a more modest level, simply by listing some immediate, pragmatic steps that seem likely to improve the quality of practice by social workers in juvenile courts, as those courts are presently organized in most jurisdictions.

1. *Appropriate Training:*
   Social workers need access to training for the roles they actually must play in juvenile court. Traditional casework skills are not enough. For instance, they need better preparation for doing legal research and giving expert testimony in court. They also badly need more skill development in practice techniques for crisis intervention and short-term counseling, so as not to short-change the cases that do not fit an intensive family therapy model. Stronger skills in program evaluation, community analysis, and organizational change techniques would also be useful (see points three and four).

2. *Better Networking:*
   Social workers within the court and those in outside social service agencies have much to gain by developing better communications with each other. A major sore point in most juvenile court systems is a lack of information about available community social service resources. A problem in many community youth services is being out of touch with how the

juvenile justice system is affecting the lives of young clients and their peers. Better networking would help solve both problems.

3. *Community Analysis:*
   Social workers in juvenile justice have a special need to understand the community context of their work—how the kids feel about the court, how the schools feel about the kids, how police and youth interact on the street, what kinds of opportunities and problems exist for youth, what the community norms are concerning pot-smoking and teenage sex, how the parents and the neighborhood feel about youth crime. These social patterns differ so much by neighborhood, social class, and ethnicity that social workers need to make a conscious effort to learn and analyze them for each of the communities with which they work. Gaining this kind of information would be especially helpful for handling the complicated "neighborhood dispute" cases that are usually the bane of a juvenile court social worker's existence.

4. *"Education" of Other Juvenile Justice Professionals:*
   Rather than reacting with hostility to the interprofessional frictions of their work, social workers in juvenile justice should set about demonstrating the value of their contributions. One way is through evaluation research, choosing measures that will command the attention of other court professionals: for example, lowered recidivism rates or more efficient use of probation staff. Another way is through organizational politics. Social workers should recognize that in the juvenile justice system practicing social work involves more than simply delivering service to clients or advocating for them as individual cases. Being effective requires knowing something about how bureaucratic organizations operate and, in particular, how they react to programmatic innovation. The social worker should be prepared to undertake advocacy for programs and policies, as well as for clients.

5. *Recruitment of More Social Workers:*
   Despite its problems, work with juvenile offenders remains a field with tremendous gratifications for social workers. Job opportunities in juvenile justice should be better publicized in social work schools and associations, in order to attract

enough people with social work training and orientation to form a "critical mass" of mutual support.

REFERENCES

Abadinsky, H. The status offense dilemma: Coercion and treatment. *Crime and Delinquency*, 1976, *22*, 456–460.

Abadinsky, H. *Social Service in Criminal Justice*. Englewood Cliffs, N.J.: Prentice-Hall, 1979.

Bernstein, B. The social worker as a courtroom witness. *Social Casework*, 1975, *56*, 521–525.

Bernstein, B. The attorney ad litem: Guardian of the rights of children and incompetents. *Social Casework*, 1979, *60*, 463–470.

Brennan, W. C., & Khinduka, S. K. Role expectations of social workers and lawyers in the juvenile court. *Crime and Delinquency*, 1971, *17*, 191–192.

Bruce, N. Children's hearings: A retrospect. *British Journal of Criminology*, 1975, *15*, 333–344.

Cicourel, A. V. *The Social Organization of Juvenile Justice*. New York: Wiley, 1968.

Cohen, L. E. *Delinquency Dispositions: Analytic Report 9*. U.S. Department of Justice, Law Enforcement Assistance Administration, National Criminal Justice Information and Statistics Service. Washington, D.C.: Government Printing Office, 1975.

Creekmore, M. Case processing: Intake, adjudication and disposition. Pp. 119–151 in Sarri, R., & Hasenfeld, Y. (Eds.), *Brought to Justice? Juveniles, the Courts, and the Law*, National Assessment of Juvenile Corrections, Ann Arbor: University of Michigan, 1976.

Cressey, D. R., & McDermott, R. A. *Diversion from the Juvenile Justice System*. National Assessment of Juvenile Corrections. Ann Arbor: University of Michigan, 1973.

Davidson, W. S., & Rapp, C. A. Child advocacy in the justice system. *Social Work*, 1976, *21*, 225–232.

Dietrich, S. G. The probation officer as therapist. *Federal Probation*, 1979, *43*(2), 14–19.

Emerson, R. M. *Judging Delinquents: Context and Process in the Juvenile Courts*. Chicago: Aldine, 1969.

Empey, L. T. *American Delinquency: Its Meaning and Construction*. Homewood, Ill.: Dorsey Press, 1978.

Eskridge, C. W. Education and training of probation officers: a critical assessment. *Federal Probation*, 1979, *43*(3), 41–48.

Gilbert, N., & Specht, H. Advocacy and professional ethics. *Social Work*, 1976, *21*, 288–293.

Hasenfeld, Y. Youth in the juvenile court: Input and output patterns. Pp. 60–72 in Sarri, R., & Hasenfeld, Y. (Eds.), *Brought to Justice? Juveniles, the Courts, and the Law*, National Assessment of Juvenile Corrections, Ann Arbor: University of Michigan, 1976.

Howlett, F. W. Is the YSB all it's cracked up to be? *Crime and Delinquency*, 1973, *19*, 491.

Keve, P. W. Administration of juvenile court services. Pp. 172–199 in Rosenheim, M. K. (Ed.), *Justice for the Child: The Juvenile Court in Transition*, New York: Free Press, 1962.

Lindner, C. *In the Best Interests of the Child: Social Work in the Family Court*. New York: Federation of Protestant Welfare Agencies, 1978.

Martin, L. H., & Snyder, P. R. Jurisdiction over status offenses should not be removed from the juvenile court. *Crime and Delinquency*, 1976, *22*, 44–47.

Miles, A. P. The reality of the probation officer's dilemma. *Federal Probation*, 1965, *29*(1), 18–23.

National Advisory Commission on Criminal Justice Standards and Goals. Juvenile intake and detention. Pp. 247–272 in *Corrections*, Washington, D.C.: Government Printing Office, 1973. (b)

National Center for Juvenile Justice. *Juvenile Court Statistics, 1974*. Pittsburgh: National Council of Juvenile Court Judges, 1977.

Needleman, C. E. *Screening Juvenile Offenders for Court Appearance: An Empirical Test of Positivist and Labelling Theory Interpretations*. Unpublished dissertation, Washington University in St. Louis, 1978.

Needleman, C. E. Discrepant assumptions in empirical research: The case of juvenile court screening. *Social Problems*, 1981, *28*, 247–261.

Pabon, E. A re-examination of Family Court intake. *Federal Probation*, 1978, 42(4), 25–32. (a)

Pabon, E. Changes in juvenile justice: Evolution or reform. *Social Work*, 1978, *23*, 492–497. (b)

Parsloe, P. *Juvenile Justice in Britain and the United States: The Balance of Needs and Rights*. London: Routledge & Kegan Paul, 1978.

Platt, A., & Freidman, R. The limits of advocacy: occupational hazards in juvenile court. *University of Pennsylvania Law Review*, 1968, *116*, 1156–1184.

President's Commission on Law Enforcement and Administration of Justice. *Task Force Report: Juvenile Delinquency and Youth Crime*. Washington, D.C.: Government Printing Office, 1967. (a)

Rosenheim, M. K. *Justice for the Child: The Juvenile Court in Transition*. New York: Free Press, 1962.

Rosenheim, M. K. Notes on helping: Normalizing juvenile nuisances. *Social Service Review*, 1976, *50*(2), 177–193.

Sarri, R., & Hasenfeld, Y. *Brought to Justice? Juveniles, the Courts, and the Law*. National Assessment of Juvenile Corrections. Ann Arbor: University of Michigan, 1976.

Scherrer, J. L. How social workers help lawyers. *Social Work*, 1976, *21*, 279–283.

Schultz, L. G. The adversary process, the juvenile court and the social worker. *University of Missouri at Kansas City Law Review*, 1968, *36*, 288–302.

Schur, E. M. *Radical Non-Intervention: Rethinking the Delinquency Problem*. Englewood Cliffs, N.J.: Prentice-Hall, 1973.

Treger, H. Reluctance of the social agency to work with the offender. *Federal Probation*, 1965, *29*(1), 23–28.

Chapter 11

SOCIAL WORK IN COMMUNITY-BASED GROUP CARE FACILITIES

Tom Roy

INTRODUCTION

Historically, young people have been viewed as chattel—the personal property of their parents—and the latter's chief perspective on their offspring was economic. So long as a child was needed and useful around the farm, he/she was cared for within the family. When a child no longer had an economic function at home, he/she was expected to leave. Those youth who ran afoul of the law were treated like adults. Those who, being below a prescribed age, were believed to be too young to commit crimes willfully, were taken under the community's care and generally apprenticed out to families.

During the late nineteenth century, concern over the horrors and excesses of adult courts was reinforced by a belief that young people, as future citizens, were the state's most valuable assets. The state, therefore, had to equip youth for responsible citizenship and this meant governmental authority over youth had to be expanded. This led to the establishment of separate institutional rules and structures for youth including the juvenile court system. The new juvenile codes covered not only youths formerly subject to adult courts but they invented new categories of youthful behavior (incorrigible, runaway, truant) that had not been viewed previously as requiring formal societal intervention (Platt, 1977).

Legal justification for this intrusion of the state into the behavioral lives of children was justified under the concept of *parens patriae*, the duty of the state to protect children from all that might harm them. States chose generally to discharge their *parens patriae* responsibilities by placing young people in juvenile correctional institutions. Set apart in environments distinct from society, institutionalized youth were powerless to improve how they were treated since the state, acting as the ultimate parent, did not develop in its juvenile codes the due process and procedural safeguards for youth found in the adversarial, adult correctional system.

Through a series of Supreme Court decisions in the 1960s, some basic legal rights were extended to youth within the juvenile justice system. Simultaneously critics were assailing the system's use of correctional institutions for having failed to achieve their purposes of nurturing and rehabilitating youth. They called for alternative approaches, one such being community-based group home care (Bakal, 1973).

The 1970s saw the burgeoning of the community-based group care movement for troubled children and youth. This movement gained impetus from the normalization, deinstitutionalization, and right to treatment approaches begun in the fields of adult mental health and mental retardation (Dore & Guberman, 1981). This approach of focusing care and service at the community level has been institutionalized for children and youth through such federal legislation as the Juvenile Justice Act and Title XX of the Social Security Act.

Community-based services for troubled children and youth are of many types: in the area of living outside the family, for example, Anthony Maluccio has identified ten forms community-based child placement might take (Maluccio, 1977). Among the most popular of these community-based child placement forms is group home care. One commentator has observed that, "a new group home is probably established each day somewhere in the nation" (Gula, 1973).

Group homes vary depending upon the nature of agency ownership, the age and status of the youth served, the size of the facility, and the size and training of the staff. Nevertheless, group home care can be defined generically as, "a community-based program for children who are unable to tolerate the intimacy of a small family but who do not need the structure of an institution" (Maluccio, 1977).

A close reading of our generic definition of group home care underscores our lack of sophistication about which types of children and youth are served best in which forms of group homes. Youths are referred through the juvenile court system to group homes as delinquents (committed a crime that would be a felony if were an adult), status offenders (indulged in behavior deemed inappropriate because of one's age), and as youth in need of care (abandoned, dependent, neglected). There is a presumption within the juvenile justice system that delinquents and youth in need of care should not be placed within the same group home facility. Placement of status offenders is more problematic. Often these youth are the most difficult and troubled in the juvenile system and the decision as to their placement is dictated by the availability of group home resources and agency preferences.

While some work has been done to relate the needs of children and youth to types of community-based group home care, our knowledge and practice skills in this matching game are still primitive. Moreover, these efforts contain a contradiction. The purpose of community-based services is to provide care within as normal an environment as possible. To match youth behavior more precisely to type of group home requires a system of labeling. Labeling leads to stigmatizing and scapegoating, both major liabilities of the system of institutionalizing youth that community-based facilities seek to change (Harrington, 1980). This is one reason observers have noted that placing programs, including group homes, in a community has not in itself guaranteed normalizing experiences for youth (Dore & Guberman, 1981).

A more pragmatic approach to improving the quality of group home care has been to focus upon the functions and tasks required of staff in group home settings without concern for the etiology of the children's and youth's problems or status. Generally, apart from maintenance personnel, two levels of staff function have been depicted. On one level are the direct service workers known variously as child care workers, group parents, houseparents, or family-teachers. These persons provide a major portion of the around-the-clock care, supervision, and resources for children and youth in a group care setting (Maier, 1977). At another level are the indirect service workers, identified as social workers or home administrators. While these persons provide some primary care to the children and youth within the home, their primary function is to provide social supports to the youth and the staff through their roles as coordinators, program developers, trainers, and interpreters.

Definitionally, this notion of two levels of staff responsibility within group homes cuts cleanly, but it blurs much in reality, especially with respect to the social workers' roles. Most group care facilities or homes are operated by small, local nonprofit agencies. Where social workers are employed at all, they are moving continuously between direct and indirect service roles. Given the anticipated rollbacks in federal financial support of group home care, this tendency to expect social workers in group home settings to be "jacks of all trades" will intensify.

DIRECT SERVICE FUNCTIONS: SOCIAL WORKERS PROVIDE CARE

In a recent study on the tasks performed by social workers in group care facilities, Pecora and Gingerich found that while social workers do function more as program developers and representatives of the program to the community than child care workers, they do, nevertheless, spend considerable time in direct care giving tasks. Indeed, social workers within the group homes they studied ranked providing therapy as their number one task (Pecora & Gingerich, 1981).

The therapy or direct care social workers provide, however, must be compatible with the case plan developed for each youth. The agencies that have legal custody over youth—the police, probation, welfare, aftercare, or child and family service agencies—develop with the group home staff a case plan for each youth they place. The houseparents or child care staff are responsible for parenting the youth and working with the placement agencies to implement each youth's care plan. Since the placing agencies have final responsibility for removing as well as placing youth, they theoretically control the case plan and hence the direct services offered within the homes.

The social worker's role as a direct care provider then is circumscribed by the degree and amount of service provided by the houseparent staff and by the case plan that ultimately reflects the thinking of the placing agency. Within these real constraints, however, there are opportunities for the social worker in group homes to provide care services to youth, staff, and youth's parents.

Providing Care to Youth

The populations of group homes can be characterized as being comprised of children and youth from backgrounds so troubled that they cannot make it in a family situation. When you house anywhere from six to fourteen such youth in a single residence, the demands upon the primary care staff, the houseparents, or child care workers are overwhelming. There are a number of legitimate opportunities, then, for social workers to provide direct care to these youths. We shall describe five.

PROVIDING SHORT-TERM TREATMENT. Agencies sometimes place youth in group care facilities for what they intend to be a short time (two to seven days). In these situations, the social worker may provide primary—or at least share primary—care responsibilities for the youth. This occurs because of the intense and often highly specialized work that needs to be done in a short period. House-parents often are not trained in short-term crisis techniques, and even if they were, to ask them to take primary responsibility would upset the home's routine and could jeopardize interpersonal dynamics that they have spent months nurturing. An example might clarify the types of situations where short-term care by the social worker is required.

Jane, an eleven-year-old, awoke one night to the smell of smoke. When firemen arrived, they detected arson and suspected Jane's mother, who appeared to have fled. Jane was taken to a group home and the social worker assumed chief responsibility for providing care to Jane. Initially the social worker sought to locate relatives; that failed, and in the process, Jane, gasping and sobbing, explained how her mother and she had been arguing and fighting for months. Before the social worker could find an appropriate placement for Jane, she needed to help her work through her intensely ambivalent feelings of guilt and joy over her mother's disappearance and her genuine sense of loss and abandonment coupled with anger and hatred that her mother had tried to burn her alive. Jane needed the skilled help and attention of staff unencumbered by responsibilities for keeping the rest of the group home going. Providing direct care to Jane through short-term treatment and crisis intervention was an appropriate social worker role within that group home.

PROVIDING RESOURCES FOR YOUTH. Fortunately, most youth enter group home care under less precipitous circumstances than Jane, giving the placing agency and group home staff a chance to prepare an individual case plan for them. Once a youth is placed and his case plan becomes operative, the most common form of care provided by the social worker is to refer or link him to a resource he needs or wants. A worker, for example, may determine that a youth would benefit from a Big Brother or Sister, a job, or some special education or training. If done properly, the worker's referral work is perceived by the youth as expressing genuine care and concern for him.

PROVIDING GROUP COUNSELING FOR YOUTH. Peers clearly influence a youth's behavior and the home provides a setting for using group approaches to individual problems. Ted, for example, was a sullen, withdrawn seventeen-year-old with a long history of being physically and verbally abused. Prior to Ted's entering the home, the worker shared, at the weekly group meeting, something about Ted. The group, which had been aggressive and direct towards one another, determined after several weeks of discussion that they should be more considerate and supportive in their remarks so as to encourage Ted's participation. They devised a penalty system for members who became aggressive.

Ted did not speak in group the first three weeks, and in the fourth was led into discussion about purchasing a dog for the Home. Over the next weeks, Ted began to open up, and by his fifth month in residence, he had emerged as the Home's leader. More important to the worker, the group, in trying to accommodate Ted's sensitivities, had itself become much less aggressive. Through the group, members had learned that one can speak one's mind and still be cordial. That's a survival skill the worker had been seeking to engender.

The worker's role in the group depends upon the group approach used: behavioral-teaching, ecological, guided intervention, and reality therapy are among the models used. More commonly, however, the worker employs an eclectic approach based upon his perception of what would work best for the group's successfully dealing with a particular problem.

PROVIDING FRIENDSHIP TO YOUTH. Often youth in group homes feel "counseled" to death. What they may need or want is an adult friend or confidant readily available whom they can trust, but who does not have direct responsibility for and thus authority over them. While social workers should not necessarily seek to offer this friendship role to all youth in group home care, youth, nevertheless, may turn to them for this. This is especially so when the social worker, albeit distant from the direct daily caring for the youth, makes an appropriate referral for him. Youth may read this provision of concrete service as an expression of worker friendship and interest in them.

John, an aggressive sixteen-year-old, had a caseworker, a probation officer, a counselor at the mental health clinic, a special school counselor, and a clinical psychologist in the group home working with him. He did not lack for concerned adult direction!

John wanted to get into Outward Bound; he felt, however, that none of his counselors would see this as appropriate. He casually mentioned his interest in Outward Bound to the social worker who had driven him to a doctor's appointment when no one else was available to do it. The worker remarked that maybe John would like to jog with him sometime to get in shape since Outward Bound requires physical stamina. The two met to jog several days later and in a winded voice John blurted out that he had never mentioned Outward Bound to any of his counselors because he didn't think he could get in shape to make it (he was overweight and a heavy smoker), and anyway he didn't think they would like the idea well enough to want to help him. Over a four month period of jogging with the social worker, John lost weight, quit smoking, and having rounded into shape, was subsequently accepted into Outward Bound.

John may have needed all the counseling he was receiving, but he also needed someone who could accept him as he was: a confused boy who, nevertheless, still had dreams and yearnings that required a caring adult to find expression. The social worker became that special adult friend John needed.

PROVIDING ADVOCACY ON BEHALF OF YOUTH. Situations may arise in which the youth needs someone to serve as his advocate. For instance, a houseparent may inadvertently pick on certain youths, a placing agency sometimes allows a youth to linger too long in placement, or a school can develop rules that affect youths capriciously. Precisely because the social worker is not the primary care person in a group home setting, he may have a better overview or perspective for spotting these types of situations. Whenever such situations arise, the social worker has a responsibility to act on behalf of the affected youth. Since youth in group homes are minors and nonvoluntary clients, social workers have a special obligation to protect their interests and insure respect for their rights. An example illustrates this.

Local high school policy stated that if a student missed three classes without permission, he was suspended without a hearing or notice. Hal, a fifteen-year-old educably handicapped youth who had missed three of his shop classes within the first two weeks of school, was suspended under this policy. He did not understand the reason for his suspension, but fearing he would be punished when his group home parents found out, he decided to run, thereby breaking his probation agreement. Eleven days later, he was found and arrested.

After visiting Hal in jail, the social worker urged the houseparents to readmit him into the home. Swayed by her arguments, they agreed. Days later, Hal remarked to them that he missed the shop classes because his resource room teacher, whose class preceded shop, often helped him after the bell. Afraid to be late for shop, Hal skipped the class altogether.

After hearing this from the houseparents, the social worker met with the school principal and gained Hal's readmittance. More important, she spent the next months working to have the school board change its suspension policies so that youth and parents could receive warnings and a hearing prior to a suspension being issued.

Providing Care to Staff

The role of social workers that is most often overlooked is provision of services to the houseparents. Houseparents provide primary care twenty-four hours a day for eight to twelve troubled and in trouble youth. Under these circumstances, the question arises, "Who cares for the houseparent staff?" Social workers can. They have been trained to be care providers, and they are involved in the home enough to see what is happening to primary staff, yet distant enough to have perspective.

Some group homes have institutionalized the social worker's role as care provider to the staff by setting aside specific periods each week for them to meet together. Two periods a week are suggested. During one session, the houseparents discuss with the social worker particular problems or concerns they have with youth in the home; during the other weekly session, the social worker focuses upon the houseparents' personal needs, including their own relationship.

Ann was the houseparents' favorite. She was the first group home resident to graduate from high school and to be accepted into college. In the past, she had used her charm to gain credit with merchants, passing bad checks when finally forced to pay.

She was continuously "borrowing" money from the houseparents, paying back just enough to pacify them. She used the money to support a drug habit.

The worker attempted in their weekly sessions to help the houseparents see how Ann was using them. She enabled them to recognize that their "pride" in Ann was a function of their need to see some "successes" with the kids and that it simply reinforced Ann's manipulative and acting out behavior.

The high burnout rate of primary care staff in group homes is a major problem. In Montana group homes, for example, houseparents last an average of only twelve months. Where attention has been paid to caring for houseparent staff, however, staff turnover seems to be much lower. We say seems to be because this is a subjective judgment and an area where research is needed.

Providing Care to Youths' Parents

These parents have abused, neglected, given up on, or otherwise failed to control their children, with the result that the youths have been placed in a group home. Providing care to the parents is often cited as something social workers should do, but few actually get around to doing it. This is unfortunate because group homes ostensibly were not designed as permanent placements, but as way stations preparatory to youth emancipating or returning home. Yet, painfully little is done to provide parents with the type of assistance that could pave the way for the youth's eventual return to his natural home. Instead, we retool the youth and pray that he can survive back home, at least until he becomes eighteen.

Granted, parents often are hostile, lacking in visible strengths, and some other agency's responsibility anyhow. The sad fact is, however, that unless the group home takes an interest in the youth's parents, these parents are not likely to receive help from any other source. Some group homes—the Achievement Place Homes are an example—have incorporated parent involvement and home visitations into their programs, but these are exceptions.

Some Achievement Place Homes give their residents the "weekends off." Throughout the week, youth earn points and, above a certain minimum, they gain the weekend to go home. This procedure sustains parental-youth contact and reinforces parental involvement in what Achievement Place is attempting with their youth.

Social workers in group homes who are not yet providing care to youths' parents need to develop such programs. A good place for social workers to start thinking about the best ways to involve parents is to review the extensive bibliography Maluccio and Sinanoglu have drawn up on ways to work with parents whose children are in placement (Maluccio & Sinanoglu, 1981).

In providing care within a group home setting, social workers are not doing parenting or even primary counseling. Rather they are linking youths to needed resources, acting as their friend in selected situations, and advocating on their behalf. The care they provide houseparent staff is more direct, working to assist them in carrying out each youth's case plan and offering perspective and counseling to staff on their houseparenting and personal needs. Provision of care by group home social workers to youths' parents is sporadic and requires further implementation.

INDIRECT SERVICE FUNCTIONS:
SOCIAL WORKERS PROVIDE SOCIAL SUPPORTS

In their roles as providers of care within group homes, social workers have to defer to or work with the primary care staff, usually houseparents. Their responsibilities as providers of social supports in group homes is clearer probably, in part, because nobody else claims these activities as their turf. In providing social supports social workers act as coordinators, program developers, interpreters, and trainers.

Coordinators

A multitude of individuals are frequently involved in the life of a youth placed in a group home: there are the houseparents, the placing agency's caseworker, perhaps a probation officer, a school counselor, a counselor from mental health, and an employment person. Each of these persons comes with his own organizational and professional perspective of the youth; no one comes, per se, to put it all together, to view the youth in his total environment. This is a natural role for the social worker. By training and professional inclination, the social worker has been taught to understand people as shaped both by nature and environmental nurturing. With his broader perspective, the social worker, therefore, needs to take the lead in pulling together the case plan for each youth and seeing that it is carried out responsibly and on time.

This coordinator role is political. The social worker has to ingratiate himself with these other professionals and gain their respect to succeed. He can do this by being a careful and open listener, providing useful information, following up on leads and suggestions, and taking on those assignments others are reluctant to do. In his role as coordinator of youth case plans, the social worker is guided by his commitment to move youth out of the group home as soon as termination would benefit the youth.

Program Developer

The movement to deinstitutionalize troubled and in trouble youth was based upon the assumption that sufficient services for these youth existed already in the community or that they would be readily developed. Few communities, however, had thought through the questions of who the developers would be and where they would gain their sanction. As a consequence, communities often lack the special schooling, counseling, employment-training, and other services group home youth require to survive in the community. The result is that the social worker in the group home setting must often act as a developer of programs both within the home and within the community.

Being a program developer requires a number of social work skills; a partial listing includes organizing a problem-solving group, facilitating its meetings, helping it plan, developing support for the plans, preparing budgets and raising funds, and implementing the initial phases of the program. Three examples suggest programs social workers may typically need to develop.

1. Earlier we discussed that social workers may provide care to youth through friendship. A problem arises when you have a home filled with youth who all want an adult friend. The social worker simply cannot be that friend for all youth.

Assuming that youth in trouble, and that includes all youth in group care, need an adult friend, one social worker took it upon himself to develop a program that provides volunteer adult friends to troubled youth. An unanticipated bonus of his program is that the average length a youth stays in the home is down in part because with an adult friend for social support youth are more likely to succeed in independent placements.

2. The emancipation of youth is another problem group homes face that often requires the development of new programs. The

problem is twofold. First, there are youth who are ready to move out of the group home before their majority but for whom there is no place to go. Second, there are youth who, turning eighteen years of age, become legally emancipated but who are not yet prepared to live on their own. Social workers need to watch for these issues of emancipation and determine what, if any, new programs the group home should develop.

Some group homes have developed apartment-type facilities where newly emancipated youth as well as those about to emancipate (seventeen years or older) may live singly. Youth take care of their own units, shop and prepare their own meals, and generally take on the responsibilities of living independently. Since by design these programs are beyond the control of the group home houseparents, the social worker assumes responsibility for both developing and supervising them (*Practice Digest*, 1979).

3. Another way the social worker acts as a program developer is to be the catalyst in bringing together agencies to address common concerns and facilitate their deliberations. Again, through counseling staff and seeking resources for youth, the social worker becomes aware of the community's resource base and more particularly of problems faced by youths that appear to be endemic and beyond any one agency's ability to help.

In one community, for example, twenty-eight different agencies served youth. They had been meeting once a month for several years to exchange pleasantries, share program information, and ventilate their frustrations. The group home social worker realized that over time the agencies had repeatedly bemoaned the community's lack of indoor, winter activities for youths. Because this was a real concern of the group home staff, the social worker talked informally to others and certified for himself that there was a real need. He then announced at one of the group's monthly meetings that he had scheduled a meeting specifically for those agencies interested in discussing indoor facilities for youth.

Twenty-one agencies showed up for the initial meeting which was given over largely to members exclaiming, "why didn't we get together on this earlier" or "I wish I had known you were interested in this sooner." The upshot was that within the year this ad hoc committee, led by the group home social worker, had persuaded the local Y.M.C.A. to build a new multipurpose recreation building and the "Y" had initiated a several-million-dollar fund drive. In working to find winter programs for youth in his group homes, the social worker had led the community into developing new programs to serve all youth.

Interpreter/Advocate

A variety of situations requires the social worker to interpret the group home and the needs of its youth to the community. The social worker's success at developing new programs depends upon his/her ability to interpret the need for the envisioned program to the community. New programs require new dollars—there is no escaping it—and that means the social worker must interpret or sell the program to potentially large donors within the community.

Other occasions arise that require the social worker to be an advocate. Most group homes fund their services through purchase of service agreements with government agencies or other third parties. The worker may have to negotiate the agreements, persuading politicians of the justification for a given rate request and helping them understand the importance of group home care within the broad continuum of child care of social services that they fund.

The social worker should be prepared to respond to requests that he give a talk or speech about the group home. The social and service clubs issuing the invitation want to hear what the professionals are doing and see what they look like. As invitations to speak to church groups, Kiwanis, or the American Legion come in, the social worker should view them as opportunities to help the community better understand the youths being served and his agency's program. Doing so will make it easier for the social worker to go to the community later for support of a new program.

Trainer

The social worker is in a unique position to determine what additional training or education the staff needs. While the worker does not have to provide the needed training himself, he, nevertheless, is responsible for designing a training program.

An area where all staff need training is in working with nonvoluntary clients. Most counseling and intervention models presume a voluntary or at least compliant client. Even group home models like the family-teaching construct of the Achievement Places make this assumption. Yet group homes house youth who legally and often psychologically are not voluntary clients. Indeed, they may resent being there, may be embittered about what has happened to them, and would prefer to be elsewhere. Consequently, the traditional notions of counseling typified by the so-called "fifty minute interview," just don't make sense. Social workers need to design training on an ongoing basis that helps staff develop skills for living and working with these nonvoluntary, often hostile youth (Murdach, 1980).

ORIENTATION TO THE SOCIAL WORKER'S ROLE IN A GROUP HOME

Traditionally, social workers have been trained to offer direct service and so it is not surprising that they feel most comfortable doing diagnosis and treatment-counseling. In group home settings, however, other primary care workers are there to do some or all of these tasks, and the social worker's chief responsibility may well be to provide indirect service or social supports. Since social workers are not trained specifically to do this, they must develop the requisite support skills on the job. The following is a series of activities to orient social workers to their indirect service roles. It was designed by one community-based corporation that operates three group homes. The specific activities have been organized around five topic areas, knowledge of which has been deemed essential to competent social work practice within a group home:

1. Organizational context of practice.
   - Read the annual program plan of each of the group home programs.
   - Review the budgets of each of the homes.
   - Read the quarterly reports of each of the homes for the past three years.
   - Read case files and plans on all youth currently in residence.
   - Meet with the secretary-office manager; review office and corporate procedures with her.
   - Attend a corporate Board of Directors meeting.
   - Attend all staff meetings.
   - Participate in intake, case planning, and termination meetings.
   - Attend occasionally the "House" meetings (these are meetings of houseparents and youth).

— Meet with the Executive Director of the corporation, completing above, to ask questions and discuss the above information.

2. Community context of practice.
   — Read the daily newspaper regularly; maintain a file of articles relevant to youth.
   — Attend at least one city council, one county commission, and one school board meeting.
   — Read studies and surveys done in the past five years on youth in the area.
   — Attend meetings of youth serving agencies.
   — Interview youth in the homes; ask them their concerns and impressions of community attitudes and needs.
   — Interview student leaders from the junior high and high schools asking them the same questions.
   — Attend a P.T.A. or high school parents' meeting.

3. Existing social policy.
   — Learn what attendance, suspension, termination policies are at the schools.
   — Attend another school board meeting.
   — Interview a counselor at one of the high schools and a teacher to gain their perspective on school policy.
   — Write a three-page summary of school policy on suspension or some other issue, indicating who made it and its impact upon youth.
   — Attend another county commissioners' meeting, drawing some conclusions about how sympathetic they appear to be to funding youth services.
   — Review the budgets of the homes, following them back to funding sources and specific pieces of legislation (e.g. Runaway Youth Act, Title XX).
   — Read the Acts identified above, select one, and write a two-page paper describing its impact upon youth in your community.
   — Read the juvenile code or youth court act, focusing on its classification of youth and which agencies are responsible for which youth and the process they are to follow.
   — Interview a probation officer, child care worker with the welfare department, and an aftercare worker. Compare and

contrast how they describe their jobs with what juvenile statutes decree they should be doing.

4. Awareness of community resources.
   - Develop a resource guide by problem area, e.g. employment services for youth, recreation services for youth.
   - Identify three of the most commonly utilized resources within each problem area and visit and get to know personally those agencies.
   - Participate in any communitywide meetings that focus on services to youth.
5. Assessing the group home program.
   - Review stated agency purpose and program plans.
   - Compare these against the statistics and information contained in the quarterly and annual reports of the homes; also compare these with your own impressions of what actually goes on in the group homes.
   - List all services offered by the corporation; indicate whether an evaluation is done for each and, if so, whether the evaluations are appropriate and adequate.
   - For those services where evaluation is inadequate, indicate why you think so and what you would suggest instead.

These activities develop the social worker's knowledge and skill base for providing social support services. Simultaneously, they nurture worker sensitivity to the support needs of youth, staff, and the community. The intended effect is to politicize the worker to the environments outside the group home that define what it is possible for youth, staff, and the agency to do.

CONCLUSION

We have seen that no set of universal roles or tasks is available to guide social workers practicing in community-based group care facilities within the juvenile justice system. The specific roles and tasks any given worker undertakes are a function of factors like worker attitudes and training, the size and clientele of the group home, the tasks of the primary care staff, and the resources available in the community. Generally, however, the social worker provides some direct care duties within the home but primarily serves in an indirect role providing social supports. While not typically trained for this latter role, we have indicated how social workers can develop their support skills and sensitivities.

The importance of social worker sensitivity to larger economic, political, and social forces needs to be underscored. In the crush of meeting the daily needs of youth in group home care, staff need to be reminded that, simply stated, we do not know what to do as a society with our adolescents. Our failure to articulate a viable role for young people may be instrumental to increases in the number of adjudicated status offenders, and it is the increasing number of status offenders that is keeping our group homes filled. As persons interfacing between youth and society, social workers in group homes have an experienced perspective to share that could enable all of us to rethink what we as a society expect and want of our youth. Without this reconsideration, group homes will continue to expand in numbers to care for America's thrown away youth.

REFERENCES

"Alternatives to Foster Care for Older Adolescents." *Practice Digest*, September 1979, *2*, 13–15.

Bakal, Yitzhak. *Closing Correctional Institutions*. Lexington Books, D.C. Heath and Company, Lexington, Massachusetts, 1973.

Dore, M. M. and Guberman, K. "Two Decades of Turmoil: Child Welfare Services." *Child Welfare*, June 1981, *LX*, 371–382.

Gula, Martin. "Community Services and Residential Institutions for Children" in *Closing Correctional Institutions*, edited by Y. Bakal. Lexington Books. Lexington, Massachusetts, 1973, pp. 13–18.

Harrington, W. A. "Labeling Theory in the Juvenile Justice System." *Child and Youth Services*, 1980, *III* 1, 15–23.

Maier, H. W. "Child Welfare: Child Care Workers." *Encyclopedia of Social Work, 17th Edition*. N.A.S.W., Washington, D.S., 1977.

Maluccio, A. A. "Community-Based Child Placement Services: Current Issues and Trends." *Child and Youth Services*, 1977, *I*, 1–12.

Maluccio, A. A., Sinanoglu, P. A. "Social Work with Parents of Children in Foster Care: A Bibliography." *Child Welfare*, May 1981, *LX*, 275–304.

Mayer, M. F., Richman, L. H., Balcerzak, E. A. *Group Care of Children: Crossroads and Transitions*. Child Welfare League of America, New York, 1977.

Murdach, A. D. "Bargaining and Persuasion with Non-Voluntary Clients." *Social Work*, November 1980, *25*, 458–461.

Norman, J. S. "Short Term Treatment with the Adolescent Client." *Social Casework*, February 1980, *61*, 74–82.

Pecora, P., Gingerich, W. J. "Worker Tasks and Knowledge Utilization in Group Care: First Findings." *Child Welfare*, April 1981, *LX*, 221–232.

Platt, Anthony M. *The Child Savers: The Invention of Delinquency*, 2nd edition, Chicago: University of Chicago Press, 1977.

Stein, T. Book review of Frank Ferro's "Child Welfare Strategy in the Coming Years." *Children and Youth Services*, 1980, *4*, 438–442.

Section V

PROBATION, PAROLE, AND COURT SETTINGS

INTRODUCTION

It is a sad fact that the antisocial attitudes and behavior patterns of some offenders will not change as a result of social work intervention. No matter how competent the probation officer may be, nor how intensive the group therapy, drug therapy, and/or vocational training may be, some offenders will never change. Even with the most valid assessment instruments, it is difficult to identify this type of offender. However, there are many offenders who are capable of positive change; social work intervention can help to bring it about.

Social workers employed in probation and parole settings play a pivotal role in helping change come about for the probationer. "Probation officers work with probationers at a crucial time in their lives: a time when they can seize opportunities for renewal and change.... Offenders frequently are able—with the help of probation officers—to say, 'The cycle of my life' did change'" (Havenstrite, 1980).

The ultimate value of a probation and parole department is based on three major components: (1) the ability of the probation officer to facilitate positive change with offenders under supervision, (2) the ability of the probation supervisors to enhance the line social worker's ability to effect those changes, and (3) the ability of probation and parole administrators to perform the managerial functions of planning, organizing, staffing, directing, leading, and controlling. These functions are carried out simultaneously in the day-to-day work of the administrator.

In Chapter 12, Frank B. Raymond focuses on administrative functions and explains how these functions can be optimally carried out in the day-to-day work of the administrator. He discusses the effectiveness of social work education in preparing graduate students for management positions in probation and parole departments. Raymond also acquaints the reader with a contingency perspective on management theory. The usefulness of the five functions of management are illustrated through a detailed case illustration of a social work administrator's application of these management fundamentals.

In Chapter 13, Gloria Cunningham points out that psychotherapy and other types of individual counseling for offenders has been devalued on the basis of the conclusions of effectiveness studies. She also cautions that it is inappropriate to assume that the goal of treatment is the modification of the offender's personality. The author questions both the accuracy of effectiveness studies and the need to define treatment in such narrow terms. The probation officer's role is reexamined in view of evolving methods of social work intervention. In contrast to traditional psycho-dynamic approaches, Cunningham identifies the target of change as being the offender, as well as the offender's spouse, family system, and/or community. She views the probation officer's role as an advocate and broker of services in addition to being a therapist, counselor, and teacher.

In Chapter 14, Robert Scheurell discusses the applicability of ethics to corrections, probation, and parole work. He emphasizes the need for every social worker in these settings to internalize the behavior and ethical standards of the social work profession. Scheurell is cognizant of the limitations placed on probation and parole officers by court mandates and the objectives of individual agencies. These limitations are readily apparent with regard to the ethical concerns of client self-determination and confidentiality. The correctional social worker must attempt to balance the needs of clients with the objectives of the agency. Since these needs are often contradictory, it is recommended that social workers develop their own general guidelines on the utilization of social work ethics and develop their own style of behavior in balancing the demands of practice.

REFERENCE

Havenstrite, Al. "Case Planning in the Probation Supervision Process." *Federal Probation*, *44*:2 (June, 1980) 57–66.

Chapter 12

ADMINISTRATION IN PROBATION AND PAROLE

FRANK B. RAYMOND III

INTRODUCTION

Administrators of probation and parole agencies come from a variety of backgrounds. Their education and practice experience cover a wide range. In recent years, however, increasing emphasis has been placed on recruitment of administrators who have graduate training in social sciences, with a concentration in management. Social work has proven to be one of the best equipped disciplines to provide this kind of educational experience. Accordingly, a number of probation and parole departments now give priority to hiring administrators who have graduate training in social work.

Social work education is especially effective in preparing students for management in probation and parole agencies for several reasons. First, graduate study of social work provides one with a broad understanding of the field of social services rather than a focus on one narrow component. Such a perspective is important for a probation or parole administrator who must be concerned with relating the agency appropriately to a wide variety of other systems—employment agencies, counseling services, welfare departments, educational institutions, volunteer organizations, and so on. Second, master's degree programs in social work are longer than most other graduate degree programs in human services and usually require two years of study beyond the B.A. degree. Moreover, this extensive experience generally includes four semesters of field work, whereas other types of degree programs may require little or no field work. This field experience, a hallmark of social work education, is particularly important in enabling students to go beyond the acquisition of knowledge and develop skills in applying this knowledge in real life situations. A third advantage of graduate study in social work in preparing probation and parole administrators is its humanistic orientation. While it is granted that other disciplines, such as business administration, may teach many of the same management theories as social work, they do so from a different philosophic orientation. Social work education stresses values and emphasizes that services to clients should be planned, organized, and delivered with a humanitarian objective. Thus, for example, while the administrator with a social work background and the administrator with a business administration background may be equally trained in techniques of cost-benefit analysis, philosophic differences may influence the ways in which they would define benefits and, consequently, make programmatic decisions.

Graduate programs in social work have increasingly offered specializations and concentrations. This trend has resulted partly from the tremendous growth of bachelor's degree programs in social work and the consequent need for more advanced training at the graduate level. Opportunities to specialize in administration and/or concentrate in corrections are now widely available in graduate social work programs. More than ever, M.S.W. programs are equipped to educate students specifically for practice as probation and parole administrators.

It should be emphasized, however, that neither social work nor any other academic discipline concerned with preparing probation and parole administrators utilizes a distinct body of knowledge concerned with probation and parole agency management. Such a body of knowledge does not exist. Historically, in fact, little discussion has appeared in the corrections or social work literature regarding administrative practices in probation and parole. While certain aspects of the administrator's role have been addressed, such as caseload management and personnel supervision, a thorough body of knowledge has not yet been developed in this field. It is interesting that so little has been written on this subject, given the importance of the administrator's job.

There are several possible reasons why so little discussion has appeared in the literature regarding management techniques in probation and parole. First, the wide variation in the organizational structure of probation and parole offices makes it particularly difficult to develop managerial principles that would be universally applicable. Furthermore, since the legal basis for agency structure varies from jurisdiction to jurisdiction, there is limited opportunity to develop organizational configurations around principles of organizational theory. Instead, management principles must be adapted to existing structures. Second, the traditional structure of probation and parole offices relative to legal systems has caused administrators to feel they have little opportunity to develop policies concerning the operation of their organizations. Rather, they often see their role as that of implementing policies and procedures that have been determined legislatively or judicially (Latta & Cocks, 1975). Third, the lack of literature regarding administration in probation and parole may be attributable to the fact that many probation agencies are relatively small and fractionalized, resulting in a reliance by administrators on management strategies and techniques borrowed from social work or other disciplines or developed through personal experience (Allen, Carlson, & Parks, 1979).

It is unfortunate that a systematic body of literature regarding administrative practices in probation and parole has not yet been developed. Probation and parole agencies, like other components of the correctional system, have been criticized increasingly during recent years for inability to demonstrate effectiveness. A number of studies have pointed to the failure of correctional systems to achieve a high degree of success in rehabilitating offenders (Cohn, 1973; Bennett, 1973; Martinson, 1974; Amos & Newman, 1975; Smith & Berlin, 1976). If administrators of probation and parole agencies are to modify their programs in order to achieve greater effectiveness and efficiency, they need a thorough understanding of managerial principles. Certainly there are factors related to agency success that may be beyond the control of administrators, such as the decisions to grant, deny, or revoke probation, or the length of the probation period (Allen, Carlson, & Parks, 1979). However, there are many aspects of agency operation for which administrators have considerable responsibility and authority, and they are accountable for the agency's performance relative to these areas. In order to make appropriate decisions in those areas where they have managerial discretion and thus enhance agency effectiveness, administrators need to be knowledgeable of organizational and management theory.

Probation and parole administrators have learned management theory in the disciplines of social work, business administration, public administration, social psychology, and political science. Theoretical perspectives acquired in these disciplines have been applied by administrators in different ways, as they have attempted to relate them to their individual organizations and particular needs. Since this approach does not result in a unique theory of management that can be uniformly applied to probation and parole administration, it may be challenged by those who desire simple answers and pure models. Indeed, a number of organizational theorists have sought to develop management theories that prescribe *the best* ways of managing organizations (Taylor, 1947). During recent years, however, there has been a trend among organizational theorists towards contingency, or situational, approaches to management. That is, rather than advocating the one best way of managing an organization, these writers contend that management theory should develop knowledge of fundamental relationships and basic techniques that can be applied to a given practical problem for the purpose of achieving the best possible results for *that* situation (Koontz & O'Donnell, 1976).

The following pages of this chapter will reflect a contingency perspective on management theory. Given this perspective, the social worker's role as administrator of a probation or parole agency will be discussed in terms of operational functions. That is, management theory will be presented regarding the five basic functions of all managers—planning, organizing, staffing, directing and leading, and controlling. This operational perspective assumes that the fundamentals of management are universal and apply in all kinds of enterprises, including probation and parole agencies.

The five managerial functions can best be understood when illustrated by example. Thus, a case situation involving a probation and parole agency will be presented below, and this situation will be dealt with throughout the chapter in terms of application of the five functions of management.

Case Example: The Situation

During the past year, the Lowman County Probation and Parole Agency has received a great deal of public criticism. This criticism, which was triggered by several notorious crimes involving parolees, became focused on the overall ineffectiveness of the agency as measured by recidivism rates. The administrator resigned under pressure of the adverse publicity and Mark Donaldson was hired to replace him.

Mark received his MSW degree from the local university and for the past five years had served as assistant director of a community-based social services program. Upon arriving at the Lowman County Probation and Parole Agency, he found the program in a state of turmoil. In his first meetings with his twenty-one member professional staff, Mark discovered that there was a diversity of opinions as to whether the agency was supposed to function as a control entity or as a treatment program. Staff who had been with the agency for most of its existence tended to operate as control agents, while newer staff (those who had been employed for two years or less) generally tended to be more treatment oriented. The previous administrator had utilized a philosophy of letting each staff member function as s/he thought best, using any style of client supervision. Those who functioned as controllers complained to Mark that staff who focused on treatment spent too much time with their clients with little results. Staff who were treatment oriented charged that the controllers were ineffective in changing client behavior and, therefore, did little to reduce the high recidivism rate.

After investigation of the personnel records, Mark determined that the newer staff had been hired from among the graduates of the university's six-year-old BSW program, while older staff had a variety of backgrounds in terms of education and experience. Further, no staff had received any training after initial orientation. An annual evaluation sheet was completed for each staff member, but all agents received good to excellent ratings each year.

There were no intermediate supervisors in the agency. Meetings between the previous administrator and staff had been held infrequently and had consisted of the administrator's report of new policies received from the central office. The policy manual was a hodgepodge of central office directives stuffed into a folder in the administrator's office.

A file on caseload assignments revealed that these were made by the administrator's secretary who used a random assignment method. Agents' last names were alphabetically listed and a running tally was kept of cases assigned. When a new case came in from the court or the parole board, it was given to the next agent named on the list, even though other agents may have conducted previous presentence investigations or parole investigations on that case.

PLANNING

In creating within the probation and parole office an environment for the effective performance of personnel, the first essential task of the administrator is to see that purposes and objectives, and methods of attaining them, are clearly understood. If the probation or parole agency is to be effective, agents and other staff must know what they are expected to accomplish. This is the function of planning, which is the most basic of all the managerial functions. Simply stated, planning is deciding in advance what to do, how to do it, when to do it, and who is to do it.

Since the probation and parole administrator's other functions of organizing, staffing, directing and leading, and controlling are designed to support the accomplishment of the agency's objectives, planning logically precedes the execution of all other managerial functions. In other words, planning must occur in order for the administrator to be able to establish the objectives of the agency, create the kind of organization that can best attain these objectives, decide the type of personnel that are needed, determine how these personnel are to be directed and led, and define the kinds of control to be applied to ensure that objectives will be achieved.

Like managers of other social agencies, probation and parole administrators often feel that their potential for planning is severely restricted, given the constraints within which they must operate. These constraints include factors such as the legal structure of the organization, caseloads whose size cannot be predetermined or controlled, conditions of probation and parole that will affect the work of probation agents, staff size, and so on. However, the manager of any organization is faced with constraints, although they may be of a different nature, and these constraints do not preclude successful planning. Given the constraints that may affect planning, the administrator can still exercise a wide range of choices in developing plans; for example, even though the geographic boundaries of the agency may be established, the administrator may have flexibility in determining the most feasible location of local offices. Or, although it may not be possible to control caseload size or staff size, caseload management techniques that will enhance the efficiency of the probation agents can be planned.

Finally, while conditions of probation and parole may be set by the court or parole board, alternative ways of supervising clients and ensuring compliance with these conditions may be planned.

If planning is to be effective, the administrator must recognize that there are many different types of plans that are appropriate for the probation or parole agency. Since a plan encompasses any course of future action, plans are varied. They are often classified in the literature as purposes or missions, objectives, strategies, policies, rules, procedures, programs, and budgets (Koontz & O'Donnell, 1976). These various types of plans are interrelated. The degree of the probation or parole administrator's involvement in each of these areas of planning will vary relative to agency structure and one's position within the organizational chain of command.

In order for planning to be successful, the administrator should involve probation agents and other staff in the planning process. As a result of this involvement, employees have a clearer knowledge of what is expected of them, and they have a higher commitment to carrying out plans and achieving objectives that resulted from decisions they helped make; for example, by participating in the development of a mission statement, probation agents are forced to clarify their philosophy regarding the old issue of treatment versus control (Raymond, 1974), or in helping to decide the types of treatment programs to be used in the agency, probation and parole agents may have to examine new and different alternatives and evaluate the efficacy of traditional approaches. As a final example, if agents participate in defining treatment objectives and establishing how the attainment of these will be measured, it will be necessary for them to differentiate between administrative and operational definitions of "success," which will undoubtedly benefit them in evaluating their own supervisory efforts (Latta & Cox). Thus, while final responsibility for planning must rest with the administrator of the probation or parole agency, many benefits can be realized from including staff in the decision-making process.

All planning is ultimately aimed at the attainment of the agency's objectives. Indeed, unless objectives are clearly established during the planning process, there will be no way that the administrator can subsequently evaluate the results of a program and determine whether or not planning was successful (the control function of management). The National Advisory Commission on Corrections has emphasized that in order for a probation agency to be effective it must develop a goal-oriented service delivery system and specify measurable objectives based on priorities and needs assessment (National Advisory Commission on Criminal Justice Standards and Goals, 1973).

Because of the importance of establishing clear and measurable objectives in the planning process, during recent years administrators of social agencies in general and correctional managers in particular have given increasing attention to programs of managing by objectives or results (Koontz, 1971; McConkie, 1975). One of these approaches, Management by Objectives, is a systematic approach to managerial problem-solving and decision-making. It is a process whereby managers and subordinates engage in the process of identifying organizational goals and objectives and structuring the agency's operation around these goals and objectives. The process focuses attention on solving problems and attaining results rather than on activities that lead to those results. The basic concern is setting measurable objectives and providing avenues for achieving them. Thus, Management by Objectives entails a highly formalized, systematic approach to planning, involving administrators and other personnel. Because of its many advantages, this system of management has been adopted by many correctional agencies, including probation and parole departments (McConkie, 1975).

Case Example: Planning Function

In the previously cited problem situation at the Lowman County Probation and Parole Agency, Mark Donaldson determined that the first need of the program was to facilitate the development of a management plan. He believed the agency must be concerned with both control and treatment in order to be of benefit to the clients and the community. Expanding on the statutory mandate for the agency, Mark wrote a statement of purpose (or mission) that encompassed these two functions. He then established a task force to develop the actual goals and objectives based on the purpose/mission statement. In selecting the task force, which he chaired, Mark was careful to include representatives from each of the two philosophical persuasions.

The task force was divided into three subcommittees and instructed to develop appropriate goals relating to designated areas within the agency's purpose, measurable objectives for each goal, and a reasonable time frame to test out the attainment of each objective. One subcommittee was assigned responsibility of developing plans relative to presentence investigations and parole investigations. A second subcommittee was to develop plans regarding supervision of probationers and parolees. A third subcommittee had the responsibility of making plans relative to agency policy, staff management, and community relations. Each subcommittee was given two weeks to prepare its initial draft.

At the next meeting, the proposals were presented. After a great deal of discussion, the task force completed an overall plan that was basically agreeable to all members. The draft plan was then distributed to the entire staff for additional comments and suggestions. After further revisions, the final plan was prepared. Goals included, for example, "to create a community advisory board," and "to reduce the recidivism rate by 5 percent during the next 12 months." An example of an objective included was "to prepare complete presentence investigation reports on all cases within two weeks after assignment." A staff meeting was held, during which Mark and the task force members fully explained the plan and answered questions about it.

It was explained to the agents that they would be expected to develop individual objectives relating to their work. These objectives would be based upon and supportive of the goals and objectives of the agency. For instance, an agent developed as one of his objectives the following: "to offer group counseling sessions during one evening each week for clients whose circumstances preclude daytime meetings." It was explained to agents that part of their annual evaluation would be based on how well they achieved their objectives.

It was decided to test the new plan for a six-month period. At the end of that time, the rate of success in attaining individual and organizational objectives would be determined. The task force would then compile the results, make revisions as needed, and develop a one year plan using the six month plan as a basis.

ORGANIZING

The second major function of the administrator of a probation and parole agency is organizing. Simply stated, organizing means creating a structure by establishing relationships between people, work, and physical resources. The purpose of organizing is to provide a framework within which people can work together effectively, utilizing resources, to achieve common goals in an optimum manner (Eckles, Carmichael, & Sarchet, 1974).

An important question related to organizing in probation and parole administration is whether probation services should be centralized or decentralized—a common concern of social agencies. Generally, the organizational structure of the probation service of a given jurisdiction is outlined by statute. However, detailed structure and procedures may be determined by administrative regulation, in which case the administrator can have considerable authority in determining the extent to which services within the jurisdiction will be centralized or decentralized.

Corrections literature presents arguments supporting both centralization and decentralization. The most frequently cited arguments in favor of centralization are that a centrally administered system is more free of local political considerations, it can develop uniform policies and procedures, leading to a greater likelihood that the same level of services will be provided to all clients, it contributes to greater efficiency in the disposition of resources, and it has greater potential to develop innovative programs, demonstration projects, and correctional research. On the other hand, arguments supporting decentralized arrangements include local probation or parole programs can generally develop better support from local citizens and agencies, local units can be more flexible and less bound by bureaucratic rigidity, and probation agents working for a local unit are more likely to be thoroughly familiar with the local community (Allen, Carlson, & Parks, 1979; Killinger, Kerper, & Cromwell, 1976).

While the probation and parole administrator's authority to determine the degree of centralization/decentralization may be limited by statute, there are other means of organizing that may be employed; for example, the administrator may develop departments or divisions based on function. Departmentation by function means the grouping of activities on the basis of similarity of skills required or on basis of a common purpose (Koontz & O'Donnell, 1976). This is perhaps the most common type of departmentation among all types of organizations, including social work agencies. When probation and parole agencies are organized around groupings of tasks and activities into relatively discrete functions, this usually involves assignment of agents to either investigation or supervision functions. This type of functional specialization in probation and parole has the advantages of enhancing the development of expertise, facilitating supervisory control of performance, and eliminating neglect of one function in favor of the other. On the other hand, it may be argued that such specialization results in unequal workloads with consequent morale problems and that probation agents who handle both investigation and supervision will have a greater knowledge base and repertoire of skills than those who specialize (Czajkoski, 1969).

The administrator of a probation or parole agency may also organize the department based upon caseload assignment of probationers or parolees. There are five major caseload assignment models (Carter & Wilkins, 1976). First, the conventional model utilizes the random assignment of probationers to available probation officers. Second, with the numbers game model, the object is to balance numerically all of the caseloads within the agency. Third, the conventional model with geographic consideration restricts caseloads to clients living in specific geographic areas. Fourth, the single factor specialized model assigns probationers to caseloads on the basis of a single shared characteristic, such as drug abuse, mental deficiency, or type of offense (Latessa, Parks, Allen, & Carlson, 1979). Fifth, the vertical model is based on classification by a combination of characteristics. Each of these models has advantages and disadvantages, and too little research has been done to conclude which caseload management strategy is more effective or efficient (Allen, Carlson, & Parks, 1979). The administrator must consider the unique needs and circumstances of the probation and parole agency in determining the caseload assignment model that will be most appropriate.

The chief administrator of a probation and parole agency will likely have subordinate administrators, such as supervisors or agents-in-charge, unless the agency is particularly small. In developing an organizational structure with several administrative positions, the chief administrator of a probation or parole agency should keep in mind several important principles of organizing. First, the line of authority from the chief administrator to every subordinate position should be clear, if effective communication and responsible decision-making are to occur. Second, subordinate administrators should be delegated adequate authority to enable them to do their job. Third, it should be made clear that subordinates are responsible to their superiors and that the superiors cannot escape responsibility for the organization activities of their subordinates. Fourth, insofar as possible, each individual should have a reporting relationship to a single superior in order to avoid a problem of conflict in instructions and to enhance the feeling of personal responsibility for results. Fifth, subordinate administrators with authority to make certain decisions should be required to make these decisions and not be allowed to refer them upward in the agency structure (Clegg, 1970; Koontz & O'Donnell, 1976). When these principles are followed, the job of every administrator in a probation and parole agency becomes easier and the operation of the agency becomes more effective.

Case Example: Organizing Function

Mark Donaldson recognized he had two primary problems in the organization of his agency. The first was the absence of intermediate supervisors to help assume some of the responsibility for overseeing staff functions and responding to problems. He was particularly aware of the potential for staff resentment of his interference in their daily schedules since he was the new administrator who had already begun changing a system in which staff had become comfortable if not satisfied. He also believed his time could be better spent in activities other than direct supervision. Since he had developed a close working relationship with the staff members who composed the planning task force and had been favorably impressed with their ability to communicate and reach compromises for the benefit of the agency, he asked these people to serve as the personnel committee to recommend persons to serve as intermediate supervisors. Based on their recommendations, Mark promoted four agents to supervisory positions. Each intermediate supervisor was assigned five to seven staff members to direct.

Mark's second organizing problem pertained to the assignment of caseloads. The arbitrary random assignment that had been used caused agents to spend valuable time traveling from one end of the county to the other. Given this system, agents were unable to develop a thorough knowledge of a community or establish a relationship with any particular neighborhood. Furthermore, this method of case assignment ignored the fact that individual agents were more skilled in working with certain kinds of problems than others. To address this problem, Mark met with his intermediate supervisors and developed a new organizational plan. The county was divided into four separate regions, and each officer was assigned cases in one region only. Furthermore, each supervisor was responsible for supervision of agents in a single region. Additionally, several officers who appeared to have exceptional skill in working with youthful offenders were assigned caseloads comprised predominantly of this type of client. Every effort was made to equalize caseloads among agents, although it was recognized this could not be completely accomplished.

STAFFING

The third function of the administrator of a probation or parole agency is staffing, which has to do with selection, appraisal, and development of personnel to fill the roles designed into the organizational structure of the agency. The ultimate success of the agency is largely dependent upon the manner in which the administrator carries out these three elements of staffing.

There is great discrepancy among jurisdictions as to the preservice educational requirements for probation and parole officers, more than for most social agencies. Requirements set by statute or administrative regulation vary from high school or less to graduate degrees plus prior experience. The American Bar Association (1970) and the National Advisory Commission (1973) standards call for a minimum educational requirement of a bachelor's degree for probation agents. The American Bar Association also suggests the need for postgraduate study and recommends uniform state standards for all probation officers. The American Correctional Association (1977) also stresses the value of undergraduate and graduate degrees. Furthermore, it is generally accepted by criminal justice planners, administrators, and educators that a university graduate is more capable and competent as a probation or parole officer (Carter & Wilkins, 1976; Newman, 1971). It is this writer's belief that social work education offers the best preparation for work in probation and parole settings. It should be noted, however, that there is little empirical research to demonstrate what type of preservice training is most effective in enhancing the overall performance of probation and parole officers (Eskridge, 1979). More research needs to be done in this area.

In the selection of probation and parole officers, a number of merit systems and agencies use some form of written examinations

(Newman, 1971). Some systems require the utilization of mass produced employment tests. Because of problems entailed when such tests are used in the selection process, every effort should be made by the administrator to conduct personal evaluations of potential staff (Cunniff, 1968). Usually the administrator of the probation or parole agency participates in some phase of the selection process. If a subordinate administrator is to serve as immediate supervisor of the individual being selected, however, this supervisor should also participate in the selection process.

The staffing function also includes the provision of in-service training, and there are two types. The first type, orientation training, should be provided as soon as possible after the employee is hired. This training for the probation or parole agent generally includes a combination of classroom and on-the-job training. In training new employees, many probation and parole agencies are now making greater use of technical aids such as projecters, tape recorders, television, and professional films. Regardless of the type of orientation training offered, it is essential that it cover five important areas: the goals of the agency, the policies of the agency, the organizational structure, the objectives that the agent being trained is to accomplish, and the roles to be performed by the agent.

The second type of in-service training is developmental training. This type of training tends to concentrate on the development of specialized treatment modalities or case supervision skills. In probation and parole agencies, this training is usually conducted by the immediate supervisor. Several methods may be used. First, if several people are to be trained and the training involves dissemination of concepts and details for the first time, the lecture may be the most effective method. Second, when the training is concerned with common problems experienced by agents, such as how to deal with certain types of clients, the group conference may be the most appropriate method. Third, simulation and role playing are effective methods of helping agents develop treatment skills. Fourth, individual conferences involving personal instruction and guidance are helpful in enabling the agent to develop knowledge and skills through solving real-life problems. Fifth, in those probation or parole agencies having specialized tasks, such as investigation and supervision, job rotation may be used to enable the agent to learn more about the agency's overall structure and functioning (Eckles, Carmichael, & Sarchet, 1974).

The third element of staffing is appraisal, which is a formal rating of how well the employee has handled job duties during a given period of time. Performance appraisals have three purposes: to determine the agent's job competence, assess his/her need for further training and development, and help determine compensation and promotion decisions. Given these purposes, performance appraisal should be regarded as an ongoing process. That is, although the formal evaluation must be completed at prescribed intervals, the administrator should let the agent know how s/he is performing on a day-to-day basis through supervisory conferences. In this manner, the results of the formal evaluation entail no surprises.

The type of evaluation often used in probation and parole agencies, as in most social agencies, is the "trait appraisal." Trait-rating evaluation systems generally include several items related to personal characteristics such as leadership, industry, or judgment, as well as several work oriented characteristics such as job knowledge, casework skills, or performance of tasks on time. This type of evaluation is highly problematic in that the items are very subjective, the criteria are nebulous, the items may have little to do with the probation agent's actual performance, and because of the foregoing problems, administrators often tend to rate employees too positively (Koontz & O'Donnell, 1976).

A better tool for probation and parole administrators to use in appraising agents and other employees is a system of evaluating performance in terms of the individual's accomplishment of verifiable objectives. As noted earlier, clear objectives should be established for the agency and specific objectives should be defined for each employee based on the agency's objectives. These objectives should be made clear to the agent during the orientation phase, work should be structured around these, and the performance appraisal should be in terms of the agent's attainment of these objectives (Latta & Cocks, 1975). In establishing specific objectives for the probation agent, the administrator should involve the agent in the process. This involvement not only helps the agent understand what is expected but serves as a motivating factor. The development of individual objectives is clearly illustrated in the Management by Objectives system, although such objectives can be developed when other systems of management are used (McConkie, 1975).

Case Example: Staffing Function

In reviewing his staffing policies and determining needs, Mark found that a bachelor's degree in "criminal justice or a human services field" had been a requirement of the central office for six years. All members of the current staff met this requirement, but their backgrounds varied and included the fields of criminal justice, social work, sociology, psychology, education, and religion. Their previous employment had included law enforcement, teaching, social work in public agencies, and the ministry. Several agents had been hired upon graduation from a BSW program and had no previous experience.

Given this variety of backgrounds, Mark felt it would be helpful for the staff to consider together the philosophical issue on which they seemed to be in greatest disagreement—the control/treatment dilemma. He decided an in-service training program was needed for this purpose. He set up four one-day sessions and brought in consultants from the academic setting to guide the sessions. In addition to leading discussions on these issues, the consultants employed role playing, small group simulations, and values clarification exercises help the agents examine their beliefs, values, and practice orientations.

After these initial sessions, Mark held monthly follow-up sessions. These were more informal and focused on particular problem situations of clients served by the agency. Mark or one of the immediate supervisors led these sessions. Based on the material used in the initial and follow-up sessions, Mark developed an initial orientation and training program to be used for future training of new agents.

After their appointment, the intermediate supervisors were sent to a three-day training session on the fundamentals of staff supervision. This session was sponsored by the state central office. A supervisor orientation manual was also developed by the intermediate supervisors for future use.

Staff evaluation became Mark's next area of concern. Because of state policy, he had to continue using the evaluation forms already available, but he made changes in the procedure. Mark instituted an additional evaluation system whereby each agent was rated according to his achievement of specific objectives that he helped set. These individual objectives, it will be recalled, related to the goals and objectives that were developed for the agency. The intermediate supervisors were given the task of evaluating the agents under their direction. Since the supervisors met with their agents on a regular basis, the completion of periodic evaluation forms simply formalized what each supervisor and individual agent already knew about the agent's job performance.

DIRECTING AND LEADING

The fourth function of administrators of probation and parole agencies is that of directing and leading the agency employees. Directing and leading are the interpersonal aspects of managing by which employees are helped to understand and contribute effectively and efficiently to the attainment of the agency objectives. This function has to do with establishing the proper relationship with employees, communicating effectively with them, supervising them appropriately, motivating them, and helping them work towards the achievement of the agency's objectives. Administrators with graduate training in social work generally have a good grasp of this function.

It is probable that the administrator of a probation and parole agency will relate to employees on the basis of his/her assumptions about human nature and behavior. Douglas McGregor (1960) identified two opposite orientations of administrators based on their assumptions about human beings. Theory X managers assume that people have an inherent dislike for work; they must be coerced, controlled, directed, and threatened to get them to pursue organizational goals; and the average person prefers to be directed, wishes to avoid responsibility, has little ambition, and wants security above all. Sigurdson et al. (1973) contend that most probation agencies operate according to these suppositions; for example, the emphasis on maintaining tight schedules, the importance of documentation of one's work, and the insistence on conforming to agency regulations are evidences of a Theory X orientation.

Sigurdson and his associates emphasize that the administrator of a probation or parole agency should strive for a Theory Y approach to management (1973). According to McGregor, an administrator with a Theory Y orientation assumes that physical and mental work is as natural as play or rest; people are self-directed and will strive to achieve objectives to which they are committed; people not only accept but seek responsibility; and most people have high degrees of imagination, ingenuity, and creativity which they will use to solve organizational problems if given the opportunity. The administrator with this orientation will seek to maximize human growth and development and will do so by creating an organizational environment in which individuals realize that they can achieve their own goals by directing their efforts toward the achievement of the organizational goals. Sigurdson and his associates state that in a model probation department a Theory Y orientation to management should prevail; for example, open communication should occur at all levels, the administrator should involve staff in decision-making insofar as possible, individuals should be involved in setting their work objectives and in evaluating their effectiveness, and a client orientation rather than a bureaucratic orientation should be encouraged (1973).

There has been substantial research in social work and other disciplines to support the relationship between the administrator's supervisory style and the response on the part of the persons supervised. It has been well documented that an autocratic style of leadership results in poor morale and, generally, inefficient work among employees. Furthermore, the *laissez-faire* type leadership produces frustration among employees, poor commitment to organizational goals, and poor quality work. The democratic style of leadership, on the other hand, typically results in more effective and efficient work performance and greater job satisfaction among employees (Austin, 1981; Odiorne, 1970). While these findings generally apply to most organizations, the administrator of a probation or parole agency should realize that different situations call for different types of leadership; for example, it may be necessary for the administrator to assume more of an autocratic style in supervising some agents, whereas other agents may function better under a *laissez-faire* type of leadership. Furthermore, a situation in which a large number of presentence reports must be completed in a short period of time may call for a rather autocratic style on the part of the administrator.

In carrying out the function of directing and leading, the administrator of a probation and parole agency needs to give attention to those factors that produce the greatest motivation among employees. The best known research on this topic is that of Herzberg (1968).

Herzberg made a distinction between two types of factors related to motivation. The first group of factors, called "maintenance" or "hygiene" factors, includes such things as agency policy and administration, supervision, working conditions, interpersonal relations, salary, status, and job security. Herzberg found that the presence of these factors will not motivate people in an organization; yet they must be present or dissatisfaction will arise. The second group of factors, called "motivators," all relate to job content and include such things as achievement, recognition, challenging work, advancement, and growth on the job. Their existence will yield feelings of satisfaction, and they are, therefore, real motivators.

Since probation and parole agencies are public organizations, the administrator may have little control over some of the "maintenance" factors. However, through the appropriate leadership style, s/he can see to it that many of the true "motivators" are present in the agency; for example, the administrator can recognize the accomplishments and achievements of probation agents or other staff, or job rotation can be used in agencies having specialized functions in order to present agents with the challenge of learning new tasks. Finally, giving the probation agent increased responsibility as a result of demonstrated competence can be a successful technique for motivating (Smith & Berlin, 1976).

Case Example: Directing and Leading Function

Mark approached his leadership role with a goal of obtaining maximum staff input in decision-making. He had involved staff in the beginning during the development of the agency's goals and objectives, its policy manual, and its organizational structure because he believed staff would be more supportive of any plan they had helped create. He continued this practice by submitting drafts of major intra-agency policies to his supervisors and instructing them to review these with all agents for comments prior to finalization.

Mark held weekly meetings with his supervisors to discuss progress and problems. These supervisors then met with their staff members to report on the administrative meeting. Mark met with the total staff once a month.

Mark also saw the value in providing staff with opportunities to associate with their peers from other agencies. He believed such meetings stimulated ideas about how others in the field dealt with problems and made improvements in agencies. Furthermore, the break in the routine could help reduce tensions created by the job. Within budgetary limitations, he tried to create as many opportunities as possible for supervisors and agents to attend conferences and other workshops. He tried to ensure that all agents were provided these opportunities for continuing education.

Another technique Mark implemented within a few months after coming to the agency proved to be particularly useful in motivating staff. He initiated agent-led seminars on a bimonthly basis. Agents selected to conduct the seminars were chosen on the basis of demonstrated excellence in a particular area such as report writing or working with drug abusers. This approach not only stimulated other agents to revise their own methods and develop new skills but it also served as a reward of recognition for those who excelled in a given area.

CONTROLLING

The final function of probation and parole administrators is that of controlling, which is the measurement and correction of the performance of activities by subordinates in order to make sure that the agency's objectives and the plans devised to attain them are being accomplished. In order for this function to be performed, it is necessary that the probation or parole agency have clearly stated objectives and a data system that can measure the effectiveness of various probation service components. Unfortunately, these two prerequisites have traditionally been absent in probation and parole departments, as is true for most social service organizations.

Several events have occurred during recent years, however, which have caused probation and parole administrators to give more serious attention to the function of control. First, the growth of the criminal justice system in general and the consequent operational problems have caused public attention to be focused upon the structure and functioning of the system's components, including probation and parole services. Second, the increased general emphasis on accountability of all public agencies during the past decade has created public scrutiny of probation and parole agencies. Third, the lack of demonstrated success of all components of the criminal justice system has caused administrators to look for more effective and efficient treatment programs and better means of measuring effectiveness and efficiency. Finally, the growing utilization of computerization has facilitated the establishment of management information systems in all areas of human services, including probation and parole, and such systems make control more feasible. That is, these management information systems enable the administrator to gather client information in order to monitor, evaluate, and ultimately improve client services (Fein, 1974; Hoshino & McDonald, 1975; Raymond, 1981; Young, 1974).

In order for the administrator of a probation or parole agency to carry out the control function, it is necessary that the agency's objectives are clearly identified. These objectives should be as specific and quantitative (and hence measureable and verifiable) as is possible. Thus, it is not adequate for the agency to express objectives in terms such as "to rehabilitate individuals who are placed on parole." Instead, objectives must be stated in terms such as "to reduce by 10 percent the number of parolees returned to confinement within the next twelve months" (McConkie, 1975). As stated earlier in this chapter, the planning function of the administrator should involve the development of objectives such as these.

In performing the control function, the administrator of a probation or parole agency must have sufficient flexibility to develop an organizational structure that has the greatest potential for achieving the stated objectives of the agency. That is, the administrator should be able to create the necessary work units, develop appropriate policies and procedures, and design and implement programs aimed at the achievement of the agency's objectives. As stated earlier in this chapter, this effort comprises the organizing function of the administrator. Unfortunately, factors such as staff size, caseload size, and legal mandates occasionally militate against the creation of an organization that can fulfill the agency's objectives in an optimum manner. Nonetheless, operating within these constraints, the administrator must seek to achieve maximum agency effectiveness and efficiency through designing the program structure and continually modifying it as needed based on feedback concerned with the degree of achievement of agency objectives.

Finally, then, in order for the control function to be carried out, the administrator of the probation and parole agency must design some type of information system that can provide accurate, detailed data that can be rapidly procured and is specifically related to decision-making requirements, planning requirements, and measurement of agency objectives. There are two basic models for information systems for social agencies: administrative management information systems and caseload management systems. Administrative management information systems serve three functions: to control and coordinate employee behavior, provide information for long-term planning, and provide information to external groups. Systems of this type have the capability of generating point in time reports, period in time reports, and notification reports that are automatically initiated by conditions that vary from previously established standards (Allen, Carlson, & Parks, 1979; Coffey, 1974). Caseload management information systems utilize information for line level decision-making. The functions of this type of information system are to control client behavior, provide information for individual agent planning, and provide information for management use (Allen, Carlson, & Parks, 1979).

The probation and parole administrator can utilize a comprehensive information system in order to determine what the agency is doing that is effective for selective offenders, ascertain what the agency is doing that is not effective for selective offenders, and identify areas in which changes might be made to increase the overall performance of the agency. It is possible through computer technology to construct a mathematical model of a probation agency. Such a model can be used to analyze a wide variety of program possibilities and conduct "experiments" where real-life experimentation is not feasible (Austin, 1981; Sigurdson, McEachern, & Carter, 1973; Raymond, 1978). Computer technology also makes it possible to conduct cost/benefit analyses to evaluate existing program components in terms of efficiency or the relative costs involved in achieving program objectives through alternative approaches (Nelson, 1975; Raymond, 1981). During recent years, computers have been increasingly used by social agencies for all of these purposes.

In addition to the monitoring of programs and program components to ensure agency effectiveness, the control function of administrators includes the ongoing assessment of the performance of individual staff members. At this level, also, effectiveness is measured in terms of the attainment of stated objectives. If the probation or parole administrator has established with each probation agent clear and measurable individual objectives that grow out of and support the agency and program objectives, the evaluation of each individual's effectiveness will be a part of the total system evaluation. Consequently, during the process of performance appraisal the probation agents can see clearly how their roles fit into the overall agency structure and how their performance contributes to the general success of the agency.

Case Example: Controlling Function

The weekly meetings between Mark and his supervisory staff were spent in part on reporting and assessing each unit's progress on agency objectives and discussing problems therein. In addition, Mark met with individual units as needed to address problems and explore alternatives.

Supervisory reports generally included a statistical breakdown of number of clients contacted, categories of services provided, and hours spent per client during the week. These data were compiled and submitted to the central office on a quarterly basis and analyzed by Mark and the supervisors in relation to the goals and objectives that had been established for the agency; for example, at the end of six months, Mark reviewed the report on staff hours and realized most agents were having to work a good deal of overtime to complete all of their presentence investigations. This was partially due to their attempts to meet the objective of preparing complete presentence investigation reports on all referrals within two weeks. Given the fact that each agent was preparing an average of four presentence reports each week, it became obvious that the objective was unrealistic. Accordingly, it was decided that rather than preparing complete presentence reports on all cases, partial reports would be developed for appropriate clients based on certain criteria. This plan proved to be more effective.

After a six-month period, it was also determined that supervisors and their agents were spending relatively too much time discussing individual cases. A decision was made to initiate client staffings as a means of dealing with client problem situations in a way that could be educational for all agents. Each supervisor began to meet with the agents under his supervision twice monthly. During staffings, agents would review selected cases relative to plans of action developed by the agent, tasks undertaken with the client, and problems encountered. In addition to being an effective means of problem-solving and staff development, this process also helped Mark and the supervisors assess the abilities of the agents.

Case Example: Conclusion

At the end of the first twelve months, Mark and his staff had sufficient data to develop a five year plan and document to the central office the need for additional staff to conduct the work of the agency. The recidivism rate had been lowered by 3 percent and public criticism of the agency had virtually ceased. The community advisory board had proven to be particularly helpful in achieving "good press" for the agency, developing job placement sources for clients, and securing the assistance of civic and religious groups when needed. Mark had lost five staff members during the year — two obtained other jobs, one returned to school, and two left due to dissatisfaction with the changes. The operation appeared to be running smoothly, and a positive working atmosphere prevailed. While Mark had not achieved all he had hoped and a number of problems still existed, his sound management practices had obviously produced many positive results.

CONCLUSION

This chapter has considered the role of the probation or parole administrator from an operational perspective. That is, attention has been focused on the major managerial functions are performed by probation and parole administrators. These functions include planning, organizing, staffing, directing and leading, and controlling.

These five managerial functions are performed by administrators at all levels in probation and parole agencies, just as they are carried out by administrators at various levels in any type of social agency or other agency. The degree to which each function is performed by probation and parole administrators may vary, of course, from one managerial level to another. Furthermore, the degree to which these functions are carried out may vary from agency to agency. Regardless of the statutory, judicial, or other conditions affecting the operation of the probation and parole agency, however, agency administrators inevitably perform all of these functions.

It is obvious that the five managerial functions discussed in this chapter are interrelated. Sound planning, including the establishment of clear objectives, is necessary in order for the probation and parole administrator to know what kind of organization is necessary to achieve the objectives. The establishment of objectives and the development of an organizational structure helps the administrator know what kind of people will have to be hired, what type of training they will need, and how they will be evaluated. The probation or parole agency's objectives, the organizational structure, and the people hired will affect the kind of leadership and direction provided by the administrator. Standards of control can be established only after measurable objectives have been planned, and the administrator can keep the agency goal-directed through changes in the organizational structure, changes in personnel, and changes in methods of leadership and directing.

It is understandable that the managerial functions performed by the probation and parole administrator would intermesh in this manner. The tasks of the administrator of a social agency are never discrete, and any actions in one area of work inevitably affect other areas. Thus, the administrator does not typically perform the functions of planning, organizing, staffing, directing and leading, and controlling in a sequential fashion. Rather, these functions are carried out simultaneously in the day-to-day work of the administrator. A sound knowledge of these managerial functions and an awareness of how they interrelate will enhance the administrator's performance of the challenging job of managing a probation or parole agency.

REFERENCES

Allen, H. E., Carlson, E. W., & Parks, E. C. *Critical issues in adult probation.* Washington, D.C.: U.S. Government Printing Office, September 1979.

American Bar Association. *Standards relating to probation.* New York: American Bar Association, Project on Standards for Criminal Justice, 1970.

American Correction Association. *Manual of standards for adult probation and parole field services.* College Park, Md.: American Correctional Association, 1977.

Amos, W. E., & Newman, C. L. (Eds.). *Parole.* New York: Federal Legal Publications, Inc., 1975.

Austin, M. J. *Supervisory management for the human services.* Englewood Cliffs: Prentice-Hall, Inc., 1981.

Bennett, L. A. Should we change the offender or the system. *Crime and Delinquency,* July 1973, pp. 332–342.

Carter, R. M., & Wilkins, L. T. (Eds.). Caseloads: some conceptual models. *Probation and parole* (2nd ed.). New York: John Wiley and Sons, Inc., 1976.

Clegg, R. K. *Probation and parole.* Springfield: Charles C Thomas, 1970.

Coffey, A. R. *Administration of criminal justice.* Englewood Cliffs: Prentice-Hall, Inc., 1974.

Cohn. A. W. The failure of correctional management. *Crime and Delinquency*, July 1973, pp. 323–331.

Cunniff. J. Employment tests deprive business of good workers. *Reporter Dispatch*. 1968. *52* (18), 18.

Czajkoski. E. H. Functional specialization in probation and parole. *Crime and Delinquency*, April 1969. p. 238.

Eckles. R. W., Carmichael. R. L., & Sarchet. B. R. *Essentials of management for first-line supervision*. New York: John Wiley & Sons, Inc.. 1974.

Eskridge. C. W. Education and training of probation officers: a critical assessment. *Federal Probation*, 1979, *43* (3), 41–48.

Fein. E. A data system for an agency. *Social Casework*, 1974, 20 (1).

Herzberg. F. One more time: how do you motivate employees. *Harvard Business Review*, 1968, *46* (1).

Hoshino, G. & McDonald, T. P. Agencies in the computer age. *Social Work*, 1975, *20* (1).

Killinger. G. C., Kerper, H. B., & Cromwell, P. F., Jr. *Probation and parole in the criminal justice system*. St. Paul: West Publishing Co., 1976.

Koontz. H. *Appraising managers as managers*. New York: McGraw-Hill, 1971.

Koontz. H. & O'Donnell, C. *Management: a systems and contingency analysis of managerial functions* (6th ed.). New York: McGraw-Hill. 1976.

Latessa. E., Parks, E., Allen, H. E., & Carlson, E. Specialized supervision in probation: implications, research, and issues. *The Prison Journal*, 1979, *59* (2), 27–35.

Latta. R. M. & Cocks, J. Management strategies for federal probation officers in metropolitan areas. *Federal Probation*, 1975, *39* (3), 10–17.

Martinson, R. What works—questions and answers about prison reform. *Public Interest*, September 1974, pp. 22–54.

McConkie. M. L. *Management by objectives: a corrections perspective*. Washington. D.C.: U.S. Government Printing Office, 1975.

McGregor, D. *The human side of enterprise*. New York: McGraw Hill, 1960.

National Advisory Commission on Criminal Justice Standards and Goals. *Corrections*. Washington, D.C.: U.S. Government Printing Office, 1973.

Nelson, C. W. Cost-benefit analysis and alternatives to incarceration. *Federal Probation*, 1975, *39*, 43.

Newman, C. L. *Personnel practices in adult parole systems*. Springfield: Charles C Thomas, 1971.

Odiorne. G. S. *Training by objectives*. London: Macmillan Publishing Co., Inc., 1970.

Raymond. F. B. Program evaluation. In R. M. Grennel, Jr., *Social Work Research and Evaluation*. Itasca: F. E. Peacock Publishers, Inc., 1981.

Raymond. F. B. The cybernetic model as a means to accountability: an agency example. *Arete*, 1978, *5* (1), 23–35.

Raymond, F. B. To punish or to treat. *Social Work*, 1974, *19* (3), 305–311.

Sigurdson. H. R.. McEachern. A. W.. & Carter, R. M. Administrative innovations in probation service: a design for increasing effectiveness. *Crime and Delinquency*. 1973. *19* (3). 353–366.

Smith. A. B., & Berlin. L. *Introduction to Probation and Parole*. St. Paul: West Publishing Co.. 1976.

Taylor, F. *Scientific management*. New York: Harper & Brothers, 1947.
Young, D. W. Management information systems in child care: an agency experience. *Child Welfare*, 1974, *53* (2).

Chapter 13

SOCIAL WORK AND CRIMINAL JUSTICE: NEW DIMENSIONS IN PRACTICE*

GLORIA CUNNINGHAM

At a workshop several years ago a respected colleague with over 40 years of practice in the field of juvenile justice confided to the rest of the participants that among the benefits of becoming a senior citizen was knowing what "new" approaches were worth getting excited about and which were simply old ideas being rediscovered by a new generation. There is, indeed, a depressing regularity about the cyclical quality of alternating philosophies of rehabilitation and control in criminal justice as succeeding generations of helping professionals become disenchanted with one approach or another having failed to take into consideration the inherent vulnerability of any argument concerning something as poorly understood as human behavior. In frustration we are inclined to look for someone or something to blame for our failure to predict with accuracy how thousands of unique individuals in unique environments will respond to our helping effort. Sometimes we blame the clients and declare them "untreatable." We blame our theoretical forebearers; Freud, Skinner, or Mary Richmond or our methodologies. Most often we blame one another for not having all the right answers, and our professional name-calling makes us vulnerable to attacks by others, especially in the light of the escalating competition for dwindling funding resources. Frequently concern for the client and the community get lost in the midst of these polemical discussions and everyone is the loser. It would be a genuine mark of professional maturity if criminal justice practitioners could acknowledge openly what we know to be the truth; that people can be helped in a variety of ways, that no one

*From *Federal Probation*, 1980 44(1), 64–69. Reprinted with the permission of the publisher.

approach will work with everyone, nor will any one approach work with the same person every time.

For some time now direct counseling efforts have been the methodological scapegoats in criminal justice for their failure to deliver what they promised 20 or 30 years ago in terms of altering the course of criminal careers. There is no question that social workers and other mental health practitioners naively promised too much, but the claims that casework is a "dead-end" as far as criminal justice is concerned or that psychotherapy in general is "ineffective" can be challenged. Some of the points to be made in this article are: First, that arguments about effectiveness are sometimes political and not accurate reflections of the services being offered; second, that some of the problems we experienced in applying counseling techniques to criminal justice clients were the result of narrow and unselective application of treatment models which did not take into consideration the profound treatment significance of many of the routine interventions of probation officers; and finally to make the point that counseling approaches with individuals and families have not remained static but have evolved in ways which make them more relevant to a wider range of clientele. There is much in these contemporary approaches to social treatment that is consistent with evolving views of community-based corrections.

HOW EFFECTIVE ARE EFFECTIVENESS STUDIES?

Most of the claims for the ineffectiveness of psychotherapy and one-to-one counseling originated in Esynick's studies published in 1959 and 1965. Esynick's pronouncements about the ineffectiveness of conventional psychotherapy have assumed the status of the graven tablets of Moses in spite of the fact that Esynick has been challenged on the basis of his methodology, his scholarship and his conclusions. For example, Esynick's first report was based on only four studies of psychotherapy when 30 were available, many of which indicated effectiveness (Meltzoff and Kornreich, 1970, p. 973). By 1964 there had been at least 70 control studies on the effects of psychotherapy, but again Esynick's 1965 conclusions were based on a small unrepresentative example of the available evidence. Meltzoff and Kornreich comment, "the widespread myth that controlled, evaluative studies have not been done has been passed along to those of us who relied upon Esynick's reviews but did not ourselves examine the literature in depth. It had become almost customary for researchers and reviewers alike to introduce their papers with the erroneous observation that few studies on the effectiveness of psychotherapy exist" (Meltzoff and Kornreich, 1970, p. 74).

Meltzoff and Kornreich conducted their own review of 101 studies on the effectiveness of psychotherapy. They concluded on the basis of their review that the weight of experimental evidence is sufficient to enable them to reject the null hypothesis that psychotherapy is ineffective. Far more often than not, psychotherapy of a wide variety of types and with a broad range of disorders has been demonstrated under controlled conditions to be accompanied by positive changes in adjustment that significantly exceed those that can be accounted for by the passage of time alone. In addition they found that the more carefully controlled the study, that is, the more sophisticated the research methodology, the more likely the study was to demonstrate the effectiveness of psychotherapy (Meltzoff and Kornreich, 1970, p. 100).

It is important at this point to make clear that this is not an argument for psychotherapy or intensive treatment of all criminal justice clients, nor is it a denial of the fact that treatment often is ineffective and even destructive. The point is being made that the polemical discussions about what approach to helping works or does not work are often waged without any serious consideration into the validity of the arguments or the actual relevance of the method to the clients involved. Academic careers are often built on the basis of such publicized debates. Academic institutions and other service organizations are frequently dependent financially on the grant research money, and the eventual findings of the research are often immaterial. The politics of funding are such that the funding resources are much more anxious to make money available to constituencies with more clout than helping professionals have, and to claim that a particular group "has failed to demonstrate their effectiveness" is a handy excuse, valid or not, to redistribute the funds in other ways. Wilks and Martinson refer to the way in which findings of their study on the effectiveness of incarceration were used to support arguments for mandatory sentencing in spite of their findings that offenders placed on probation almost inevitably perform better relative to recidivism than do those of similar background and criminal history who are placed in prison (Wilks and Martinson, 1976, p. 3).

We are also becoming more aware of the fact that many of the effectiveness studies reflected not so much the ineffectiveness of casework or psychotherapy as it did the ineffectiveness of the research methodology to measure such variables. There are many areas of specialization within research, and researchers trained in survey, evaluation, and other forms of research dealing with aggregate data are often not knowledgeable about some of the special problems involved in conducting research on clinical treatment models.

UNDERSTANDING "REAL TREATMENT"

In the past, "treatment" of the criminal offender tended to be viewed undimensionally with little recognition of the reality that no one model will be equally relevant to all types of correctional clients. In addition, the nature of criminal justice practice is such that we are often involved in long-term relationships with our clients and that unique adaptations of existing models must be made in order to accommodate to this fact and other realities of correctional practice. For example, long-term or intensive clinically oriented treatment may be relevant to a relatively small portion of offenders. It may be most relevant early in our contact with them or at points of crisis, but we know from experience that long-term intensive clinically oriented counseling geared toward personality restructuring is neither relevant nor necessary with the *majority* of our clients. By the same token, although we can derive much that is useful from short-term treatment models, the nature of our extended relationship with probationers and parolees means certain adaptations must be made in short-term treatment models.

An unfortunate side effect of a too narrow view of "treatment" is the fact that probation officers are prevented from recognizing the value of what they do, those tasks that are not included within more traditional definitions of counseling or therapy. Narrow methodological adherence promotes the idea that anything less than long-term, intensive counseling oriented to achieve personality restructuring is second best or "band-aid" help. Because this clinical model was upheld as a *sine qua non* of professional practice, we do not value the important, significant and highly skilled work we do with people in other ways. We depreciate our high level performance in the difficult tasks of working effectively with a client's environment to promote a more receptive milieu that helps modify destructive behavior. We are led to believe that anything short-term, reality oriented, or concerned with concrete services and environmental intervention is somehow not "real treatment." It is important to understand that "real treatment" is a status game that professionals play with one another. It has very little to do with actual, significant help to people in need. Real treatment can be understood as any kind of purposeful intervention rendered within the context of an ethically bound professional relationship and directed toward aiding the client in easing some problematic aspect of his or her functioning. The "realness" of the treatment should not be based on the extent to which it adheres to a particular theoretical framework or how much other professionals are impressed by the technique. A more rational basis for evaluation is in terms of the extent to which it is appropriate to the client and the particular case situation. Is it meeting some real need? Is it likely to produce some real change in the situation for the better? Can the client and other people involved make some real use of the help you are offering?

Some of the narrower treatment methodologies assumed that the individual client was inevitably the target of change. Whether or not one talked in terms of short-term or long-term treatments or intensive or nonintensive psychotherapy the basic assumption was the person who needed changing was the client. Practice wisdom tells us that this is not always the case. Sometimes the most realistic target for change is a significant person in the client's environment. Sometimes it is the family system or the larger society which has denied resources and opportunities to the client to fulfill necessary role expectations. Sometimes it is, indeed, the client who must change, but our knowledge of the situation tells us that change can be induced more readily if changes in other systems occur first. The relevance of this point is that the adjustment of the individual can be enhanced by intervention in a variety of ways, and that no one single technique is necessarily more likely than another to produce more positive social functioning. Periodic interviews with a client's wife may be much more effective than long-term intensive interviews with the client himself. Using your clout to relieve a client of a dunning creditor may be more significant than helping the client ventilate his anger and rage over the experience. We are not talking in either/or terms. We are saying that no technique is inherently better than any other technique, or is a more "real" form of treatment, and that the final decision rests on the basis of the professional judgment of the practitioner who bases his decision in turn on an indepth knowledge of the client, his situation, and the interventive alternatives available. Many probation officers have conducted their practice in this way for many years, and for them there is nothing new in such a point of view. What may be new is the acknowledgement that this represents the highest form of professional service, one which involves a myriad assortment of skills, knowledge and expertise.

SOCIAL WORK INSIGHT FOR CRIMINAL JUSTICE

In spite of the scapegoating role social work has assumed in recent years it still has much to offer the criminal justice practitioner and client including the broadened perspective on direct treatment outlined above. Some of these insights represent discoveries of old truths rather than new knowledge. Application of new concepts arising from systems theory has helped social work clarify the significance and implications of its long-term traditional focus on the "person-in-the-environment" and the nature of the interaction between the two, a focus, incidentally, particularly relevant to criminal justice practice. Social workers are also developing techniques of assessment and intervention focused on current functioning and ongoing social interaction rather than on psychosexual and early childhood development. They are redefining their professional activity in terms of the multiple forms of activities they perform with a wide range of clients in many different types of service settings, activities which include but which are in no way limited to direct counseling with individuals around psychological and personality problems. A typical listing of such role behaviors includes professional tasks involving advocacy and brokerage functions in addition to those of therapist, counselor, and teacher.

The role of the advocate is a familiar one to probation officers, and it is likely that the advocate role is assumed more frequently in behalf of a client outside of rather than in the courtroom. Probation officers must frequently act as an advocate with employers, with family and neighbors, with public welfare agencies, or investigative agents, "pleading the cause" for clients who lack the skill, opportunity or the influence to do so for themselves. Advocacy assumes a broad and sophisticated attitude toward assessment or "diagnosis" that recognizes from the outset that some of the options for bringing about change in a situation lie in the environmental systems impinging on the client. It further assumes a complicated array of skills and knowledge in dealing with many different kinds of individuals, groups and organizations in ways that will enhance rather than alienate their interaction with the probationer.

Brokerage functions are also familiar to probation staff and there is one school of thought that suggests this is the only real function probation officers should render, the linking up of the client with community based agencies that can do the therapy, the counseling, the employment placement, and all the other types of services probationers and parolees need. The experienced practitioner knows that this is a very involved and time-consuming function, one which requires much more than developing a list of agency names and telephone numbers which can be handed over to the client. If this is all there was to it a part-time clerk could do the job. *Effective* brokerage services mean knowing both the client and the community resources very well. It means constant surveillance of these resources to keep up-to-date on policy and personnel changes, shifts in service philosophy, special programs, and how individual staff are going to receive and follow through with the correctional client. It often means a massive education task with community resources to preclude their overt or passive rejection of clients simply on the basis of their being offenders (and therefore psychopaths and therefore untreatable). Effective brokering also requires a sensitive awareness of the particular stresses and strains the client and family may be experiencing relative to a referral to another resource, and the skill to use this understanding to maximize the chances that the referral will "take." Finally, it means sticking with the client to see what does happen and if a first referral falls apart, to hang in there until the need is met in some way. This is a valuable service, indeed, but whether it is the only one that probation officers should offer seems unrealistic given the practice reality.

By using some of the skills mentioned above, the probation officer can greatly increase the probability that the client will receive needed services from those community based resources best equipped to provide them, and this is a most efficient use of everyone's time and money. The reality is, however, that there are many communities lacking the needed resources. If the resources exist they may be poorly run, inadequately staffed or funded, just generally incompetent or reluctant to include offenders in their client group. Even when adequate services exist the client may be unwilling or unable to make the best use of them. In those situations it is not acceptable to just throw up one's hands and give up. Probation officers have the responsibility to do what they can within the limits of their skill and what the client is willing to accept to remedy the situation in some way. If the local family service agency has a 3-month waiting list it is unrealistic to ignore the current marital pressures a client is experiencing if the probation officer has the skill to intervene in a situation to prevent it from escalating or to bring about some positive improvement. A timely, short-term intervention by a probation officer who has already developed a trust relationship and who has demonstrated consistent interest and concern may be far more potent than a new relationship with an unknown counselor no matter how skilled that person may be.

In addition we must keep in mind the significance of the probation and parole officer as a "teacher" or educator. Some of our clients come from backgrounds in which they had not had the opportunity to understand the expectations of normal role behavior. It is difficult for a young adult to perform adequately in the role of worker if no one in his family has ever been employed in a well-paying, steady, secure job for a long period of time. It is difficult for individuals who have themselves never experienced a stable family life or mature nonpunitive parenting to know what is required in the establishment of a marital relationship and the rearing of children. It is difficult for any individual to make a transition from an institutional life with its unique set of role behavior and interpersonal transactions to have to learn or relearn different modes of behavior in the free community.

A recent development in criminal justice which has confused practitioners as to their counseling role with clients has been the increasing emphasis on civil rights of offenders and some question as to whether or not we have the right to do anything other than provide control and surveillance. Clearly there are politics involved in that debate also, but as professionals there are certain ethical and value positions that must be explicated. Many of the abuses of clients' rights as far as "treatment" was concerned occurred because helping professionals assumed that all offender clients were psychiatrically disabled patients. It was assumed further that because of their offender status and the presumed threat to the larger community they were a captive clientele and could be subjected voluntarily or not to any effort on the part of helping professionals intended to "make them well" or protect the community. The fact is that being an offender is a legal definition and not a psychiatric diagnosis. The offender group is probably much more like the population as a whole than most people are willing to acknowledge, if self report studies of crime and delinquency are any indication. Our pragmatic experience tells us that those factors that determine when and how a person first becomes labelled as deviant and is processed through the criminal justice system have little or nothing to do with the innate psychological makeup of the individual involved.

But criminal justice clients are human beings and they function in a real and problematic world. They, like all of us, will have ongoing problems in social functioning. They experience the predictable traumas of adolescence, marriage, ill health, aging, and a range of other kinds of crises that occur in the life of most of us. In addition they will have to deal with other types of problems of interaction with their environment because they are probationers or parolees. We have the skills to enhance their ability to cope with these problems more effectively and to help moderate, relieve some of the stresses of the environment by intervening with family, employer, mental health or welfare agencies and other significant institutions as described above. We have the professional training, the experience and the skill to assist clients in more effective problem-solving generally, to direct them to more effective styles of living, and to provide linkages for them with resources in the community that can help them live more satisfying lives. To refuse to offer these services to offender clients in the name of their "civil rights" seems a very perverse, cynical and unrealistic view of the total situation.

We do have to be clear about rights' violations. We do not impose our helping efforts on someone who clearly sees no need, will not benefit or refuses to cooperate in these efforts. We do have a responsibility, however, to interpret to all clients the availability of such services, our skills in helping them to negotiate ordinary and extraordinary developmental or life stage problems, and our conviction, when it exists, that we can make a significant and positive impact on their lives by so doing. We have, in short, the right to "sell" our skills to clients. This does involve the conviction, however, that we do have an important function to perform, that rights will be protected in the process and that the services we have to offer are professional, effective and of real worth.

The message is that we have to develop an accurate perception of what probation and parole services have to offer offenders and their communities, and the skills to document and communicate these perceptions to one another, to clients, to administrators and to funding sources. How we define our services need not be methodologically respectable or "fashionable" as long as we render it responsibly with due recognition of client rights and assume as part of our professional responsibility our ongoing, unbiased and nonpolitical assessment of its effectiveness. It is often suggested that helping professionals avoid evaluations of effectiveness out of fear of having their inadequacies exposed; however, there is evidence to suggest that rational, well-designed studies may turn out to be our ace in the hole.

REFERENCES

Meltzoff, J. and Kornreich, M. *Research in Psychotherapy*. New York: Atherton Press, 1970, p. 973.

Wilks, J. and Martinson, R. "Is the Treatment of Criminal Offenders Really Necessary?," *Federal Probation*, 40:1, p. 3.

Chapter 14

SOCIAL WORK ETHICS
IN PROBATION AND PAROLE

ROBERT SCHEURELL

INTRODUCTION

A ll helping professions have developed a set of ethical principles that are to guide professional practice in working with people. Social work as a profession is not an exception (see National Association of Social Workers, Code of Ethics, 1979). Ethical principles in the helping professions are a reflection of the values of the broader society. In the United States, this is evident by the high premium placed on the values of individualization, uniqueness of the client, confidentiality, and self-determination, which are consistent with the larger values of American society.

Ethics in a helping profession are not general ideals to be "sought for," but should be internalized in the behavior of the helping professional. Many individuals have felt that professional ethics are esoteric statements of conduct, for which one is not really accountable. Yet, the professional is accountable to ethical standards morally and more recently legally. Until the 1960s, few courts would accept cases involving violations of professional ethics. Since 1960, the court system has accepted cases involving professional ethics such as *Tarasoff v Regents of the University of California*, 1974 (threat to a third party). The helping professions in the 1980s are expected to be operating from an ethical position, and the individual professional is to be held accountable. In the area of corrections, the question of ethics is becoming crucial, since the correctional system is under pressure from politicians, legislators, and the public. The correctional system is open to public scrutiny from these groups. Professional ethics, then, are no longer esoteric idealistic standards, but rather ground rules

241

of expected behavior for which the individual professional is to be held accountable.

GENERAL SOCIAL WORK ETHICS

In reviewing ethical concepts and their application in corrections, there are five general categories of concern: clients, colleagues, employer, broader community, and the Social Work Profession.

Some of the general ethical concerns in each of these categories are described as follows:

RELATIONSHIP TO CLIENTS. Some examples of ethical concerns in this category include acceptance of the individual, confidentiality, nonjudgementality, client priority, self-determination, competency, honesty and integrity, nonexploitation of clients, fair fee assessment (in payment situations), avoidance of conflicting personal relationships with clients, and nondiscriminatory behavior.

RELATIONSHIP TO COLLEAGUES. Some examples of ethical concerns in this category include not publicly maligning colleagues (respect, courtesy), knowing limitations (not accepting work one is unable to perform), confidentiality in colleague consultation, honesty and integrity, and pulling one's own weight in work load.

RELATIONSHIP TO EMPLOYER. Some examples of ethical concerns in this category include presenting agency in a positive light, supporting agency to meet social work goals, and adhering to legal and societal commitments of the agency.

RELATIONSHIP TO BROADER COMMUNITY. Some examples of ethical concerns in this category include promoting the general welfare of society, acting in a manner that would minimize or prevent discrimination, providing emergency public service, promoting changes in public policy and legislation, and participating in community affairs to inform the public on issues related to social welfare policy and encourage respect for diverse groups in society.

RELATIONSHIP TO THE SOCIAL WORK PROFESSION. Some examples of ethical concerns in this category include individual competence (know one's limitations), continuing education (professional and self-development), open representation of qualifications and areas of competence, distinguish between professional and personal viewpoints, personal (private) behavior is a reflection of professional behavior, and to make contributions to the advancement of the social work profession.

These general ethical concerns of social work are modified for various practice settings, such as education, physical health, mental health, and corrections. At times, some of these ethical concerns are in conflict with a practice setting, consistent with a practice setting, or indifferent to a practice setting. Because of the legalistic nature of corrections and the general obligation of "protection of society," conflicts between these ethical concerns and correctional practice is rather common.

APPLICABILITY OF SOCIAL WORK ETHICS TO CORRECTIONS

Corrections is a diverse system that includes jails, institutions, probation and parole, community facilities, and private agencies. The degree of potential conflict between ethical concerns and practice concerns will vary, depending upon which part of the correctional system one is describing; for example, in jails and institutions, potential conflict with the ethical value of client self-determination is more evident than in probation and parole, or private agencies. Conversely, in probation and parole, potential conflict with the ethical value of nonexploitation of the client or professional association is more evident than in jails and institutions, where the client is not seen outside working hours.[1]

Instead of attempting to describe potential conflicts between ethical concerns and correctional practice across the board, selected examples of social work ethics and potential conflict in corrections for each of the five categories of ethical concerns described above will be discussed.[2]

RELATIONSHIP TO CLIENTS. Some of the major areas in which potential conflicts emerge between ethical concerns and correctional practice are in client self-determination, confidentiality, and acceptance.

In corrections, the concept of *client self-determination* has a dual perspective: to what degree can the client self-determine behavior based upon his/her legal status, and what authority (legal and social) does the social worker have over the client? Client self-determination does not mean an absolute freedom of choice or

---

[1] In this discussion, the term agent refers to a probation/parole agent.

[2] Examples of the potential conflict between ethical concerns and correctional practice are drawn from the author's experience in working in Probation/Parole both as an agent and an assistant supervisor and from experiences of placing social work students in correctional settings at both the undergraduate and graduate level.

license to engage in any behavior one desires. Generally, the concept of client self-determination is limited by physical and mental capability, degree of rationality, perception of reality, moral and ethical codes, and in the corrections field by legal restrictions. Legal restrictions on behavior means the probation and parole agent or institutional social worker will set limits on client behavior or use "authority"; for example, an agent may set limits on a parolee's physical movement both in-state or on leaving the state. The agent finds out that a parolee has left the state on two occasions, the local community on two occasions, and has not notified the agent of these physical movements. Upon verification of the circumstances for which the parolee left the state or metropolitan area, the agent could recommend revocation of parole. In situation A, the parolee left the metropolitan community and the state to visit a sick mother-in-law with his wife. The agent was not notified of the parolee's leaving the metropolitan area or state, which is a technical violation of parole (in Wisconsin) and grounds for revocation. If investigation of the circumstances indicate that the parolee did visit a sick mother-in-law, the agent could recommend continuation of parole, provided the parolee was making a satisfactory adjustment. In situation B, the parolee and his wife left the metropolitan area and the state without the parole agent's consent and visited "unknown" friends. The issue becomes whether the parolee engaged in illegal behavior such as using drugs or carrying a firearm while in the other state. In this situation, the agent upon confirming that the parolee did use drugs and carry a firearm would recommend revocation of parole, especially if the parolee was making a marginal adjustment.

In corrections, the concept of *confidentiality* is limited by the broader objective of "protection of society." Confidentiality and privileged communication are not synonymous. Confidentiality refers to an ethical principle that mandates that discussions between a client in corrections and the social worker, discussions with other agency personnel, and records of the client are held in a confidential nature. This is different than privileged communication, which is the confidential nature of the client-worker relationship, which is sanctioned by law. In general, privileged communication involves four conditions: communication originates in confidence, communication is essential to maintain relationship, communication is essential to foster relationship, and communication nondisclosure is of greater benefit to society than disclosure. These four conditions are spelled out by John Wigmore in *Evidence in Trials at Common Law* (1961). Even where privileged communication between a client-worker exists, various state courts have tried cases where privileged communication was upheld and rejected (New York).

The social worker in corrections does not have privileged communication, consequently, numerous conflicts emerge around what is confidential and not confidential material. Corrections employees, as part of the criminal justice system, are obligated to report new offenses and suspected offenses to law enforcement officials when these are reported to an agent in a confidential manner. Two contrasting situations in the area of confidentiality are as follows. In situation A, a juvenile is with a group of teen-agers who take a joyride for five miles in a car. The car is returned with no damage and the group fills the gas tank so the owner doesn't notice. The specific parolee did not drive the car and did not break into the car. The owner never realizes his car was taken, yet the juvenile parolee admits this to his/her agent. If the juvenile is making a satisfactory adjustment, the agent would probably recommend continuance on parole since the danger to society seems to be limited. On the other hand, if the parolee admitted to driving the car or breaking into the car and is making a marginal adjustment, the agent would recommend revocation of parole. A recommendation of a parole revocation is based upon a parolee's overall unsatisfactory adjustment, and a joyride in a car with the active participation of the parolee in the offense is an indication of poor adjustment, in contrast to a temporary lapse of judgment in the previous situation. In either case the situation should be reported to appropriate authorities.

Situation B is a juvenile female, who has run away and admits that the reason for running away is her father. The father has been engaging in sexual relations with her (incest). The incest behavior has not previously been reported by the girl or her family. The agent in this situation has an obligation to break confidentiality ethics, since the father's behavior may result in other problems for the family or for the runaway juvenile female. In other words, a correctional client should be aware that confidentiality in a relationship is limited by the greater good of society. In questionable cases, the agent must also look at the implications of a decision on a specific client for the agency and the community at large. Confidentiality in a corrections setting is limited by the threat of a new offense (third party threats), commission of a new offense, and knowledge of a new offense (accessory to or a participant). Other examples of confidentiality could be used, such as use of records, peripheral information, and so on.

An ethical concern such as *client acceptance* at first glance seems to be easy to obtain. Yet, in corrections there are potential conflicts in this area. In some jurisdictions in probation and parole, female agents have male parolees and vice versa. In situation A, a young female agent has transvestites and prostitutes on her caseload. This specific agent is attempting to define and feel comfortable with her own sexual identification. The potential result could be explosive with the agent not accepting these clients and their behavior and could lead to identity and psychological problems for the agent. On the other hand, the female agent, may have a clear self-concept, with no problems of sexual identification. In this case, the agent could accept the clients and their behavior (not condoning the behavior), with no deleterious psychological or emotional result. The same situation could occur with a male agent.

In situation B, a young male worker has individuals with sexual problems on his caseload; for example, individuals who engage in bestiality (intercourse with animals), multiple incest, etc. If this agent has rigid perceptions of sexual behavior, the result could be nonacceptance of the client and outright hostility toward the client. On the other hand, one can have clear perceptions of acceptable sexual behavior and still accept the client, however not condoning the behavior. The same situation could occur with a female agent.

RELATIONSHIP TO COLLEAGUES. A potential area of conflict between ethical concerns and practice in corrections is *respect and courtesy for colleagues*. In the frustration of day-to-day working with people, individuals may become careless with whom and about whom one speaks; for example, an agent may be on friendly terms with a parolee who is supervised by another agent. The agent may discuss freely with the parolee his/her negative feelings about the parolee's agent or question the competency of the parolee's agent in front of the parolee. This type of behavior is clearly a violation of the ethical concern of treating colleagues with respect. This behavior also results in tension between the two agents, the parolee and his/her agent, and more than likely between the agent who has befriended the parolee and the parolee. Other examples of colleague relationships could be used such as maligning a person in public or only providing a supervisor with the facts of a situation he/she needs to know. This means stating the facts of a situation for a recommendation of continuation or discontinuation of probation or parole for an individual based upon biases and prejudices, instead of objectively reviewing a case.

RELATIONSHIP TO EMPLOYER. In corrections, the primary objective of the agency is "*protection of society*" (legally) and secondarily "rehabilitation of the client." The social worker, regardless of individual perspective of a client's behavior, is expected to maintain protection of society as a priority in making case decision; for example, if a seventeen-year-old male juvenile is drunk one night, takes a .22 caliber rifle, and begins to shoot toward cars driving on a freeway, the agent would have to make a judgment whether this behavior warrants revocation of parole. The agent could respond to the behavior by a *moralist approach* arguing for revocation of parole since the behavior was illegal (possession of a firearm, drinking, and could have resulted in harm to someone); this argument defines the behavior as unacceptable regardless of circumstances. A *realist approach* could be taken, arguing for revocation of parole because the parolee could have seriously hurt someone and that it was only an accident that no one was hurt; this argument looks at the specific behavior and the situation before making a decision. Or an *individualist approach* could be taken, arguing for continuation of parole since no one was hurt. This argument looks at the benefit of the client first. In this case, the argument for revocation of parole is appropriate since the primary objective of the agency is to protect society. Hopefully, the agent makes a recommendation based on a realist basis and not a moralist basis.[3] The argument for continuation of parole is inappropriate, since it clearly violates the primary goal of the agency.

---

[3]For a more detailed discussion of the moralist, realist, and individualist value orientations in corrections, the reader is referred to Scheurell, Robert. "Valuation and Decision Making in Correction Social Work," *Issues in Criminology*, Vol 4 #2 (October 1969), pp. 101–109.

On the other hand, the social worker, although arguing for revocation, should encourage the use of counseling techniques to have this particular juvenile accept responsibility for his/her behavior.

Another potential conflict area between the employer and the social worker is when an agent deliberately does not follow *agency policy*; for example, an agency may have regulations restricting the off duty association of probation/parole agents with current and former correctional clients. An agent who becomes close friends with a parolee is in potential violation of the agency's policies and is subject to disciplinary action; for example, situations have developed where an agent dated and had sexual relations with a parolee or an agent attended and participated in "pot smoking" with parolees. In these situations, there is a clear conflict between the agency and individual interests. A reasonable solution to the dilemma is for the agent to clearly define his/her relationship with the parolee, avoid discussion of cases and agency policy, and avoid illegal behavior. Concurrently, the agent should attempt to have the agency more clearly define its regulations on association of agents with current and former correctional clients. In large urban communities where a probation or parole agent has lived their entire life in the community and has gone to school with current parolees when they were younger, the issue of association between an agent and a parolee becomes difficult to manage. In some cases, parolees may live on the same street, know the agent's relatives, or may even be a relative. The fact one becomes a probation or parole agent changes relationships with people one has known for a long time and creates some difficulties in how one deals with "old friends" who are now on parole.

RELATIONSHIP TO THE COMMUNITY. One of the ethical concerns is to inform the community of issues as they relate to social welfare and in this case correctional policy. The social worker is expected to discuss issues in public to inform the public of facts when necessary about correctional programs and their outcome; for example, many communities are concerned about the establishment of community-based treatment facilities. The community in general is unaware of the fact that usually the "least risk" clients are placed in community facilities. The social worker would need to present facts on the outcome of establishing a community-based program and how they operate. In relating to the community the need for a community-based facility, the agent is generally representing the agency and the social work profession. A conflict can occur when in a public meeting to build support for a community-based facility one denounces the agency's intentions to build a community-based facility or indicates personnel views that may be against the community-based facility. One should at all times clearly *indicate the distinctions between the agency perspective, professional social work perspective, and individual perspective.* To develop community-based programs, the politicians and the local citizens need to support the concept of community corrections. This means having them participate in meetings and in various steps of the decision-making process. The net result is that one may actively participate in changing zoning laws and other aspects of local politics.

RELATIONSHIP TO THE SOCIAL WORK PROFESSION. Some of the ethical concerns as they relate to corrections include *professional behavior in one's private life, distinguishing between one's professional and personal viewpoints, and professional competency. Professional behavior in one's private life* means not to violate the laws such as the use of drugs and exploitation of clients for one's personal needs, either psychological or physical; for example, as a professional social worker in corrections, one should not use drugs (since it is illegal). This behavior usually results in disciplinary action or release from a position. A common occurrence for the inexperienced agent is asking many detailed questions about a client's sex life when the questions are peripheral to the investigation for a social history. There is a temptation to obtain more detailed and tantalizing information, which serves vicariously the psychological need of the agent and not the client. In a social investigation, information requested should have a direct bearing on the facts of the case and a direct bearing on a psychosocial diagnosis.

In discussing an agency's policies in the broader community and with professional colleagues, one should make a clear *distinction between one's professional views, personal views, and agency policy*; for example, if an agent is concerned about police brutality and belongs to a group advocating police reform, he/she may be asked to prepare a position paper on police brutality. As a professional social worker holding personal viewpoints about police reform, it is appropriate to prepare a position paper. However, it is unethical to use agency stationery for circulating the position paper. The reason is that the use of agency stationery gives the impression that the correctional agency has taken a position, which may not be the case. This behavior could lead to an administrative reprimand or possible suspension. Similarly, if one is discussing legislation relating to the legalization of marihuana or prostitution and one is personally in favor of it but professionally is against the legislation, the difference between the two perspectives and reasons for the difference in perspective should be made clear.

Professional competency should not be misrepresented. If one is an expert on alcoholism and is asked for "expert advice" by a court on the causes of sexual assault, one should decline to provide "expert advice." Conversely, if one is an expert on alcoholism, and is asked for "expert advice" on alcoholism, one should be willing to provide needed information. In effect, agents should be aware of their own limitations and competency, and not misrepresent themselves to the public and the agency. A different aspect of professional competency is *continuing education.* A social worker in corrections should be reading current material in the correctional area and participating in staff development and other forms of continuing education. A conflict can occur in this area, when research and other studies indicate psychoanalytic casework is only one tool for working with people, yet the agent refuses to read or learn about different modalities in working with people.

SUMMARY

Social work ethics, in corrections, similar to other fields of practice, are modified, based upon the legal parameters and objectives of the agency. In corrections, protection of society comes first and rehabilitation of the client second. There are clear limitations to ethical concerns such as client self-determination and confidentiality. Situations of potential conflict between the worker and client and worker and the agency are common. Each social worker in the correctional area, based upon experience, needs to develop general guidelines on the utilization of social work ethics in corrections. In general, the social worker in corrections will be balancing the needs of clients with the objectives of the agency. All persons working in corrections need to develop their own style of behavior in balancing these contradictory demands.[4]

---

[4]For further details on social work ethics, the reader is referred to the following sources: National Association of Social Workers. "Code of Professional Ethics." Washington, D.C.: National Association of Social Workers, 1979; Biestek, Felix and Clyde Gehrig. *Client Self Determination in Social Work.* Chicago, Illinois: Loyola University Press, 1978; Council on Social Work Education *Casebook in Correctional Practice.* New York, New York: Council on Social Work Education, 1958; Levy, Charles. *Social Work Ethics.* New York, New York: Human Services Press, 1976; Mills, Robert. *Offender Assessment: A Casebook in Corrections.* Cincinnati, Ohio: Anderson Publishing Co., 1980; Studt, Elliot. "An Outline for the Study of Social Authority Factors in Casework," *Social Casework,* Vol. 35 #6(June 1954) pp. 231–238; Van Hoose, William and Jeffrey Kottler; *Ethical and Legal Issues in Counseling and Psychotherapy,* San Francisco, California: Jossey-Bass Publishers, 1977; Wigmore, John. *Evidence in Trials at Common Law* Vol. 18: Boston, Massachusetts: Little Brown and Co., 1961, and Wilson, Susanna. *Confidentiality in Social Work.* New York, New York: The Free Press, 1978. In addition, one should read specific state statutes as they relate to licensing, certification of social workers, and ethical codes for governmental employees; for example, Wisconsin has a code of ethics for state employees (State Bureau of Personnel Ch. Pers. 24).

Section VI

CORRECTIONAL SOCIAL WORK

INTRODUCTION

Prison conditions are worsening. The arbitrary, harsh, and often inhumane conditions of many state prisons have resulted from irrational sentencing policies and prison overcrowding. In June, 1981, state and federal prisons held 349,118 felons in confinement (Bureau of Justice Statistics, 1981). This was a gigantic increase from the total at the end of 1971 of 198,061 (Hindelang, Gottfredson, Flanagan, 1981). Deplorable prison conditions are particularly apparent in some of the southern states, which imprison as many as 250 offenders in a dormitory and confine two inmates to cells that measure less than fifty square feet.

Reports abound by members of the mass media on escalating crime, long delays before a defendant's going to trial, and overcrowded prisons. However, the media does not usually report on the small, yet growing reforms within corrections that have been effective in changing inmates' behavior and reducing recidivism. Many jurisdictions are searching for methods to alleviate prison overcrowding and develop humane methods of changing offenders' behavior. This section describes workable alternatives to the mounting crisis in corrections.

In Chapter 15, David Showalter and Marian Hunsinger describe the role and function of social workers in a maximum security penitentiary. Special consideration is given to the knowledge and skills necessary to prepare a professional to work in a prison. Social work skills such as advocacy, mobilization of resources, and familiarity with minority problems are stressed as being especially useful in a prison setting.

The following chapter, by Jack G. Parker and John A. LaCour, explores an area of program development fraught with problems — the development of volunteer programs in correctional facilities. In order to have effective volunteer programs, the authors recommend that volunteers be educated about the stress that is characteristic of correctional environments and the awesome responsibility of wardens and superintendents. They emphasize the importance of keeping recruitment and selection efforts consistent with the objectives and attitudes at each institution.

In Chapter 17, Judith F. Weintraub identifies several of the crisis points most frequently encountered by prisoners' families: arrest and arraignment, sentencing, initial incarceration, and pre– and postrelease. Weintraub recommends ways in which both public and private agencies can act to meet such problems, with maximum use of volunteers and minimum financial expenditure.

In Chapter 18, Susan Hoffman Fishman and Albert S. Alissi present a case illustration of an innovative volunteer service agency, Women in Crisis. The authors demonstrate the effectiveness of this model program in meeting the needs of family members at times of crisis and in strengthening the family as a stable source of help to the offender. This practical and cost-effective program is based on the following underlying premises: "1) the use of volunteers as service providers, 2) the relationship as the primary tool of the volunteer, and 3) advocacy as a role of the volunteer" (Fishman & Alissi).

REFERENCES

Hindelang, M., Gottfredson, M., and Flanagan, T. *Sourcebook of Criminal Justice Statistics*. Washington, D.C.: U.S. Government Printing Office, 1981.

Bureau of Justice Statistics Bulletin. Prisoners at Midyear, 1981. Washington, D.C.: U.S. Department of Justice, September, 1981.

Chapter 15

SOCIAL WORK WITHIN A
MAXIMUM SECURITY SETTING

DAVID SHOWALTER AND MARIAN HUNSINGER

R esidents of our penitentiaries are individuals who most often
come from low socioeconomic backgrounds. They are usually
poorly educated, many times not having completed high school.
There is a disproportionately high number of inmates from minority
groups such as blacks, Chicanos, and Indians. Many times, they
are unskilled and have little or no hope of obtaining adequate
employment. Many come from broken homes, while a significant
proportion were abused as children. Most inmates have a relatively low self-concept and many emotional problems. The majority have probably abused drugs or alcohol consistently. Generally,
inmates have little trust or respect for their fellow human beings.
They usually possess poor social and communication skills. In
essence, our prisons are full of people extremely short on resources and long on problems.

Working within the walls of a prison challenges the staff with a
very tough double bind. On one hand, the employee is forced to
work in a negative and restrictive environment. On the other
hand, the employee is forced to work with clients with severe
problems who are in the institution against their will. The worker
must face overwhelming problems with very few resources available to improve the environment or to provide alternatives to
their clients. Working in an environment under constant conflict
with strong forces pulling in opposite directions, the worker is
faced with the difficult task of maintaining his own emotional
stability. Failure to handle the stress in a positive manner will
result in a burnout for the worker. The worker then would become
one more negative factor in an already negative situation. The

authors contend that social work is an excellent profession to effectively cope with the various problems and stress of working in a prison. First, social workers are trained to study the effects of the environment. The well-trained social worker can then develop a realistic plan for changing the environment or help the client develop more effective skills to cope with the environment. Second, the social worker is trained to analyze the individual and make an assessment of the behavior and attitudes creating problems. The social worker, through clinical treatment, helps the client recognize his problems and develop a more effective pattern of behavior and attitudes. Third, the social worker is trained to develop a high level of self-awareness. This is extremely important in being able to cope with the problems and stress of working in a prison. The social worker should have an advantage over most professions in recognizing his own stress when it reaches a high level. He also has the knowledge and training to be able to choose a positive method to cope with the stress and tension. The result can be an individual effectively functioning under high stress while members of other professions are burning out.

In recommending social workers as employees for prisons, the authors would like to point out that we have in mind individuals trained at an accredited school of social work. The authors feel that a Bachelor of Social Work is the minimum amount of formal training necessary to meet the advantages we have outlined for social workers. There is no way to ensure that individuals without the formal degree will have had access to the knowledge and skills necessary for functioning effectively in a prison. Working within a prison is a challenge that social workers need to look at more seriously. It could possibly open up a new field of employment for social workers at a time when many positions are being cut. A real challenge is provided for individual social workers who appreciate the rewards of successfully meeting a challenge. Within this chapter the authors hope to provide information that will help the reader understand the role and function a social worker can fill in a prison setting. We also hope to identify some of the special problems facing social workers within the correctional institution. Perhaps this information will enable some social workers to make the decision to seek employment in a prison setting.

SOCIAL WORKER AS THERAPIST

Perhaps one of the most important and, at the same time, toughest roles a social worker can fill is that of therapist. As pointed out in other parts of this chapter, the issues of confidentiality and a security role provide tough double binds for the social worker. This makes the role of therapist even more difficult. Both of these issues affect the trust that the inmate is willing to offer the therapist. If the inmate believes the social worker will break the confidentiality bond or if the inmate perceives that the social worker is acting in a strong security role, the inmate will refuse to trust the social worker. Thus, one of the very essential elements of the therapeutical relationship is lost from the very beginning.

One of the most important foundations of social work is the idea of client self-determination. The concepts involve the idea that the more an individual can accomplish for himself, the more confident an individual will become in his own abilities to handle problems and responsibility. The concept also involves recognition of the right of an individual to decide his own fate.

Incarceration within a prison provides barriers to an inmate being able to use self-determination. The inmate is allowed very little responsibility. Instead, the whole environment is one that encourages dependency. The reason for this is obvious. It is essential that order and control be maintained within a prison so that escapes and people being hurt are kept to a minimum. There are many rules and regulations that govern the inmate's daily life. He is told when to eat, when to lock up, etc. Jobs are assigned to him that usually do not keep him busy and do not involve much skill. There are usually very few activities and recreation from which he can choose. In short, being in prison takes away the individual's right to decide many things and offers few choices for those decisions that are allowed.

A second major barrier to client self-determination is the inmate himself. A large number of inmates are very angry individuals who tend to blame families, friends, society, police, courts, and prison officials for their problems. Many of the reasons for their anger are legitimate such as abuse as a child, discrimination because of minority status, miscarriage of justice, lack of educational or employment opportunities, etc. However, there are many instances in which the problems are magnified out of proportion or non-existent. In any case, it is very scary for these inmates to be presented with the idea that they are responsible for their decisions and actions. It is much easier to focus blame and responsibility elsewhere besides self. This gets in the way of the individual's growth and development. In fact, it is highly likely that until an inmate is willing to accept responsibility for his actions and decisions, he will be unable to adjust successfully to society.

Following a policy of client self-determination is essential if a social worker is to function effectively. The client must come to understand that even within the rigid confines of a prison he can determine some of the direction for his life. Since the inmate may very well blame others for his actions and situation, it is likely to be very difficult. Learning to make choices about his life in prison can help him understand that a person can usually make choices concerning his life if he is willing. This is an important step for the client. He can learn to gain control over his life by accepting responsibility for himself. The social worker will have to be creative and imaginative to help the client find ways to follow a course of self-determination. However, if the social worker is willing to look, he will be able to find several issues over which the client can have control. The key is to make sure that the issues are realistic, within the bounds of prison rules, and within the capacity of the client. Most importantly, the issues must have value for the client. The following is a case example in which a social worker helps an inmate develop a new perspective. The power of the new perspective enables the client to improve his personal relationships and helps him to develop a sense of self-responsibility.

The inmate in this case is a short black man who is thirty years of age. Presently this man is serving his second term in a maximum security prison. His present sentence is five years for robbery. He had earned his living while in society by pimping. His women friends would support him by selling their sexual favors or by getting a job and giving him their paycheck. The inmate will be referred to hereafter as Sam.

Sam sought help from the social worker because he was bitter, resentful, and fearful of the direction his life had taken so far. He tended to blame his father and the criminal justice system for the problems he had in life. The immediate crisis that prompted him to seek help was the fact that one of his girlfriends had just given birth to his first child. Parenthood struck him hard. He started seriously thinking about marrying the woman, we will call her Nancy, and settling down to raise a family. From his perspective, the problem was that Nancy wanted little to do with him. She visited only a few times and usually did not answer his letters. She had been one of the women who had supported him by working and prostitution. It was quite evident from her behavior since his incarceration that she had ambivalent feelings about him at best. Counseling during the first few months focused on trying to help him resolve the relationship. During this period of time, other important facts came to light. Sam was extremely tired of his life-style and of having to serve time in prison. As he put it, "I am getting older and there is no retirement plan for people with my life-style. Either people die young in my life-style, spend most of their lives in prison, or end up friendless and penniless." Another important piece of information was that he held women in contempt. He viewed them as robots that he could get to do anything he wanted. He bragged that he chose his girlfriends young and trained them to think and act as he desired. He stated that he did not believe they could think on their own. He had no respect for them as people.

After a couple of months, it became very clear that the relationship with Nancy would not work out. She refused to visit, write, or come in for a counseling session. During this period of time, the social worker had attempted to help Sam realize his attitude toward women and behavior toward Nancy had probably helped create her unwillingness to get back under his control once she had escaped as a result of his incarceration. Sam resisted this idea very strongly. During a counseling session Sam asked the social worker, a male, what a woman's perspective on his problem might be. The social worker suggested that Sam might be able to discuss the problem with a female social worker on staff. Sam's immediate reaction was one of surprise and fear. He made it very clear that in no way did he want to talk with the female social worker directly. The male social worker confronted him about his fear. After a considerable amount of confrontation mixed with encouragement and support, Sam was able to admit that he was scared of women who were not under his control. Sam admitted that he had never felt accepted by women and was afraid of rejection. He had solved his problem in several ways. First, he was the first to reject a woman before she had a chance to reject him. Second, he only chose to be around women with very low self-esteem and who were very dependent upon their men. Third, he became involved with his girlfriends when they were young and taught them to be dependent on him. Sam admitted being too scared to even talk with a woman if she was independent and self-assured. The social worker pointed out that this perspective of women was unhealthy, which by now Sam was able to admit. Sam informed the social worker that one of the reasons he wanted to maintain his relationship with Nancy was because she was somewhat more independent than the others, for which he respected her. This is probably the reason she was able to maintain her distance once she was able to establish it. Soon thereafter, Sam was able to decide that he wanted to change the way he thought about women and related to them. He set a goal for himself to be able to think of women and treat them with respect.

Sam has made very positive progress toward this goal through therapy. He is now able to carry on a normal conversation with self-assured women. He no longer encourages women to send him money, nor does he lead them on with promises of a permanent relationship when he gets out of prison. Instead, he asks women to write or visit as friends and clearly lets them know the only thing he can offer or wants is friendship. This behavior is new for Sam but has been very rewarding. He feels more self-confident and does not fear rejection as much. He hopes that upon his release he will be able to establish a relationship with a woman independent enough to be a partner for him instead of his being the dominant one.

This particular issue has been an important turning point for Sam. It helped him realize that even while in prison he can determine what direction some of the important issues of his life will take. Sam has made several positive changes. He is trying to develop good work habits, something he never had. Sam is now the inmate leader of a small group of prisoners who are seeking ways to improve their lives with the aid of an outside social worker. Finally, Sam is developing a positive attitude toward life. He is learning that he can control his own destiny even while in prison if he is willing to take responsibility for himself and make what positive choices are available to him.

From their training and experience, social workers understand the importance of environment and significant others in the life of their clients. This knowledge can be very useful in a penitentiary. The inmate's family is very important to him because it is the only thing of value in his life. It represents his hopes for the future. Since the family is so important to the inmate, it can be used as a lure to help encourage the inmate to seek treatment. Unfortunately, for many reasons, family counseling is not widely practiced in prisons. This problem is discussed in an article entitled "Marital and Family Counseling in Prison" in the May 1980 issue of *Social Work Journal* (Showalter & Jones, 1980).

Social workers employed within a prison could have a positive influence on this problem. They could use their knowledge to encourage prison administrators to pursue a policy of supporting marriage and family counseling. In the California Corrections System, Norman Holt and Donald Miller found strong evidence that family support helped inmates do their time with less rule violations and increased chances for successful completion of parole (Holt & Miller, 1972). There certainly are indications that such a policy would be of benefit to the inmate and to the prison.

Following is a case example of how a social worker successfully used marriage and family counseling within a prison. Names are fictitious.

Ralph is a twenty-six-year-old white male serving a long sentence for murder. His father had served time in prison when he was young. Ralph is married with three young children. He had served time before on drug charges.

Ralph approached the social worker for help when he found his wife had gone on a vacation to another state with his uncle. He was afraid of sexual involvement and was thinking seriously of divorcing his wife. The social worker suggested that he get his wife to come in for a counseling session. Ralph agreed and was able to convince Kathy, his wife, to come in. The first couple of sessions were exploratory in nature, and several serious problems were identified. First, Kathy had been very dependent on Ralph when he was free and let him make all of the decisions. Now that he was locked up, she resented him trying to control her life by demanding she stay home all the time and care for the kids. She denied doing anything wrong by taking a vacation. Second, Ralph had a strong need to retain his control over Kathy and his children. He was unable to express trust for her. Third, Ralph's mother was creating problems for Kathy, interfering with the way she raised the children. Ralph supported his mother over Kathy. Fourth, Adam, the oldest child at eight, was starting to become a behavior problem and refused to obey Kathy. Fifth, Ralph had gotten Kathy into legal trouble by having her bring drugs to him when he was in jail. She was on probation. Counseling sessions were set up and continued over several months. There was significant success but also a rather dramatic failure. One of the approaches used by the social worker was to help Kathy develop a more positive self-image. The social worker used assertive training to help Kathy learn to stand up to Ralph for her rights. There was a failure in that against her better judgment she let Ralph persuade her to smuggle money into him during visits. She got caught and the marriage counseling sessions had to be stopped as a result.

However, there were a number of successes as a result of these counseling sessions. First, Ralph decided not to pursue a divorce. Second, Ralph learned not to try to exercise so much control over Kathy's life. He learned to trust her to go out and have fun. Third, Kathy did learn to speak up to Ralph about her rights on many important issues even though she failed on the one. Fourth, Ralph learned to support Kathy when his mother began to interfere. Fifth, Ralph was able to explain to Adam why he was in jail and help the boy recognize that he was still loved. Both Ralph and Kathy were able to recognize Adam's problems as being serious, and Kathy took him to a private therapist. Ralph learned not to put so many financial demands on Kathy, since she was struggling to support the family. Seventh, Kathy learned to start looking for new interests for herself. Presently, she is going to school to study to be a nurse. Finally, Ralph was able to adjust to serving his time better. He is creating fewer problems for the prison administration because he is more content.

Minority groups are vastly overrepresented in our prisons by population. There is a far higher percentage of them in prison population than in society. Each minority group has somewhat different culture, customs, and values than the general society, sometimes including a language difference, as is the case with many Spanish-speaking Americans. There is strong evidence that their overrepresentation in prison is partly due to these differences. The minority inmates must try to cope with a system designed to meet the minimum needs of a white Anglo-Saxon group. On the other hand, prison administrators must try to make their system flexible and endeavor to meet some of the needs of the minority without adequate funds or resources. There are many harsh double binds for both groups.

The social worker can be useful in this situation, as he is taught to be sensitive to the various minority group members' needs. First, he can provide emotional support for his minority clients and treat their values and beliefs with respect. Second, he can help his clients rationally explore what legitimate avenues there are to pursue their customs and values. Third, the social worker can work toward helping the overworked prison administration to be more sensitive to the various minority groups' needs. Many times, the administrator may be insensitive unknowingly or unintentionally.

STRENGTHENING SUPPORT SYSTEMS

Acceptable social support systems are often a weak area in the life of an inmate. Family and marital relationships may be tenuous. Trust or confidence in social service agencies can be nonexistent. Their use of friends as a support system has often been in a negative direction. Even their criminal support system, i.e. "inmates stick together" or "honor among thieves," is proved over and over again to be unreliable. Thus, the social worker needs to work with the inmate to strengthen the support he does have and develop support in other areas he has never used.

Marital relationships can be one of the best support systems an inmate has going for himself. However, many factors of incarceration work at weakening this bond. The greatest assistance toward strengthening this tie will come from the treatment staff. One such program developed at Kansas State Penitentiary is called "A Marriage Workshop." Approximately fourteen hours of a single weekend are devoted to individual couple and small group work with inmates and their spouses. Specific time is given to learning and evaluating good communication skills. Emphasis is placed on problem-solving techniques and the opportunity for each couple to pick a specific problem and work through it in the presence of a therapist.

A committed effort is necessary to sustain a healthy relationship. Some couples try to ignore the fact that incarceration makes a change in their relationship. New problems have developed because of the separation. The inmate, for the most part, has no chance to provide financial support. Old problems have possibly intensified. If trusting each other was a problem in the past, this new arrangement will exploit that condition. If the wife was too dependent, it is a rude jolt to now be in charge, and if she was too independent, circumstances will force her to capitalize on that quality. If these matters are not dealt with, the partnership will deteriorate to an empty shell and divorce will probably result. This is a common occurrence for a number of inmates. For those who continue their marriage, it is useful to consider the changes brought on by incarceration before they get paroled and are overwhelmed by them on their release.

One couple who participated in the workshop had a special problem. Ted was arrested the same day Sue had their only baby. Consequently, he had never lived at home anytime in the four years of the child's life. Ted would soon be eligible for parole and back living with the family. Special attention had to be given to the possible problems that might arise. Normal conflicts in family building were discussed as well as some signs and situations to be alert for as needing professional help. This opportunity for preparation gave the transition a better chance to succeed.

Sometimes the support most needed is the support to let a relationship end. An inmate, George, tried on two occasions, months apart, to set up weekly marriage counseling sessions for himself and his wife. Both times the wife offered a few weak excuses why she could not make it to the sessions. The therapist was able to help George admit that the relationship was over, even though that was not the way he wanted it to be. While an inmate is incarcerated, his family is often seen as the most important thing to him and it is hard to relinquish that. George resisted handling his feelings of loss in a positive way. The therapist pointed out to him how damaging his anger and resentment could be, but he chose not to participate in individual counseling.

The normal support system of friends is often overlooked by inmates. The people they chose to believe or trust in the past have often had a negative influence on their life. Some decided they did not want any friends, as a means of avoiding being hurt in life. If they had a history of being abused as children, it is hard to open up to the idea that there is support that can come from people. Sometimes the social worker can use friends as a tool in therapy. Jim was an inmate who had successfully completed counseling. By mutual agreement, he sat in on a session with Bill who was having a hard time seeing the social worker as someone who wanted to help him instead of making his time harder. Jim and Bill had known each other on the street. Bill would listen to Jim and sought him out as a friend in prison. Likewise, when inmates work on the same job and develop a friendship, they can help each other in therapy by giving feedback on progress they see daily. Also, fellow group members can turn into friends. During therapy, an inmate can take a good look at the people he chose as friends in the past and discover some of the reasons why.

Another reason for friends as a support system was noted in an article written by Fred for the Lifer's Club magazine. Fred, halfway through for a parole eligibility on his life sentence, wrote

> Any effort to develop friends, and constructive acquaintances, allows us to strengthen our ability to co-exist with different types of individuals, (regardless of "where"), and also helps us to understand and cope with individualized attitudes and life styles. These "prison formed" friendships are sometimes used for escape from physical attacks, i.e., the more "friends" an inmate has, the less likely he is to be physically abused, for fear of retribution from that inmate's friends. This is a very real faction of prison life, and "prison friendships", to be considered.
>
> ... friendships among inmates many times tend to be more closely knit, more open and honest, in the emotional sense, there are, in reality, no "secrets" about one's personal life in prison. Everyone knows, (or can easily find out if he so desires), where another inmate lives, where he works, whether or not he is interested in sports and what kind, whether or not he gambles, if he is an aggressive person; a multitude of personal facts are evident to all. Considering that these and many other subjects are openly known about other inmates—when one strikes up a friendship on the inside—personal high-lights of another's behavior and/or life style is apparent.

Most inmates distrust social service agencies. Even when they knew things were falling apart for themselves on the streets, they did not ask for help that might have prevented their incarceration. Either pride or distrust contributed to them missing out on available help. The social worker can do many things to change this for the future. Simple explanations of some known agencies help the inmate know some types of assistance is available. Assertiveness will teach an inmate how to ask with a good chance of receiving aid. Often, the inmate has now learned the value of therapy and will seek it on the streets to insure he maintains his freedom. If nothing else, the social worker has modeled what social services can do if given the opportunity.

ADVOCACY AND MOBILIZING RESOURCES

One of the key functions of a social worker is that of advocate. Sometimes his clients are trapped within a situation where they are unable to effectively speak for themselves. At these times social workers have stepped into the role of advocate and promoted their client's case.

In many instances the client is without adequate resources to meet his needs. The resources may be unavailable or the client may lack the influence that would enable him to obtain the services or material that he needs. In these cases, social workers have traditionally intervened for their clients to mobilize whatever resources were available. The social work intervention then enables the client to obtain services that will enable him to cope more effectively with his problems and start to make changes.

Within a prison setting, the inmates are without official power or influence. There is a very real scarcity of resources available for prisoners. The social work skills of advocacy and mobilization of resources can be essential for helping a client cope within a prison. Without social work intervention, the inmate may find himself in a powerless position without being able to find an effective way to cope. The social worker's intervention may provide the inmate with some hope for the future. Following is a case example of a social worker using such skills for inmates in a helpless position. The names are fictitious.

Don was a twenty-eight-year-old black man serving a mandatory fifteen years sentence for murder. He was attacked by another inmate with a knife over a misunderstanding between the two of them. As a result of the attack, Don was completely paralyzed from the neck down. He had no feeling or movement in any of his limbs or the trunk of his body. Don was kept in the infirmary of the prison. He was fed by hand by the infirmary staff. His body waste was removed on a regular basis, and he was given daily sponge baths. Before the attack, Don was known as a self-reliant person who was happy and friendly. He was well liked by both inmates and staff. After the attack, he became very angry, withdrawn, bitter, and resentful. No matter how much attention the staff was able to pay him or what they did for him, Don continued to withdraw into himself.

Julia, one of the staff social workers, became aware of his situation after several weeks had passed. She went to the infirmary to talk with him, trying to find ways to be of help. He was very bitter and frightened about having to spend the rest of his life paralyzed and dependent upon others for his needs. He was deeply concerned that he still had five years to serve on his sentence with no chance for parole before then. He complained that he was developing bedsores because the staff did not have enough time to turn him over often enough. He also felt that his body waste was not being removed often enough. The most severe problem was simply that nobody was working with him to help him start learning how to cope with his feelings of being paralyzed.

Julia decided to work with Don to see how she could help improve his situation. First, she assured him that she would visit him regularly to let him discuss his feelings. She set up a schedule to visit with him three times a week for a half hour. Second, she talked with the infirmary to see if Don could be turned over more often and his body waste picked up more regularly. The infirmary was simply unable to make such a commitment because of staff and time shortages, although they were quite concerned about Don. Julia then approached several inmates who had been Don's friends before the attack. Don had ignored their attempts to be friendly since the attack. When Julia asked for their help, they were happy to volunteer.

She then asked the Deputy Director of the institution if the inmates could be allowed to work with Don. The Deputy Director approved the idea. Julia next discussed with Don the idea of letting his friend help him and convinced him to try it. A regular schedule was set up for Don's friends to visit with him, remove his body waste, turn him over, exercise his limbs, and feed him. This arrangement proved to be highly satisfactory. Don's physical needs received more than adequate attention. Don was able to start discussing his feelings with people that he felt cared. Over the months, he became less frightened and angry. He started learning to develop a more healthy and positive attitude toward himself.

After Julia had mobilized resources for Don, in this instance a number of friends to provide a support network for him, she turned to the more difficult issue of advocacy. She felt there would be no useful purpose for Don to spend another five years in his present position. The only possibility for early release would be a pardon from the Governor. This is a very difficult process. Very few pardons are granted, and the process takes a lengthy amount of time. She contacted the Governor's office and discussed the case with the Pardon Attorney. He encouraged her to pursue the case but told her the road would be difficult.

Julia spent six full months working on obtaining the pardon. The details are too complex to list here, but a summary of the accomplishments could help enlighten the reader on what a social worker can accomplish when determined. Julia had a full medical evaluation completed on Don by outside medical experts to provide proof of his total disability. She contacted his family and worked with them on forming a realistic plan to cope with Don if he were released. She contacted a nursing home and obtained their agreement to accept Don as a patient for several months. She acquired the agreement of a physical therapist to work with Don to try to rehabilitate his limbs to some degree. She contacted the vocational rehabilitation services and they agreed to pay for the nursing home and physical therapy.

Midway through this process, it was discovered that a detainer had been placed on Don from another state for a crime ten-years-old. The effect of the detainer would be that if Don received a pardon, he would be transferred to the new state to face charges there. This development was highly discouraging. Julia contacted the state and asked them to withdraw their detainer. The new state was reluctant to do so. The result was several weeks of negotiations in which Julia finally convinced the other state to withdraw their detainer. She accomplished this by first convincing them Don really was paralyzed and, second, pointing out that they would have to assume financial responsibility for him if they insisted upon keeping the detainer on him.

Don finally received a pardon and was released through the hard work of Julia. She was able to get him physical and emotional help while he was incarcerated. She was able to obtain a pardon through a very difficult and lengthy negotiations process. She enabled the family to develop realistic plans for his release, which included services from a nursing home and a physical therapist. Through her efforts, a detainer was removed that would have made the whole effort worthless. Finally, she was able to help Don start to come to grips with the fact he was paralyzed for life. This was probably her biggest accomplishment, as Don was deeply withdrawn into himself when she first started working with him. This case illustrates very clearly the positive work a social worker can accomplish by applying knowledge and skills. Through the use of advocacy and mobilization of resources, Julia was able to manage a positive outcome for a case that seemed totally hopeless. A social worker was able to successfully manage this case when all other correction officials had given up hope.

SECURITY ROLE AND CONFIDENTIALITY

Security is the primary purpose of a penitentiary. This is a fact that a social worker employed within a prison setting must learn to cope with. The social worker must come to grips with the fact that security will get first consideration over treatment at all times out of necessity. Little can be accomplished by constantly fighting this concept. Much can be done if the social worker will adopt the idea of treatment being in a working relationship with security. The social worker needs to be security minded for his own safety and the appropriate operation of the institution.

One of the benefits of social workers to the operation of a penitentiary is that they can create and implement programs that may reduce some security problems. Most inmates need to learn good communication skills they can use in dealing with other inmates and civilian and security staff. Assertiveness training is an example of a program that can be helpful in teaching effective communication. Guards also can be taught this method of dealing with inmates to improve their interactions with these individuals. Inappropriate ways of handling anger cause many problems within the penitentiary. Learning how to handle feelings in a positive manner can make a difference in how inmates respond to anger and frustration. Drug and alcohol abuse is another common source of security problems. Many methods of counseling can be effective in helping inmates learn to reduce stress and tension and not need a chemical crutch. In this manner, social workers can make a significant contribution in the area of security. Programs that teach inmates to communicate effectively and cope with their feelings contribute to security because it helps reduce stress and tension.

These contributions of the social worker to the security force will be of an indirect nature. There must be a clear understanding on both sides that the treatment staff will not be a spy network for security use. Occasionally, the social worker will provide information to security, but that should not be a regular occurrence. The guard force may find out the same information that the social worker knows, but seldom should the source of that information be the social worker.

Basically, one of the requirements of any employee in a prison is to be an extension of the security force. In whatever capacity they have, caution and good sense is necessary for the reasonable functioning overall of the institution. The social worker must see that inmates do not misuse programs. If marriage counseling sessions are used for the spouse to smuggle in contraband to the inmate, those sessions must stop. The social worker can reinforce the essential premise of the institution that the inmate is responsible for his actions and that he is responsible for the consequences of his actions. During a marriage workshop, as described above, the social worker must be alert that it is not used as just extra visiting time or for unauthorized physical contact. In developing innovative programs, the security risks and needs should be openly dealt with. It is unrealistic to feel that nothing can happen, since the project is treatment oriented. The social worker can role model that reasonable rules can be followed and beneficial results obtained. Too often, inmates have a distorted view of rules and their value. This is another opportunity for the social worker to use the inmate's present situation as a teaching tool.

Confidentiality is an equally important factor that needs special emphasis in a penitentiary setting. Most inmates by nature do not trust authority or official people, and the social worker usually fits that definition. Consequently, the worker must make a special effort to establish trust and prove that confidentiality is possible and honored. As sometimes happens in relationships, there will be testing to see if the social worker backs up his word. That should be expected and handled with consideration.

The inmate has a right to expect that he can say things in confidence as a client and not be penalized. This helps build the clinical relationship that must be based on trust, openness, and honesty. For many, they are not used to admitting anything, thinking that will protect them. Consequently, the honesty demanded in therapy is frightening. It takes time to build up the trust level.

Once they learn the liberating experience of honestly confronting themselves, therapy sessions may resemble a confessional and should be treated similarly.

Under certain circumstances, the security role of the social worker will require that the confidentiality bond be broken. Any information regarding an inmate planning to harm himself or another inmate or attempting to escape would be dealt with from a different point of view. The appropriate people must be notified, even though the information was gained in confidence. Here a social worker walks a tightrope between treatment and security, but some guidance is given by the Code of Ethics of the National Association of Social Workers which states in II-H-1: "The Social Worker should share with others confidences revealed by clients, without their consent, only for compelling professional reasons." The social worker should make this position clear to the inmate at the start of therapy.

As an example, an inmate had been in therapy for several months. During a session, Tom mentioned that he had heard other inmates asking around the mess hall for contribution of packs of cigarettes to have a certain staff member killed. Although Tom admitted he did not like this staff member, he did not feel he should be killed. Tom was told by the social worker that this information would be passed on to the proper people but he would not be named as the source. If it became important for his name to be given, the social worker would discuss with Tom the reasons why that was necessary before proceeding to give Tom's name. Tom accepted this procedure and the therapeutic relationship continued.

As with most situations in life, there will be circumstances that do not fit neatly into categories of how to be handled. How does the social worker respond to an inmate saying, "I was so mad at one inmate the other day I got a knife and was going to go find him, but decided not to do it?" Basically, the worker must make a judgment, depending upon the therapy session and how much, if any, danger still exists. There is no simple answer to how this should be handled. Professional skill and reasoning will be the best guidance.

CONCLUSION

Social work within a prison is an area that has not received much attention from the profession or social workers as individuals.

There is an overwhelming amount of problems within a prison that demand effective methods of coping. The problems produce great amounts of stress and tension for the individual who is employed in such an environment. Coping with the problems and stress requires a professional who is successfully able to cope with the kinds of people in such an institution. Social work certainly provides the training, knowledge, and skill for such an undertaking.

The work provides a real challenge to the individual who enjoys accomplishing worthwhile objectives under difficult conditions. It is by no means impossible, as a large number of individuals from many professions successfully work in such an environment. The satisfaction from accomplishing a difficult objective in a prison environment is very great. The individual has to learn to keep his expectations of himself realistic. There certainly is no lack of realistic challenge for an individual. The creative individual who is willing to spend time and energy working on a problem will find solutions that can be rewarding to himself and his clients.

The authors encourage social workers to consider a prison when thinking about a place of employment. The social worker will find a working environment full of challenges that has great potential for achieving professional growth and development. On the other hand, prisons will gain the benefit of the expertise of the social worker. It can be a rewarding experience both ways.

REFERENCES

Bartollas, C. "Sisphus in a Juvenile Institution". *Social Work*, 1975, *20* (5), 364–368.

Brown, B. S. "The Casework Role in a Penal Setting". *Journal of Criminal Law, Criminology, and Police Science*, 1967, *58* (2) 919–196.

Handler, E. "Social Work and Corrections. Comments on an Uneasy Partnership". *Criminology*, 1975, *13* (3), 240–254.

Holt, Norman, & Miller, Donald. "Explorations in Inmate-Family Relationships". California Department of Corrections, 1972, Research Report #46.

Holtman, P. "The Prison Social Worker". *Process*, 1979, *58* (6), 159–165.

Kelling, George. "Caught in a Crossfire—Corrections and the Dilemmas of Social Workers", *Crime and Delinquency*, 1968, *14* (1), 26–30.

Showalter, David, & Jones, Charlotte Williams. "Marital and Family Counseling in Prisons", *Social Work*, 1980, *25* (3), 224–228.

Stafvaltz, Z. "The Social Worker in Prison With Special Reference to Two Projects". *Staffälligenhilfe*, 1978, *27* (4), 217–221.

"The Prison Social Worker". *Process*, 1979, *58* (4), entire issue.

Chapter 16

COMMON SENSE IN CORRECTIONAL VOLUNTEERISM IN THE INSTITUTION*

JACK G. PARKER AND JOHN A. LACOUR

That the development and operation of an effective volunteer program is complex and difficult is axiomatic. The development and operation of a volunteer program for offender clientele is even more difficult. The reasons for this are at the same time both obvious and subtle. It is to this point that this article is directed.

Our purpose is not to dwell on the "how to" of establishing traditional volunteer programs. Certainly, there is substantial literature on this subject as some scholars have devoted their entire professional careers to its development. There is no dearth of organizational theory, small group theory, and guidelines for volunteer selection and training that applies to volunteer development across the board. For those who are seriously considering establishing a volunteer program, it is recommended that they become familiar with this theory.

Traditional volunteer efforts share a body of theory and experience; this has lead to a sharing of operating assumptions as well. As a matter of fact, there are a series of basic assumptions that are made and might be examined in the light of corrections institutions.

Assumption: The whole volunteer movement is well established and is welcomed as a positive force for the well-being of differential clientele.

This assumption could be considered to be true in some areas, such as mental health and geriatrics. However, it is suggested that in the broad field of corrections this is an a priori assumption.

*From *Federal Probation*, 1978 42(2), 45–50. Reprinted with the permission of the publisher.

There are many areas of corrections where volunteers are not welcome and, in fact, have not proven themselves to be of value. One might say that it is the practice of volunteerism in a hostile environment. The source of the hostility, however, is not from anger or contempt for the volunteer, but is from concern over the tremendous responsibility we place on our wardens and superintendents. Volunteers add to this responsibility.

In educating the corrections volunteer we should make him aware of this environment so that there will be fewer injured egos and, more important, less loss of motivation. It is important that we make prospective volunteers aware of multiple roles of wardens and superintendents and of the roles that are both appropriate and inappropriate for volunteers within the system.

Volunteer programs have had greater acceptance and effectiveness in Juvenile Courts or other community-based programs. Their successes in these structures have been well documented. However, the span of responsibility can allow more flexibility in quasi-official influences in probation cases than in cases where the client is incarcerated.

Effective volunteer programs can be established in the more traditional institutional programs. The first task is to show your warden or superintendent the efficacy of having such a program. To accomplish this one might prepare himself by asking the following questions:

(1) What is the task or mission of the institution?

(2) What *realistic* goals can volunteers accomplish within this mission?

(3) What are the tasks that volunteers *cannot* realistically be asked or expected to accomplish?

(4) What interface is appropriate between the inmate and volunteer population?

(5) How can you measure the effectiveness of the program within your respective institution?

(6) Will the program be an asset or burden to the institution thereby adding to or reducing the responsibilities of the warden?

It is not our purpose to depict the warden as some kind of ungrateful or uncaring person. Certainly we see enough of that on television and film. Our purpose is the necessity of making prospective volunteers aware of his pressing responsibilities so that they will have greater appreciation of his concerns and needs.

In the words of a popular song of a few years past, you might help volunteers to "walk a mile in his shoes." The result might very well be the greater introduction of effective volunteer programs in correctional institutions.

Assumption: Most people will respond to the sincere care and concern shown to them by volunteers, which will aid them in becoming more productive citizens.

This assumption is more true for mental health programs and community-based corrections programs. Unfortunately, it is often not true for institutions. The difficulty here is to point out the differences in thinking and behavior of most offenders and that of other people without sounding dramatic. However, for those who have worked in correctional institutions this is nothing new. Dr. Stanton E. Samenow, of St. Elizabeth's Hospital in Washington, D.C., has published a two-volume work entitled *The Criminal Personality*. This is the culmination of 16 years of N.I.M.H.-sponsored research into the personality of the offender. Essentially, Dr. Samenow depicts the criminal as a personality that is deceitful and void of the normal value system because he chooses to be that way. Albeit somewhat controversial, Dr. Samenow's study provides us valuable insights into the criminal personality.

What does this have to do with volunteerism? A great deal! Prospective volunteers must be made aware of the kinds of individuals with whom they will be working. Most volunteers will approach their new experience with sincere and altruistic motives. There is an innate risk of loss of motivation and personal emotional damage to the volunteer if these efforts are manipulated by the inmates for their own illegitimate gains. As an example, the most sincere volunteer might be manipulated by a skillful inmate into breaking institutional rules or even bringing in forms of contraband. Let me hasten to add that the volunteer would not knowingly be a party to this behavior. However, this is precisely the point; the unsuspecting volunteer probably would not even be aware of the subtle manipulation by an inmate.

Volunteers in the correctional institution should be given enough insight into the criminal personality to prevent their being victims of such manipulations. The question becomes one of how to accomplish this without inducing undue fear in the prospective volunteer or making him feel unneeded and unwanted. The most appropriate approach appears to be one of graduated volunteer involvement. In other words, if the volunteer is slowly introduced into the correctional system, he will become cognizant of the various forms of manipulation and subsequent problems involved. The failure to initiate graduated involvement for volunteers could place the entire volunteer program in jeopardy.

Assumption: Volunteers are people who have a great deal of warmth and caring to share with their clients; therefore, creative efforts on their part are to be encouraged.

This assumption is true, but has limited application in the correctional institution. On many occasions I have witnessed the creative efforts of volunteers with mental patients, elderly people, and young offenders in juvenile court. Much of the excitement and reward of being a volunteer comes from this personal creativity; therefore, to limit creativity does harm to both the volunteer and to the program. Why limit creativity? This has already been alluded to in our discussion of the criminal personality. The overzealous volunteer might very well become involved in situations with inmates for which they are not professionally or personally prepared. It is appropriate, then, to limit the volunteers' involvement to those areas where they have abilities. They must learn that in the correctional institution volunteering to play a musical instrument, provide entertainment, or organize recreational programs are examples of some of the most worthwhile contributions they can make. The volunteers should not feel that they are unwanted because they are not becoming deeply involved with the inmate's personal life. To the person who has been locked away from society the mere presence of a concerned volunteer is therapeutic in itself. Care should be taken to inform prospective volunteers that honesty, concern, friendliness, and helpfulness are characteristics that will be more meaningful to their function than the practice of insight therapies that will only serve to further frustrate the inmate. Most correctional institutions have a well-trained clinical staff who are familiar with the individual cases of inmates and "therapy" should be left to these people.

Assumption: The correctional system is in need of reform and this is because people who work in correctional institutions are callous, cold, and sometimes brutal.

To make such an assumption to the experienced reader is ludicrous. However, this is the image that many people have of the institutions and those of us who work in them. They have been told by media and scholar alike that correctional institutions are failures, and that rehabilitative efforts are futile. I have met many people who project the blame for these failures strictly on the personnel in the institution. The truth of the matter is that this is an easy explanation for a very complex problem.

How does a volunteer become involved in this dilemma? For one thing, many prospective volunteers might feel that the above assumption is correct, and that their efforts will be toward alleviating staff callousness. Clearly conflict can develop from this type of attitude. It is necessary that the prospective volunteer be educated in the elements of the correctional system. The need for security, disciplinary action, and inmate control should be made clear to them, and only those who are able to appreciate and understand these needs should be accepted. Life within the correctional institution is one of reality and one of survival where disruptive influences cannot be tolerated.

Recognizing that volunteers and correctional staff are often at loggerheads over these assumptions, specific strategies for teaching both parties some things they need to know about the other are necessary.

In order for correctional administrators, wardens, and superintendents to be more open to the utilization of volunteers in their institutions, they must know how such a program will benefit their institutions. It is not enough to say that inmates enjoy having volunteers work with them. What must be clear is how such a program will not increase, and better yet, will reduce the problems (and thus pressures) of operating such a facility.

The problems of an institution may vary with the objectives of the institution. If the staff sees its objective as being "keeping the criminal off the street," problems surrounding security issues will be most prominent. Institutions whose goal is rehabilitation may have more concerns about creating behavior and attitude change in inmates. Volunteers can be helpful in either or both situations.

Where security is the primary goal, volunteers can help by reducing the amount of "dead" time available to inmates. This is time when there is nothing to do. The less there is to do to keep inmates busy, the greater the security problems. By providing recreational activities, educational opportunities, or direct assistance (i.e., writing letters, repairing radios, etc.), volunteers reduce the rate of rule violations in the institution. They also create a larger number of rewards and privileges to be made available to inmates who behave well. The result is that inmates have a better institutional experience and the staff's job is more pleasant because they have more control of the system.

At facilities where the primary concern is rehabilitation, volunteers can be effective in catalyzing attitude change. A recent study (Andrews, 1973) demonstrated the efficacy of having a group of volunteers meet each week with a group of inmates simply to talk about the law, the value of education, working, and similar topics. After a period of a few months, they found that the "straight" attitudes of the volunteers had modified the attitudes of the inmates considerably, certainly to be helpful in future law-abiding efforts.

Just as correctional staff must learn how volunteers can benefit their institution, volunteers must learn how correctional institutions differ from other institutions (i.e., for the mentally ill or mentally retarded). Perhaps the most unique difference is the greater emphasis on issues of due process. Legally, certain procedures must be followed; this includes the necessity to adhere to rules governing security. Courts mandate that institutions carry out their sentence in a constitutional manner. Because the judicial system specifies the actions of correctional facilities to such a degree, the parameters within which volunteers must operate are different than whose to which they may be accustomed. These differences should be explained to volunteers during orientation and training sessions prior to actually working in a facility.

Not only is the correctional institution unique, but so is its clientele. How do we get volunteers to be aware of the manipulative nature of inmates and to behave accordingly (i.e., not doing "favors" for inmates, bringing in contraband, etc.)? The answer lies in selection and screening activities.

This process will ultimately establish the quality and tenor of the volunteer program. It is here that the program will assess the potential volunteer — and where the volunteer will assess the program.

In order to reach this point of mutual assessment, some method of contact must occur. The logical technique to recruit volunteers is to make broad public appeals through a number of media (newspaper, radio, television) and by speaking before large groups. These are not likely to prove successful techniques. Rosenbaum (1955) suggests that the failure of such efforts is due to the act of volunteering being an act of social conformity rather than an individual act. Thus, a person is more likely to volunteer if he observes others doing so, but is much less likely to volunteer if others refuse. The broad appeal is best used as an information-giving device.

Volunteers can best be recruited by the personal referral of people who are friends of program personnel. This will allow the program to begin with a sound nucleus of concerned, responsible people. It will grow as the initial few volunteers begin to refer their friends, a process described by Likert's "linking pins" concept (Weick, 1969). This method of recruitment will serve two functions simultaneously—*good* volunteers will be selected and the initial screening function will be enhanced. Persons referred to be a volunteer are likely to be similar to the person referring them (Duck, 1974). Typically, the person directing the volunteer program at an institution will be more mature and should have experience in corrections. Too, the referred person is more likely to consider the possibility of being a volunteer since a close friend who is already a participant has suggested him for membership in the volunteer program. The person referred by a friend who is a volunteer will have a higher level of investment than a person who is more randomly selected for membership.

When a volunteer program depends upon the heterogeneity of its volunteers to meet the variety of demands of its program, the difficulty of selecting the best mix of volunteers becomes more difficult. However, by requiring the potential volunteer to demonstrate qualities of responsible behavior prior to acceptance into the program, screening will be more efficient and less prone to subjective bias. This is done as the potential volunteer is required to come to the program's office initially and perhaps again for a followup session. By the act of attending, his level of investment increases, responsible behavior is demonstrated, and program personnel have an opportunity to discover the source of the person's interest in the volunteer activities offered by the program. At the followup meeting, the volunteer can be assigned to a particular activity; the type of activity should include direct contact with the inmate unless a unique situation arises that might not allow this (Katz, 1970). Where questions of the volunteer's readiness to work with inmates remain after the initial few meetings, it is best to have him perform a series of approximations of the volunteer task. This may include working with a group of volunteers who are setting up a birthday party for an inmate. This way he will be doing a service but with less autonomy than he may later experience. If he is able to perform tasks satisfactorily, it is likely that he can function more independently; if not, he can be moved to a less responsible job in the program (i.e., typing, collecting magazines for the institution, etc.), thus averting potential program problems.

Emphasis on behavior should be part of a volunteer effort to help the inmate as well as to screen volunteers. Volunteers are not needed to explore the psyche; they can have a greater impact through activities *with* the inmate, not *to* him.

The importance of *doing with* a client cannot be overemphasized in programs having direct client contact. By doing, rather than discussing the reason why a client should do (e.g., going with a client to apply for a job rather than suggesting that he do so, helping an inmate with math rather than telling him to get an education), two powerful forces are brought into play that encourage behavior change. The first is modeling behavior (Bandura, 1974). Much of what we learn is through watching the behavior of others and the resulting rewards or lack of rewards for the behavior. By sitting with a client and discussing future behavior with him, a volunteer, by his presence and attention, rewards not the *activity* but merely the *discussion* of future behavior. The client learns to talk seriously about the future but only sees rewards linked to the discussion and not to the act. A second force related to behavior change is the concept of "cognitive dissonance" (Festinger, 1957). The notion that behavior change follows attitude change has been demonstrated to be false. Instead, the reverse is true and is explained by a person's need for consonance between actions and feelings. If a person feels that he does not like camping but finds himself in a tent, he is in a state of dissonance that must be resolved. To do so, he must either deny his statement of feelings or his behavior. The resolution invariably chosen is in favor of behavior. The person will find a "reason" for what he has done. It is obviously important that the behavior for which a person finds a rationale be an appropriate behavior. A number of these can be engaged in by the inmate that will be useful after release from the institution. The process of dissonance resolution strongly maintains the behavior performed.

As inmates find value in doing new behaviors through cognitive dissonance, so do volunteers and staff learn to value the roles each may play. As volunteers meet with inmates, they must also inter-face with institution staff. Through observing each other they discover they do not have mutually exclusive concerns but instead can see value in what they each do. If this does not occur, the volunteer program will not survive.

McClelland (1965) has suggested 11 propositions that will in-crease motivation. These should be applied to institution staff who will interface with volunteers as well as to volunteers.

(1) The more reasons a person has to believe that he should develop a motive in the program, the more likely he is to do so;

(2) A person must feel his involvement is consistent with de-mands of reality and reason;

(3) A person will be more highly motivated if his definition of his motivation is clearly consistent with that of the program;

(4) There must be a clear link between the program's actions and the volunteer or staff member;

(5) The motivation of the program must be linked to events in the person's everyday life;

(6) He must perceive and experience new motivation as an improvement in current cultural values;

(7) A person should achieve concrete program goals that also relate to his own life;

(8) He should keep records of progress toward his goals;

(9) The atmosphere of orientation should be warm, honest, and supportive; a person should be respected as someone who can guide and direct his own future behavior;

(10) Orientation should dramatize self-study and lift it out of the routine of everyday life; and

(11) Motivation is more likely to increase and persist if the new motive is a sign of membership in a new reference group. What-ever changes occur must be consistent with the person's self-image if he is not to reject them.

The eleventh proposition is most critical. For the volunteer to remain, he must become friends with other volunteers *and* insti-tution staff. Ideally, staff and volunteers will like each other and will do things together away from the institution. When this occurs, it is a clear sign of establishing the setting for program success. Friends working together are more effective than people who are suspicious and untrusting.

As we consider the ramifications of these assumptions, we see why volunteer programs are so difficult to establish and maintain. It is easy to get the impression that volunteer programs are unwanted and unwelcome in the institution. This should never be the case. There is no place where willing people from society are needed more. These restrictions should not deter the institution from actively seeking volunteers, nor volunteers from making contributions to the institutions. It is only that the practice arena has a few more necessary rules that must be followed. Within these restrictions, the volunteer can make tremendous contributions, and the institution can benefit greatly from well-established volunteer programs.

REFERENCES

Andrews, D. A., J. G. Young, J. S. Wormith, Carole A. Searle, and Marina Kouri. "The attitudinal effects of group discussions between young criminal offenders and community volunteers." *Journal of Applied Behavioral Sciences*, *1*, 4 (October 1973): 417–22.

Bandura, Albert. "Behavior theory and the models of man." *American Psychologist* (December 1974): 851–69.

Duck, Steven. "Friendship, similarity and the reptest." *Psychological Reports*, *31*.1 (August 1974): 231–34.

Festinger, Leon. *A Theory of Cognitive Dissonance*. Evanston, Illinois: Row, Peterson, 1957.

Katz, Alfred. "Self-help organizations and volunteer participation in social welfare." *Social Work* (January 1970): 51–60.

McClelland, David C. "Toward a theory of motive acquisition." *American Psychologist*, *20*,5 (1965): 321–33.

Rosenbaum, Milton and Robert R. Blake. "Volunteering as a function of field structure." *Journal of Abnormal and Social Psychology*, *50*,2 (1955): 193–96.

Weick, Karl E. *The Social Psychology of Organizing*. Reading, Mass.: Addison-Wesley Publishing Co., 1969.

Chapter 17

THE DELIVERY OF SERVICES TO FAMILIES OF PRISONERS*

JUDITH F. WEINTRAUB

Traditionally, very few social service agencies, either governmental or voluntary, have identified families of incarcerated
individuals as needing specific informational, counseling, and
other supportive services. Departments of correction generally
formulate their programs only with regard to the offender in their
care. When the National Conference of the Association of Social
Workers committed themselves in 1973 to working in the corrections field, it totally omitted any mention of families of prisoners.
These families, in situations of acute emotional disequilibrium,
do require a range of services. They need basic information on
which they can proceed to structure their lives. They need counseling to assist them in reformulating their new family unit.

A family member of an incarcerated individual may indeed
receive social work services from one of a number of agencies but
it is rare that the special problems arising out of the incarceration
of the family member will be recognized and dealt with properly.
In addition, there is no formal mechanism to deliver basic information about the jails, the courts, the prisons and what is happening
to an individual who passes through them. It is therefore necessary
to identify the families of the incarcerated individuals as a discrete
client group with specific problems and to have the appropriate
agencies assume responsibilities for dealing with these problems.

IDENTIFICATION OF CRISIS POINTS

Four specific crisis points have been identified for the family of
an individual passing through the criminal justice system. They

---

*From *Federal Probation*. 1976 40(4), 28–31. Reprinted with the permission of the publisher.

are arrest and arraignment, sentencing, initial incarceration, and immediate/pre/post release. An examination of the crisis points showed that families experience a twofold need which is common throughout the system (Schwartz and Weintraub, 1974).

SPECIFIC RECOMMENDATIONS

Arrest and Arraignment

The obvious first crisis of the family comes when the family member is arrested and arraigned. If the arrested individual is remanded to detention there may be a lapse of time before the family is notified by the inmate. Such notification, when and if it comes, will not necessarily include such important information as the name by which the individual is known to the institution, the exact location of the institution, how to travel there, what restrictive rules govern visiting, writing, and packages, and what requirements apply to bail.

All families of arrested individuals have in common the problems of discovering the name of the defense attorney if he is from the public defender's office or appointed by the court, when the next court appearance will be, what happened at the last court appearance, and what is the approximate period of time it can be expected that the proceedings will take.

To begin to meet these basic informational needs, it is recommended that the institutional authorities provide a preprinted, when appropriate bilingual, form to every individual remanded to a detention facility. The form should include the name and address of the institution, the nearest public transportation, visiting hours, the name by which the individual is known to the institution, and a telephone number to call for further information.

It is further recommended that the governmental agency with the responsibility for maintaining detention institutions should establish a centralized office which can provide information on location of individual inmates, location of institutions, means of transportation to them, visiting hours and regulations, and the names and telephone numbers of voluntary agencies which can provide further services to families. The telephone number of this office should be the one which appears on the forms mailed out by the detainees. This service lends itself to the use of paraprofessionals and/or volunteers.

Sentencing

The second crisis point for the families of individuals going through the criminal justice system is at the time those persons are sentenced to prison. Once again, the families generally cannot obtain information as to which facility their family members will be sent, approximately when they will be transferred there, where the institution is located, how to travel to that institution, what are the regulations for visiting, what must be done to write to the individuals, what are the regulations on sending packages, transfer of money, and most simply, how long is the sentence and when is the earliest possible release. This is in addition to the problems of need for financial assistance, be it welfare or work, problems with housing, and outstanding bills (especially for installment buying). There is also a plethora of internal family problems relating to the need to redefine the family unit in the absence of the incarcerated individual. These problems are especially critical when children are involved. Whether the children remain within the family or with some other family member, or whether they are placed in care, there is still the question of interpreting to them what has happened to the incarcerated parent and why. Questions concerning communication (including institutional visits) must be addressed. The whole continuing relationship between the children and the incarcerated parent must be carefully evaluated on the merits of each individual case.

To meet these problems it is recommended that there be established in the court building itself an office which would assume the responsibility of providing information to families at the time of sentencing. Such an office could be sponsored by a public agency such as probation or the public defender, or by a voluntary agency. The staffing of such offices could well be supplemented by the use of volunteers, especially persons who have been or are at that time members of families of incarcerated individuals. The family would be notified of the availability of this service at the time the defendant is sentenced. At the Family Assistance Office, families would be given a bilingual (where appropriate) printed brochure which would include the location of the facility to which the individual is being sent, how to find out when that transfer has taken place, how to travel to the institution, including reference to free bus services which might be available, regulations on visiting, correspondence, and packages. Staff personnel would give as much of this information as necessary orally, paying particular attention to explaining the minimum release date. If the family so wished, staff would also make an appointment with a private agency for further counseling within as short a period of time as possible.

In order for these to be effective services for families of incarcerated individuals, voluntary agencies doing casework with the general public as well as those programs designed specifically for offenders must be involved.

It is therefore recommended that those voluntary agencies already providing services to the general community identify the members of their clientele who are families of incarcerated individuals. Agencies dealing with children in care should identify which of their clients have incarcerated parents. These agencies should provide orientation and training for staff to enable them to recognize the specific problems of this subgroup and to deal with those problems effectively.

Wherever possible, the voluntary agencies should establish regularly scheduled group sessions for families of incarcerated individuals. These groups, which can effectively utilize volunteer and peer group resources from the community, would focus on problems with children, redefining the family structure, relationships between the family and the incarcerated individual. Any specific problems needing more intensive attention that are identified within the group sessions would be referred to an individual counselor in the same agency or referred to an outside service agency. (It should be noted that provisions for child care and carfare are of essential importance to the success of such a program.)

Further, it is essential that those agencies presently working with offenders recognize that the problems of the family are the problems of the offender also. Whenever possible, a program servicing offenders should work with the individual in the context of his total family.

Institutionalization

The third crisis point occurs at the time that the individual is sent to prison to serve his sentence. The family must redefine itself in the absence of the incarcerated member in such a way as to still include him. In addition, the newly incarcerated individual will rapidly begin to interact with his new milieu. His natural effort to adapt may impose one more strain on the family. The incarcerated person makes demands on the family which they have no way of validating and which they often cannot meet.

In addition to these internal problems, the family must learn to cope with a bewildering new bureaucracy. Traditionally, departments of correction have not established services to meet the needs of families, even on the simplest levels. There is no formal structure to which the family can relate to obtain the information they need about the functioning of the institution and particularly about the status and problems of the incarcerated family member. There is no one to whom the family can give and from whom they can get information. In addition, the varying institutional rules from one facility to another even within one state (or the Federal) system creates confusion.

A far step toward reducing confusion would be accomplished if uniform regulations were established for all institutions within the same system on what can be sent by the family to the incarcerated individual and what constraints are put on visitors with regard to visiting room regulations.

In addition, all reception institutions should provide the inmate with a bilingual (where appropriate) informational mailing containing the location of and traveling instructions for all institutions, rules and regulations on writing, visiting, and packages, and the department in each institution to be contacted if there are any questions. (If all rules are standardized, this can be one mailing from the reception institution.)

Families should be notified *immediately* when an individual has been transferred to another institution and they should be given the reason for the transfer. Family needs should be taken into consideration in any assignment to an institution when possible.

Departments of correction, local, state, and Federal, should accept their responsibility for the families of inmates by:

1. Establishing a coordinating function for all program and services to families. This would include developing and coordinating those programs that exist within a department, such as family visitation services, volunteer and institutional information services, and other department-wide programs for families. It would also include acting as liaison between the department and the community agencies providing services to families of incarcerated individuals.

2. Establishing a family visitation service which would provide at least free transportation from the nearest point of public transportation to a given institution.

3. Initiating programs in the institutions to deal with problems which families may be having with the incarcerated individuals or with the institutions themselves. Such a program can effectively utilize individuals who themselves have been members of families of incarcerated individuals.

4. Developing within the institutions social service units the capability to work with any other program providing service to families or directly with the families themselves. It should serve as a liaison between the inmate with regard to the problems of his family and those community agencies which can deal with the problems.

Prerelease and Parole

The last crisis point occurs when the individual returns to his family. During the period of incarceration, the family has made an adjustment to continue a stable existence without the presence of that family member. The incarcerated individual has adapted to existence in the prison society. There is presently minimal attention given to preparing the incarcerated individual to return to his family or preparing the family to receive him. There is little or no continuity between planning which may be done for the individual in the institution and agencies which may have been working with the family in the community and the field parole office.

At the time the inmate is to meet the parole board, the department of parole should provide families of prospective parolees with information as to the parole process, how they can possibly influence it, when the inmate will meet the parole board, the amount of time after parole is granted before the individual will actually be released, and the general rules and regulations of parole. The parole officer should also ascertain if the family is receiving any services from a community agency. If not, and the family so wishes, he should refer them to an appropriate agency for prerelease adjustment counseling.

If the family of an incarcerated individual has been known to a community agency, that agency should be invited to submit recommendations to be incorporated in the parole plan for the incarcerated individual.

Community agencies should develop group sessions similar to

those described earlier to help families identify those problems which can be expected when the incarcerated individual is released. (Whenever possible, the agency should continue to work with the family and the releasee after his return to the community.)

Prerelease orientation sessions for inmates within the institutions should include discussion of problems to be encountered in reentering the family structure. Whenever possible there should be consultation between those dealing with the families in the community agency and those running the prerelease orientations.

Once an individual is approved for parole, a meeting should be arranged between the inmate, his family, and a parole officer who has responsibility for the case at that time. Whenever possible, this meeting should be prior to release, with the inmate attending on furlough. If the individual is being transferred to a Community Residential Facility, a representative from that facility should be present at the meeting.

If an individual's parole is revoked, immediate notice (bilingual where appropriate) should be sent to the family including the name and location of the institution in which the individual is detained, traveling instructions to that institution, regulations for writing and visiting, the date that the hearings will be held and what representation and documentation is permitted at them. Consideration should be given to allowing the family to be present at the revocation hearings.

CONCLUSION

Many of the suggestions in this article can be implemented at little expense. The primary need is to recognize the families of prisoners as a group with specific problems needing specific responses. It is not necessary for a local bureau of child welfare to hire an expert on the problems of children of incarcerated parents. It would be sufficient to orient the already existing workers that such problems do exist and provide training as to how to deal with them.

Many of the services suggested can be well provided by volunteers, especially ones who themselves have had a family member in prison. More and more departments of correction are establishing volunteer services. It costs no additional money for such an office to establish a volunteer-operated desk in the visiting room of a prison to which families can go for assistance. Many problems can be answered by the dissemination of printed materials. Since most prisons have printshops, it should be an easy matter to have such forms duplicated.

There are no major or insuperable bars to providing many of the services required by prisoners' families. What is needed is the recognition by both private organizations and public agencies that an offender's family will generally have a strong effect on his postrelease behavior. It may be one of positive support, which argues for a maintenance of the family unit during the period of imprisonment. It may be one of negative pressure, which strongly suggests the need for programs to deal with the root problem. Whether for good or ill, the family exists and it behooves the public and private correctional establishment to recognize that fact.

REFERENCE

Schwartz, Mary C. and Weintraub, Judith F. "The Prisoner's Wife: A Study in Crisis," *Federal Probation*, December, 1974, 20–26.

Chapter 18

STRENGTHENING FAMILIES AS NATURAL SUPPORT SYSTEMS FOR OFFENDERS*

Susan Hoffman Fishman and Albert S. Alissi

S ervice programs in the field of corrections traditionally focus their efforts on rehabilitating, controlling, or otherwise "treating" the individual offender, while little systematic attention is given to spouses, parents, children, relatives, and other significantly related individuals whose well-being is often placed in jeopardy as a result of the offender's incarceration. Although the offender in prison is provided with food, clothing, shelter, some opportunity for job training, and other types of physical and emotional support, the family, specifically the woman, he has left behind has had to deal with all their needs alone. Not only must the woman establish a new life, care for her children, and withstand the type of social criticism that can occur as a result of the crime committed by her loved one but she must also learn to cope with the unfamiliar and often frightening court and prison systems in order to maintain meaningful contact with the offender (Schwartz & Weintraub, 1974).

It has been documented that inmates who do maintain family ties while in prison have a better chance of remaining out of prison after their release. Drawing from a study of 412 prisoners of a minimum security facility in California, Holt and Miller (1972) concluded that there was a strong and consistently positive relationship between parole success and the maintenance of strong family ties during imprisonment. The study suggests that family members, as a natural support group for offenders, have a tremendous potential for assisting in the reintegration of the offender to community life.

---

*From *Federal Probation*. 1979 43(3) pp. 16–21. Reprinted with the permission of the publisher.

Since family members themselves, however, are under new pressures and face new financial and emotional burdens during the separation process, they are usually not in a position to serve in an effective helping capacity until they stabilize their own lives and adapt to the "crisis" situation brought on by their loved one's incarceration.

Judith Weintraub and Mary Schwartz recognized and documented the need and importance of prompt assistance for families of offenders (Schwartz & Weintraub, 1974; Weintraub, 1976). It is these individuals who must be helped to sustain themselves and maintain stable relationships during separation so that the family unit can offer an offender the support and security he will need upon his release. Although specialized assistance to prisoners' families can be essential to the well-being of the family members themselves and their corresponding ability to assist in the reintegration process of the offender, recognition of the unique needs of these families and appropriate services are not available through existing social service agencies. And even though existing literature on families of offenders clearly indicates the specific needs of this special group, it presents little guidance on concrete, practical service programs that can effectively address such needs (Bakker et al., 1978; Schneller, 1975; Zemans & Cavan, 1958; Wilmer et al., 1966; Morris, 1967; Friedman & Esselstyn, 1965; Fenlon, 1972).

The purpose of this article is to describe an innovative pilot program in Connecticut that was designed to meet the special needs of offenders' families and has been formally evaluated as being highly successful in accomplishing that task.

Women in Crisis is a private, nonprofit program that utilizes trained volunteers to support and assist women from the Greater Hartford area whose husbands, boyfriends, or sons have been sentenced to prison for the first time. Women in Crisis was implemented in March of 1977.[1] During the planning stages of the project, the Advisory Board of Women in Crisis developed several basic, underlying concepts and premises upon which the program itself now operates: (1) the use of volunteers as service providers, (2) the relationship as the primary tool of the volunteer, and (3) advocacy as a role of the volunteer.

---

[1] Much of the early leadership in developing the program came from Margaret Worthington, a retired social worker, who conceived of the program in 1975 and served as the first President of the Women in Crisis Board of Directors.

THE USE OF VOLUNTEERS AS SERVICE PROVIDERS.

The first decision reached by the planners of Women in Crisis was an overwhelming commitment to the use of trained women volunteers as the primary service providers to clients. The Board and staff reached this decision after carefully documenting available research and observing the experiences of numerous women whose men were sent to prison. They realized that women whose men are sentenced to prison experience what is usually termed as a "crisis" in their lives, a short-term situational disturbance. Except in unusual circumstances, they are not pathologically damaged (Schwartz & Weintraub, 1974). Based on this information, the Board concluded that most women could adjust to the abrupt and distressing change in their life-styles with the help of an informed, sensitive individual (volunteer).

In September of 1978, a study on the first eight months of the program's operation was completed under the supervision of the University of Connecticut School of Social Work (Women in Crisis Program Evaluation, 1978). The researcher drew a total population sample including all clients and volunteers engaged in the Women in Crisis Program from March 1, 1977, through October 31, 1977. Interview schedules and questionnaires were developed, pretested in the field, and administered. Clients and volunteers were contacted using all available information on record at the Women in Crisis office. In all, twenty-two out of a total possible sample of forty clients were administered a personal interview; sixteen were unable to be contacted, and two refused to be interviewed. In addition, fourteen of the fifteen volunteers who had provided the services to the clients in the sample were identified and interviewed. The interview procedure was standardized and systematically applied to clients and volunteers alike. The study offered evidence that those volunteers who had been recruited from the community, trained by the program, and assigned to assist families of offenders had been highly successful in their roles and offered invaluable services to their clients. In addition, statements made by volunteers, clients, and representatives from the community agencies connected with the program stressed several important reasons why volunteers can and should be major service-givers for the Women in Crisis Program. All of these factors have universal implications:

(1) Volunteers as helpers are not seen by potential clients as

professional "do-gooders" or as part of any system connected with their recent experiences, but rather as concerned people addressing basic human needs.

(2) Volunteers as private citizens, taxpayers, and community participants have a vested interest in the functioning of the correctional process. Their involvement in this process not only serves as a means of monitoring the system but can also serve as a tool for its improvement. One fine example of volunteers as pacemakers for change has occurred over the past year-and-a-half at Superior Court in Hartford. Volunteers from Women in Crisis are present in court each sentencing day to approach and assist families immediately after an offender is sentenced and taken away. When the program initially began this service, court officials were suspicious of the volunteers and seemed indifferent to the needs of families in the court setting. For months, however, they have observed the positive effects resulting from information and support provided to families in court, and as a result, the sensitivity level of these court personnel has changed dramatically. Prosecutors, public defenders, and sheriffs are now personally escorting families to Women in Crisis volunteers for assistance and are openly acknowledging an understanding of the stress being experienced by the families.

(3) As a result of their participation in the program, volunteers receive personal satisfactions and opportunities for education and growth. All volunteers are required to complete the intensive Women in Crisis training program before assignment is made. Training consists of four classroom sessions, each three hours in length. Topics include an introduction to the criminal justice system, values clarification, interpersonal skills, crisis intervention, the culture of poverty, and a description of resources in the community. In addition to the classroom sessions, volunteers are also provided with orientations to Correctional Institutions and Superior Court. Periodic in-service training sessions are held throughout the year in order to provide detailed information on specialized topics of interest to Women in Crisis volunteers.

This growth and increased awareness of volunteers, in turn, affects the attitudes of others in the community with whom they come in contact. Women in Crisis volunteers interviewed for the program study highlighted some additional benefits gained through their involvement with the program. Half of the women interviewed observed an increase in their own sensitivity to the problems and strengths of others; approximately one-third of the volunteers felt that their communication skills became more highly developed; and one-third emphasized the satisfaction they received from making new acquaintances and coming to know women from different social and economic backgrounds.

(4) The participation of volunteers as the primary service providers to families of offenders is economically feasible for the program itself in a time when costs of services continue to increase.

RELATIONSHIP AS THE PRIMARY TOOL OF THE VOLUNTEER

A second major concept, which was substantiated by data in the evaluation study of the program, identified the informal, personal, and nonprofessional relationship between the volunteer and her client as the most important factor in the client's adjustment to her new life. At certain times, particularly on sentencing day, on the first visit to the institution, and during the first few weeks of adjustment, the "woman in crisis" was in crucial need of the human, practical, and uncomplicated assistance that was offered by an objective, informal volunteer.

SENTENCING DAY. Regardless of the nature of the crime committed by an offender and the likelihood that the offense would necessitate his incarceration, most families are not prepared for the possibility that the man will, in fact, be going to prison for an indefinite length of time and, as a result, display symptoms of shock, panic, or emotional turmoil in court when sentencing does occur. Therefore, Women in Crisis was structured in such a way that volunteers, under the supervision of a court liaison staff person, would be available in court each sentencing day to provide immediate information on court procedures and prison rules as well as practical guidance and emotional support. The evaluation study substantiated the assumption that Women in Crisis clients would need and respond positively to informed, well-meaning volunteers in court, regardless of differences in race or social background.

Eighty-nine percent of those clients interviewed felt that it was important for them to have had someone in court to assist them on sentencing day and the vast majority of clients stated that the race of their volunteer made no difference to them. The type of human support that volunteers provide each week can best be understood by examining the specific experiences of Mrs. S and her volunteer, Jan.

> Mrs. S., a woman in her fifties, is a widow with five sons. Her eldest son was in court to be sentenced for a sexual offense. Mrs. S. spoke in open court to the judge. She told him how she had tried to help her son and how difficult it had been for her. Jan approached Mrs. S. after the judge had sentenced the young man, explained who she was, and asked if she could be of any assistance to her. Mrs. S. and Jan sat down together in the hallway, whereupon Mrs. S. put her head on Jan's shoulder and wept. She then expressed her feelings of frustration and shame in speaking before the judge. Jan assured her that her comments had made a great impact on the court. After talking with Jan for another fifteen minutes, Mrs. S. told Jan that "just as I thought I didn't have anyone to turn to, you were there to help me."

FIRST VISIT. The first visit by a woman to her loved one in prison is usually a very difficult experience. There are a great many specific regulations and a precise visiting procedure outlined by the institution that can be overwhelming to a family member who is unaccustomed to expressing feelings in such a structured environment. The location of the prison itself can often present an insurmountable problem to a family without access to private transportation.[2]

The ability of a family member to acquire the appropriate information and support necessary to overcome these practical and emotional obstacles can determine her feelings towards subsequent visits. For this reason, the initial Advisory Board and staff of Women in Crisis felt that it was imperative for a volunteer, as part of her job responsibilities, to accompany a woman on her first visit to the prison. The volunteer would, in no way, be part of the actual visit itself but would be available to guide the woman through the procedure and discuss her reactions to it before and after the visit itself. In addition, by offering private transportation during weekday hours, the volunteers would be providing the "woman in crisis" with the opportunity to visit for the first time

---

[2]Somers Correctional Institution in Somers, Connecticut, is the primary intake prison for adult male felons in Connecticut and, like many prisons throughout the country, is located in an area of the state that is not on any preestablished, major passenger routes. Until April of 1978, when Women in Crisis successfully advocated on behalf of its clients for increased public bus service to Somers, there was only one bus per week, which traveled from Hartford, the major urban area serviced by the program. This bus traveled only on the weekend when visiting hours are shorter and when the visiting room is the most congested. There is, however, no regular public transportation from other areas of Connecticut to Somers.

under less crowded conditions and for a longer period of time.

The evaluation study of Women in Crisis supported the program's commitment to the use of volunteers as helpers on the first visit. Over half of the clients interviewed experienced fear and nervousness before their first visit to the institution. Two-thirds of the clients interviewed indicated that they talked with their volunteers about their feelings prior to the first visit. Over 85 percent of the clients who were accompanied by their volunteers on their first visit said they relied heavily on the volunteer's presence. When asked whether it was helpful to have had a volunteer go with them on the first visit, 93 percent of the clients responded positively. Only those clients who were already familiar with the procedure felt that the volunteer's assistance was not imperative. It would seem, therefore, from this data that the presence of a caring, objective person at this critical time in the family's adjustment process is very helpful. One volunteer described a client's first visit and her own role as an important helper:

> When I met Dee for the first time, I was amazed that she seemed so calm and so much in control of herself. Until we went up to the prison together for that first visit, I wasn't sure what I could offer her. We talked quietly during the drive to Somers, but as we approached the parking lot of the prison, I noticed that her expression suddenly changed. We walked together to the metal detector and into the first waiting area. At this point, Dee completely broke down, refused to go any further and insisted that she would never come to this awful place again. I sat with her as she cried and quietly encouraged her to go into the visiting room, since her husband was probably just as nervous and anxious to see her as she was. After what seemed like hours, she did finally go in. Later she told me that she would never have done so if it had not been for me.

It should be mentioned at this point that Women in Crisis volunteers are instructed to accompany a client *only* on this first critical visit. The program does not want the volunteer to spend her time simply as a chauffeur. Nor does it feel that it is helpful for the "woman in crisis" to develop a dependency on the volunteer for transportation over a long period of time. Clients are, therefore, encouraged to develop their own resources. Since many clients mentioned during the evaluation interviews that the institution was frightening for them only until they became familiar with the visiting routine, it is apparent that continued volunteer support on additional visits is unnecessary.

THE SIX– TO EIGHT-WEEK ADJUSTMENT PERIOD. In addition to the critical support that a volunteer provides to her client at the specific points of crisis on sentencing day and on the first visit, a volunteer is also available as a resource on a continuing, intensive basis for the six– to eight-week period, which usually reflects the average critical adjustment time for a woman whose loved one has recently been incarcerated. Periodic follow-up can continue until the point when the man is released from the institution if the family desires this support. Clients interviewed indicated that of all the types of assistance provided by the volunteers during this adjustment period it was the most helpful to have been able to relate on a human level to another person, to have "someone to talk to." The following letter, which one client wrote to her volunteer, describes the impact that their relationship had on her life:

Dear Meg:
    I wrote you this letter to know how you field. I wish that when you recive this letter you are in good condition of health.
    Mrs. Meg, I wish you have a good luck in your summer vacation, I meet you because you was a wonder-women, who I was the pleasure to know. I would never forget the day I know you because you bring me your friendly when I was alone.
    Have a great summer vacation with all of your families. Stay as nice as you are. I will always remember you.

                                            Sincerely,
                                            Your friend, Maria.

ADVOCACY AS A ROLE OF THE VOLUNTEER

Although the initial Board of Women in Crisis considered the emotional support and assistance provided to a family member by a volunteer to be of critical importance, it also recognized additional concerns of clients that could not be addressed through emotional support alone. Families in turmoil need accurate information in order to make rational decisions about their future. They need to identify and establish contact with the appropriate personnel at the institution so that their concerns and fears about their loved ones can be expressed and addressed. They may need practical, professional services or crisis intervention to alleviate ongoing or emergency situations. Many families facing problems so soon after the offender's incarceration feel helpless and over-whelmed. For this reason, the planners of Women in Crisis concluded that it would be important for well trained, informed volunteers, as part of their job assignment, to assume a role of advocacy on behalf of their clients. They, as vocal representatives of an established organization, could serve as liaisons and investigators to gather and interpret necessary information and steer clients towards appropriate, existing services. They could also intervene on issues relating to the prison if the client had a justifiable complaint and received no satisfactory response to it.

Since March of 1977 when the program began operation, volunteers have assumed advocacy roles in specific cases. Various types of services that volunteers have provided and the results of their intervention are summarized below:

An agitated mother called her volunteer because her son had been writing to her and complaining that he was being heavily drugged at the prison. Since the mother was unable to clarify the situation, the volunteer called the institution as a representative of Women in Crisis and established, to the mother's relief, that the inmate was not being medicated.

In her conversations with a young family member, one volunteer discovered that, as of mid-October, the woman had not enrolled her children in school. The woman was embarrassed that the youngsters did not have proper clothing to wear to school. The volunteer suggested to the woman that they visit a local clothing bank together. When the woman acquired sufficient clothing for her children, she and the volunteer went to the school and registered the children in classes.

A volunteer whose client was being evicted from her apartment spent countless hours with her as the woman searched for suitable living quarters for herself and her small children.

A volunteer whose client was lonely and isolated in a suburban town arranged for a scholarship to a class at the local Y.W.C.A. for the woman so that she could meet and be with other women during the day.

An offender contacted the agency for help in reestablishing a relationship with his three and one-half-year-old son who was living with his former wife's parents. The parents had never responded to any of the offender's letters to them. A volunteer wrote a letter to the in-laws informing them of the man's desire to see his son upon his release from prison. When the in-laws responded to the letter, the volunteer was able to reassure them about the man's intentions and his awareness of the difficulties such a visit might cause. The in-laws were appreciative of the support offered by the volunteer and agreed to one initial visit between the child and his father. Subsequent visits ensued.

ADDITIONAL SERVICES

Although Women in Crisis was established to address the needs of offenders' families during the critical period immediately following the man's sentencing and initial incarceration, the program has begun to develop services at other key points in time when family members are equally in need of vital assistance. Judith Weintraub, in her article, "The Delivery of Services to Families of Offenders" (1976), identifies arrest and arraignment and pre– and postrelease as additionally turbulent and bewildering periods of crisis for families of offenders. The experiences of Women in Crisis over the past two years have substantiated her observations.

When loved ones cannot raise bail and must remain incarcerated for varying lengths of time prior to sentencing, families face practical, emotional, and financial burdens as a result of the man's abrupt absence from the home. Vital information on court and jail procedures is as confusing and difficult to obtain as it is once the man is sentenced. Family members whose men have served their time and are preparing to reenter community life have adjusted to new roles and taken on new responsibilities during the man's absence. Their expectations may not be consistent with those of the offender whose life in prison has been so vastly different from their daily existence on the street. Common goals and realistic plans must be established between the man and his family so that the offender may experience a smooth transition between prison and community life.

Women in Crisis volunteers have begun to provide support services to families of felony offenders who remain incarcerated prior to sentencing. These family members (whose loved ones are classified as "transfers") receive the same type of services provided by the agency to families of sentenced offenders. Counselors and other personnel at the correctional facility, private attorneys, public defenders, and bondsmen refer "transfer" families in need to the agency on a regular basis.

Within the "Return to Community" component, a family counselor is available to assist an offender and his family establish realistic goals and facilitate effective communication among family members. The family counselor is in the process of determining methods for utilizing trained volunteers within this new project.

Women in Crisis also runs "personal growth classes" and group activities for family members of offenders. These sessions not only provide the opportunity for women to gather socially but also allow them to discuss common problems and learn new skills that may be valuable to them as they adjust to new lives on their own. Some of the topics that have been addressed in the past include single person parenting, money management, and interpersonal communication.

SUMMARY

Existing literature is limited in that it hypothesizes on the various means for meeting needs of offenders' families but does not present concrete programs and methods for dealing with these specific needs. Women in Crisis authenticates a method of providing services that has major advantages. In the first place, it is practical and can be offered with limited financial resources because it utilizes trained women volunteers as primary service providers. In addition, it provides the opportunity for volunteers, as representatives of their communities, to serve in a positive way and contribute to the adjustment process of offenders' families. Not only do these volunteers realize personal rewards and satisfactions but they also offer an effective, straight-forward form of assistance that is viewed as genuine by family members "in crisis." To the extent that families are assisted in dealing with crises, there is every reason to believe that they can be strengthened to become a major source of support in furthering the rehabilitation of the offender as well.

REFERENCES

Bakker, Laura J., Morris, Barbara A., and Janus, Laura M. "Hidden Victims of Crime," *Social Work*, 23:2 (March, 1978).

Brodsky, Stanley. *Families and Friends of Men in Prison*. Lexington, Mass.: D.C. Heath & Co., 1975.

Fenlon, Sister Maureen. "An Innovative Project for Wives of Prisoners." *FCI Treatment Notes*, 3:2 (1972).

Friedman, Sidney, and Esselstyn, T. Conway. "The Adjustment of Children of Jail Inmates." *Federal Probation*, 29:4 (1965).

Holt, Norman, and Miller, Donald. *Explorations in Inmate Family Relationships.* Research Division, California Department of Correction Report Number 46. Sacramento, CA, January, 1972.

Morris, Pauline. "Fathers in Prison." *British Journal of Criminology*. Vol. 7 (1967).

Schafer, N. E. "Prison Visiting: A Background for Change." *Federal Probation*, 42:3 (September, 1978).

Schneller, Donald. "Some Social and Psychological Effects on the Families of Negro Prisoners." *American Journal of Correction*, 37:1 (1975).

Schwartz, Mary, and Weintraub, Judith. "The Prisoner's Wife: A Study in Crisis." *Federal Probation*, *38*:4 (December, 1974).

Wilmer, Harvey A., Marks, Irving, and Pogue, Edwin. "Group Treatment of Prisoners and Their Families." *Mental Hygiene*, Vol. 50 (1966).

Weintraub, Judith. "The Delivery of Services to Families of Prisoners." *Federal Probation*, *40*:4 (December, 1976).

Women in Crisis Program Evaluation: March 1, 1977–October 31, 1977. (Hartford, Conn.: Women in Crisis) 1978. Unpublished document.

Zemans, Eugene, and Cavan, Ruth Shonle. "Marital Relationships of Prisoners." *Journal of Criminal Law, Criminology and Police Science*, *47*:1 (1958).

Section VII

SPECIAL ISSUES AND
OFFENDER GROUPS

INTRODUCTION

G enerally speaking, services for offenders and their families are inadequate. The problems of being labelled a felon are often compounded for those offenders with special needs. The offender's potential for change is sometimes aggravated or complicated by special problems. This section examines the special offender groups that are increasingly represented in the criminal justice system.

Because systematic research on special offender groups is relatively scarce and research on the effectiveness of programs developed for these groups is even more scarce, the effects of special problems on behavioral change and rehabilitation have not yet been clarified. Nevertheless, recent practice and research reports suggest that special offender groups can benefit from services and programs that are responsive to their needs and life experiences.

In Chapter 19, James D. Jorgensen provides a model for assessing the degree of dangerousness among offenders as well as the offender's capacity to be changed and deterred. Much of the impetus for violent and dangerous behavior rests in felt powerlessness. People who feel they are insignificant or discounted are candidates for the commission of violent acts as a means for making their presence felt. The preventive strategy proposed by Jorgensen as an alternative to traditional psychotherapeutic approaches incorporates the concepts of empowerment and mastery to reduce dangerousness. Integral to the proposition is that the social worker assume six central roles: advocate, broker, mediator, guardian, enabler, and conferee; the focus of the strategy should be that of linking the offender and the community to one another by directing change efforts at both entities.

In Chapter 20, Kay Seeley Hoffman explores the correctional treatment provided to female offenders. At the outset, Hoffman examines the prison conditions, special problems, and needs of women offenders. She then identifies important roles for social workers in servicing women offenders. The importance of community-based programs is stressed. Through the application of systems theory and case vignettes, the roles of enabler, broker, and advocate are described.

In Chapter 21, Dan W. Edwards delineates the special concerns and behavioral problems of the following offender types: alcoholic offenders, drug abusers, sex offenders, and older offenders. These types of offenders are represented in growing numbers in criminal justice settings. Edwards points out the need for designing programs around the unique needs of prisoners with special problems. Large numbers of offenders are afflicted with complex behavioral problems such as drug addiction, sexual deviance, psychopathy, and sociopathy. Criminal justice practitioners should become cognizant of the psychodynamics of each disability, as well as the community resources for intervening on behalf of the offender.

In Chapter 22, Joseph Palenski explores the increased interracial violence and strain among prison inmates. The often unpredictable and volatile environment in most American prisons poses new obstacles to developing a correctional social services program. This chapter examines some of the factors important for an understanding of the role race plays in prison. It discusses how these race configurations have changed, while touching on the ways these changes impact on the delivery of services. Social workers need to be sensitive to the racial suspicion and tension that permeates prison life. They also need to develop a range of advocacy and mediation skills in order to serve clients within turbulent prison environments.

Chapter 19

ASSESSMENT AND MANAGEMENT OF POTENTIALLY DANGEROUS OFFENDERS

JAMES D. JORGENSEN

W hen discussing the "potentially dangerous" offender, it must be recognized there is a glaring lack of clarity about the meaning of the term. Is a potentially dangerous person different from a dangerous one? If so, how? What constitutes dangerousness? Given that we could agree on what dangerousness is, could we agree on who is potentially dangerous?

According to a *Harvard Law Review* article (1974) on civil commitment laws for the mentally ill, the criteria the states employed in committing individuals to institutions included the following: (a) is dangerous to self or others (29 states), (b) is in need of care or treatment or is a fit subject for hospitalization (29 states), (c) is unable to care for his physical needs (15 states), and (d) requires commitment for his own welfare or others' (7 states). These criteria are vague and confusing, and they do little to help us understand dangerousness.

The Model Sentencing Act identifies two types of dangerous offenders: "(1) the offender who has committed a serious crime against a person and shows a behavior pattern of persistent assaultiveness based on serious mental disturbance, and (2) the offender deeply involved in organized crime" (National Council on Crime and Delinquency, 1973). This categorization of dangerousness, while somewhat more helpful, still leaves us searching for a more precise definition.

This writer contends that the terms "dangerous" or "potentially dangerous" ascribe to individuals so labeled a higher probability of hurting people, damaging property, or taking a human life than is ascribed to the general population. In reality, the difference, if any, between dangerous and potentially dangerous is negligible.

309

The working definition of dangerousness employed herein is *the extent or degree to which a person is viewed as likely to inflict physical injury, harm or violence, or cause death to another person or to self.*

Social workers and other professionals working within the criminal justice system make daily decisions affecting the lives of people who have been described as dangerous. Each such decision reflects the predictions made by the decision-maker about someone's dangerousness. The question is, can we accurately predict who will be dangerous?

Item: A forty-eight-year-old man confronts his estranged forty-two-year-old lover as she returns to her apartment with a new boyfriend. After a brief argument he shoots her with a shotgun, then turns the weapon on himself. The police report describes the incident as a murder-suicide.

Item: A thirty-three-year-old man is advised by his thirty-four-year-old male roommate, source of financial support and friend of thirteen years, that he is planning to be married in the near future and will be leaving the house they had both occupied. He is further advised he will have to pay the rent alone and support himself. In the panic that ensues, the disappointed roommate kills his "best friend." An autopsy reveals that the victim had been beaten on the head, stabbed in the neck, and strangled.

Item: A forty-two-year-old male security guard, employed by a large national discount store, is informed by the store manager that he is to be fired. The guard produces a .38 caliber revolver and shoots the store manager several times, killing him. He also critically wounds the manager of security. He later seeks out his friend, a policewoman, who induces him to surrender.

Item: A twenty-four-year-old babysitter becomes "mad and upset" over her inability to stop an eleven-month-old baby's screaming and crying. She slaps her and the child falls to the floor and stops breathing. The babysitter revives her by blowing into her nose. Later she shakes the child, attempting to get the lethargic baby to respond to her. The child loses consciousness and dies the next day of a fractured skull.

The above vignettes are actual accounts of dangerous people. None of them had previously been arrested or known to be violent. All were described by those who knew them in such terms as, "upstanding," "decent," or "quiet and mild-mannered." It is doubtful that anyone considered them capable of taking someone's life, or even as potentially dangerous. Yet all four of these people were lethal. They killed fellow human beings and, in so doing, added to the growing number of homicides committed in the United States.

Is the state of the art such that the dangerousness of these four people could have been predicted? It is one thing to exclaim in retrospect as we often do that, "They were time bombs waiting to explode." It is quite another to say, "this person will kill."

Perry Smith and Dick Hickock, convicted killers of the Clutter family in the best seller, *In Cold Blood* (Capote, 1965), are excellent examples of walking time bombs. Smith, who actually pulled the trigger in these murders, would probably not have killed without the deadly presence of Hickock. While both men were time bombs waiting to explode, many human time bombs never go off, not because they don't have the capacity to do so, but because they fortunately never encounter the type of interactional situation that triggers the explosion.

One could easily take the position that anyone has the potential to kill another human if the stakes are high enough. In the case of the four individuals described above, the stakes were loss of friendship, love, financial security, and control, high stakes to be sure. If in fact we all have homicidal potential, we are in a most uncertain and unsettling environment in which to assess each other's potential for dangerousness!

An abundance of literature supports the premise that *dangerousness cannot, at this point in time, be reliably predicted*. In reviewing this literature, Monahan (1981) delineated the issues and discussed them in detail. For our purposes, however, suffice it to say that predictions of dangerousness are fraught with many legal, ethical, and practical problems, and we who attempt to make them face a high rate of error.

If we cannot predict dangerousness, what can we do about it? First of all, we can study its dynamics: by observing people who have acted out their dangerousness, we can become more sensitive to the characteristics of dangerous persons and the force field in which they were operating. When we learn more about what triggers violent behavior, we can expand the area of our concern beyond the violent person. Dangerous behavior, like other kinds of behavior, occurs as a transaction between the individual and the environment. The latter is often ignored in our concern for the "pathology" of the offender.

Finally, we can frame our study of dangerousness in the context of two other concepts that are vitally important to social workers in criminal justice: modifiability and deterrability. By so doing, we allow ourselves to discuss potential for change and potential for prevention of behavior as well as potential for dangerousness.

May (1972) convincingly makes the point that the chief source of violence lies in felt powerlessness, impotence, and apathy.

> As we make people powerless, we promote their violence rather than its control. Deeds of violence in our society are performed largely by those trying to establish their self-esteem, to defend their self-image, and to demonstrate that they, too, are significant. Regardless of how derailed or wrongly used these motivations may be or how destructive their expression, they are still the manifestations of positive interpersonal needs. We cannot ignore the fact that, no matter how difficult their redirection may be, these needs themselves are potentially constructive. Violence arises not out of superfluity of power, but out of powerlessness.

This simple yet profound concept is vital to our thinking about violence and dangerousness, because it helps us not only to comprehend these phenomena but to formulate plans for intervention.

Much of the current legislation formulated to deal with violent offenders centers around "incapacitation," a polite term for incarceration. While incapacitation may seem inviting as a short range response, it reflects a shortfall of other solutions. Pragmatic in the sense that it removes dangerous people from the streets and, in so doing, satisfies public opinion, imprisonment is most expensive and has serious long-term implications. If we were to follow May's cue, our response to dangerous people would be to find ways to empower them.

TWO ROUTES TO DANGEROUSNESS

Turning away from the source of dangerousness for a moment, let us examine briefly the process by which people become violent and endanger others. A great deal can be learned by monitoring the routes people take in moving from manifest to actual dangerousness. Two distinct routes emerge.

Route one is the short route. It begins with passive or subassertive behavior that changes rapidly and dramatically to behavior of violent and dangerous proportions. Route one people suppress a great deal of anger for a time; they appear outwardly to be quiet, kind, and helpful, terms that have, incidentally, been used to describe many of our contemporary assassins. Unable to deal with their powerlessness or threatened with serious loss, they erupt in violence and leave their admirers in a state of shock, dismay, and disbelief.

The second route to dangerousness is more of a continuum, and the end behavior holds fewer surprises to the observer. Route two is more typical of the path followed by correctional agency clientele; it begins with aggressive behavior, a term Bandura (1973) defines as, "... behavior that results in personal injury and in destruction of property. The injury may be psychological (in the form of devaluation or degradation) as well as physical." This behavior, reinforced, leads to violence and subsequent dangerousness.

Our two routes to dangerousness are shown in Figure 19-1.

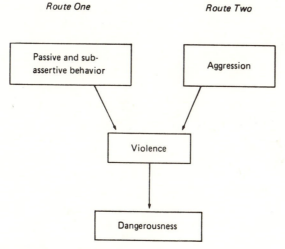

Figure 19-1. Two Routes to Dangerousness.

It should be recognized that aggression and violence have positive support in our culture; for example, one has to be aggressive, we're told, to survive, to make sales, to get ahead, and to compete successfully in the world of work and on our unsafe streets. Violence is considered an essential ingredient of human nature. Lorenz (1963) refers to "militant enthusiasm" as a "specialized form of communal aggression."

If we reject the idea of violence, we nevertheless reinforce its continued presence. Football coaches admonish their players for not being violent enough or for being reluctant to hurt people. Beyond that, we sanction the discharge of violence by whole armies of people, whether Central Intelligence Agents or Green Berets. Killing, legitimized in the jungles of southeast Asia, comes back to haunt us years later in the form of dangerous Viet Nam veterans suffering from "delayed stress syndrome."

THE ROUTE TO SAFETY

Noticeably absent from our discussion on dangerousness is the term "assertiveness." There is ample reason for this: the assertive person, whether through social learning or formal training, has arrived at a balance between indiscriminate discharge and total suppression of aggression. The assertive person has been empowered to decide rather than to react. A decider selects from a range of choices on how to deal with people and situations. Thus, assertiveness becomes a pivotal position, leading the individual away from either subassertiveness or aggression—dangerousness—to safety.

We might call this road to safety via assertiveness "alternative route three" and map it as shown in Figure 19-2.

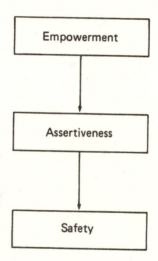

Figure 19-2. The Route to Safety.

THREE DIMENSIONS: DANGEROUSNESS,
MODIFIABILITY, AND DETERRABILITY

As was mentioned earlier in our discussion, two important dimensions must be considered in addition to the dimension of dangerousness. These are modifiability, the degree of change that can realistically be expected from an offender, and deterrability, the degree to which social controls can be expected to dissuade an offender from further violent conduct.

Modifiability, as we will discuss it here, goes well beyond the traditional concept of "treatability." It relates to a broader question, namely to what extent can the offender's behavior and environment be changed? Phrased in this way, the query addresses potential for change resulting from counseling and psychotherapy and from education, training, and environmental and community intervention. This expanded question opens up a wider array of roles on the part of the worker, because answering it demands the worker become engaged in intersystemic intervention.

The third concept, deterrability, concerns the degree to which the offender will refrain from further violent behavior as a result of the aversive nature of prosecution and correctional experience, including fines, loss or threat of loss of freedom, the stigma of conviction, and other kinds of punishment. The meaning of social control to the offender is important in this respect.

The worker, in this construct, is faced with ultimately determining whether an offender is dangerous, modifiable, and deterrable. The three concepts are weighed against each other and an offender is classified within one of the following categorizations:

1. Dangerous, deterrable, modifiable.
2. Dangerous, deterrable, not modifiable.
3. Dangerous, not deterrable, modifiable.
4. Dangerous, not modifiable, not deterrable.
5. Nondangerous, deterrable, modifiable.
6. Nondangerous, deterrable, not modifiable.
7. Nondangerous, not deterrable, modifiable.
8. Nondangerous, not deterrable, not modifiable.

Classification within one of these categories is no simple task. It requires first answering a bank of questions that are not always easy to answer. To these, we now turn our attention.

Dangerousness Questions

    I. Stresses the offender was under at the time of the offense.
       A. Was the offender provoked?
       B. Would the offender behave in a similar way again?

Discussion: The importance of these questions is that external factors often enter into a violent act. Provocation by someone, particularly if one's "honor" is at stake, can result in a violent response. It is important to assess the likelihood of a similar provocation, as well as the likelihood of a similar response to it.

       C. Was the offender led?
       D. Does the offender bend to peer pressure?

Discussion: We should keep in mind that people who are easily led may be coerced to commit dangerous acts. The individual who seeks to prove self-worth or please others is likely to lack the critical judgment necessary to weigh social situations.

    II. The instant offense.
       A. Did the instant offense involve violent behavior?
       B. Has the offender been involved in violent behavior recently?
       C. Was the offense situational or planned?
       D. If planned, to what degree was the offender involved in the planning?

Discussion: These questions are aimed at two aspects of the offender's behavior. How close at hand is the behavior? How involved was the offender in the act? If the behavior is recent and responded to quickly, we are in a more favorable position to intervene. Knowing the degree of involvement in the planning of the act on the part of the offender can provide a clue as to whether the act was intentional or situational.

    III. Meaning of the offense to the offender.
       A. Does the offense reflect a high level of criminal sophistication?
       B. Was the defendant armed? Did he use a weapon in committing the offense?

    C. Did the offender inflict bodily injury in connection with the offense?

    D. To what extent were victims harmed in connection with the offense?

Discussion: These questions reflect a concern about the offender's intent to do violence and the extent to which he carried out his intentions by injuring others.

  IV. Prior record of criminal behavior.
    A. What is the frequency of the behavior?
    B. How serious has previous behavior been?
    C. At what age did the offender first come into contact with the criminal justice system?
    D. What is the offender's age now?
    E. What patterns or types of offenses have been in evidence in the offender's past?

Discussion: One of the strongest indicators of potential for violence is the extensiveness of previous criminal behavior. Monahan (1981) notes that the likelihood of future crime increases with each prior criminal act. In terms of age, we know that juveniles between fifteen and twenty years of age, while representing 8.5 percent of the population, constitute 35 percent of arrests for violent crime (Zimring, 1978). The age at which one enters the system is also significant (Wolfgang, Figlio, & Sellin, 1972). One is more likely to become an adult offender if one is a juvenile offender.

  V. Childhood experiences.
    A. What childhood losses has the offender suffered?
      1. Have these losses been resolved?
      2. How?
    B. Did the offender experience childhood burns?
    C. Did the offender experience physical abuse?
    D. Did the offender experience emotional abuse?
    E. Did the offender experience emotional neglect?
    F. Did the offender experience physical neglect?
    G. Was the offender sexually abused?

Discussion: The above questions are particularly important in view of recent observations that abusive parents report being abused as children (Steele & Pollock, 1968).

VI. Behavioral patterns.
   A. What is the offender's pattern in terms of aggressive or assaultive behavior?
      1. Does the offender place himself in high-risk situations?
      2. Does the offender seek out trouble?
   B. Is the offender impulsive?
      If so, is the impulsiveness linked to criminality?
   C. Has the offender been steadily losing control over time?
   D. Do drugs and alcohol play a part in the behavior?
   E. Is there a history of use of weapons?
   F. Have there been suicide threats? Attempts?
   G. Has the offender previously damaged property?
   H. Is there a history of arson?
   I. Does the offender enjoy inflicting pain on others?
   J. Is there a history of spouse abuse?
   K. Is there a history of mutilating animals?
   L. Has the offender experienced psychotic episodes?
      If so, did these episodes include fantasies of violence toward others?
   M. Do psychological tests point to violence?

Discussion: Most of the above questions are self-explanatory. All are designed to determine whether the offender's loss of control over behavior is increasing and how imminent a threat the offender presents to others.

VII. Demographics.
   A. What is the sex of the offender?
   B. Is the offender married, either legally or by common law arrangement?
   C. Is the offender's income high or low?
   D. Is the offender skilled or unskilled?
   E. Is the offender well educated or poorly educated?
   F. Is the offender living in a rural or urban community?

Discussion: An unmarried male with a low income, poor education, few marketable skills, and residing in an urban environment presents greater potential for criminal and dangerous behavior than males without those characteristics.

Modifiability Questions

    I. Stresses the offender was under at the time of the offense.
        A. To what extent did emotional problems contribute to the offense?
        B. Were any physical or mental handicaps operating at the time of the offense?
        C. What is the intelligence of the offender?

Discussion: Several factors may be operating at the time of an offense that may not be subject to change. Intelligence will remain more or less constant, whereas handicaps and emotional problems may be overcome.

    II. Meaning of the offense to the offender.
        A. Did the behavior meet physical, social, or psychological needs?

Discussion: Someone who commits an armed robbery of a taxi driver to obtain money to send to a sick mother is meeting a need different from the one met by someone who enjoys watching the victim shrink in fear as a pistol is placed next to his head. The latter offender is likely the more dangerous of the two.

        B. Is the offender remorseful?
        C. How well does the offender understand and own up to his responsibility for the offense?
        D. What degree of anxiety does the offender exhibit?
            If anxiety is present, is it based on concern about the behavior or concern over being apprehended?
        E. Does the offender wish to be different than he is?
            If so, can he describe how he would like to be?

Discussion: These questions are posed for the purpose of revealing the extent to which the offender feels the need to change and the urgency of the need. How the offender intends to change and to what end are also pertinent questions here.

III. Environmental considerations
  A. Is the offender's family a resource?
  B. What are the likely effects on the offender's family if he is imprisoned?
  C. Will the community accept the offender back into the community?
  D. What are the present police attitudes toward the offender?
  E. Is the victim living in the same community as the offender?
  F. What is the tenor of public opinion regarding the offender? What impact would public attitudes have on efforts to change the offender's behavior?
  G. Are any codefendants presently living in the offender's community?
  H. Are appropriate community resources available?
    1. Are schools, employment, and vocational training available?
    2. Are health, welfare, and mental health services available?
  I. Is adequate housing available for the offender?
  J. Are there significant others available to the offender?
  K. Are recreational opportunities available to the offender?
  L. Does the offender have immediate financial resources?

Discussion: Even though the offender may be highly motivated to change, prospects for modifiability may be seriously threatened if the offender's environment cannot or will not support these change efforts. The worker can commit a well-intentioned offender to failure if the plan for integration is faulty. If the response to many of the above questions are negative, intervention may be necessary in order to assist the community to better adapt to the offender.

IV. Perspective of the future.
  A. What are the offender's goals and objectives?
    1. Are they realistic?
    2. Are they achievable?
  B. How far can the offender project into the future?
  C. Does the offender believe his behavior has any relationship to his future?

    D. Is the offender amenable to counseling and reeducation?
    E. Would the offender view corrective efforts positively or negatively?
    F. Would the offender be amenable to making restitution?

Discussion: Efforts to involve the offender in any rehabilitation plan will ultimately depend upon his view of and plans for the future. The above questions are designed to determine the extent to which the offender is either "time bound" or capable of looking beyond the present.

Deterrability Questions

  I. Attitude toward the criminal justice system.
    A. Is the offender fearful of the system?
    B. Does the offender express a desire to be incarcerated?
    C. Does the offender constitute a danger to others if not incarcerated?
    D. How well has the offender performed under previous probation or parole supervision?
    E. Does the offender view himself as a criminal?
    F. Does the offender view himself as violent?

Discussion: The offender's attitude about himself and his relationship to the criminal justice system constitute important data in measuring deterrability. These questions get at the offender's view of himself as an enemy of society, or at the other extreme, a nonparticipant in society, and his expressed or unexpressed desire to live in prison.

  II. Legal issues.
    A. How do mandatory sentencing provisions influence decision making regarding the offender?
    B. Are there detainers from other jurisdictions?

Discussion: In some jurisdictions the legislature has preempted decisions by the criminal justice system. In those instances, our deterrability questions may be moot.

  III. Perspective of the future.
    A. How would probation be viewed by the offender?
      1. Would it be viewed as assistance?
        An inconvenience? Punishment? Freedom?

2. Would the probation officer focus on surveillance, counseling, brokerage, or all of these?
3. Would the offender comply with the terms of probation?

Discussion: Since there is a definite guardianship component in managing dangerous offenders, it is important to determine the extent to which the social control aspects of supervision would be abided. These questions seek to facilitate that determination.

DANGEROUSNESS, MODIFIABILITY, DETERRABILITY: MANAGEMENT CONSIDERATIONS

Having asked the above questions, the next task is that of getting the answers. The worker should be aware that many of the questions will be answered "unknown." Others will be answered only in part; still others will not be answered at all. Many of the questions are sensitive, and the worker should be alert to those that may, in and of themselves, trigger violent responses.

Once the answers are in place and the offender relegated to one of the eight categories, recommendations must be formulated and action plans designed. These action plans should take into account the realities posed by all facets of the case, and be implemented accordingly; for example, as guardians we may be sensitive to the damaging life experiences that have led to dangerousness, yet more responsive to the imminent danger presented by the offender to the community. Decisions under such circumstances are painful, but necessary. Let us now discuss recommendations and planning considerations for each of the categories.

DANGEROUS, DETERRABLE, MODIFIABLE. The first and most obvious question to arise with such an individual is, "how dangerous?" People classified as dangerous, but who are considered both deterrable and modifiable might well be placed in residential facilities within the community if supervision is adequate. Halfway houses might also provide the coercive structure to implement rehabilitative measures, such as psychotherapy or group counseling. A lengthy, suspended sentence may provide the punishment and threat necessary as a deterrent.

DANGEROUS, DETERRABLE, NOT MODIFIABLE. Someone described in these terms has only one thing operating for him: deterrability. One strategy aimed at deterrence might be a short "shock" experience in a closed facility followed by surprise release and surveillance-oriented supervision in the community. A lengthy suspended sentence might be useful as well.

DANGEROUS, NOT DETERRABLE, MODIFIABLE. An individual so described would best be processed under civil commitment proceedings. A closed psychiatric facility with rigorous standards for release is indicated in this case. Counseling-oriented aftercare would be a necessity.

DANGEROUS, NOT MODIFIABLE, NOT DETERRABLE. These are the people for whom prisons are the best resource available. Charles Manson comes to mind as a prototype of this classification. Sentences in these cases should be long enough to insure incapacitation of the offender until he reaches the age when dangerousness is no longer a reality.

NOT DANGEROUS, DETERRABLE, MODIFIABLE. These individuals can benefit from fines, suspended sentences, restitution, and human relations-oriented probation.

NOT DANGEROUS, DETERRABLE, NOT MODIFIABLE. A fine, a suspended sentence, and surveillance-oriented probation might be in order for these offenders.

NOT DANGEROUS, NOT DETERRABLE, MODIFIABLE. An example of this offender group is the habitual exhibitionist who, unresponsive to jail sentences, does respond to court ordered psychiatric treatment. An appropriate plan for this person might be a suspended sentence with court ordered treatment as a condition of suspension.

NOT DANGEROUS, NOT DETERRABLE, NOT MODIFIABLE. This offender is often a skid row resident who seeks ways to be jailed when the first snowflakes fly. He may throw a brick through a window and wait to be caught. There are few ready answers for this person. Release to a mission might be preferable in such cases. If this is not feasible, perfunctory probation with the offender being assigned to a "paper caseload" is recommended.

Before leaving this discussion, the reader is cautioned to remain ever alert to behavioral changes that indicate the need to reclassify individual offenders. We should look for signs that dangerousness is on the wane or that modifiability is more in evidence. The tentative nature of these categorizations cannot be overemphasized. No human assessment should be chipped in stone!

PREVENTIVE STRATEGIES FOR REDUCING DANGEROUSNESS

As this is being written, a bipartisan commission is preparing a report to the President on policy recommendations to deal with violent crime. While the scope of this paper does not allow for a detailed discussion of those recommendations, the commission openly pleads for more prisons and more federal aid to build them. This plea flies in the face of May's argument (1972) and certainly runs counter to the spirit of this paper. A strategy of incarceration is inherently dangerous because it increases the sense of powerlessness and loss of control that ultimately translates into violence. Any movement to reduce dangerousness must begin with a lobbying effort to combat the construction of more cell space.

Toffler (1980) discusses the need to attack loneliness if we are to combat violence.

> To create a fulfilling emotional life and a sane psychosphere for the emerging civilization of tomorrow, we must recognize three basic requirements of any individual: the needs for community, structure and meaning. . . . To begin with, any decent society must generate a feeling of community. Community offsets loneliness. It gives people a vitally necessary sense of belonging.

Both Toffler and May sense the root causes of violence lie in societies where people are discounted and rendered powerless. While they offer no easy answers to remediate the lives of those who have struck out in fury, they do provide clues for a preventive strategy.

If people are to take their place on this planet, it is crucial that the individual societies on the planet have plans to accommodate them. This includes providing social roles so that people "matter."

Once a part of the society, there is another fundamental requirement: that the individuals be provided assistance in mastering their world. This requires a strategy of empowerment. Again, to quote Toffler:

> At the very simplest and most immediate level, why not create a cadre of professional and paraprofessional "life organizers"? For example, we probably need fewer psychotherapists burrowing mole-like into id and ego, and more people who can help us, even in little ways, to pull our daily lives together.

Toffler's point is well taken. We would do well to rethink the time-worn medical and psychiatric treatment approach to problems that have ecological causes. The criminal has never been comfortable in the role of patient because he is, for the most part, not a patient. Monahan's observation (1981) warrants mention:

> With the exception of a higher prevalence of the "disorders" of alcoholism and drug dependence, prisoners do not appear to have higher rates of

diagnosable mental illness than their class matched peers in the open community.

If a preventive strategy of empowerment were to be developed, how would it look? How does one combat powerlessness and loneliness when working on the human service delivery line?

The indications are that social work is developing some promising, although untested, alternative approaches to social service delivery. Social work literature now features more material envisioning the social worker as a "generalist" (Anderson, 1981; Middleman & Goldberg, 1974). The generalist would be equipped to engage with other professionals in interdisciplinary approaches to complex social problems. Viewing social problems as a complicated interactional system, workers take on the primary professional roles of conferee, advocate, broker, enabler, mediator, and guardian. A more detailed discussion of these roles is in order.

Broker

The practitioner, operating in this role, is not unlike a stock broker. Both study the market. The social service broker's market, however, is consumer demand for social services, the relationship of the consumer to the social service network, the social services, and the resources they control. Knowing the state of the services and resources as well as the consumer's quality of life, the broker's task is to match community resources to consumer needs. Instead of asking, "What kind of character disorder is present in this offender?" the broker inquires into the offender's quality of life. Does he require training? Employment? Medical care? The social broker strengthens consumer linkages with the community through resource management, creating a greater sense of consumer belonging and community responsibility.

Enabler

A social enabler could be described as a manipulator of resources, people, and events. The enabler is a facilitator whose business it is to empower people through "how-to" instruction. The social worker who operates in this role is capable of establishing self-help networks, facilitating consumer groups, and training consumers to help other consumers. Enablers may be found conducting training sessions on such subjects as stress management, dealing with anger, parenting, budgeting, problem-solving, decision-making, interviewing for employment, and similar human relations concerns. Truly, this person fits the description of Toffler's "life organizer."

Advocate

Advocacy is a scary concept for many social workers because it is often viewed as a high-conflict, high-risk activity. Visions of picketing and rent strikes overshadow some of the other advocacy activities. Even though advocacy does involve conflict and risk, much of the advocate's work is the quiet, low profile work of developing community resources where they don't exist. Grant writing, community education, and public information activities all fit well within this role. Advocates do plead the cases of powerless people, but the empowering function lies in the transferring of power to the consumer.

Mediator

Unskilled as the powerless are in dealing from the "one down" position and accustomed as they are to ending up in a "you lose" situation, they often require assistance in negotiating disputes. As a mediator, the worker performs at the interface of troubled relationships between consumers and their spouses, employers, teachers, school principals, and the like. From this buffering position, the worker can negotiate and, more importantly, model the skills needed to deal with conflict in a nonviolent, nondangerous manner.

Conferee

This role is the one with which social workers are most familiar, probably because they have performed in it very often to the exclusion of the others. From the generalist perspective, the social worker and consumer confer for the purpose of addressing, solving, or managing problems. Over the years, correctional social workers have been conferring with their clients with mixed results. The offender, whether a probationer, parolee, ward, or inmate, has been wary of our "services." The services have not always appeared relevant to the client's perceived needs and his response to them, as viewed by workers, is embodied in the term "unmotivated."

Perhaps we could overcome this impasse if we become more concrete in what we confer about. The consumer of correctional services needs to be empowered, not dissected. Were we to use our time with offenders to model and teach such skills as problem-solving, decision-making, and other tools for mastering the environment, we may find the market for our services turning bullish.

Guardian

Guardianship has been a difficult role for many social workers to accept, in that it requires use of power and authority, which runs counter to the high value social workers place on freedom of choice and democratic process. Many workers report they do not perform well in this role, but feel trapped in it. Yet, social workers generally, and social workers in criminal justice settings in particular, cannot escape the fact that they have been delegated a social control function. Guardians protect people from other people and at times from themselves. They protect the larger society from some of its more dangerous members. In an imperfect society, this cannot and should not be avoided. Rather, it should be carried out in such a way as to give meaning to the word "justice."

We cannot escape the fact that violent and dangerous people continue to exist in a society that has not found legitimate roles for all its citizens. Powerlessness prevails when nothing one does matters. At this point in our national life, many dangerous people, people who have given up hope of ever mattering, will remain dangerous, undeterred, and unchanged. This is a reality.

Our challenge as a society, indeed our very hope for a civil alternative to a handgun society, may rest on how large we allow this powerless segment of our population to grow. As social workers we must empower ourselves to assist our nation to find and develop new responses to the problem of powerlessness and dangerousness.

REFERENCES

Anderson, Joseph. *Social work methods and processes.* Belmont, California: Wadsworth Publishing Co., 1981.

Bandura, Albert. *Aggression: a social learning analysis.* Englewood Cliffs, N.J.: Prentice-Hall, 1973.

Capote, Truman. *In Cold Blood.* New York, N.Y.: Random House, 1965.

Developments in the law: civil commitment of the mentally ill. *Harvard Law Review,* 87:1190–1406, 1974, pp. 1389–1394. In David B. Wexler, J. D. Criminal commitments and dangerous mental patients: legal issues of confinement, treatment, and release. *Crime and Delinquency Issues: A Monograph Series,* 1976, DHEW (ADM) 76-331, p. 31.

Lorenz. Konrad. *On aggression.* New York, N.Y.: Harcourt Brace & World Inc., 1963.

May. Rollo. *Power and innocence: a search for the sources of violence.* New York: W. W. Norton & Company, Inc., 1972.

Middleman, Ruth R. & Goldberg, Gale. *Social service delivery: a structural approach to social work practice.* New York, N.Y.: Columbia University Press, 1974.

Monahan, John. The clinical prediction of violent behavior. *Crime and Delinquency Issues: A Monograph Series,* 1981, DHHS (ADM) *81-921,* pp. 3-20.

National Council on Crime and Delinquency, Board of Directors. The non-dangerous offender should not be imprisoned: A policy statement. *Crime and Delinquency,* 1973, *19,* 449-456. In John Monahan. The clinical prediction of violent behavior. *Crime and Delinquency Issues: A Monograph Series,* 1981, DHHS (ADM) *81-921,* pp. 3-4.

Steele. B. F., & Pollock, C. B. A psychiatric study of parents who abuse infants and small children. In R. E. Helfer & C. H. Kempe. *The battered child.* Chicago: U. of Chicago, 1968. In John M. Macdonald (Ed.). *Psychiatry and the criminal, a guide to psychiatric examinations for the criminal courts* (2nd ed.). Springfield, Illinois: Charles C Thomas, Publisher, 1969.

Toffler, Alvin. *The third wave.* New York: Bantam Books, Inc., 1980.

Wolfgang, M., Figlio, R., & Sellin, T. *Delinquency in a birth cohort.* Chicago: University of Chicago Press, 1972. In John Monahan. The clinical prediction of violent behavior. *Crime and Delinquency Issues: A Monograph Series,* 1981, DHHS (ADM) *81-921,* p. 72.

Zimring. F. Background paper. *In confronting youth crime: report of the twentieth century fund task force on sentencing policy toward young offenders.* New York: Holmes and Meier, 1978, pp. 27-120. In John Monahan. The clinical prediction of violent behavior. *Crime and Delinquency Issues: A Monograph Series,* 1981. DHHS (ADM) 81-921. p. 72.

Chapter 20

WOMEN OFFENDERS AND
SOCIAL WORK PRACTICE

KAY SEELEY HOFFMAN

INTRODUCTION

As the number of women who are arrested and incarcerated increases and as the condition and needs of women offenders become known, the profession of social work must reassess its historically minor involvement with female offenders.

Social work has not been active in the criminal justice system, although some rehabilitative work, including prison counseling, community placement, job placement, and community supervision, have been filled by social workers. Still, the profession has had little involvement in or impact on policy decisions. Furthermore, the work done in corrections by social workers has been done largely on behalf of men.

The purpose of this chapter is to discuss women offenders as a "forgotten minority," describe their past and current treatment, and then relate how the profession of social work can become involved in working effectively with female offenders.

Forgotten Minority

Until recently, women offenders have been the forgotten minority of the criminal justice system. Their small numbers and a misunderstanding of their needs have been the excuses for excluding women from vital vocational training programs in prisons, from development and placement of women in community corrections, and from job counseling and job finding after prison. Even research on women offenders has been scarce, thus effectively blocking recognition of their particular needs to correctional professionals, to politicians who allocate funds for programs, and to the public at large.

While women continue to be denied access to "equal treatment" in the penal system, their incarceration rates are increasing at a faster pace than arrest rates. In a recent study at The University of Michigan School of Social Work, it was reported that during the decade of 1968 to 1978 incarceration rates for women in Michigan rose by 26 percent, far greater than the increase in female crime (Figueria-McDonough, Inglehart, Sarri, & Williams, 1981). Therefore, more women than ever are becoming subjected to the low status that women experience in the criminal justice system.

Although literature on women offenders is relatively scarce, a minor surge has begun in the past decade. This interest has not been kindled by the criminal justice system, but instead has been undertaken by representatives of the women's movement. Feminist scholars, attorneys, women professionals in criminal justice, and women offenders themselves are beginning to examine conditions for women in the penal system, and they are beginning to ask why women have been effectively excluded from meaningful programming. Their findings offer a major critique of the system.

For example, Simon (1975) found that in women's prisons few vocational programs were available. "While the average number of vocational programs for a men's prison is ten, the average number for women is 2.7" (Klein & Kress, 1976). Many of these programs are actually aimed at maintaining the institution such as "housekeeping training," rather than programs that might actually lead to meaningful employment on the outside.

The treatment of women offenders in the criminal justice system has been not only neglectful but based on myth. The lack of vocational programs in prisons and other correctional programs has been attributed to the small numbers of women in the system and falsely to the belief that women do not need vocational training. Facts on female offenders indicate that they are unskilled, poorly educated of low socio-economic status, and heads of households without active spouses (American Bar Association, 1976). It is obvious that training and opportunities for meaningful work are significant needs for this population.

The criminal justice system has further neglected the needs of women offenders by not addressing the problem of incarcerated women and their children. According to most research, between 60 percent and 80 percent of imprisoned women are mothers with dependent children. What happens to the children of these women when their mothers are imprisoned? How does imprisonment impair a woman's ability to be a nurturer after confinement? What is the criminal justice system doing to prepare female offenders to resume and improve their roles as mothers after imprisonment? These questions are seldom addressed by the criminal justice system. Yet, of all areas of neglect, this may be the most serious because so many innocent and vulnerable people are involved and because the impact of separation of parents and children can have ongoing and even future generational significance.

Child Welfare and Women Offenders

Social work has been involved with offenders in the area of child welfare. Social workers have often dealt with the children women who are incarcerated leave behind, and according to some researchers, their contacts have been, too often, ineffective.

Most children of incarcerated women live with relatives, especially maternal grandmothers; however, the threat of the child welfare system looms large in their lives (Hoffman & Larson, 1981). McGowan and Blumenthal (1978) studied children of incarcerated women and indicated the child welfare system for inadequate response to the needs of women and their children. Their indictment rests on the fact that child welfare services are often too narrow and in too intensive a range to be of service to the many needs of children of incarcerated women. In other words, women whose children are serviced by the child welfare system during their incarceration too often lose their legal rights to their children or those needing supportive services do not receive them. They find themselves in a "Catch-22" situation. If they have lost their rights, they are hopeless that they will regain custody. And because of the fear of losing rights, they do not avail themselves to existing supportive services. Unfortunately, the fear of losing their children often forces incarcerated women to leave their children in undesirable situations. Research by Hoffman and Larson (1978) showed that women offenders had as one of their constant fears losing their children.

The child welfare system along with criminal justice has failed to help mothers plan realistically for their children. Children of imprisoned women are placed in foster homes that are not accessible to women in prison (McGowan & Blumenthal, 1978). Therefore, the separation can lead to irreparable estrangement in the parent-child relationship. When a woman is released from prison, there is seldom an available means to obtain assistance in regaining her children. At the other extreme, women who have avoided the child welfare system very often find their children "dumped" on their doorstep as soon as release from prison occurs, because the temporary child providers have grown tired of their duties. In a pilot follow-up study of women offenders, Hoffman and Larson (1981) found that impaired parent-child relationships lasted long after the mother's release from prison and that reluctance to seek help with problems was the norm.

A More Effective Role for Social Work with Women Offenders

The legacy of social work and women offenders is, unfortunately, not positive. However, current developments in the criminal justice system offer the opportunity for growing and important roles for social workers in servicing this population.

The indications of the wastefulness of human and economic resources in our society's overreliance on prisons, coupled with a new impetus toward the development of community corrections, make this a particularly ripe time for social work to take a more aggressive role in both direct service to women offenders and policy development.

Prison Wastefulness

Because female offenders are part of a growing trend of increased incarceration and longer sentences, the economic and human wastefulness of the prison system must be addressed by the social work profession. Although women's crimes continue to be overwhelmingly nonviolent, the use of prisons for punishment of these crimes grows, especially among the minority population. In Michigan, during the ten year period, 1968 to 1978, the percentage of minority women sentenced to prison increased by 368 percent and for white women by 120 percent (Figueria-McDonough et al., 1981).

Prison overcrowding is a concern in many states, and the reaction by the public, politicians, and many in the criminal justice system is to build more prisons to accommodate this burgeoning population. It is assumed that growing crime rates dictate prison construction and that, although it is costly, the public safety must be protected. Research indicates that longer sentences and the increased use of prisons for nonviolent crimes are the real culprits in the overcrowding problem (Figueria-McDonough et al., 1981).

Because of increasing incarceration, many states are experiencing prison overcrowding. The public is led to believe that overcrowding is a result of growing crime rates and do not question the millions upon millions of dollars spent to build more prisons.

The trend toward prison construction is dangerous, because prisons have been found not only to be costly but to be ineffective as well. Prison wardens themselves are beginning to ask whether or not all those who are imprisoned ought to be or whether other more effective systems should be sought. Vernon Housewright, Warden of the Vienna Prison in Illinois, stated, "I admit that some prisons may do more harm than good" (*Chicago Sun Times*, April 11, 1975).

The harm is experienced not only by those currently serving in prisons for lengthy sentences but by society at large. When prisons are built, they tend to be filled regardless of the real need. In other words, the net of social control simply widens.

The profession of social work has certainly not promoted the growth of prisons, but unfortunately, neither have social workers been involved in movements and policies to decrease the use of prisons. One way that social workers could become active in these needed changes is through the promotion of humane alternatives to prison.

Community Corrections and Social Work

Even as prisons continue to be overcrowded, community corrections is on the upswing. Because of social policy directions, there is a growing recognition that individual communities must begin to take responsibility for offenders from their own areas. It is possible that community corrections could relieve the growing prison population as it prepares people more effectively to a life after criminal activity. On the other hand, the growth of community corrections might also simply widen the net of social control in this society by defining more behaviors as criminal while it "stores" people in "smaller warehouses," closer to their homes.

The profession of social work can have a positive impact on community corrections for women. Some community programs are those that have grown out of a felt need in the community rather than through the dictates of the larger correctional system. These community programs offer a wide variety of services to women including vocational training, counseling, teaching of parenting roles, job placement, and residential living (Hoffman, 1979). Social work's experience in the development of community programs of many different kinds could be used by the growing number of community programs for women offenders.

Such programs suffer from the identical plights of other fledgling programs such as lack of secure funding, program underutilization, and lack of community acceptance, which causes it to be a victim, too soon, of the vagaries of our system. The lack of secure funding places on administrators of community-based programs for women offenders the burden of seeking continued financial support at the sacrifice of program and staff development. It may lead to the closing of effective programs before they have had a chance to mature because stable funding mechanisms are not planned.

One community-based program evaluated by this author cited its difficulty in maintaining an adequate flow of potential clients from prison or the courts. It is doubtful, given the huge increase in sentenced and incarcerated women, that there are not enough people to fill community programs. Rather, it is the correctional system's intractability in developing and making use of alternative programs that limits the number of women served in community corrections.

Even though community-based programs for offenders can grow out of a felt need in a community, community acceptance of such programs is not assured. The desire of a community to meet the needs of its elderly, handicapped, or mentally ill population does not translate directly into the building of nursing homes, senior citizen apartments, or group homes for the physically and mentally handicapped. Community programs for these groups have met with much opposition.

The problems of gaining and maintaining community support are especially difficult for community-based programs for offenders. It is essential to consult with communities where potential programs are targeted before the site is determined. When programs are placed in communities solely for the convenience of corrections departments, without community acceptance, the entire community corrections movement is undermined.

Financial incentives are often suggested as methods to pave the way for community acceptance. The idea is that finances provide a fair exchange for the community's allowing offenders into their collective lives; for example, in Minnesota, the Community Corrections Act authorizes the payment of subsidies to counties that develop and provide community corrections programs for their offenders. Payments are based on a complicated formula that includes per capita income of the county as well as the number of convicted felons in a particular county in a given year. Although each county must have a Community Advisory Board, the existence of such a board does not insure community acceptance nor does the use of financial incentives.

It is possible that finances may have a short run, positive effect; however, in the long run, such incentives can become road blocks in the continuation of programs. Financing becomes a facade for community acceptance and when the finances are inevitably withdrawn, community corrections are not only faced with fiscal problems, but also with a community that does not support its prolongation because grass-roots work with residents has never really begun. Currently, the Minnesota program is under review.

Beyond the issues of ongoing or initial acceptance is the question of what kind of a geographical setting is preferable. The tendency to place these residences in high crime and high drug availability areas is often due to necessity rather than to desirability. On the other hand, putting a site in a rural area with local, rural personnel is the opposite and unworkable extreme. Agencies that desire to locate in urban communities should engage the community in finding local people to participate in the search. Such an approach is responsible and based on the social work value of self-determination.

The three problems of financial insecurity, program underutilization, and community acceptance are not owned exclusively by reformers of the criminal justice system. They are problems that social work has dealt with over the years in serving the vulnerable populations of this society. Therefore, the profession is fully equipped to become a part of this change movement.

GUIDELINES BASED ON THE DEVELOPMENT OF PRINCIPLES, POLICIES, AND PHILOSOPHY FOR SOCIAL WORK INVOLVEMENT WITH WOMEN OFFENDERS

In the preceding discussion, social work's role with women offenders has been both criticized (in the case of child welfare) as well as theorized (in the case of community corrections). At this point, specific guidelines arising from social work philosophy and principles will be presented to build a case for social work involvement with women offenders.

Person-Situation Interaction

The emphasis in social work practice is the person-situation configuration. It is a multidimensional view that considers not only the dynamics of the individual or group but also the complexities of a dynamic, ever-changing environment. Social workers are skilled at assessing and intervening at the interface of the person and his or her environment (Compton & Galaway, 1979). This special framework and way of thinking can be utilized to understand the unique problems of women offenders and can motivate social workers to become involved in setting correctional policies.

We have discussed the overuse of prisons in our society. Too many women who are imprisoned receive lengthy sentences for crimes on which the prison experience has little positive impact; for example, most women are sentenced for property crimes, and during the years 1968 to 1978 in Michigan, the length of sentences increased as well as the percentages of women sentenced to prison. "Despite the fact that the percentage of female prisoners convicted of serious crimes has declined, the length of sentences has increased" (Figueria-McDonough et al., 1981).

The prison experience is almost void of preparing women for success in society upon release. It isolates women; they lose contact with their families and often build resentment toward society during their prison experience. The prison experience is the most extreme example of the "unresponsiveness of social and physical environments" (Germain & Gitterman, 1980).

Accepting the principle that people need to interact with an environment that is growth producing in order to grow themselves clearly implicates the prison as the placement of last resort for the female offender. An understanding of the unresponsiveness of the prison experience is best illustrated by an offender's own experience.

Case Example: Ms. Jenson

Ms. Jenson is a black, thirty-four-year-old mother of four children who has served four years of a seven to ten year sentence for armed robbery. Her children are staying with the maternal grandmother because the children's father died during Ms. Jenson's imprisonment. The grandmother has grown very dependent on the children and is controlling them by not allowing them to visit their mother. None of Ms. Jenson's friends have visited, and she does not really know what is happening at home. Two of her children are teenagers, and Ms. Jenson worries that they will follow in her footsteps. She wants to help them avoid her pitfalls, but knows she cannot.

In the meantime, Ms. Jenson is not taking advantages of any of the meager opportunities for personal growth in the prison. She hesitates to even talk about herself because it stirs up feelings that she does not know how to handle. She is angry but fears she will explode and therefore remains aloof, attempting to cope alone.

Ms. Jenson's prison experience is not uncommon. Her alienation from her family and friends, her isolation of the world at large, her bitterness toward society, and her loss of self-esteem will make her eventual reentry into society perilous and very possibly unsuccessful.

Social Work Practice in Prison

Fully acknowledging the negatives of the prison experience, social work can be practiced even in the hostile prison environment; for example, social workers might be challenged to help women prisoners make use of any and all resources, however scarce, the prison has to offer. Perhaps more realistically, social workers in prison must begin to develop services for women. The following case example is illustrative of the many needs of women in prison.

Case Example: Ms. Phillips

Helping prisoners arrange for family visits on visiting day can be of enormous assistance for women who wish to maintain ties with their children. Ms. Phillips, an incarcerated woman interviewed by this author indicated that visiting day was her only time to do all of her "mothering." Her children brought school work in for her to check, and they brought accounts of problems with family and friends. Ms. Phillips found her tasks to be enormous and stated that she is "barely holding on." She had no contact with a counselor or social worker with whom she felt she could discuss her family concerns. There was no institutional support for her continuing in the role of mother.

Ms. Phillips was a particularly resourceful woman, but it is doubtful that she can continue "holding on" without support. Clearly, a social work response to her situation is needed.

For example, social workers in prisons must be encouraged to recognize the importance of continuation of the mothering role even for women who are incarcerated. Through individual work with prisoners, social workers might help women face their losses in their roles as well as accept the aspects of mothering than can be continued. For greater impact, social workers in prison must develop such services as parenting classes for young mothers, groups for mothers of teenage children to help with acting out behaviors, and classes on substance abuse and its effect on fetal development. Such services can provide not only essential information but can serve as incentives for keeping women involved in the lives of their families, an essential aspect of the person-situation configuration.

In some other countries, notably Mexico and West Germany, the role of the social worker is to engage the inmate in contacts with the outside world, especially the family.

Although inmate need for family contact is acknowledged in prisons in the United States, it is not incorporated into most penal systems. Incarcerated women are seldom treated as persons with family responsibilities and obligations or as persons with familial needs. Instead, their definition, and, thus, their treatment represents the singular view of woman offender as prisoner, to be confined and excluded from society.

In addition to working with women and their families, social workers in prison must be aware of any community placements available to women after their minimum stay is fulfilled. In interviews with prison counselors, Hoffman and Larson (1978) found that the underutilization of community programs in Michigan could be traced to prison counselors' unawareness of programs. For prison counselors who were aware of community programs, lack of referrals was related to heavy workloads in institutional maintenance type services. In other words, prison counselors were too busy meeting the demands of working in an overcrowded prison to refer people for screening and evaluation for community corrections.

A detailed discussion of roles for social work practice with women offenders is found later in this chapter.

Systems Theory and Its Relation to Servicing Women Offenders

Of all theoretical underpinnings of social work, systems theory seems best suited to providing a framework for social work with women offenders.

Earlier, the isolation of the prison experience illustrated its negative impact on an incarcerated woman. A systems theory framework can help criminal justice practitioners recognize the effect that separating a family member from her family system can have, not only on the prisoner herself but on her children and even on the future of her children.

Colleen Russell had been released from prison for two years when she was interviewed by the author for a research project. She completed her last year of her sentence for grand larceny in a community treatment program for offenders where she received vocational training as a secretary. Ms. Russell is an especially attractive well-spoken black woman of thirty. She found immediate work at a public utilities company upon release, but soon moved from that job to a similar position at a human service agency because she felt isolated and discriminated against at her first job. Ms. Russell progressed very well during her first few months after release. She was a "success story."

However, about three months after release, her family system began to break down. Her two younger children, age eight and ten, demanded to be placed back in the home of the paternal grandmother where they had stayed during their mother's incarceration. Ms. Russell allowed them to return because she felt she had no right to question their desires. After all, she had been separated from them for a long time, and the grandmother had provided for them.

Ms. Russell's thirteen-year-old daughter, Andrea, became pregnant. Andrea decided not to continue school and began spending her days watching TV and her nights "running around." Ms.

Russell was not able to convince her daughter to go to school or even to take care of her health.

Because of frequent absenteeism, Ms. Russell lost her job at the human service agency. She applied for A.D.C. During these stressful months, Ms. Russell's mother died. This was a blow that Ms. Russell felt she couldn't handle, and she began drinking, a pattern she had developed before incarceration, but had managed to avoid for several years.

Ms. Russell was fearful of any counseling for herself or her daughter. She had no real plans for her future. She had told her parole officer none of her concerns and problems.

It may be that Ms. Russell's troubles did not begin with involvement in the criminal justice system. However, her time in prison, her separation from her children, and her consequent guilt and fear certainly caused more problems not only for her but also for her family. Changing one unit of a system, such as the family, invariably has an effect on all other units. It is the lack of understanding by the criminal justice system of its impact on the individual as well as its transformation of related individuals that is so harmful. Criminal behavior does not occur in a vacuum, nor does the state's judgment and treatment of the offender.

A social work perspective with its common sense use of systems theory is badly needed in the courts, the penal system, and parole and probation. Women offenders have special needs because they are so often the sole providers in their families. Therefore, the responsibility of the criminal justice system extends not only to incarcerated women but also to their families.

Social Work Values and Women Offenders

Social Work has long associated itself with the values of self-determination and the uniqueness and dignity of the individual. However, actual practice has also found social work in roles of social control.

Practicing social work with its underlying values in an institution such as corrections, so obviously an arm of social control, therefore, has certain dilemmas. It is difficult for the profession to come to terms with the coercive powers found in the corrections field. This is especially difficult in prisons and in programs that offer few meaningful services to offenders.

Community Corrections and Values

One of the reasons that social work can find a more comfortable and consistent position in the newer community corrections program for women has to do with the question of values. Women who are serving time in community corrections must take responsibilities upon themselves, and they must be accountable for their activities. In other words, the value of self-determination is part of the programs; for example, in a residential program located in a community, offenders have access to the same services in the communities that nonoffenders do. Inmates come and go (within appointed hours and under certain conditions); they shop in stores, ride buses, eat in restaurants, and walk the streets, just as nonoffenders do. All the while, they are under the auspices of the criminal justice system. However, the value of self-determination along with its inherent responsibility and self-discipline is reinforced in the internal structure of the program.

Small programs, so often a hallmark of community corrections for women, offer many more opportunities for offenders to be treated as unique individuals with their own strengths and weaknesses. In Project Transition in Detroit, a program evaluated by this author, vocational and personal counseling programs are individually tailored for each woman. There are vocational programs in secretarial studies, medical records, power sewing, data processing, and welding that are available to inmates. Women attend a variety of schools throughout the city.

Social workers at Project Transition agree on individual contracts with each offender concerning vocational goals, counseling goals, and environmental changes. The small size of the program allows individual needs to be addressed and the uniqueness and dignity of the individual to be taken seriously by the staff.

ROLES FOR SOCIAL WORK PRACTICE WITH WOMEN OFFENDERS

There is currently a growing cadre of critics who say that rehabilitation within the criminal justice system is not possible. The famous study by Lipton, Martinson, and Wilks (1975) has been used to reinforce the punishment ethic and eliminate possibly effective programs before they have had a chance to be tested. The old "social work ideal" of rehabilitation, of extending opportunities, and of providing vocational training is not in vogue.

For women offenders, this turn of events is especially cruel. Glick and Neto (1977) surveyed women's correctional programs in the United States and found, "Treatment in correctional institutions was conspicuous by its absence." The Lipton, Martinson, and Wilks critique could not have included women because rehabilitation has not even been attempted except by a small band of community programs listed by Glick and Neto.

Rehabilitation has been measured almost exclusively by a single measure: recidivism. This exclusive focus has led researchers and policymakers away from serious questions about the lives of inmates, their needs, their strengths, and what helps in a correctional setting. Instead, we know only the number of times persons are returned to the criminal justice system.

The most obvious drawback of recidivism data alone is that it tells us nothing about reintegration into society by ex-offenders. Therefore, it can tell us nothing about the conditions within correctional institutions that aid or detract from positive reintegration.

Hoffman and Larson (1978, 1981) evaluated a community corrections program and conducted a pilot study of female offenders that addressed helping roles within community corrections that seem to aid the female offender.

The findings are congruent with the social work roles of enabler, broker, and advocate; these roles are discussed below.

Enabler

The role of enabler, an established role within the social work process, is used particularly in one-to-one situations and can be quite effective in working with offenders. In the role of enabler, the social worker's activities, "are directed toward assisting clients to find the coping strengths and resources within themselves to produce changes necessary for accomplishing objectives of the service contract" (Compton & Galaway).

At Project Transition, the community corrections program evaluated, the significance of the enabler role was determined both by the success of the inmate in the corrections program and by her positive judgment of her correctional experience after release.

Women who were involved in one-to-one relationships with

counselors, who used their time with counselors to work on coping abilities, and who were committed to change successfully completed the corrections program at a much higher rate than those who were not engaged in the helping process.

Later, women who had been at Project Transition were interviewed about their correctional experiences. They cited the opportunity to discuss their problems with interested and skilled people as significant in gaining belief in themselves and, in their viewpoints, a growing self-esteem helped them cope on the outside.

It is unfortunate that so few programs for women offenders incorporate the enabler role. Because these women have committed felonies, there is a mistaken belief that they cannot gain control over their own impulses and that "talking therapies" are ineffective. For some women, this may be true, but it is an untested hypothesis that is largely accepted.

Broker

The function of the broker in social work is to link clients with community resources that the client needs for the enhancement of social functioning.

For the female offender, the work of the broker is essential. Female offenders in prisons, in community programs, and on parole are all in need of resources from the community. The imprisoned woman may need help planning for her family and, thus, is in need of such community services as protective services, foster home placements, or a combination. The prison social worker has an important function in alerting service providers to the special needs of the female offender and her family.

Women in community corrections are attempting to learn, among other things, what community services are available and how such services can be obtained. Project Transition workers arrange for appropriate vocational training for women; they assist in arranging medical appointments; they put offenders in touch with drug rehabilitation programs. The broker services are both extensive and significant.

Creative use of community resources can be an efficacious tool for women after release when they are back with their families and dealing with the real world of children, men, and work.

Women interviewed after their correctional experience by Hoffman and Larson (1981) did not know how to effectively use community resources. They were fearful of entanglement with the law and generalized this fear to any sanctioned agency. Their life situations, evidenced by extensive interviews, indicated a need for the continuation of the broker role by community-based correctional programs.

Advocate

Of all disadvantaged groups in society, women offenders are among those with the fewest advocates. Female offenders upset the ideal in our society of what women "ought to be." In addition, their relatively small numbers as compared to men do not invite great interest. Therefore, those working with women offenders must not only advocate for individual women but they must also advocate for them collectively.

According to Compton and Galaway, "As advocate, the social worker becomes the speaker for the client by presenting and arguing the client's cause . . . " (1979).

The setting and instances when social workers may be called upon to act as advocates for individual female offenders are extensive.

Women in the entire criminal justice system are so handicapped by their weak positions in society that advocating for their special needs must be an integral part of social work services.

Many times, women in prison are not aware of the limited services available to them. Social workers in prison must be sure that inmates receive proper medical care, participate in visiting hours, take part in appropriate vocational and educational experiences (if available), and act upon community placement or parole when eligibility occurs. Women inmates must have access to legal services, and social workers can facilitate such access.

In communities, women in placements and on parole are faced with inequities that the social work advocate can help to change; for example, offenders have enormous need for vocational training and employment, and the advocate can represent the offender to increase her opportunities.

In their follow-up study, Hoffman and Larson (1981) found that women offenders were very critical of community programs where advocacy did not exist. One traditional community halfway house in Detroit, which is understaffed and nearly void of programming, demands that inmates "get on the streets and find a job before the day is over." No consideration is given to the lack of opportunities and the indignities and effronteries heaped upon offenders when they meet the world of work. Too many correctional programs offer no preparation for job interviewing. In addition, women are not made aware of basic rights in the work place, nor are they aware of paths for redress when their rights are violated. One woman interviewed in the follow-up study who had served time in a community program lacking advocacy stated that it was "worse than prison."

Although the needs the individual has for advocacy are tremendous, the collective needs of female offenders are even more awesome. Recently, some feminist attorneys and women offenders themselves have taken up the question of inequities within the criminal justice system. The lack of vocational training has been the focal point for this small group of advocates.

For example, women in Michigan have sued and won a case against the state for providing unequal vocational training programs for women in prison (Hoffman, 1979). Work is currently underway to implement vocational training programs in the state prison facility. This was a landmark case, and its effect can be generalized to other parts of the country if advocates for women offenders act prudently and efficiently.

Another imbalance faced by women in the criminal justice system concerns community-based programs, which have grown at a much slower rate than they have for men. Justification of this fact has been based on the belief that it is too expensive to provide such specialized programs and, besides, women do not need them. Haft (1974) reports on a lawsuit won by women offenders in New Mexico charging the state with unequal treatment under the provisions of the fourteenth amendment. Women offenders, they argued, do need community-based programs and the services they provide such as vocational training and job experience.

The unjust structure of the criminal justice system in relation to women offenders must be addressed by social workers. Social workers' knowledge and training as well as the ethical base of the profession are qualifications that enable us to act as advocates on behalf of women offenders. Women offenders' rights, their treatment, and their opportunities for rehabilitation are all areas that the profession of social work must address. Specifically, poor medical care, loss of parental rights, lack of vocational training and job opportunities, drug dependency, mental health problems, and support services for families of offenders are all areas requiring the services of the social work advocate.

SUMMARY

In this chapter, the conditions of female offenders within the criminal justice system have been described. The need for social work involvement with women offenders has been stated along with the complexities of an increased participation. Given the inherent philosophical difficulties of social work in prison, significant contributions by the profession can still be made. The growing trend toward community corrections for women as a more complementary setting for social work was discussed. Community-based programs, probation, and parole when guided by the special expertise of social workers has the potential for development into meaningful experiences and truly corrective experiences for the female offender.

REFERENCES

Compton B. and B. Galaway. *Social work processes.* Homewood, Illinois: The Dorsey Press, 1979.

Female offenders: Problems and programs. Washington, D.C.: American Bar Association, Female Offender Resource Center, 1976.

Figueria-McDonough, J., A. Iglehart, R. Sarri, and T. Williams. *Women in Prison, Michigan 1968–1978.* The University of Michigan School of Social Work and the Institute for Social Research, Ann Arbor, 1981.

Germain, C. and A. Gitterman. *The life model of social work practice.* New York: Columbia University Press, 1980.

Glick, R., and V. Neto. *National study of women's correctional programs.* Washington, D.C.: NILECJ, LEAA, U.S. Department of Justice, June, 1977.

Haft, M. Legal challenges to unequal treatment of women offenders, *The Woman Offender Report,* July–August, 1975, 1 (3), pp. 1–2.

Hoffman, K. and E. Larson. *A follow-up study of women offenders from three correctional programs; a pilot project.* Unpublished research, available through the Whitney Foundation, Detroit, Michigan and Marygrove College, Detroit, Michigan, 1981.

Hoffman, K. *Variables relating to program outcomes in a community-based program for women offenders.* Unpublished doctoral dissertation, Wayne State University, Detroit, Michigan, 1979.

Klein, D. and J. Kress. Any woman's blues: A critical overview of women, crime and the criminal justice system, *Crime and Social Justice,* Spring–Summer, 1976, pp. 34–49.

Larson, E. and K. Hoffman. *An evaluation of project transition: An innovative approach to community corrections for women.* Unpublished research, available through Marygrove College, Detroit, Michigan, 1978.

Lipton, D., R. Martinson, and J. Wilks. *The effectiveness of correctional treatment: A survey of treatment evaluation studies.* New York: Praeger Publishers, 1975.

McGowan, B. and K. Blumenthal. *Why punish the children; a study of children of women prisoners.* Hackensack, New Jersey: National Council on Crime and Delinquency, 1978.

Minnesota Department of Corrections. *The Community Corrections Act*, St. Paul, Minnesota, August, 1979.

News Article. *Chicago Sun Times*, April 11, 1975.

Chapter 21

SPECIAL PROBLEM OFFENDERS

DAN W. EDWARDS

A single chapter on special problem offenders that would satisfy everyone in the criminal justice field would be impossible to write. Therefore, the development of this chapter included an earnest attempt to consider a balance of regional, practitioner, as well as academic and administrative viewpoints.

It may be of some interest to note that the first prison in America was opened in the state of Connecticut in 1773, which placed adults, children, women, and the sick together. Since that time, the criminal justice system in America has seen fit to separate and, in some instances, develop specific institutions and programs for certain types of offenders.

Apparently, this society has come to recognize that a single approach to treatment has represented a futile attempt at rehabilitation. The primary reason for this stems from the fact that it is all but impossible for the typical correctional agency or institution to offer viable treatment programs for special problem offenders, while at the same time maintain a treatment program for others who comprise the majority of offenders.

ALCOHOLIC OFFENDERS

In some states, such as the state of Florida, where the author directed a large comprehensive alcohol counseling center, public intoxication has been decriminalized. More specifically, the Myers Act of the state of Florida decriminalized public intoxication and declared alcoholism to be a disease deserving specialized treatment rather than prosecution and punishment.

It is also not an uncommon practice for police to detain indigent alcoholics through civil commitments to detoxification programs.

This practice also serves to divert alcoholics from the criminal justice system (Duffee & Fitch, 1976).

A two-year follow-up study focused on 100 indigent male alcoholics and 100 indigent female alcoholics who were brought to a detoxification program for public intoxication. Interestingly, only nineteen of the males and eight of the females came into official contact with the criminal justice system during this time. However, six females and eleven males could not be accounted for at the conclusion of the study (Edwards, 1977). Furthermore, as recently as 1980, the office of Substance Abuse of the Louisiana State Department of Health and Human Resources was awarded a federal grant for the purpose of developing an interface between substance abuse and the entire state criminal justice system. One result, while the author was serving on the state task force, was the development of a model program in a single parish (county) that accepted substance abusers, and at the discretion of the District Attorney, received suspended sentences pending completion of the treatment program. Plans for evaluating the program have been implemented but are incomplete at present. However, it would tentatively appear that an implication for social policy may be that diverting alcohol and other substance abusers from the criminal justice system and referring them for treatment may indeed be a viable alternative.

Offenders with alcohol and related problems is also a concern for probation and parole. The present trend appears to be for probation and parole to assume primary responsibility for identifying offenders who have experienced or who may be developing problems and referring them to appropriate community programs for treatment.

Most correctional institutions presently offer some type of treatment for offenders with alcohol related problems; for example, a number of institutions utilize the resources of Alcoholics Anonymous, which is a self-help organization developed for the purpose of mutually helping alcoholics attain and maintain sobriety. A unique characteristic of Alcoholics Anonymous is that all of its members have experienced problems with alcohol abuse.

DRUG ABUSERS

Both residential and nonresidential treatment programs for drug abuse are similar to such for alcoholics. This becomes readily apparent when one realizes that alcohol itself is a depressant drug. It may also be of interest to note that a recent investigation indicated that 62 percent of 100 probationers referred for treatment at an alcohol counseling center were found to be multidrug users (Edwards, 1978). Nevertheless, programs and treatment techniques for drug abusers remain somewhat diverse.

The following is an excerpt of an interview the author had with Mr. Junior Braud, a recovering alcohol and drug abuser and pardoned ex-offender. Mr. Braud is presently employed as a drug and alcohol counselor for the Louisiana State Department of Corrections, in the Adult Division.

"I was the only child of a fairly wealthy family in New Orleans. I was spoiled and pampered and never really had to take much responsibility. My first contact with drugs was sometime during the fifties when I became part owner of a bar in New Orleans. There were a lot of women, drugs, and alcohol around, and I became caught up with trying to be someone important, even though I knew that I never really liked myself. During the next few years I drank a lot of booze and graduated to shooting up on heroin. My heroin habit became more and more expensive, and my need to impress other people became even greater. I was caught, convicted, and sentenced for selling marijuana. Later, I was convicted for the same thing and decided while I was in prison this time that I would never get out."

Needless to say, Mr. Braud did "get out," and received a full pardon in 1972. He attributes this and his present recovery from alcohol and drug abuse to his involvement with Alcoholics Anonymous during and following release from prison. Mr. Braud presently travels from institution to institution, offering counseling for offenders with both alcohol and drug abuse problems.

In 1962, the Supreme Court of the United States ruled that narcotic addiction was basically a medical problem and could not appropriately be treated as a criminal offense (*Robinson u. California*, 1962). Narcotics is a drug class that includes pain-killing drugs derived from opium, such as heroin, codeine, morphine, paregoric, and several synthetic drugs, including methadone.

Methadone maintenance is a treatment approach for heroin addicts that came into vogue around 1964. The treatment simply involves withdrawing the addict from heroin and substituting regular doses of methadone. However, methadone maintenance has met with considerable controversy; for example, Dupont reported that this approach was economical for the criminal justice system and that persons participating in such programs remained away from criminal acts at a higher rate than heroin addicts who did not participate in such programs but were supervised on probation and parole (Dupont, 1971). However, another study suggested that unborn children of pregnant women on methadone have been born addicted (Rector, 1972). Other opponents argue that such an approach merely substitutes one addiction for another and fails to address the social and psychological aspects. Increasing reports of untoward side effects and overdoses have raised serious questions about methadone maintenance.

Marijuana has been around for a long time but never really received much attention in this country until the fifties and sixties. Due to the fact that marijuana is readily available, relatively inexpensive, and does not ordinarily cause extreme effects, most crime associated with this drug is usually illegal sale or illegal possession of certain quantities. Apparently though, some users do graduate to other more serious drugs (Saltman, 1969).

Both alcoholic and drug abuse offenders share an additional characteristic that most other offenders do not. Specifically, all offenders may be considered to be two-time losers in the sense that they failed to make it in society or to be successful at crime. However, alcoholic and drug abuse offenders share the additional failure of not being able to cope with life without the use and abuse of substances. For this reason, it is recommended that serious consideration be given to further experimentation and evaluation of diversionary programs that provide these offenders with treatment rather than criminal prosecution. Future social policy might focus on requiring the criminal justice system to provide specific treatment programs for this segment of the offender population. Also, more attention needs to be placed on training personnel in the criminal justice system to be able to identify and respond appropriately to the special needs of alcoholic and drug abuse offenders (Edwards & Bragg, 1979).

SEX OFFENDERS

Dr. Richard von Krafft-Ebing was probably the first person to write and publish about sex offenders. He published his treatise, *Psychopathia Sexualis*, in 1886, which in addition to his frequent "expert testimony" throughout Europe significantly influenced subsequent social policy and legislation. Dr. Krafft-Ebing described psychopathia sexualis as deriving from a combination of heredity, brain deterioration, and physical degeneracy and purported such to be incurable. Unfortunately, his descriptions of sex offenders promoted an image of some type of morbid, sadistic fiend, rather than a person who was sick and in need of treatment (Klaf, 1965).

Today, the relatively few sex offenders who murder, mutilate, and physically torture their victim seldom if ever reach treatment programs for sex offenses. An attempt was made to verify this statement by telephoning personnel at three separate treatment programs for sex offenders. All of the persons communicated with indicated that they not only did not have this type of offender but that they did not want to accept them, knew of no effective treatment for them, and that most spend the remainder of their lives in maximum security facilities.

The 1960s evidenced a liberalization of attitudes toward sex in this country. In fact, current policy in most state and local jurisdictions border on permitting almost any form of sex between consenting adults in private. Given this, along with plea bargaining associated with the majority of nuisance and minor sex offenses, the typical offender in specialized treatment programs is somewhere between those who engage in public nuisance sex offenses for the first time and those who have committed henious and brutal sex offenses. Of course, many offenses are never reported because of guilt, fear, and shame. It must therefore be assumed that these offenders seldom if ever receive treatment.

On the other hand, a recent investigation suggested that sex offenders made up approximately 12 percent of the total population of those committed to a special forensic unit because of being adjudged not guilty by reason of insanity. Furthermore, most of the sex offenders came into contact with the criminal justice system early in life. It was also discovered that the vast majority of those sex offenders were males who abused alcohol or other drugs and had been arrested for aggravated rape an average of two times (Edwards, Gaines, & Goodman, 1981). A case example was a twenty-three-year-old white male of lower socioeconomic status. He was presently committed to the facility relative to probation violation from being adjudged not guilty by reason of insanity. His original charge was aggravated rape, and the reason for his probation being revoked was in relation to an alleged attempted rape. He also had an extensive drug history, and psychological testing suggested that he had tendencies toward passivity and dependency, with moderate chronic depression.

Apparently, sufficient data is not yet available to meaningfully assess the effectiveness of the few sex offender programs presently operating in this country. Obviously though, one key variable to be examined will be the recidivism rate of those sex offenders treated. Further, a 1965 study of sex offenders treated on an inpatient basis in Wisconsin suggested that only twenty-nine, or 6 percent, of 461 offenders treated and released on parole committed subsequent sexual or other offenses at the conclusion of a two-year follow-up study (Roberts & Pacht, 1965).

Several considerations for social policy may be offered. Namely, it would appear prudent for a great deal of local, regional, and national planning to occur as new programs will inevitably develop throughout the nation. Experimentation with diversionary programs that emphasize early intervention and specific treatment for sex offenders would also appear to be worth considering. It would also appear to be worthwhile for community programs to be able to provide a reasonable period of time in custody for observation, diagnosis, evaluation, and recommendation prior to any formal sentencing. For more serious offenders, consideration might be given to training a cadre of existing personnel in the treatment of sex offenders and to housing sex offenders separately, but within existing minimum, medium, and maximum security institutions. Such an approach may serve to limit the amount of additional funds required to provide treatment for institutionalized sex offenders and provide adequate security. Finally, based upon the author's personal experience as a part-time certified sex therapist, it may be helpful if more community programs were developed and confidentiality laws could be modified to permit the provision of treatment for persons who voluntarily presented themselves for such. More attention might also be focused on providing services to child victims, in view of the fact that the majority of child abusers were found to have been victims of child abuse themselves.

EMOTIONALLY DISTURBED OFFENDERS

The treatment of emotionally disturbed (criminally insane) offenders remains extremely varied within the United States; for example, a few states have special forensic units or hospitals for psychotic offenders, whereas other states vary from placing these offenders in the general prison population to providing special units within the correctional system.

One of the primary means of being committed to a forensic unit or hospital is for a defendant to be declared not guilty by reason of insanity. It should be emphasized that the concept of insanity is a legal term and has nothing to do with psychiatric diagnosis. Two other reasons that offenders are admitted to forensic units is for the purpose of observation and testing to make a competency determination or for an offender to become mentally ill while serving their sentence. In 1972, the National Institute of Mental Health attempted to identify institutions for adult mentally disordered offenders. The following types were identified: (1) security hospitals, (2) mental health facilities whose primary mission is to treat the mentally ill who are not offenders, and (3) correctional institutions with on-site psychiatric units for offenders who become mentally ill during the course of being incarcerated (Eckerman, 1972).

Ordinarily, a jury makes the final determination of not guilty by reason of insanity, but usually with the benefit of psychiatric evaluations. The McNaughten Rule has come to be the primary test of insanity. A number of states have also adopted the "irresistible impulse" rule, which suggests that while a person may know the difference between right and wrong, the person experienced an irresistible impulse that prevented him or her from acting on that knowledge. Unfortunately, policies vary a great deal in terms of identifying and processing such cases, which renders any attempt to determine specific numbers or to compare one jurisdiction with another totally impossible.

The issue of competency to stand trial is illustrative of legal and scientific problems within the criminal justice system. Competency is also a legal concept that refers to the accused person's ability to understand the nature of the proceedings against him or her and to participate adequately in the defense. However, this does involve a diagnosis, which addresses issues of pretrial competency that are primarily legal (McGarry et al., 1972). The criteria for competency primarily focus on protection of due process rights of the accused, in that the person must not only be able to cooperate with legal counsel but also understand the proceedings and potential consequences. Proceedings are suspended until such time as the person is able to satisfy the criteria for competency, provided the accused is found not competent to stand trial. Unfortunately, descriptions of persons based upon psychiatric diagnosis frequently have no relevance to competency. For this reason, McGarry and others developed a set of more objective procedures for determining competency. This approach focuses on in-depth assessment of specific areas of psychological functioning which have direct relevance to what is required by the legal issues (McGarry et al., 1972).

Emotionally disturbed children who come into contact with the juvenile justice system are commonly referred to as special children, who are either emotionally disturbed or retarded. Those who are fortunate enough to be identified are usually diverted from the juvenile justice system and referred to appropriate public or private programs and institutions. However, many may be unable to take advantage of existing legal opportunities. For this reason, it would appear that a need exists for social policy to focus on requiring special training in this area for law enforcement personnel, probation and institutional personnel, as well as juvenile court judges.

OLDER OFFENDERS

A quick look at the literature reveals a paucity of information on older offenders. Yet, as early as 1957, it was reported that 342,956 of 2,068,677 total arrests (16%) involved persons aged fifty and over (Uniform Crime Reports, 1957). More recently, it was reported that in 1979 almost 40 percent of defendants in U.S. district courts were thirty-five years of age or older, whereas convicted defendants in this same age group represented only 33 percent of the total number of convicted defendants (Federal Offenders in United States District Courts, 1979).

Currently, 11 percent of the total population in this country are comprised of twenty-five million men and women over sixty-five years of age. It is anticipated that by the year 2000 the number will reach thirty-three million, and by the year 2035 these men and women are projected to number fifty-eight million or 19 percent of the projected population of the United States (Edwards, D., 1981).

In the midst of these facts and projections, it would appear that we can no longer afford to ignore the older offender and his or her special needs and problems. Certainly one thing we can reasonably expect is for the number of older offenders to increase for the next few decades.

A recent study of older incarcerated offenders in Louisiana revealed that over 50 percent committed crimes against persons of a violent nature. There were also a considerable number of rape and carnal knowledge offenses, however, only 2.5 percent were habitual offenders suggesting that the majority of older offenders in this study were first offenders. Further, most of the older offenders committed crimes late in life when their physical capacities diminished, which may account for overreacting that resulted in crimes of violence (Edwards, D., Roundtree, G., & Schaffer, E., 1981).

Discussions with various personnel in criminal justice settings throughout the nation revealed that very few correctional programs have special geriatric facilities. Those correctional programs that do tend to have them within institutions rather than entirely separate facilities. An additional note of interest was that a large number of wardens expressed that they had found older offenders to have a positive or settling influence with the general population, as well as experiencing less difficulty adjusting to prison life; for example, one older offender in a maximum security institution appeared to represent a father figure for younger offenders and was frequently requested to talk with them when they became upset or depressed.

On the other hand, older offenders do experience problems that younger offenders usually do not have. Fortunately, there does exist a growing body of professional research and literature on gerontology and aging that should have relevance for better understanding and programming for older offenders. The major areas of consideration would appear to be physical (medical), psychological, and social.

More specifically, the major and most frequent problem area identified by several correctional personnel were basic gerontological medical problems. Among those cited were cardiovascular and respiratory and related problems, including other degenerative problems. It is also not infrequent for older offenders as well as for older people in the free society to require special diets.

Both psychological and social considerations are perhaps the least understood. More specifically, it would appear that numerous stereotypes of aging continue to persist in spite of contradictory evidence (deBeauvoir, 1972). Coping with negative stereotypes about aging would certainly appear to be deserving of serious consideration by those who deal with this segment of the population in criminal justice settings; for example, the stereotypical claim that, "you can't teach an old dog new tricks," is entirely erroneous, and increased attention is currently being placed on providing older adult students with better lighting, larger print in written materials, as well as content that has been found to be of greater interest to older adults. Finally, the question must be raised as to whether or not criminal justice settings are adequately addressing adaptational needs peculiar to older offenders in adapting to or reintegrating back into the free society. More specifically, to whom can or do older offenders turn for psychological, social, and economic support when their friends and relatives are dying, their children are taking care of the needs of their own families, and they are no longer desirable in the economic market place? Obviously, this is one area in which social work can and should provide extensive intervention, both before and following release. Such an effort would require not only preparing the older offender as an individual for return to free society but also involve extensive efforts in advocating for and mobilizing resources in the community to be responsive to the unique needs and problems of older offenders. In this same vein, it would appear to be extremely important to begin prerelease planning for older offenders as early as possible, as they may have even fewer resources than do other offenders.

IMPLICATIONS FOR SOCIAL WORK PRACTICE

Unfortunately, social workers have historically been underutilized in corrections as well as in settings for special problem offenders. This may largely be attributed to the position social work took during the 1930s when the American Correctional Association requested social workers to define their area of expertise. Obviously, the definition presented was based upon a narrow clinical perspective due to social work having a close relationship with psychiatry at the time.

Fortunately, in 1945, Dean Kenneth Pray pointed out at a National Conference of Social Work that social workers could be effective in authoritative settings. This has resulted in social work and all of the social work methods slowly becoming more visible throughout all criminal justice settings.

More specifically, beyond merely providing therapy for offenders, the social work practice role in criminal justice settings is beginning to expand. This role expansion and the continued need for such has become heightened in conjunction with increasing emphasis on questioning credibility and demanding accountability. Two articles focused on the effectiveness of treatment programs in criminal justice settings and reported that treatment has had little if any significant impact on rehabilitating offenders or in reducing recidivism (Martinson, 1974; Robinson & Smith, 1971). Of course, this research did not focus exclusively on the practice of social work in criminal justice settings, but it does provide at least some justification for expanding the role of social work beyond traditional treatment methodology.

The social work practice role with special problem offenders could be expanded to include a number of things; for example, further and more extensive research needs to be undertaken to provide a better understanding of the unique needs and differences of special problem offenders. Such information may provide social workers with a valuable data base from which to assume a more active role in restructuring present programs and participate more intelligently in planning, organizing, and implementing alternative strategies that may be more responsive to special problem offenders. Further, social work has a stake in emphasizing and innovating more effective means of mobilizing resources, strengthening social supports and advocating for special problem offenders. Finally, any such expansion of the role of social work with special problem offenders will require social work education to place more emphasis on skill development and knowledge building of organizational management and administration in authoritative settings for special problem offenders.

SUMMARY

Special problem offenders in criminal justice settings represent a segment of the population whose problems may be defined as being physical, psychological, social, cultural, or various combinations of such. Policy and practice issues can only be intelligently addressed by developing an increased understanding of the unique needs and differences of each type of special problem offender. For this reason, continued scientific investigation and careful experimentation with new and innovative policies and methods needs to be undertaken in view of what little is presently being achieved.

The time, effort, and expense of developing programs for special problem offenders may prove to be more effective than simply placing them with other offenders in criminal justice settings. In any case, the potential for such may be enhanced by designing the programs around the unique needs and differences of special problem offenders.

REFERENCES

Brecher, E. M. and Penna, R. D. Health Care in Correctional Institutions, Sept. 1975, National Institute of Law Enforcement and Criminal Justice. Law Enforcement Assistance Administration, U.S. Department of Justice, pp. 33–35.

Burkhart, K. *Women in Prison.* New York: Doubleday, 1973.

DeBeauvoir, Simone. *The Coming of Age.* New York: Putnam, 1972.

Duffee, D., and Fitch, R. "Other Correctional Strategies on the Community Level." *An Introduction to Corrections: A Policy and Systems Approach.* Santa Monica, California: Goodyear Publishing Co., Inc., 1976, pp. 248–290.

Dupont, Robert L. "How Corrections Can Beat the High Cost of Heroin Addiction," *Federal Probation.* 35, No. 2 (June 1971): 43–50.

Eckerman, William C. A Nationwide Survey of Mental Health and Correctional Institutions for Adult Mentally Disordered Offenders. Rockville, Md.: National Institute for Mental Health, 1972.

Edwards, Dan W. "A Two Year Follow-Up Investigation of 100 Indigent Male Alcoholics and 100 Female Alcoholics Admitted to a Detoxification Program for Public Intoxication." An unpublished manuscript.

Edwards, D. and Bragg, R. "Study of Alcoholism and Substance Abuse," News and Views, Federal Probation Division, Sept. 3, 1979.

Edwards, Dan W. "Sex Role Attitudes, Anomie, and Female Criminal Behavior," submitted for publication consideration to *Journal of Probation and Parole,* 1981.

Edwards, Dan W. "Assessment of a Group Intervention Model for Facilitating Movement of Needy Aged into Unsubsidized Employment." Accepted for publication in the Winter, 1981 (Volume 4, Number 2) issue of the *Journal of Gerontological Social Work.*

Edwards, D., Gaines, M. and Goodman, C. "An Investigation of Sex Offenders Committed to a Louisiana Forensic Unit Having Been Adjudged Not Guilty by Reason of Insanity" (unpublished research).

Edwards, D. W., Roundtree, G., and Schaffer, E. A Descriptive Assessment of Older Incarcerated Offenders in Louisiana, submitted to *Corrections Today,* in consideration for publication.

Federal Offenders in United States District Courts, 1979, p. 4.

Krafft-Ebing, Richard von. Psychopathia Sexualis. Franklin S. Klaf, Trans. New York: Stein and Day, 1965.

Martinson, Robert. "What Works — Questions and Answers About Prison Reform," *The Public Interest* (Spring 1974), pp. 22–54.

Robinson, James and Smith, Gerald. "The Effectiveness of Correctional Programs," Crime and Delinquency, Vol. 42 (1971), p. 67.

McGarry, A. L. et al. Competency to Stand Trial and Mental Illness, Final Report on NIMH Grant R01-MH18112. Boston Mass.: Harvard Medical School Laboratory of Community Psychiatry, 1972.

Milton G. Rector. "Heroin Maintenance: A Rational Approach," *Crime and Delinquency, 18*, No. 3 (July 1972): 241.

Roberts, Leigh M. & Pacht, Asher R. "Termination of Inpatient Treatment for Sex Deviates: Psychiatric, Social and Legal Factors." *American Journal of Psychiatry*, v. 121, No. 9, March 3, 1965.

Robinson v. California, 370 U.S. (1962).

Roundtree, G. A., Edwards, D. W. and Parker, A. D. "A Survey of the Types of Crimes Committed by Incarcerated Females in Two States, Who Reported Being Battered," Presented at the Thirty-Ninth Annual Conference of the American Association of Mental Health Professionals in Corrections, New Orleans, La., Feb. 25–27, 1981.

Saltman, Jules. What About Marijuana? Public Affairs Pamphlet No. 436. New York: Public Affairs Committee, 1969, p. 3.

Schwartz, B. "Legal Training for Women Inmates," The Women Offender Report, No. 1 (March–April 1975), p. 5, published by the National Resource Center on Women Offenders, Washington, D.C.

Sorenson, V. "Educational and Vocational Needs of Women in Prison." *Corrections Today*. Vol. 43, No. 3, May–June 1981.

Steffensmeier, D. and Steffensmeier, R. "Trends in Female Delinquency." *Criminology, 18* (1980):62–85.

Uniform Crime Reports, Vol. 28, No. 2, 1957, p. 114.

Uniform Crime Reports, 1980.

Ward, D. and Kassenbaum, G. "Homosexuality: A Mode of Adaptation in a Prison for Women," *Social Problems, 12* (Fall 1964), pp. 159–77.

Chapter 22

RACE RELATIONSHIPS IN PRISON:
A CRITICAL SOCIAL WORK CONCERN

JOSEPH E. PALENSKI

It is now nearly twenty years since America experienced the
chain of racial unrest beginning with the race conflict in the Los
Angeles community of Watts during the mid-1960s. Perhaps no
other event could better demonstrate the anger and frustration of
black Americans than the random destruction of their own community. While urban unrest was not new to America, events such
as the Watts riots sparked a new interest in the problem of race and
its impact on being processed in the American justice system.
Consequently, new insights appeared on the manner in which
race permeated relations between minority Americans and the
justice system; for example, Kuykendall and Burns (1980) have
noted numerous instances of racial prejudice in the treatment of
blacks by police. They noted the systematic tie between treatment
in the justice system and treatment in a larger American social
structure.

The President's Commission on Law Enforcement and Administration of Justice (1967) and the President's Commission on Civil
Disorders (1968) identified race as the critical ingredient in improving both the rates and patterns of crime in the United States.

> "When all offenses are considered together," the President's Crime Commis-
> sion noted, "the majority of offenders arrested are white, male and over
> twenty-four years of age." Even so, race is almost as much a factor as sex in
> determining the likelihood of arrest in our society. Though blacks comprise
> only 11 percent of the population, their rate of arrest is disproportionately
> high for all but two of the offenses.
>
> (Wickman & Whitten, 1980)

It is not feasible to recount here all of the changes that grew
from the unrest of the sixties. In general, it can be said that black

363

and hispanic Americans took greater opportunity to scrutinize the work of the criminal justice system and to enter it as workers in greater numbers. For example, Kuykendall and Burns (1980) report approximately a 33 percent increase in the number of black officers working in U.S. departments between 1960 and 1970. Moreover, Americans were, for the first time, approving legislation that made provision for the planning, improvement, and research of crime control issues (Omnibus Crime Control and Safe Streets Act of 1968).

Unfortunately, despite reforms in the criminal justice system, America's jails and prisons have received little assistance when compared to the rest of the criminal justice system. Nowhere is this more dramatic than in the matter of race relations and the American prison. Until recently, little attention has been given to the matter of race and prison despite the dramatic shift in the racial composition of American prisons. As noted by Jacobs (1983):

> Blacks, Mexicans, Puerto Ricans and members of other racial minorities now constitute the majority of American prisoners. Behind the walls, white, black and Spanish-speaking inmates exist in separate conflict-ridden social worlds. While the racial composition of American prisons is often reported by the media and is obvious to prison employees, inmates, and visitors, most sociologists who have studied prisons have ignored race relation entirely.

To date, the national incarceration rate for blacks is 600 per 100,000 as compared to 70.8 for whites (Christianson 1980). The 1973 Law Enforcement Assistance Administration statistics on state prisoners report 48.1 percent of American prisoners as black (U.S. Department of Justice, Census of Prisoners in State Correctional Facilities, 1973).

The purpose of this chapter is to explore the topic of race and its impact on social work in prisons. The objectives of this discussion are threefold: first, to provide an understanding of the dimensions of race conflict in prisons; second, to demonstrate that the traditional avenue of assistance open to prisoners, namely the courts, may have exacerbated the question of race in prison; and third, to provide social workers with strategies for lessening racial conflict in prisons.

RACE AND THE NEW INMATE RELATIONSHIP

Since the latter part of the 1960s, working in an American prison has required the recognition that a new inmate has emerged

—an inmate who is sensitive to the circumstances of the world he will eventually reenter and the important role race plays in day-to-day survival. As John Irwin (1980) observed:

> Toward the end of the 1960's in California and other states, many prisoners began redefining their relationships to each other, the prison, the system (the criminal justice system), and the society in a more politically radical fashion. Many black leaders became Marxists, most Chicanos developed a Chicano political identity, and most whites, though not becoming radical, developed a sense of injustice about their legal status. The spread of these more radical perspectives stalled the drift toward racial segregation, hostility, and violence and supplied a basis for a new unity among prisoners.

Perhaps it should be no surprise that race exists as a pivotal factor in today's prisons, given the historically benign racial neglect character of the American prison.

However, race difference is not the only factor inmates have come to see as critical to defend themselves against. How prison staffs view race is also a problem. Irwin (1980) noted:

> Guards' racism takes three forms. First, they do not like, and in fact often hate, non-whites. A guard who had denied to the Attica Commission that there was racism at Attica explained why prisoners practiced voluntary segregation in the mess hall: "How would you like to sit between two coloreds while you were eating?" Moreover, most white guards believe that non-whites are inferior. Another officer explained to the Attica Commission that black and Spanish-speaking prisoners had the undesirable jobs in the prison, because they were "better suited for these jobs," and another stated that "it is hard to find coloreds who can do good clerical work." (In truth, 17 percent of the black prisoners, as compared with 28 percent of the white, had finished high school.) Finally, the guard force with a rural background and poor education, misunderstood the perspective or subcultures of most prisoners, particularly of non-white, urban prisoners.

Given the circumstances of prison life that confront inmates, racial pride and the violence that flow from it may be a truly practical coping mechanism. We may wish to look at the "new inmates" as a response to the succession of threats leveled at them over the years. Often, inmates have only their race as a source of strength and unity during incarceration. In attempting to grapple with day-to-day deprivation, inmates must provide explanations to themselves and other inmates about what is taking place. For minority inmates the indignity of prison is but one more example of how a majority white society has the power to both make and enforce rules. That blacks constitute a minority outside the prison and a majority inside is confirmation to blacks that they are indeed victims by virtue of their race. Often such realizations turn to anger, which then is immediately directed toward white inmates — the perceived majority. While this process of race identification, conflict and ill feeling is not always the case, minority inmates must at least "publicly" rally around their own race, and white inmates must do likewise. To do otherwise is to relinquish even more links with their former identity. The prisoner who feels rage against fellow inmates, corrections staff, or administration along racial lines is in a sense salvaging self through group solidarity. Race thus becomes helpful to inmates in a situation that is otherwise impersonal, derogatory, and destructive to self. Threats to other inmates, violence, sexual attacks, and control of contraband within and between one's race can be viewed as a source of strength in that it gives attention to persons who biographically are often very marginal people. As Jacobs (1983) points out:

> It is hard to imagine a setting that would be less conducive to accommodative race relations than the prison. Its inmate population is recruited from the least successful and most unstable elements of both majority and minority racial groups. Prisoners are disproportionately representative of the more violence-prone members of society. As a result of crowding, idleness, boredom, sexual deprivation, and constant surveillance prisons produce enormous interpersonal tension.

Given the critical role played by inmates' race, social workers must never lose sight of this variable. Unlike the theories of the past (see Clemmer, 1940; Cressey, 1961), prison is no longer a homogenous community of inmates supporting other inmates. It is rather a "community of communities" separated by color and race. And it is this color and race dimension that often shapes the other daily routines that constitute prison living.

THE PRISON AS A FORGOTTEN TERRAIN

Prisons have never been easy places in which to work. Prisons stand as fairly "low visibility" settings that have an awesome impact on newcomers. Everything that goes on in prison gets shaped and distorted by the ultimate concern of prison, namely security. The new social workers coming to the prison must orient themselves to a world of new concerns and new vocabularies; for example, new social workers must learn how difficult it is to move around in a prison. They must learn they are dependent on correctional staffs. They must also learn the role boredom plays in prison and that there are few resources available (unlike the outside) to combat boredom in prison.

Given the new inmates and potential violence that exists, the problem of limited resources in prison influences race in three ways. First, inadequate manpower jeopardizes the enforcement of rules in prison, forcing some inmates to become victims of violence or violent sexual assault. As one inmate and corrections spokesperson suggested to a New York City reporter, these assaults often have racial overtones (Piloggi, 1981):

> ... sex between consenting inmates is common, but sexual assault is not. Fifty-seven sexual assaults were reported to authorities last year; more probably took place. Are sexual assaults racially motivated? "How you going to know what's inside a man's head?" says Sky, a member of the Savage Nomads who comes from the Bronx and is something of a Rikers Island habitue ("Seems I'm here every summer"). "But if you're slight and white you stand just as good a chance of getting raped as if you're slight and tan or slight and black. It's up to yourself. You got to fight for your manhood, man.
> "The first time you're there it's tough," Sky goes on. "You got to be cool. They might mess around. They might jump you. They can do it even with the C.O. watching.

Second, scarce resources limit the administrator's ability to segregate prisoners, which often leads to race and violence confrontations.

Third, scarce resources often make it impossible to assist inmates who report race conflict (as well as other types of conflict). Investigating allegations of one inmate about another is a serious and time-consuming matter. Allegations of assault between and among races often demand that an individual inmate agree to enter protective custody or recount the embarrassing and humbling experience of being a prison victim.

For those inmates who choose to go to protective custody, there looms the problem of returning to the general population. Inmates who do return often have to cope with the dual reputational problems of being labeled weak and pressured (Doran, 1977) or selling "woof" tickets (tough guy). Often the number of inmates to be counseled on the decision to segregate makes it impossible to service all inmates and thus ensure an inmate's safety.

Traditionally social workers as well as other prison advocates looked toward the court for help in assisting inmates gain a reasonable level of survival in prison (Berkman, 1979). However, court intervention, while helpful, brought with it some unanticipated consequences with long range negative results for inmates. On the question of race and racial coexistence in prison, the court has failed to recognize (1) the existence of competition between the races while in prison, (2) the prejudice brought into the prison, (3) the significant role race plays in sustaining a feeling of self-worth, and (4) the fact that prisons are unlike other organizational settings we encounter in our lives.

Jacobs (1983), commenting on this point, has argued forcefully against making comparisons between such places as prisons and schools.

> Legal analysis of prison race relations has, from the beginning, been distorted by the school analogy. Prisons should not be equated with schools; they have different populations, different social functions, and different administrative problems. Behavior taken for granted in prisons would be considered aberrant in schools, indeed, probably in all other social contexts. No other institution so thoroughly controls and regiments its inmates or clients, denying them privacy and freedom of choice. In no other institution are relations so fraught with violence. It is a serious mistake to believe that what makes sense in the educational environment is appropriate for prisons.

Recent court decisions on prison race relations have made desegregation imperative without taking into account the way in which race is a "pivot" to other activities in prison.* While achieving one's sense of worth through social identity may be a healthy experience, in prison it is often done at the expense of another racial group. Moreover, it has made social work in prison problematic. The periodic failure of the court to permit assignment by race in prison cuts off a legitimate avenue of assistance to social workers. Inmates who would otherwise be segregated based upon expressed racial violence escape such designation. Such court decisions ignore the coercive forced nature of prison and fail to see the implications for inmates who refuse to engage in the atrocities of their own race or fall victim to acts between races.

ON A CONVERGENCE OF CONCERNS: RACE AND CLIENT CARE

The major responsibility of the prison social worker has been to assist in the adjustment and welfare of prison inmates. Consider-

---

*For recent court decisions see *Thomas v. Pate*, 1974, 493F.2D151 (Seventh Circuit), Illinois State Penitentiary at Joliet.

ing the rise in prison conflict and the race animosity that surrounds prison conflicts assisting inmates is no longer a matter of routine assessment, classification, and counseling. Today's inmate has grown suspicious of all correctional personnel, including the social worker. Consequently, today's correctional social worker requires skills that will allow for service delivery, despite the constant tension generated through strained race relations. Thus, the following suggestions are put forth as a guide to social workers within correctional settings.

The Development of a Mediator-Facilitator Role

Given the amount and sources of racial conflict in prison, an important role for social workers could be the mediation of race tension through the use of conflict resolution techniques. Because social workers typically possess information on the problems and preferences of inmates, they could apply such information to assist in the resolution of conflict. Unlike either prison administrators or inmates themselves, social workers are not in direct competition with inmates. Thus, social workers may be in the strongest position within the prison to resolve race conflict and reduce competition among inmates. Social workers would serve as third party mediators or "architects" for ways in which prison inmates might manage their own race conflicts. A social worker, in the course of acting as a "third party mediator" would not impose solutions but rather would make suggestions to clients in conflict. In doing so, the responsibility for a solution would rest in the minds and activities of the conflicting parties (not the social worker or institutional staff). Similarly, when an agreement is reached via specific measures such as mediation, the specific provisions of the agreement are created by the disputants themselves. In this role, the mediator resolution technique is not aimed at a final solution, i.e. fault finding, but rather at creating an agreement that is acceptable to both inmates and that will result in peaceful coexistence and minimization of violence. This mediation approach is in keeping with the definition put forth by McGillis and Mullins (1977) concerning mediation:

> Mediation involves the active participation of the third party in the processing of a dispute. This participation can range from minor involvement in which an individual who is essentially a conciliator offers some advice to the disputants regarding a possible resolution to highly structured inter-

action with the disputants. Some organizations which attempt to mediate disputes adhere to detailed procedures whereby the two parties meet together and discuss their perceptions in turn, then leave the room while the mediators formulate a plan for further mediation, then return to the room separately to discuss the issues in individual caucuses, and finally meet together again, hopefully to achieve a resolution.

Fostering a Role of Noncoercive Problem Solving

Much of what takes place in prison is of a coercive nature (Irwin, 1971). Inmates are kept on a set schedule that offers them very little in terms of independence or self-development. This often fuels conflict, as it adds to a prisoner's feeling of being "out of control." The social worker could serve to reduce the coercion of prison by giving inmates greater participation in noncoercive problem-solving activities; for example, social workers could recruit volunteer inmates to inform "new" inmates about the constant problems of violence and reprisal in prison. Behavior options could be provided to inmates as to how to manage specific conflicts or, more importantly, how to prevent conflict in prison. While to some degree inmates already guide each other on the "norms of prison living" (Irwin, 1971), this approach would differ in that a range of alternatives would be presented to inmates. Inmates would not feel the "pressure" that accompanies living in a coerced setting of trial and error survival. Social workers in conjunction with inmates themselves could develop an information program for inmates concerning drug abuse problems, legal services, children-family problems of inmates, inmate threats, and protective custody. These are the sorts of matters inmates always seek assistance on. With social workers using the insights of some inmates to manage the problems of other inmates, the stage is partially set for inmate participation. As inmates often report little appreciation for or assistance with their personal problems, self-participation might demonstrate to inmates that they do have some degree of control over their personal problems. Moreover, inmates, using the structure provided by social workers, can in part minimize the conflict and coercion that surround daily life in prison. Without being more than administratively "forced" into solutions, we cannot expect race inmate violence to subside. Inmates must be brought firsthand into recognizing that options exist to violent confrontations with each other.

Tragically, prison social work perspectives are often ignored in prison (see Colvin, 1982). This should not be the case. If social work is to remain some degree of viable assistance to inmates, it must form interest alliances with inmates and administration. Unless all three groups merge their common interests into a routine political statement and coalition on prison, the drama of violence and victimization will continue. As a power and influence unit, social work has achieved little in prison. It is the basic arrangement of little power and influence that social work must change.

REFERENCES

Berkman, Ronald. *Opening the Gates: The Rise of the Prisoners' Movement.* Lexington Books, Lexington, Massachusetts, 1979.

Blumberg, Abraham. *Criminal Justice.* (2nd Edition), Quadrangle Books, Chicago, Illinois, 1970.

Bowker, Lee H. *Corrections: The Science and the Art.* Macmillan Publishing Co., Inc., New York, 1982.

Carroll, Leo. *Hacks, Blacks and Cons: Race Relations in a Maximum Security Prison.* D. C. Heath & Co., Lexington, Massachusetts, 1974.

Clemmer, Donald. *The Prison Community.* New York: Christopher Publishing, 1940.

Cressey, Donald, ed. *The Prison: Studies in Institutional Organization and Change.* New York: Holt, Rinehart and Winston, 1961.

Colvin, Mark. "The 1980 Mexico Prison Riot," *Social Problems,* Vol. 29, No. 5, June, 1982, pp. 449–464.

Doran, Robert E. "Organizational Stereotyping: The Case of the Adjustment Center Classification Committee," in *Corrections and Punishment,* David Greenberg, ed., Beverly Hills, CA: *Sage Publications,* 1977.

Huff, C. Ronald. "Prisoner Militancy and Politicization: The Ohio Prisoners' Union Movement," in *Corrections and Punishment,* David Greenberg, ed., Beverly Hills, CA: Sage Publications, 1977.

Irwin, John. *The Felon.* Englewood Cliffs, New Jersey, Prentice-Hall, Inc., 1970.

_____. *Prisons in Turmoil.* Boston: Little, Brown and Co., 1980.

Jacobs, James and Norma Meacham. *Guard Unions and the Future of Prisons.* Ithaca, New York: Institute of Public Employment, Cornell University, 1968.

_____. *New Perspectives on Prison and Imprisonment.* Ithaca, New York: Cornell University Press, 1983.

Kuykendall, Jack L. and David E. Burns. "The Black Police Officer: An Historical Perspective," *Journal of Contemporary Criminal Justice,* Vol. 1, No. 4, November, 1980.

Mathiesen, Thomas. *The Defenses of the Weak.* London: Tavistock Publications, 1972.

McGillis, Daniel and Mullen, Joan. *Neighborhood Justice Centers: An Analysis of Potential Models.* Washington, D.C.: Law Enforcement Assistance Administration, October, 1977.

Morris, Norval. *The Future of Imprisonment.* Chicago: The University of Chicago Press, 1974.

Pileggi, Nicholas. "Inside Rikers Island," *New York Magazine*, June 8, 1981.

Scharf, Peter, Joseph Hickey and Thomas Mott Osborne. "The Limits of Democratic Reform," *The Prison Journal*, Vol. LVII, No. 2, Autumn, Winter, 1977.

Skolnick, Jerome, ed. *The Politics of Protest.* Simon and Schuster, 1969.

Toch, Hans. *Living in Prison: The Ecology of Survival.* New York: The Free Press, 1977.

————. *Violent Men.* (Second Edition). Cambridge, Massachusetts: Schenkman Publishing Company, 1980.

Von Hirsh, Andrew. *Doing Justice: The Choice of Punishments.* New York: Hill and Wang, Inc., 1976.

Wickman, Peter and Philip Whitten. *Criminology: Perspectives on Crime and Criminality.* Lexington, Massachusetts: D. C. Heath & Co., 1980.

Wright, Erik Olin. *The Politics of Punishment.* New York: Harper & Row, 1973.

INDEX